CATEGORIES

**STUDIES IN PHILOSOPHY
AND THE HISTORY OF PHILOSOPHY**

General Editor: Jude P. Dougherty

Studies in Philosophy
and the History of Philosophy   Volume 41

Categories
Historical and Systematic Essays

Edited by Michael Gorman and
Jonathan J. Sanford

THE CATHOLIC UNIVERSITY OF AMERICA PRESS
Washington, D.C.

Copyright © 2004
The Catholic University of America Press
All rights reserved
Printed in the United States of America

The paper used in this publication meets the minimum requirements of the American National Standards for Information Science—Permanence of Paper for Printed Library materials, ANSI Z39.48–1984.
∞

LIBRARY OF CONGRESS CATALOGING-IN-PUBLICATION DATA
Categories : historical and systematic essays / edited by Michael Gorman and Jonathan J. Sanford
    p. cm. — (Studies in philosophy and the history of philosophy ; v. 41)
  Includes bibliographical references and index.
  ISBN 978-0-8132-3205-8 (alk. paper)
    1. Categories (Philosophy) I. Gorman, Michael., 1965– II. Sanford, Jonathan J., 1974– III. Title. IV. Series.
  BC172.C38 2004
  110—dc22

Contents

Introduction   vii

PART I. THE ARISTOTELIAN TRADITION

1. JONATHAN J. SANFORD, Categories and Metaphysics: Aristotle's Science of Being   3
2. HELEN LANG, Aristotle's Categories "Where" and "When"   21
3. ELEONORE STUMP, Aquinas's Metaphysics: Individuation and Constitution   33
4. WILLIAM E. MCMAHON, Reflections on Some Thirteenth- and Fourteenth-Century Views of the Categories   45
5. MAY SIM, Categories and Commensurability in Confucius and Aristotle: A Response to MacIntyre   58

PART II. MODERN APPROACHES

6. TIMOTHY SEAN QUINN, Kant: The Practical Categories   81
7. CARL R. HAUSMAN, Charles Peirce's Categories, Phenomenological and Ontological   97
8. DAGFINN FØLLESDAL, Husserl and the Categories   118
9. NEWTON GARVER, Language-Games as Categories: An Aristotelian Theme in Wittgenstein's Later Thought   136

PART III. NORMATIVE CONSIDERATIONS

10. MICHAEL GORMAN, Categories and Normativity   151
11. DAVID WEISSMAN, Categorial Form   171

PART IV. EPISTEMOLOGICAL AND METAPHYSICAL CONSIDERATIONS

12. MARIAM THALOS, Distinction, Judgment, and Discipline — 185
13. ROBERT SOKOLOWSKI, Categorial Intentions and Objects — 204
14. BARRY SMITH, Carving Up Reality — 225
15. C. WESLEY DEMARCO, The Generation and Destruction of Categories — 238
16. JORGE J. E. GRACIA, Are Categories Invented or Discovered? A Response to Foucault — 268

Bibliography — 285
List of Contributors — 295
Author Index — 299
Subject Index — 303

Introduction

MICHAEL GORMAN
AND JONATHAN J. SANFORD

It is impossible to think without using categories. Consider the judgment that the rose is red. To make this judgment, one must use the category "red" and assign the rose to it; one must also, perhaps in a somewhat different way, make use of the category "rose." And what is true here about judging that the rose is red is, *mutatis mutandis*, true about asserting it, which means that categories are needed for language as well. To be sure, there is more to thinking than judgment, even as there is more to speaking than assertion. But other mental and speech acts involve categories: pondering, hoping, intending, asking, ordering, promising, and many others. Without categories we would, in short, be speechless and thoughtless.

The word "category" comes from the Greek term καταγορεύω, which means to denounce or accuse publicly; it is, in other words, to name some attribute belonging to an individual, as when someone says that George is a thief. And it was the Greek philosopher Aristotle who, building on the work of his predecessors, inaugurated the systematic discussion of categories in his work of that name. Later philosophers have not failed to notice the ubiquity of categories, nor have they hesitated to ask questions about them. The present volume is a collection of essays on categories. Before describing the essays themselves, we would like to bring out some of the main issues in category theory. A convenient way of doing so is to reflect on a simple fact: something can be a member of more than one category. This flower, for instance, is not only red; it is also a rose, a physical object, an item for sale, and so on. How is this possible?

One thing that makes it possible is that categories can be arranged hierarchically. Every rose is a physical object, but not every physical object is a rose. "Physical object" is thus a category that includes "rose" as a proper subcategory of itself, along with "car" and "stone." Hierarchy allows a particular flower to belong not only to the category "rose" but also to every category above it: flower, plant, living thing, physical object, and so on. So this brings out one important issue in category theory: hierarchy.¹

The idea that categories are related in this way suggests something else, namely, that perhaps there is a highest categorical level. And, if there is, one might ask whether there is just one category at this level, a category to which absolutely everything belongs, or whether even at the highest level there is still a multiplicity. Thinking about such matters brings us immediately to Aristotle, who used the term "category" to refer to these highest sorts of categories and who held the view that there was more than one category in this sense. Here we find one terminological issue and a host of substantive ones. The terminological issue is simply the need to keep track of when the word "category" means "highest category" and when it means "any sort of category." The substantive issues begin with the relation between the lower categories and the highest ones: in what sense are the highest ones most basic? If the answer is that they are basic in an ontological or metaphysical sense, then one might wonder about the unity of reality: if there is no single category that everything falls into, is reality ultimately fragmentary? Or, are there relations among the various categories that are sufficient to bring reality into a unity?

These are just some of the issues that arise when we use the notion of hierarchy to understand how something can belong to more than one category. But hierarchy does not always help. It can happen that something belongs to more than one category but that the categories are not related in a hierarchical way. The rose is both a plant and something for sale, but not all plants are for sale, and not all things for sale are plants. These categories, then, overlap, something that hierarchy-minded categorizers have traditionally sought to avoid.²

Thinking about how one might avoid such overlaps raises further issues, even to the point of calling into question the project of categorical metaphysics. Consider the following way of avoiding the overlaps. It is true, one might say, that a rose is both a plant and an item for sale, and it is also true that "plant" and "item for sale" are overlapping, non-hierarchical categories. But this is not a deep problem, because "item for sale" is not a natural category. Nothing is, of its own nature, for sale;

---

1. For a recent discussion of categories in hierarchical terms, see chap. 1 of Joshua Hoffman and Gary Rosenkrantz, *Substance among Other Categories* (Cambridge: Cambridge University Press, 1994).

2. See Aristotle, *Categories* 3, 1b15–20, in *The Complete Works of Aristotle: The Revised Oxford Translation*, 2 vols., ed. Jonathan Barnes (Princeton: Princeton University Press, 1984).

something belongs to this category only because human beings have made a certain decision. By contrast, a rose is, of its own nature, a plant. So, if we restrict our attention to natural categories, setting aside categories that exist only because of human concerns, we will find that a hierarchical ordering can be preserved. And perhaps this is what we as metaphysicians ought to have been focused on all along, since metaphysics is concerned with the way things are in themselves, not with the way they are relative to us.

Simply to consider such a solution—evaluating it goes far beyond the scope of this introduction—is to come up against the question of which categories are humanly constructed and which are natural. There is, to be sure, a trivial sense in which all categories are humanly constructed. We cannot think in terms of a certain category without thinking through what that category is. The category must, in other words, be something that we have "come up with ourselves." But this is not the issue. The issue is whether the categories we come up with correspond to or map onto divisions that are already there in the world or whether, by contrast, they impose divisions on the world.

That people impose divisions on the world is beyond doubt. Someone who paints lines in a parking lot is not trying to reflect any underlying structure in the asphalt, nor ought he try to. If saying this amounts to advocating a limited kind of antirealism about categories, then it would be hard to find a philosopher who is not a category antirealist. The serious question of antirealism is not this but something else. Might it be the case that no categories are real or natural, that all categories are imposed on what is, in itself, wholly devoid of structure? If so, then what of categories in metaphysics?

A related issue is the following. Reality can be looked at in a number of ways, each of which involves our thinking in terms of a particular category scheme. For example, the way in which florists divide up the world of flowers is different from the way in which botanists divide it up. From this one might be led to think that (i) there is no single right categorical scheme, and (ii) there is no single right way to relate all the schemes to one another. This would leave us with a hodgepodge of categorical schemes serving different purposes. Such a position might seem midway between realism and antirealism. Consider the islanders in Bambrough's example who think of trees as "boat-building trees," "house-building trees," and so on.[3] Their practical interests lead them to divide up the world in a way that is different from the way in which

---

3. See Renford Bambrough, "Universals and Family Resemblances," *Proceedings of the Aristotelian Society* 61 (1960–61): 207–22.

we divide it up. Suppose there are neither good reasons to prefer one scheme over the other nor uniquely right ways to construe one scheme as more basic than the other. From that it would not follow that there is no correct way to divide trees into boat-building trees and house-building trees. A relativity of category schemes might be able to coexist with a certain kind of realism about the world: which scheme we use is up to us, but once we decide on one, there is a right and a wrong way to apply it.

From what has been said, it is clear that there are many important and difficult issues surrounding the nature and use of categories. And there are many other issues that have not been discussed. For example, all the points that have been made so far about categories have been metaphysical or ontological in nature. But thinking about categories has wider relevance as well. Questions of value and morality are often closely connected to questions about the categories we put things into—think of the issues and decisions that turn on whether one considers certain living beings to be human or not. Likewise, questions of knowledge and language are often closely connected to questions about categories. And this brings us back to what was said at the beginning, that our knowing and saying involves placing things in categories.

Hence it is that categories are crucial in metaphysical, epistemological, and axiological ways. The purpose of this volume is to make available some of the best recent thinking on this topic. Before taking note of the individual essays themselves, it is well to note that the essays constitute a mix of historical and systematic reflections. Including essays of both sorts embodies the editors' conviction that philosophical reflection is best carried out in dialogue with the great thinkers of the past. Sometimes the best wine is a mix of the old and the new.[4]

In the remainder of this introduction the various wines that make up the volume are described briefly; that is, we offer but a taste here, leaving consumption to your own discretion. Five of the sixteen essays focus on categories either in Aristotle himself or in the work of figures who have adopted an Aristotelian approach to categories. Then follow four essays focusing on categories in modern philosophy. In these first nine essays there is, to be sure, systematic reflection on categories, but this

---

4. This way of making the point is Avrum Stroll's; for details on the "solera process" of making sherry and its relevance to the study of philosophy, see his *Twentieth-Century Analytic Philosophy* (New York: Columbia University Press, 2000). For related discussions, see Jorge J. E. Gracia, *Philosophy and Its History: Issues in Philosophical Historiography* (Albany: State University of New York Press, 1992), and Dallas Willard, "Who Needs Brentano? The Wasteland of Philosophy without Its Past," in *The Brentano Problem,* ed. Roberto Poli (Aldershot: Ashgate, 1998).

reflection is undertaken in tandem with explication of historically significant philosophers' reflections on categories. The last seven essays are more exclusively systematic. The first two focus on categories insofar as they bear on normative thinking, and the last five focus on categories insofar as they relate to epistemological or metaphysical concerns.

Sanford's "Categories and Metaphysics: Aristotle's Science of Being" starts us off, yoking Aristotle's earlier thought on categories to his account of the science of being in the *Metaphysics*. Sanford argues that categories are crucial for the development of any science, focusing primarily on Aristotle's account of how categories are used rather than on his account of what they are. Sanford further argues that the science of being *qua* being demands that primacy be given to being in the sense of the categories, as opposed to the other three senses of being, noting on the one hand Aristotle's insistence that metaphysics is to be a *science* of being, and on the other hand the special emphasis given to being in the sense of the categories in the central books of the *Metaphysics*. Sanford concludes with some comments on the relevance of Aristotle's take on categories and his view of metaphysics.

Lang's "Aristotle's Categories 'Where' and 'When'" brings to light important aspects of two of Aristotle's categories. She argues that the standard translations—of τό ποῦ as "place" and of τὸ ποτέ as "time"— are mistranslations, that they are grammatically deficient insofar as they treat these two categories as substantives, and that they lead to two sorts of philosophical confusion. First, Aristotle's account of place (ὁ τόπος) in *Physics* IV, 1–5, and his account of time (ὁ χρόνος) in *Physics* IV, 10–14, are sometimes muddled with his accounts of "where" and "when" in the *Categories*. Lang argues that there are systematic differences between what Aristotle examines in his *Physics* as "place" and "time" and his accounts of the categories of "where" and "when" in the *Categories*. At the same time she argues that Aristotle's accounts of place and time solve some problems he inherited from Plato. Second, the special role of the categories "where" and "when" can be obscured if we do not see them functioning within Aristotle's accounts of place and time. "Where" and "when" are better understood in their role as predicates within a view of the cosmos that already designates all natural things as being in place and within time; when these categories are employed, we can see that they indicate where and when a substance is within the ordered whole. Lang concludes by noting that when we make the effort not to confuse "where" and "when" with "place" and "time," we can better see the relevance of Aristotle's *Categories* as not just a logical work but as one that intends to give us a better purchase on reality.

Stump's "Aquinas's Metaphysics: Individuation and Constitution" moves us beyond Aristotle to one of his most prominent philosophical successors. Stump focuses on the role of Aquinas's view of things for his metaphysics. By "things" Stump means "not only substances and artifacts but also at least some of the parts of which substances are constituted." She explores the individuation, identity, and constitution of things, and especially of human things, in Aquinas's work in order to show the importance of his theory of things for his philosophical and theological views generally.

McMahon's "Reflections on Some Thirteenth- and Fourteenth-Century Views of the Categories" traces some of the first substantive refinements and rejections of the Aristotelian—and for a long time standard—account of the categories. The philosophers he deals with—Henry of Ghent, John Duns Scotus, William of Ockham, and John Buridan—are still working within the Aristotelian tradition, but at the same time they open the door for some of the wholly different views on categories that one finds in Kant and other modern figures. The four thinkers McMahon touches upon begin to tinker with such claims as that there are only ten categories and that these categories exhaust the senses of simple categorematic terms. The essay shows how thirteenth- and fourteenth-century thinkers in the Latin West began to reexamine the accepted view of the categories and their relation both to how we think and to how the world is organized.

Whereas McMahon's essay signals the beginning of the end of Aristotelian dominance in thought concerning the categories, Sim's "Categories and Commensurability in Confucius and Aristotle: A Response to MacIntyre" reasserts the pervasiveness of Aristotle's view of the categories. She makes the case that the relevance of Aristotle's account of the categories is not just a phenomenon of the West, but that one finds similar lines of thought in Confucius and his successors. Sim challenges MacIntyre's claim that there is a breach of incommensurability between Confucians and Aristotelians. She builds her case by looking at each of Aristotle's categories and demonstrating how Confucius employs the same categories in his writings. Underlying Sim's paper is the presupposition that the Aristotelian categories are not just the products of Aristotle's imagination, or just the product of a Western mind; instead, they manifest the way in which human beings in general encounter the world. Sim's paper thus widens the discussion of categories in two ways: first, she moves consideration of categories beyond Western philosophy; second, she broaches the subject of the relation between categories and ethical thought.

We find in modern and contemporary thinkers approaches to the categories that are neither Aristotelian nor even explicitly concerned with reacting to the Aristotelian view of categories. Quinn's "Kant: The Practical Categories" is the first in our next set of essays. Rather than dealing only with Kant's theoretical categories and their deduction, an issue that has been belabored in Kant scholarship, Quinn focuses on the relation between categories and ethical thought. The goal of his essay is to explain Kant's idea of the practical categories and what those categories reveal about the way in which reason acts in the world. Quinn accomplishes this goal through several steps. First, he introduces us to Kant's theoretical categories as a help to understanding the practical categories. Second, he explains Kant's practical categories. Third, he compares the practical and theoretical categories. Quinn is then able to draw some general conclusions about the role of categories in Kant's thought, arguing that the practical categories are more evocative of reason's unique power than are the theoretical categories.

Hausman's "Charles Peirce's Categories, Phenomenological and Ontological" explains that Peirce's categories, known alternately as Oneness, Twoness, and Threeness, or as the monad, dyad, and triad, are generated logically as well as phenomenologically. Though these methods of generating the categories differ, on both the logical and the phenomenological accounts the categories are seen to have ontological bearing, for, as Hausman argues, Peirce's categories reveal features of reality. After discussing the generation of the categories, Hausman turns his attention to the relation between Peirce's categories and his unique evolutionary realism. To explore this issue, Hausman explains certain features of Peirce's view of evolution as it is found in his early and in his later works. He then looks explicitly to the connection between the categories and Peirce's mature view of evolution. Hausman concludes by arguing that the relation between Peirce's categories and his evolutionary realism can be seen to be complete only when we also introduce the role of Peircean agape into the account.

Føllesdal's "Husserl and the Categories" introduces us to the ways in which categories are employed within Husserl's phenomenology. This is, Føllesdal says, not an easy thing to do, because in none of his works does Husserl provide a careful analysis of categories. Instead, one has to collect Husserl's thoughts on categories from a number of his writings. In spite of the lack of an explicit formulation of a category theory, Husserl relies nonetheless on such categories as noematic, noetic, eidetic, ontic, material, and many others. Føllesdal introduces Husserlian category theory by situating it in the general context of Husserlian phenomenology, highlighting such themes as the distinction between transcendental and transcendent, intentionality and directedness, noema and hyle, and the eidetic, transcendental, and phenomenological reductions.

Garver's "Language-Games as Categories: An Aristotelian Theme in Wittgenstein's Later Thought" argues for a connection between Aristotle's account of the categories and Wittgenstein's mature work. This may seem a surprising connection, since Wittgenstein does not mention Aristotle when introducing language-games, and Aristotle's categories and the metaphysics they are often seen to support are not generally regarded as having much in common with Wittgenstein's language-games. Important to Garver's case are his claims that Aristotle's *Categories* is ambiguous as to whether categories refer to speech-acts only or also to the way things stand in the world, and that Aristotle did not necessarily intend to limit the number of categories to ten. Garver sees connections between Aristotle and Wittgenstein in their naturalistic approach to categories, in the common assumption that categories and language-games respectively are designated within the context of human activity, and in the methodology for distinguishing between different categories or language-games. Garver sees Wittgenstein to be revitalizing Aristotelian naturalism while not denying Hume's insight that it is unsatisfactory to presume necessities to be matters of fact.

Gorman's "Categories and Normativity" is the first of the last set of essays, those that deal with categories systematically. One of the goals of Gorman's essay is to argue that normativity is more bound up with our thinking than contemporary philosophers tend to acknowledge. Gorman takes a careful look at what he terms the "unity problem," the problem of giving an account of the unity of a category. After exploring several ways of thinking about the unity problem, Gorman focuses attention on the normative version of this problem. He argues that this version is best dealt with by recognizing that at least some categories are constituted, and so given their unity, by norms. After responding to some objections to his proposal, and distinguishing the sense of "normative" he employs from other senses, Gorman makes some suggestions about what grounds normative categories.

Like Gorman's essay, Weissman's "Categorial Form" explores the relationship between categories and normativity. Remarking on the split between metaphysics and ethics that is one of the chief marks of philosophy since Hume, Weissman makes clear that his aim is to "reaffirm the linkage of metaphysics and morals." Categorial form is the bridge between metaphysics and ethics. Weissman supports his proposal in several steps, among them the following: arguing that there is indeed categorial form and that there are appropriate methods for discovering it;

responding to Kantian objections to his proposal; outlining individualism, communitarianism, and holism as possible candidates of categorial form; and then drawing some practical implications from what has been argued. One of the practical conclusions that Weissman draws is that human life is not unrestrictedly variable; successful interaction among human beings is limited by categorial form.

Thalos, in her "Distinction, Judgment, and Discipline," turns our attention from normative considerations to some of the ways in which categories bear on epistemological and metaphysical concerns. Thalos focuses on categories insofar as they undergird the sorts of distinctions and judgments we make. Thalos begins by pointing to what she considers a problematic distinction common in analytic thought between fact and knowledge of fact. What is problematic about the distinction is that it gives preference to the fact over the knowledge of it. What Thalos develops in her essay is a way of distinguishing between fact and knowledge that puts neither fact nor knowledge in an independent, and so privileged, position. The linchpin of her account is the claim that the sort of distinction one makes depends on the sort of activity one is engaged in. She then explains some of the ways in which distinguishing, judging, and defining overlap in various human activities, focusing in particular on scientific activities. Thalos closes with a series of observations and questions concerning the impact of her analysis of distinction and judgment on efforts to naturalize epistemology.

Sokolowski's "Categorial Intentions and Objects" is a reprinting (with very slight modifications) of chapter 7 of his *Introduction to Phenomenology*. Because it grows out of Sokolowski's studies of Husserl, the chapter reprinted here can be compared with Føllesdal's treatment of Husserl; nonetheless, it was written without footnotes as a systematic account, not as a work of historical research, and for that reason it is included in the present volume as a systematic account of categorial intentionality. Distinguishing between the basic intentionality involved in perception and the more complex intentionality involved in categorial activity, Sokolowski demonstrates how the latter goes beyond, but is rooted in, the former. He further explains how we establish categorial objects via our categorial intentions and argues that truth or meaning is not to be found in mental or conceptual things, but rather in the successful articulation of states of affairs. Along the way, Sokolowski also clarifies a number of technical terms employed by phenomenologists when discussing categorial intentionality. He concludes first with reflections on vagueness in categorial intentions, and then, on a more positive note, with thoughts on some ways in which categorial intentionality manifests what is most distinctive about human beings: their intelligence.

Smith's "Carving Up Reality" focuses on the ways in which we partition reality. The more common way for philosophers to partition reality is to divide it into classes, elements, species, categories, and the like. There are, Smith argues, other sorts of partitionings that occur, however. For example, in perception we divide between background and foreground, and when we develop theories we divide reality into what does and what does not fall into our theory. Smith's paper seeks a general theory of the way in which we partition reality, one that is capable of accounting for the various specific ways in which we divide reality. After sketching such a theory, Smith draws out some of its implications for our understanding of categories, our understanding of vagueness, and our understanding of what he terms "the granularity of perception." Smith concludes with a reflection on the realism of his approach, central to which is his distinction between *bona fide* and *fiat* boundaries.

DeMarco's "The Generation and Destruction of Categories" investigates why human thought and language are inextricably tied to categorial formulations and why nature itself is receptive to categorial division. DeMarco's essay addresses, then, both epistemological and metaphysical concerns, while focusing in particular on the role categories play in making it possible for reason and nature to become intertwined. In building his case DeMarco clarifies what he considers to be the function of categories, the relation between categories and qualifications, the ways in which we generate categories, and what it means to categorize successfully—that is, what it means for our categorizations to allow an adequate meeting of reason and extra-mental reality. DeMarco's essay presents what he calls "a moderate realism about categories," an approach that accounts for the multiplicity and variability of categorial schemes while at the same time arguing that such schemes must be at least in part anchored to reality if they are to be intelligible.

The volume concludes with Gracia's "Are Categories Invented or Discovered? A Response to Foucault." Gracia's essay presents a valuable finale because it brings together many aspects of the inquiries into categories undertaken in the previous essays, while at the same time paving the way for further investigations. Gracia uses as his foil Foucault's influential claim that categories are a matter of invention, a claim he finds suspect, to say the least. Also suspect, however, is the claim that all categories are discovered. Gracia's essay cautions us against overly sweeping claims concerning categories. If we avoid unwarranted generalizations, Gracia argues, careful analysis is likely to lead us to recognize that some categories are, indeed, invented, others are discovered, and still others are partly invented and partly discovered. Investigations of categories are, Gracia urges, not easy affairs; but when carefully undertaken they are capable of producing important clues to how we think, how we speak, how we act, and how the world is.

Let us close with a few words of thanks. We are grateful to David McGonagle and Susan Needham of the Catholic University of America Press for their help in bringing this volume to completion, as well as to Jude Dougherty, the general editor of the series in which it appears. We are grateful to James Despres for helping to prepare the bibliography, to Jennifer Angelo for helping to prepare the indexes, to Gregory Doolan for hunting down some hard-to-find references, and especially to Jorge J. E. Gracia for first suggesting we work together on this project. Finally, we are grateful to our wives, Anne-Marie and Rebecca, and to our children, for their support.

PART I
THE ARISTOTELIAN TRADITION

1 Categories and Metaphysics: Aristotle's Science of Being

JONATHAN J. SANFORD

The relationship between Aristotle's *Categories* and his *Metaphysics* is a matter of some debate. If one assumes that the *Categories* is fundamentally a metaphysical work, then there appear to be irreconcilable differences between the notion of substance presented in the *Categories* and that presented in *Metaphysics* Z (VII). The *Categories* account of substance does not present matter as a component of hylomorphic substance, nor does it consider substance as a formal cause of unity, both of which are key ideas of *Metaphysics* Z (VII). The *Metaphysics* therefore represents a break with Aristotle's older metaphysical scheme.[1] On the other hand, if one assumes that the *Categories* is fundamentally a logical work that makes no pretence to being a work of metaphysics, then the account of substance and the other categories in the *Categories* is at worst irrelevant to, and at best only obliquely related to, what Aristotle attempts to accomplish in the *Metaphysics*.[2] I think that the truth lies somewhere between these two views. The *Categories* is best understood as both a logical and a metaphysical account. The metaphysics presented in the *Categories* is by no means complete, but Aristotle does not claim that it is. Aristotle does not, in the *Metaphysics*, break with his ideas in the *Categories*, but deepens them and works to fill out his meta-

---

1. See, for example, G. E. L. Owen, "Logic and Metaphysics in Some Earlier Works of Aristotle," in *Logic, Science, and Dialectic: Collected Papers in Greek Philosophy*, ed. Martha Nussbaum (Ithaca: Cornell University Press, 1986), 180–99; Michael Frede, "Categories in Aristotle," in *Studies in Aristotle*, ed. D. O'Meara (Washington, D.C.: Catholic University of America Press, 1981), 1–24 (reprinted in Michael Frede, *Essays in Ancient Philosophy* [Minneapolis: University of Minnesota Press, 1987], 29–48); Michael Frede,"The Title, Unity, and Authenticity of the Aristotelian Categories," 11–28, and "Individuals in Aristotle," 49–71, both in Frede, *Essays in Ancient Philosophy*.
2. See, for example, C. M. Gillespie, "The Aristotelian Categories," *Classical Quarterly* 19 (1925): 75–84; Walter E. Wehrle, *The Myth of Aristotle's Development and the Betrayal of Metaphysics* (Oxford: Rowman & Littlefield, 2000).

physics.³ In this essay I consider the relationship between Aristotle's metaphysics and his theory of categories from the perspective of the requirements of science. The *Metaphysics* presents Aristotle's science of being, but, as his logical works show, science depends on categories. Thus the *Metaphysics* cannot be understood apart from the works—especially the *Categories*, the *Topics*, and the *Posterior Analytics*—in which Aristotle explains what categories are, how they are used, and what their relationship to science is. There are indeed some difficulties in positing a close relationship between Aristotle's earlier and later works, especially in regard to what gives unity to a science and the importance of being in the sense of potentiality and actuality. Still, these problems are not so great as to constitute a disjunction between Aristotle's earlier and later works. Indeed, Aristotle's attempts to describe being in each of its four senses in the *Metaphysics* are possible only because of the close relationship between logic and metaphysics, a relationship that he elucidates in his *Categories* and some other earlier works.⁴

I. METAPHYSICS AS THE SCIENCE OF CATEGORIES: AN OVERVIEW

In the *Metaphysics* Aristotle seems to have difficulty clarifying the domain and special task of metaphysics. He alternates between several nomenclatures for this study, calling it at different times first philosophy, wisdom, the science of first causes and principles, the divine science or theology, and the science of being *qua* being.⁵ Although each

---

3. Michael V. Wedin argues that the *Categories* and the *Metaphysics* are compatible because *Metaphysics* Z is intended as an explanation of the notion of substance presented in the *Categories*. Wedin, *Aristotle's Theory of Substance: The* Categories *and* Metaphysics *Zeta* (Oxford: Oxford University Press, 2000).

4. Joseph Owens discusses some important aspects of the relationship between logic and metaphysics in "Aristotle on Categories," *Review of Metaphysics* 14 (1960): 73–90.

5. The following passage from Γ (IV) is often considered the clearest formulation of metaphysics' task: "There is a science which investigates being as being and the attributes which belong to this in virtue of its own nature. Now this is not the same as any of the so-called special sciences: for none of these others deals generally with being as being. They cut off a part of being and investigate the attributes of this part—this is what the mathematical sciences for instance do. Now since we are seeking the first principles and the highest causes, clearly there must be some thing to which these belong in virtue of its own nature. If then our predecessors who sought the elements of existing things were seeking these same principles, it is necessary that the elements must be elements of being not by accident but just because it is being. Therefore it is of being as being that we also must grasp the first causes." *Metaphysics* IV, 1, 1003a22–31. This and other translations used in this essay are taken, with a few changes, from those found in *The Complete Works of Aristotle: The Revised Oxford Translation*, 2 vols., ed. Jonathan Barnes (Princeton: Princeton University Press, 1984).

of these designations is revealing of the domain of this science, the last, the science of being *qua* being, is the most general and so capable of covering the most territory.[6] It is not immediately clear what the science of being *qua* being might be, however, for Aristotle tells us in E2 that being has four senses:[7]

> [T]he unqualified term 'being' has several meanings, of which one was seen to be the accidental, and another the true (non-being being the false), while besides these there are the figures of predication, e.g. the 'what,' quality, quantity, place, time, and any similar meanings which 'being' may have; and again besides all these there is that which is potentially or actually. (*Metaphysics* VI, 2, 1026a34–b2)

Aristotle explains here that the four senses of being are (1) accidental being, (2) being in the sense of truth and falsity, (3) categorial being, and (4) potential and actual being. Of all these senses of being, categorial being (or, as it is called here, the "figures of predication") is the one that Aristotle considers most consistently in the *Metaphysics*.[8] One reason for this is that it is only from being in this sense that philosophical knowledge can be had: it is only by means of categories that categorial propositions can be made and demonstrative syllogisms performed. Since epistemic or scientific knowledge (ἐπιστήμη) can only be had by means of demonstrations, one can build a science only by means of the categories of being.[9]

The primacy and indispensability of categorial being for the purpose of pursuing a science of being suggests that our understanding of the other senses of being is, from the perspective of Aristotle's epistemology, dependent on categorial being. That is, if we are to know the other senses of being scientifically, then they must be known through categorial being. This is not to say, however, that the three other senses of being

---

6. For two sides of the debate whether *Metaphysics* IV, 1, 1003a22–31, represents a discontinuity with Aristotle's earlier works, compare Owen, "Logic and Metaphysics in Some Earlier Works of Aristotle," and Jiyuan Yu, "What Is the Focal Meaning of Being in Aristotle?" *Apeiron* 34 (2001): 205–31.

7. Aristotle provides a fuller explanation of these four senses of being in Δ (V) 7, 1017a8–b9.

8. Robert Hanna notes this fact in an article, relying heavily on the work of Owen: "Consequently, since Aristotle appears to regard the sense (iii) of being in the categories as prior to the other senses, it seems plausible to hold that the categoreal sense of being is the *essential* sense for metaphysics. This seems particularly likely considering what Owen calls the 'pros hen' structure of the *Metaphysics* whereby there is a tendency to fuse logical priority, primary instance, and essentiality." Hanna, "What Categories Are Not," *The Monist* 66 (1983): 424.

9. On the relationship between demonstration and sciencific knowledge, see Aristotle, *Posterior Analytics* I, 1, 2; II, 8, 9, 10, 19; *Metaphysics* VII, 10.

are ontologically derived from categorial being, though this does seem to be the case with accidental being.[10] Being in the sense of truth and falsity seems only in part ontologically dependent on categorial being, and being in the sense of potentiality and actuality is altogether distinct, in terms of its ontological priority, from categorial being. Nevertheless, it is impossible to discuss the other senses of being until they have been translated into the semantics of categorial being. For Aristotle, metaphysics, insofar as it is a *science* of being, must concentrate on categorial being, while at the same time considering the other senses of being through the fulcrum of categorial being. In the next section we will look at some aspects of Aristotle's view of science in order to see the role of categories in science in general and in the science of being in particular.

II. THE CATEGORIES IN SOME EARLIER WORKS: HOW TO KNOW THINGS

Aristotle's definition of metaphysics as the science of being that explores the categories rests on his earlier investigations of categories. It will be useful, then, to look to some of his earlier thoughts on categories and science for background. In order to understand Aristotle's theory of categories, one must look to the *Topics*.[11] This may seem a surprising claim, yet it is not without precedent: Porphyry noticed long ago, in his *Isagoge*, that tackling the *Categories* requires a knowledge of Aristotle's theory of deduction.[12] Just as the best way to know what an axe is is to learn to chop wood with one, the best way to learn what categories are is to learn to use them. In the *Topics* Aristotle presents us

---

10. Aristotle dispenses quickly with accidental being, claiming that it is not particularly revelatory of being and that there can be no scientific treatment of it. See *Metaphysics* VI, 2, 1026b24, 1026b13: "Since 'being' has many meanings, we must first say regarding the *accidental*, that there can be no scientific treatment of it.... For the accidental is practically a mere name."

11. Michael Frede argues in "Categories in Aristotle" that it is necessary to understand the *Topics* in order to understand the *Categories*. Frede's arguments serve to sever the connection between the first category and substance. That is, he does not think, in spite of the weight of most interpretations of Aristotle's *Categories* to the contrary, that Aristotle meant to identify the first category with substance. His analyses deserve to be dealt with extensively. Here I have space only to register my disagreement with his main line of argumentation. It is with a different purpose in mind that I look to the *Topics* in order to understand Aristotle's theory of categories.

12. "Since, Chrysaorius, to teach about Aristotle's *Categories* it is necessary to know what genus and difference are, as well as species, property, and accident, and since reflection on these things is useful for giving definitions, and in general for matters pertaining to division and demonstration, therefore I shall give you a brief account." Porphyry, *Isagoge*, in *Five Texts on the Mediaeval Problem of Universals*, trans. and ed. Paul Vincent Spade (Indianapolis: Hackett, 1994), 1.

with an account of how to employ categories, rather than beginning with an account of what they are. Knowledge of how to use categories will shed light on what they are, and then on the ways in which they make science possible. Science is, as it were, the end of the process that begins with the categories: propositions are composed of categories, demonstrations are composed of propositions, and science follows from demonstrations.

One reason why it may seem odd to suggest beginning with the *Topics* is that the professed goal of the *Topics* is not to discuss demonstration (ἀπόδειξις), which is a deduction or syllogism proceeding from true and primary principles that secures scientific knowledge, but is rather to deal with the dialectical syllogism that proceeds from common beliefs.[13] Since the dialectical syllogism proceeds from reputable, or generally accepted, opinions (ἔνδοξα), scientific knowledge cannot be gained through such deductions.[14] Yet dialectical syllogisms provide a model for all reasoning, and they are extremely useful for, among other things, eliminating prospective candidates for true and primary premises to serve in demonstrations (*Topics* I, 1–2, 101a24–b5). They perform this task by testing reputable opinions for consistency and other signs of veracity.[15] Demonstrations and dialectical syllogisms differ, then, in so far as the former provide us with definite knowledge and the latter only with probable knowledge. They are both deductions, however, and so employ the same mechanics to reach conclusions.[16]

---

13. "Our treatise proposes to find a line of inquiry whereby we shall be able to reason from reputable opinions about any subject presented to us, and also shall ourselves, when putting forward an argument, avoid saying anything contrary to it." Aristotle, *Topics* I, 1, 100a20–22.

14. Aristotle holds that there is another type of argument, in addition to the demonstrative syllogism, that establishes knowledge, namely, induction. But this type of argument, although often more persuasive than the syllogism in common use, lacks the demonstrable weight of the syllogism. Induction cannot, then, be properly viewed as securing ἐπιστήμη in its most forceful sense: "There are induction and deduction. Now what deduction is has been said before; induction is a passage from particulars to universals. . . . Induction is more convincing and clear: it is more readily learned by the use of the senses, and is applicable generally to the mass of men; but deduction is more forcible and more effective against contradictious people." *Topics* I, 12, 105a12–18. See also *Posterior Analytics* II, 19, and *Physics* I, 1, 184a10–b7.

15. Aristotle employs this dialectical approach in many of his other works. One of the clearest descriptions of this dialectical method is provided at the outset of his discussion of incontinence in the *Nicomachean Ethics:* "We must, as in all other cases, set the phenomena before us and, after first discussing the difficulties, go on to prove, if possible, the truth of all the reputable opinions about these affections or, failing this, of the greater number and the most authoritative; for if we both resolve the difficulties and leave the reputable opinions undisturbed, we shall have proved the case sufficiently." *Nicomachean Ethics* VII, 1, 1145b1–7.

16. For the purposes of this essay, "deduction" and "syllogism" are synonymous.

It is in deductions that we see categories as the building blocks from which propositions are constructed. A deduction is a series of expressions in which one proposition is the conclusion that follows from one or more propositions, the premises.[17] Aristotle tells us that the propositions of a deduction are always composed of one of four types of propositional material: accident, genus, property, and definition.[18] And so we are looking for one of these four types of propositional material, whether pursuing the less strict type of knowledge that follows from dialectical syllogisms or strict epistemic knowledge.

In the *Topics*, Aristotle argues that by employing a syllogism we can establish the type of predication that holds for a particular problem. In other words, we can establish the strength of the principal relational property that holds between a subject and predicate. Deduction serves to prove either that a predicate is not the same with its subject as a definition, property, genus, or accident, by displaying that the conclusion does not follow from its premises. Or, deduction proves that the predicate is the same with its subject as a definition, property, genus, or accident by demonstrating that the conclusion does necessarily follow from the premises. If the conclusion is shown to have followed from the premises, then *true* predication has occurred.[19] True predication can occur within any of the four philosophical problems, but before looking more closely at it we should look to the connection between the four types of philosophical problems and categories.

The four types of philosophical problems are drawn from the "genera of predicates," that is to say, from the categories.[20] The categories or

---

17. "Now a deduction is an argument [λόγος] in which, certain things being laid down, something other than these necessarily comes about through them." *Topics* I, 1, 100a25–26.

18. "Now the materials with which arguments start are equal in number, and are identical, with subjects on which deductions take place. For arguments start from propositions [ἐκ τῶν προτάσεων], while the subjects on which deductions take place are problems [τὰ προβλήματα]. Now every proposition and every problem indicates ... either property [ἴδιον] or definition [ὅρον] or genus [γένος] or accident [συμβεβηκός]." *Topics* I, 4, 101b13–16, 101b25.

19. "For every predicate of a subject must of necessity be either convertible with its subject or not: and if it is convertible, it would be its definition or property, for if it signifies the essence, it is the definition; if not, it is a property—for this was what a property is, viz. what is predicated convertibly, but does not signify the essence. If, on the other hand, it is not predicated convertibly of the thing, it either is or is not one of the terms contained in the definition of the subject; and if it is one of those terms, then it will be the genus or the differentia, inasmuch as the definition consists of genus and differentiae; whereas, if it is not one of these terms, clearly it would be an accident, for accident was said to be what belongs to a subject without being either its definition or its genus or a property." *Topics* I, 8, 103b7–17.

20. Ibid., 9, 103b20–21.

predicates are each an uncombined word or expression that is one of the following: what (οὐσίαν, substance), how large (ποσὸν, quantity), what sort (ποιὸν, quality), related to what (πρός τι, relation), where (ποῦ, place), when (ποτέ, time), being-in-a-position (κεῖσθαι, posture or position), having (ἔχειν, state or condition), acting (ποιεῖν, action), or being-affected (πάσχειν, affection).[21] All ten categories are listed together only twice, once in the *Categories* and once in the *Topics*.[22]

The order is slightly different in the two passages, but substance is the first category listed in each case. In the *Categories*, the word Aristotle uses for the first category is οὐσία, which is almost always translated as "substance."[23] In the *Topics*, the first category is described as τί ἐστι, a phrase usually translated as "essence." Elsewhere Aristotle uses τί ἐστι and οὐσία interchangeably, and so the two terms have traditionally been considered equivalent. Aristotle himself seems to suggest this when he writes, "And indeed the question which, both now and of old, has always been raised, and always been the subject of doubt, viz., what being is, is just the question, what is substance [τί τὸ ὄν, τοῦτό ἐστι, τίς ἡ οὐσία]?" (*Metaphysics* VII, 1, 1028b3–4). It seems sensible to accept the traditional interpretation, though the issue deserves more attention than we can afford to give it here.[24]

Substance enjoys the primary position among the categories for both logical and metaphysical reasons. Primary substances are never said of a subject or in a subject, whereas all other things are said either of or in primary substances. In addition to being logically primary, substances are the ontological ground that supports the other categories:

Thus all the other things are either said of the primary substances [τῶν πρώτων οὐσιῶν] as subjects [καθ' ὑποκειμένων], or in them as subjects [ἐν ὑποκειμέναις

---

21. *Categories* 4, 1b25–28. The same list is found in *Topics* I, 9, 103b21–24, but in slightly different order.

22. See Lang's comments on the philosophical importance of translating Aristotle's categories appropriately in Chapter 2 of this volume.

23. A literal translation is "beingness." Substance comes from the Latin *substantia*, which translates τὸ ὑποκείμενον, the Greek word for subject or substratum. Since many ancient commentators saw no problem with linking οὐσία and ὑποκείμενον, "substance" has stuck as the translation of οὐσία. This link is supported by passages such as the following from *Metaphysics* VI, 3, 1028b33–29a2: "The word 'substance' is applied, if not in more senses, still at least to four main objects; for both the essence and the universal and the genus are thought to be the substance of each thing, and fourth the substratum. Now the substratum is that of which other things are predicated, while it is itself not predicated of anything else. And so we must first determine the nature of this; for that which underlies a thing primarily is thought to be in the truest sense its substance [μάλιστα γὰρ δοκεῖ εἶναι οὐσία τὸ ὑποκείμενον πρῶτον]."

24. Michael Frede rejects this traditional interpretation in "Categories in Aristotle," 36.

αὐταῖς]. So if the primary substances did not exist it would be impossible for any of the other things to exist. (*Categories* 5, 2b4–6)

Substance serves as the absolute ontological baseline in the *Categories* and other early works, as well as in the *Metaphysics*.[25]

Once again, each of the four types of philosophical problems must necessarily be in one of these ten categories or predicates.[26] But what does it mean to "be in" a category? Aristotle obviously has more in mind than a merely semantic inclusion.[27] *Topics* I, 9 speaks of a man looking at an object directly in front of him that Aristotle describes as having a substance of such and such a quality, in relation to such and such, and so on.[28] The use of this concrete example suggests that for Aristotle the categories are not just linguistic devices but accurate accounts of how things stand in the world.[29] Indeed, Aristotle goes on to say, "for each of these kinds of predicate, if either it be asserted of itself, or its genus be asserted of it, signifies what something is [τί ἐστι σημαίνει]" (*Topics* I, 9, 103b36–38).[30] To seek to clarify a philosophical problem, then, is not just to avoid various types of ambiguity and to apply properly the mechanics of deduction; it is primarily to seek to see things in the world as they really are. It is on precisely this point that one finds a radical departure in modern philosophical thought from Aristotle's understanding and application of categories.[31]

---

25. See Wolfgang-Rainer Mann, *The Discovery of Things: Aristotle's* Categories *and Their Context* (Princeton: Princeton University Press, 2000). Mann focuses on the newness of Arisotle's notion of "things"—a notion we have come to take for granted—in comparison to the metaphysical schemes of the Platonists and pre-Socratics.

26. "For the accident and genus and property and definition of anything will always be in one of these predications; for all the propositions found through these signify either what something is or its quality or quantity or some one of the other types of predicate." *Topics* II, 9, 103b24–27.

27. The inclusion might be described as logical, in Aristotle's sense of "logical." Logical formulations, for Aristotle, are always existential. Many modern and contemporary students of logic, following Boole, reject Aristotle's existential assumption.

28. *Topics* I, 9, 103b30–34.

29. Aristotle gives a similar example in *Categories* I, 4. Also, Aristotle's following statement is a strong indication that he posits existence for all the categories: "So if the primary substances did not exist it would be impossible for any of the other things [τῶν ἄλλων τι; the antecedent for which is 'categories'] to exist." *Categories* 1, 5, 2b5–6). This seems to be the first premise of a Modus Tollens argument, in which Aristotle presumes we can supply the missing premise as well as the conclusion: Premise 2: But other categories do exist; Conclusion: Therefore primary substance exists.

30. See Frede, "Categories in Aristotle," 35–37. He points to this same passage in order to make the opposite claim to the one I am making. He claims that the categories in the *Topics* cannot be identified with the categories in the *Categories*, at least not in the standard interpretation of the *Categories*.

31. For this break with Aristotle, see Quinn's and Garver's essays, Chapters 6 and 9 of this volume.

Returning now to the issue of true predication, recall that the goal of a deduction—and deductions involve formal predications within one of the four divisions of philosophical problems—is to achieve true predication. True predication ensures that the conclusion necessarily follows from the premises by combining things in thought and speech that are in fact combined in reality. The performance of a deduction is a human action, but categories are not human inventions,[32] so true predication can only obtain if the four divisions of problems and the predications that are made within them are properly (that is, adequately and truly) nested within one or more of the ten categories. We are now in a position to see the relation between categories, predication, and science: when one pursues science (ἐπιστήμη), one seeks true predication in the type of deduction called demonstration (ἀπόδειξις) —and the elemental building blocks of every deduction are categories, the premises of which are themselves true and primary or are derived from true and primary premises.[33]

One great difficulty in pursuing science is that one needs true and primary premises. Of such premises Aristotle writes:

> Things are true and primitive which are convincing on the strength not of anything else but of themselves; for in regard to the first principles of science it is improper to ask any further for the why and wherefore of them; each of the first principles should command belief in and by itself. (*Topics* I, 1, 100a30–33)

We can leave aside here the issue of how first principles make themselves evident.[34] For the purposes of this essay it is necessary only to recognize that Aristotle is suggesting that there can be an immediate connection between first principles and our intellects. These first principles are ontological and not merely epistemological. They perform a double service both as the primary principles and causes whereby the world is organized and as the first principles whereby we understand the world to be the way it is. Every first principle is necessarily expressed by means of one or more of the categories. The categories, therefore, are prior to all first principles. For example, the principle of identity depends on the category of substance. We cannot say a substance is the same as itself without the category of substance. Similarly, the principle of noncontradiction depends on the categories of substance, quality, place, and time. Such categories are more primitive

---

32. See Gracia's essay, Chapter 16 of this volume, in which he argues against Foucault's contention that all categories are invented.
33. *Topics* I, 1, 100a27–30; *Posterior Analytics* I, 1–2.
34. See *Posterior Analytics* II, 19, for a description of the process of induction.

than those principles that are at the foundation both of the world and of our thoughts regarding the world. And, just as the grasping of any first principle depends on the grasping of the categories, so too does the performance of any demonstration require that a definition, property, genus, or accident be formulated in terms of one or more of the ten categories.

Bearing in mind Aristotle's claim that a statement is true if it adequately expresses something that is the way it is in the world,[35] it becomes evident that Aristotle's claim that every division of a problem falls under the genera of predicates is grounded on the position that the world or reality or being corresponds to categorial division. The categories must then be something unto themselves—the fundamental predicates of being about which we think, speak, and make arguments—and the underlying features of the way things are. They are, one might say, constitutive elements of the world and the vehicle for the world's intelligibility.

It is the categories, then, that make possible a science of being. For without the categories, by means of which true predication can occur, there could be no premises. Without premises there could be no deductions. Without deductions as well as true and primary premises there could be no demonstrations. Without demonstrations there could be no science. And if there were no science, then surely there could be no science of being.

III. CATEGORIES AND THE 'METAPHYSICS'

Having considered some important features of Aristotle's theory of categories and the relation of categories to science, we are in a position to press the following two observations. First, metaphysics is concerned especially with being in the sense of the categories. Second, at least one important reason why this is so is that any science is necessarily grounded on categories.

A thorough defense of the claim that being in the sense of the categories plays a primary role throughout Aristotle's *Metaphysics* lies outside

---

35. *Metaphysics* IX, 10, 1051b1–4: "Being and non-being in the strictest sense are truth and falsity. The condition of this in the objects is their being combined or separated, so that he who thinks the separated to be separated and the combined to be combined has the truth, while he whose thought is in a state contrary to that of the objects is in error." Also *Metaphysics* IV, 7, 1011b25–30: "We define what the true and the false are. To say of what is that it is not, or of what is not that it is, is false, while to say of what is that it is, and of what is not that it is not, is true; so that he who says of anything that it is, or that it is not, will say either what is true or what is false; but neither what is nor what is not is said to be or not to be."

the scope of this essay.[36] The following observation can serve as a modest and incomplete defense of this claim: Book Z (VII) is in many ways and for many reasons the heart of the *Metaphysics*. This book is concerned almost exclusively with the question of what substance is.[37] Both the question of what substance is and the ways Aristotle seeks to answer this question presuppose that substance is the first of the ten categories:

> There are several senses in which a thing may be said to be . . . ; for in one sense it means what a thing is [τί ἐστι] or a 'this' [τόδε τι], and in another sense it means that a thing is of a certain quality or quantity or has some such predicate asserted of it. While 'being' has all these senses, obviously that which is primarily is the 'what' [τὸ τί ἐστιν], which indicates the substance [ὅπερ σημαίνει τὴν οὐσίαν] . . . . And all other things are said to be because they are, some of them, quantities of that which *is* in this primary sense, others qualities of it, others affections of it, others some other determination of it. . . . Clearly then it is in virtue of this [category] that each of the others *is*. Therefore that which is primarily and *is* simply (not something [i.e., qualified in some way]) must be substance. (*Metaphysics* VII, 1, 1028a10–15, 18–20, 29–31)

These opening lines of Book Z (VII) make clear the following: being in its primary sense is substance, substance is to be thought of as the first category, substance is "a this,"[38] and this first category answers the question "what is it?" Most of the rest of Book Z (VII) seeks to achieve greater clarity concerning the question of what substance is. New considerations come into play in regard to spelling out more precisely what substance is, particularly the role that matter plays in making up substance[39] and the role of substance as a formal cause of uni-

---

36. See Michael Loux, *Primary OUSIA* (Ithaca: Cornell University Press, 1991).

37. Some argue that Z17 presents a severe break with the rest of Z, and indeed there are good reasons for interpreting literally Aristotle's claim that it introduces a new line of inquiry. See, for example, Jiyuan Yu's "*Tode Ti* and *Toionde* in *Metaphysics* Z," *Philosophical Inquiry* 16 (1994): 1–25. I consider Z17 a continuation of the inquiry into categorial being, but one that also prepares the way for a discussion of potential and actual being by means of the notion of substance as a formal cause of unity.

38. Compare to *Categories* 5, 3b10–13: "In regard to the primary substances, it is indisputably true that each of them signifies a certain 'this' [τόδε τι]; for the revealed thing is individual and numerically one."

39. *Metaphysics* VII, 3, 1029a7–11: "We have now outlined the nature of substance, showing that it is that which is not predicated of a subject, but of which all else is predicated. But we must not merely state the matter thus; for this is not enough. The statement itself is obscure, and further, on this view, *matter* becomes substance. For if this is not substance, it is beyond us to say what else is. When all else is taken away evidently nothing but matter remains." *Metaphysics* VII, 10, 1034b36–1035a5: "Let us inquire about the parts of which *substance* consists. If then matter is one thing, form another, the compound of these a third, and both the matter and the form and compound are substance, even the matter is in a sense called part of a thing, while in a sense *it* is not, but only the elements of which the formula of the form consists."

ty.[40] Neither of these considerations causes substance to lose its status as the primary sense of being, as the first category, as a "this," or as that which answers the question of "what is it?" There is added to this list, however—especially when we consider substance as a formal cause of unity—the contention that substance ought to answer the question of *why* a thing is what it is.[41]

Being in the sense of the categories plays a central role in Aristotle's metaphysics because, on the one hand, the categories are for Aristotle always predicates of being. They are not merely linguistic or mental entities but the primary parts by which the world itself is organized. On the other hand, Aristotle's epistemology requires the use of these categories as the principal elements for constructing the arguments that are necessary for obtaining scientific knowledge. Aristotle tells us in Γ (IV) 1 that his inquiry is a science of being *qua* being. Since, for Aristotle, the pursuit of science requires categories as primary building blocks, the science of being, by virtue of being a science, must employ the categories. There are, however, at least two difficulties with this view of the science of being and the role that the categories play in it. The first concerns Aristotle's notion of scientific unity in the *Metaphysics*, the second the special status given to being in the sense of potentiality and actuality.

The difficulty with Aristotle's notion of scientific unity arises when one considers his claim concerning the several senses of being in relation to the already well-established notion that each science concerns the things that fall under a single genus: "A science is one if it is of one genus" (*Posterior Analytics* I, 28, 87a38).[42] A similar conviction is echoed in *Metaphysics* IV, 1–3, where Aristotle explains that a science of being *qua* being is possible because there is a single principle for each of the senses of being: "There are many senses in which a thing is said to be, but all refer to one principle [ἀλλ' ἅπαν πρὸς μίαν ἀρχήν]" (*Metaphysics* IV, 2, 1003b5–6). But is the claim that it is from a single principle or starting point, or from a central idea and single type of nature (πρὸς ἓν καὶ μίαν τινὰ φύσιν) (*Metaphysics* IV, 2, 1003a34–35), that these senses of being are related equivalent to the claim that the senses of being fall under a single genus? The answer has to be no, since Aristotle explicitly rejects the possibility that there is a single genus of being in *Metaphysics* B, for "if unity or being is a genus, no differentia will either be

---

40. *Metaphysics* VII, 7, 1041b7–8: "Therefore what we seek is the cause, i.e., the form, by reason of which the matter is some definite thing."

41. Ibid., 17, 1041b5.

42. See also *Posterior Analytics* I, 6, 74b24–26; I, 9, 76a11–12.

one or have being" (III, 3, 998b21-27). Claiming that the four distinct senses of being fall under a single genus is tantamount to claiming that they are not truly distinct senses of being.[43] We have then a single science, the science of being *qua* being, which is not a single science because it studies one genus. This prompts two questions: what is it, then, that unifies the science of being, and has Aristotle rejected his earlier view that each science studies a single genus?

Aristotle suggests that substance serves as the starting point for the science of being *qua* being:

> For some things are said to be because they are substances, others because they are affections of substance, others because they are a process towards substance, or destructions or privations or qualities of substance, or productive or generative of substance, or of things which are relative to substance, or negations of some of these things or of substance itself. (*Metaphysics* IV, 2, 1003b6-10)

It is substance, then, that is the cornerstone for the investigation of the four senses of being. The unity of the science of being is grounded upon the logical and ontological priority of substance: "Therefore to investigate all the species of being *qua* being is the work of a science which is generically one, and to investigate the several species is the work of the specific parts of the science" (*Metaphysics* IV, 2, 1003b21-23). Being is not generically one, but the *science* of being is. That the unity of the science of being is achieved not through a common genus, but through a focus on substance, suggests two possibilities with respect to Aristotle's notion of science: (1) the *Metaphysics* represents an evolution of Aristotle's general notion of science;[44] (2) Aristotle does not intend to change his former position on science in general, but the investigation of being is a special case and an exception to the rule.[45] In

---

43. See again *Metaphysics* V, 7 and VI, 2.

44. See again Yu, "What Is the Focal Meaning of Being in Aristotle?" Yu seeks to demonstrate that Owen's explanation of the "focal meaning *(pros hen)*" in Aristotle is faulty, and that in *Metaphysics* Γ Aristotle is setting forth an expanded notion of science.

45. There are indications that the science of being, and unity, represent a special case in terms of what unifies it in works that predate the *Metaphysics*. Consider the following, from *De anima* II, 1, 412b3-9: "If, then, we have to find a general formula applicable to all kinds of soul, we must describe it as an actuality of the first kind of a natural organized body. That is why we can dismiss as unnecessary the question whether the soul and the body are one: it is as though we were to ask whether the wax and its shape are one, or generically the matter of a thing and that of which it is the matter. Unity has many senses—as many as 'is' has—but the proper one is that of actuality." *Metaphysics* IV, 1-3 echoes these notions, as does *Metaphysics* VIII, 6. Being, like unity, has several senses. The primary sense of the soul is as an actuality—a notion that is echoed in *Metaphysics* VII, 17, in regard to substance as a formal cause of unity—but the soul is the essence of the compound substance which includes the body. The soul is then both a being in the sense of

either case, the dependence of science in general, and the science of being in particular, on being in the sense of the categories remains the same.

The second difficulty involves whether logical *and* ontological priority ought both to be given to being in the sense of the categories rather than ontological priority being given to being in the sense of potentiality and actuality. Being in the sense of potentiality and actuality is examined almost as assiduously in the *Metaphysics* as is being in the sense of the categories. Indeed, the work is often read as culminating with the description of the first substance in Book Λ (XII) 7, which is characterized as complete actuality. Aristotle stresses the importance of being in the sense of potentiality and actuality by making the surprising claim in Book H (VIII) that it is a mistake to distinguish between potentiality and actuality in the way in which this is done when we examine categorial being (*Metaphysics* VIII, 6, 1045a21–b7). He goes on to say:

> The proximate matter and the form are one and the same thing, the one potentially, the other actually. Therefore to ask the cause of their being one is like asking the cause of unity in general; for each thing is a unity and the potential and the actual are somehow one. (*Metaphysics* VIII, 6, 1045b18–21)

This emphasis on the unity of substance as a hylomorphism of potentiality and actuality suggests that there may be something inadequate and even obfuscatory about dividing and dissecting being the way we do when examining categorial being and applying deductions. This is not to say that in order to define substances we no longer can think of them as unities. But it is to say that the unity we conceive substances to have is quite firmly set so that we can properly calculate its relations to other substances, classes of substances, and the other nine categories. When we think of unity this way, we are thinking of what Yu calls Aristotle's "static hylomorphism." But when we think of the unity of substances in the way Aristotle does in the passage quoted above, we are thinking of substances in terms of "dynamic hylomorphism."[46] Dynamic hylomorphism goes hand in hand with Aristotle's teleology, understanding the world in its individual substances, and as a whole, to be always striving, yearning as it were, for the ultimate final cause. Further, it

---

actuality, which makes the compound substance a unified actual being, and a being that falls into the first category, substance.

46. See Jiyuan Yu, "Two Conceptions of Hylomorphism in *Metaphysic* ZHΘ," in *Oxford Studies in Ancient Philosophy*, vol. 15, ed. C. C. W. Taylor (New York: Clarendon-Oxford Press, 1997).

is in the framework of dynamic hylomorphism and its relation to the final cause that we find the justification for Aristotle's claim that metaphysics is a type of theology (*Metaphysics* I, 2; XII, 7).

Nevertheless, we are concerned here with the status of metaphysics as a science, and it is not at all clear what kind of science can be had from potential and actual being. If potential and actual being is always a unity in a substance, how can we obtain epistemic knowledge of this unity? For epistemic knowledge is gained only when predication is employed; and for predication to be employed divisions must be made concerning the object of an inquiry. In *Metaphysics* M (XIII) 10 Aristotle suggests what a science of dynamic hylomorphism might look like:

> The statement that all knowledge is universal, so that the principles of things must also be universal and not separate substances, presents indeed, of all the points we have mentioned, the greatest difficulty, but yet the statement is in a sense true, although in a sense it is not. For knowledge [ἐπιστήμη], like knowing, is spoken of in two ways,—as potential and as actual. The potentiality, being, as matter, universal and indefinite, deals with the universal and indefinite; but the actuality, being definite, deals with a definite object—being a 'this,' it deals with a 'this'....
>
> But evidently in a sense knowledge [ἐπιστήμη] is universal, and in a sense it is not. (*Metaphysics* XIII, 10, 1087a10–19, 25)

Aristotle seems to be suggesting here that there can be a science of particulars. Such a science defies any sense of what we know, from Aristotle, to be science, and so seems quite incomprehensible, for Aristotle's standard epistemology is that scientific or epistemic knowledge is always universal (*Posterior Analytics* II, 19). Such knowledge is obtained by means of true predication, which employs the categories, as already explained. So this notion of definite or particular knowledge is quite foreign. What might it be? Well, as Aristotle stated above, definite knowledge would be of things as they are in actuality; and this most vividly seems to be substance in the sense of dynamic hylomorphism. But this explains little. Whatever Aristotle has in mind in M (XIII) 10 by definite knowledge, we know that it cannot involve demonstration. This notion of definite knowledge, then, runs against Aristotle's almost constant reliance upon demonstration as the only means by which epistemic knowledge is secured.

Aristotle informs us that his metaphysical inquiry is to be a science of being *qua* being. Such a science is best understood to be, first and foremost, a science of categories. But being in a sensible substance is most fully actual in the sense of dynamic hylomorphism. In a sense, then, ontological priority is given to being in the sense of potentiality and actuality. However, a science of dynamic hylomorphism is beyond our comprehension, since it would not be a universal science. But Aristotle does present a science of substance considered as a static hylomorphism. In a different sense, then, ontological priority is given to being in the sense of the categories. It is an inquiry into substance as the combination of matter and form that is an investigation into categorial being, and such an inquiry employs the categories to generate universal knowledge of being. So, if dynamic hylomorphism is the "really real" notion of substance but cannot be understood scientifically, and static hylomorphism is a somehow "second-rate" description of reality but that which can be understood scientifically, what would be the best way to characterize the relationship between these two hylomorphisms?

It seems most helpful to think of static hylomorphism as a type of snapshot of dynamic hylomorphism. This characterization of their relationship is justified by the following passage from *Metaphysics* Θ (IX) 10:

> The terms 'being' and 'non-being' are employed *firstly* with reference to the categories, and *secondly* with reference to the potentiality or actuality of these or their opposites, while being and non-being in the strictest sense are truth and falsity. The condition of this in the objects is their being combined or separated, so that he who thinks the separated to be separated and the combined to be combined has the truth, while he whose thought is in a state contrary to that of the objects is in error. (*Metaphysics* IX, 10, 1051a34–b4, emphasis added)

We think of being primarily in terms of the categories because they are the primary means by which being can be epistemically known at all. We can think scientifically of being in terms of potentiality and actuality, then, to the extent to which this sense of being refers to being in the sense of the categories. In other words, we can scientifically know potential and actual being only insofar as this sense of being can be funnelled into being in the sense of the categories.

The last quotation speaks also of being in the sense of truth and falsity. We speak of being in the sense of truth or falsity regarding whether or not we correctly think objects to be properly combined or separated. In other words, being in the sense of truth and falsity relies on whether true or false predication has occurred. Predication can occur only through the use of the categories. Therefore, being in the sense of truth and falsity also relies upon being in the sense of the categories.

So it is being in the sense of the categories that primarily serves as the object of the science of being, metaphysics; and it is being in the sense of the categories that enables such a science to be successfully carried forward. Aristotle's categories, then, are the rudimentary building blocks of the world and of the world's intelligibility, and it is for these reasons that Aristotle's metaphysics can be called a *science* of being.

IV. CONCLUSION

This essay has focused on Aristotle's notion of categories, how categories are employed in the pursuit of knowledge, and the way in which categories are employed in pursuit of the knowledge of being. The *Metaphysics* is undergirded by Aristotle's earlier logical works, in which categories play a pivotal role. It provides, as well, a further maturation of the proto-metaphysics to be found in Aristotle's *Categories* and other early works. The metaphysical seeds and saplings, so to speak, that are cultivated in the early works are the same, I have urged, as those found in full bloom in the *Metaphysics*. I would like to conclude with a few brief reflections on the relevance of Aristotle's views.

Aristotle's notion of categories and their role in metaphysics has long been a subject of controversy. His assumption that there is some fundamental connection between the way in which we think—by means of categories—and the way in which the world presents itself—categorially—has for quite some time borne the charge of naivete. Moreover, his contention that metaphysics concerns fundamentally the way in which the world is, rather than the way in which we perceive the world, has also been criticized as inordinately presumptive of our access to the world and too restrictive a view of metaphysics.[47] But thinkers are still drawn to Aristotle's *Metaphysics*. Why? Aristotle contends that philosophy begins in wonder. The metaphysician's wonder is something unique in so far as it directs him or her to a consideration of being itself, the noblest of intellectual pursuits. However one may judge the value of Aristotle's view of metaphysics, metaphysicians, to a person, have felt the pull of what Aristotle describes in the opening chapters of the *Metaphysics* as the nobility of the pursuit of first philosophy. Even those metaphysicians who, for one reason or another, have concluded that metaphysics does not study being (and often the claim is that it

---

47. For a historical and systematic development of these and other contentions, within the context of a work devoted to understanding what exactly metaphysics is, see Jorge J. E. Gracia's helpful *Metaphysics and Its Task: The Search for the Categorial Foundation of Knowledge* (Albany: State University of New York Press, 1999). Responses to some of Gracia's criticisms of an Aristotelian approach to metaphysics can be found in Jonathan J. Sanford, "An Aristotelian Critique of Gracia's View of Metaphysics," in *Revisiting Metaphysics: Essays on Jorge J. E. Gracia's* Metaphysics and Its Task, ed. Robert Delfino (Amsterdam: Rudopi, 2004).

cannot because of epistemological roadblocks), nevertheless tacitly acknowledge the importance of the question of being in so far as they have set themselves against it. The question of where one stands on Aristotle's view of metaphysics comes down to the question of where one stands on the relationship between our minds and the world. There is, I think, plenty of reason to suppose a kinship between the two, one that is predicated on the way in which the world is and our receptivity to the world—hence the importance of categories, which are at once logical and metaphysical. There is reason, then, to claim that although Aristotle's assumption of this kinship may be naive, just such naivete may be representative of the way things are. Finally, one should note the tentative nature of much of Aristotle's *Metaphysics*. He is *pursuing* a science of being; he never claims to have completed it. Such a pursuit, it would seem, is an ongoing task.[48]

48. Thanks go to Jorge J. E. Gracia, Jiyuan Yu, and Michael Gorman for much help at various stages of this essay's development. Gorman's comments were especially helpful for getting the essay into its present form.

2   Aristotle's Categories "Where" and "When"

HELEN LANG

INTRODUCTION

The word "category" itself comes from the verb καταγορεύω, meaning "to denounce," "to accuse," or, as we shall see in Aristotle, "to be predicated." In his entry "Categories" in the *Encyclopedia of Philosophy*, Manley Thompson turns first to "Aristotelian Theory" and asserts:

> The word "category" was first used as a technical term in philosophy by Aristotle. In his short treatise called *Categories*, he held that every uncombined expression signifies (denotes, refers to) one or more things falling in at least one of the following ten classes: substance, quantity, quality, relation, place, time, posture, state, action, and passion.[1]

This list of categories is almost always attributed to Aristotle. But in fact it does not reflect Aristotle's language either in the *Categories*, which Thompson cites, or in the rest of the corpus. With the exception of the first category, substance, none of Aristotle's categories is a noun;[2] they are adjectives, adverbs, infinitives, and in one case ("relation") a prepositional phrase, made to stand as substantives. Although classical Greek certainly allows for the formation of substantives by means of a definite article, Aristotle does not always use an article when specifying categories, and even when he does, these expressions seem odd. Indeed, they are part of the reason why Aristotle's Greek is often thought of as Hellenistic rather than "classical," strictly speaking.

The question for a philosopher is not translation *per se* but what is at

---

1. Manley Thompson, "Categories," in *The Encyclopedia of Philosophy*, ed. Paul Edwards (New York: Macmillan, 1967), 2:46–47.
2. A good deal of work has been done on the etymology of Aristotle's word οὐσία. For example, see the excellent discussion in Joseph Owens, *The Doctrine of Being in the Aristotelian Metaphysics*, 3d ed. (Toronto: Pontifical Institute of Mediaeval Studies, 1978), 137–54.

stake substantively in this apparently linguistic matter. Here I shall consider two of Aristotle's categories. They appear above as "place" and "time," but I shall argue that they are more properly "where" and "when"—indefinite adverbs that are sometimes best translated as "somewhere" and "sometime." I shall conclude that the translations "place" and "time" obscure important substantive issues at stake in these categories. These issues appear clearly in both the historical origins of these categories in Plato and in the relation of these categories to Aristotle's physics.[3]

After examining "things that are by nature" in *Physics* II, Aristotle opens *Physics* III, 1, with a list of what should be examined next in order because these things are "common to everything and universal": the continuous, the infinite, and, in addition to these, place, void, and time. Because they are common and universal, these "topics" and the issues raised by them are central to physics as a science of "things that are by nature." In *Physics* IV, 1–5, Aristotle in fact discusses "place" (ὁ τόπος), which explains "where" all things that are and are moved are; and in *Physics* IV, 10–14, he discusses "time" (ὁ χρόνος), which gives an account of "when" as it applies to all things that are and are moved. In short, translating Aristotle's categories τό που and τὸ ποτέ as "place" and "time," respectively, confuses his categories of predication, expressed by adverbs and applicable to all things involving motion, with two substantive topics, place and time, examined within the science of physics. Consequently, I shall suggest that even at the cost of peculiar-sounding English, we must reproduce Aristotle's categories in language closer to their Greek originals. I turn first to "place" or, as I shall argue, "where," or even "somewhere."

WHERE

Some predicates signify "where" a thing is, and Aristotle regularly lists "where" (τό που) among possible predicates.[4] When this category is

---

3. For a discussion of Aristotle's categories as they relate to logic and metaphysics, see Jonathan Sanford's essay, Chapter 1 of this volume; and, insofar as they relate to ethics, see May Sim's essay, Chapter 5 of this volume.
4. Aristotle, *Categories* 4, 1b25–27, in *The Complete Works of Aristotle: The Revised Oxford Translation*, 2 vols., ed. Jonathan Barnes (Princeton: Princeton University Press, 1984), vol. 1. J. L. Ackrill, who translated *Categories* in this volume, translates the categories in this list with greater etymological accuracy, including "where": "Of things said without any combination, each signifies either substance or quantity or qualification or a relative or where or when or being-in-a-position or having or doing or being-affected" (ibid., 4). Cf. also Aristotle, *Metaphysics* V, 17, 1017a26. W. D. Ross, who translated the *Metaphysics* in this volume, translates the same word as "place": "Since some predicates indicate what

translated as "place," two important points, one historical and one substantive, are suppressed: (1) that anything that is "must be 'where' (or 'somewhere')" is posed as a problem in Plato and Aristotle may in some sense be addressing that problem, and (2) that "place" is a topic taken up and defined in *Physics* IV. The definition of place may be thought of as Aristotle's substantive answer to the problem of "where" —where things are. Hence it is important to keep "where" and "place" distinct.

Plato poses the problem of "where" in two very different contexts, i.e., within one of the hypotheses posed by Parmenides in the notoriously difficult *Parmenides*, and within the account of the generation of the cosmos in the *Timaeus*. In both dialogues, Plato uses the same expression—an expression that reappears in the opening lines of Aristotle's account of place in *Physics* IV: εἶναί που, to be somewhere.

In the second part of Plato's dialogue *Parmenides*, Parmenides pursues the conclusions that follow from the assumption that "the one is." Within this argument he asserts a universal claim: "Further, anything that is must always be somewhere [ἀλλὰ μὴν καὶ εἶναί που δεῖ τό γε ὂν ἀεί]";[5] his interlocutor in the dialogue, Aristoteles, promptly agrees. The same assertion is found in the very different context of the *Timaeus*. In what purports to be a story, Timaeus (a character for whom there is apparently no historical foundation) entertains the day's guests with an account of the generation of the cosmos. After an invocation of the gods, he distinguishes being and becoming;[6] but later he adds a third member to this division, the receptacle, and makes a universal claim: "and we say also that every being must be somewhere, in some place and occupying some space [καί φαμεν ἀναγκαῖον εἶναί που τὸ ὂν ἅπαν ἔν τινι τόπῳ καὶ κατέχον χώραν τινά]."[7]

Given Plato's craft not only as a philosopher but as a writer, it is difficult, perhaps impossible, to determine the status of the claim that "anything that is must always be somewhere." Perhaps it was widely accepted by pre-Socratic philosophers, perhaps it was asserted specifically by the historical Parmenides. Indeed, perhaps it had become a regular feature of cosmology. But the issue is defined clearly and is lost if we fail to be precise about the language here.

---

the subject is, others its quality, others quantity, others relation, others activity or passivity, others its place, others its time, 'being' has a meaning answering to each of these" (ibid., 2:1606).

5. Plato, *Parmenides*, 151a5. All references to Plato are to the Oxford Classical Text (O.C.T.).

6. Plato, *Timaeus*, 27c1–28a1.

7. Ibid., 52b3–5. My translation and emphasis in the Greek text.

Beyond the historical issue, the substantive issue cannot be in doubt: "where" a thing is presents a universal problem for all things that are, and any philosopher worth his salt must be able to address this problem. Aristotle's criticisms of Plato are legendary, but at the opening of *Physics* IV, 1, we see him accepting the challenge posed by this problem (which he clearly thinks he can solve): "the physicist must know place, just as also the infinite, . . . both because everyone assumes that things that are must be somewhere [εἶναί που] (for what is not is nowhere; where is the goat-stag or the sphinx?) and because the most common and noble motion is in respect to place, which we call 'locomotion.'"[8]

The first reason Aristotle gives for the importance of place resembles the *Parmenides:* it defines a universal claim for anything that is and it contrasts what is with what is not. The second reason clearly falls within physics, as Aristotle, specifically rejecting Plato's position in the *Timaeus*, defines it. That is, according to Aristotle, physics concerns natural things—things that contain in themselves a source of being moved and being at rest.[9] Plato seems to identify "being somewhere" with being in some place or occupying space, and Aristotle accepts his point as defining a problem. Indeed, at *Physics* IV, 2, 209b10–17, Aristotle praises Plato because (according to Aristotle) among his predecessors Plato alone tried to say *what* place is. Plato's solution may be wrong, but he got the problem right, and Aristotle accepts the challenge posed by Plato's problem: where are things that are? They are in place. Here again the difference between "where" and "place" appears clearly.

"Where" (τό που) is clear: it is a kind of predicate that seems possible for anything that is (but not for anything that is not) and must be accounted for as such. "Place" (ὁ τόπος) is not found on Aristotle's list of predicates; rather, it is a topic to be investigated within the science of physics. The status of place as a topic for physics and its relation to "where" as a possible predicate is a problem for serious inquiry in Aristotle's natural philosophy.

Physics, or natural philosophy, concerns things that are by nature; nature is "some source, i.e., cause, of being moved and being at rest in that to which it belongs essentially and not accidentally" (*Physics* II, 1, 192b21–23). Consequently, it is necessary to understand motion and change, if we are to understand nature (*Physics* III, 1, 200b12–14). But motion and change in their turn raise additional topics, including the infinite, the continuous, place, void, and time, that must also be under-

---

8. Aristotle, *Physics* IV, 1, 208a27–32, hereafter cited parenthetically in the text. All references to Aristotle are to the O.C.T., unless otherwise stated.
9. For this definition of nature, cf. Aristotle, *Physics* II, 1, 192b21–23.

stood (*Physics* III, 1, 200b17–21).[10] Aristotle examines motion and the infinite in *Physics* III. He takes up place, void, and time in *Physics* IV. The continuous is defined in *Physics* V, 3. In each case, the purpose of the examination is that given at *Physics* III, 1: to understand motion and ultimately nature.

In *Physics* IV Aristotle defines the problem at hand, i.e., that everyone thinks that all things must be somewhere, and he turns directly to an account of place, commenting that he has inherited nothing of value from his predecessors and asserting that the fact "that place is" is obvious (*Physics* IV, 1, 208a32–b2). Aristotle's analysis of place leads him to define it as "the first unmoved limit of that which contains" (*Physics* IV, 4, 212a20–21). This definition, Aristotle claims, solves a number of problems, including why each element (earth, air, fire, and water) goes to its respective place, i.e., up, down, or in the middle (*Physics* IV, 4, 211a3–6). Place, as Aristotle defines it, renders the entire cosmos determinate, and so defines any place within the cosmos as "somewhere," i.e., up, down, left, right, front, and back (*Physics* IV, 4, 212a24–28). Here we can locate the relation between "place" and "where."

Aristotle concludes that some things are in place *per se*, i.e., that every body that is movable is "somewhere in virtue of itself [καθ' αὐτό που]" (*Physics* IV, 5, 212b8); but other things are not in place per se: "the world as a whole is nowhere, not in some place [οὔ που ὅλος οὐδ' ἔν τινι τόπῳ ἐστίν]" (*Physics* IV, 5, 212b8–9). The larger account returns to the problem raised at the outset and stresses place, not "somewhere"; for not everything that is is in place, but only movable body. This conclusion offers an important corrective to the assumption with which Aristotle began and which we find in Plato's *Parmenides*—the assumption that things that are must always be somewhere.

Place defines "where" within the cosmos, i.e., where things are in terms of up, down, or in the middle. But the cosmos as a whole is not essentially in place—the cosmos as a whole is not "anywhere" in terms of up, down, or in the middle. In effect, physics as a science takes up place as a topic, and the investigation of place provides an account that specifies the category "where" both by defining "where things are" (i.e., they are in place) and by limiting the domain of "where"—only movable things are in place, are "somewhere."

Aristotle next takes up another term that seems to be required by motion: the void. It must be examined by the physicist in a way that parallels the investigation of place (*Physics* IV, 6, 213a12–14). Those thinkers who subscribe to the void think of it as a kind of place, al-

---

10. The terms in this list are τὸ ἄπειρον, τὸ συνεχές, ὁ τόπος, τὸ κενόν, ὁ χρόνος.

though Aristotle quickly makes clear that he thinks this view is deeply confused and must be rejected as misled in every regard. The void is an incoherent concept and it fails to serve as a cause of any kind of motion.[11]

The notion of "where" does not appear in Aristotle's arguments about the void. Some of Aristotle's predecessors propose the void as a kind of place, and so the question Aristotle poses is whether void qualifies as place. The void fails and is the only term on the list given by Aristotle at the opening of *Physics* III, 1, to be rejected. When it fails, Aristotle's own account of place remains—the winner, so to speak: place provides the true account of "where things are" and its relation to motion (and ultimately nature) clarifies which things must be "somewhere." Aristotle's final account includes an explicit correction of Plato's universal assertion: it is false that everything that is "must be somewhere" because only things that are moved "must be somewhere." Here, in the *Physics*, we see that the world is not in place, i.e., it is "nowhere," properly speaking; were we to look to Aristotle's argument in *Metaphysics* XII, we would see that the unmoved mover is unmoved both essentially and accidentally and so cannot be in place either essentially or even accidentally. Before turning to the full implications of this account, let us briefly consider another category, "time," as it is usually listed, but, as I shall argue, "when," or even "sometime."

WHEN

Aristotle's categories are usually shown as including "time," as we saw in Thompson's account; but the Greek here is, literally, "when" (τὸ ποτέ). Grammatically, it offers a perfect parallel to "where." "When" is one of the kinds, or classes, in which predication may occur. As we have already seen, time (ὁ χρόνος), like place and void, is found at the beginning of *Physics* III in the list of things that seem to be necessary for motion and ultimately nature. A full examination of time (ὁ χρόνος) appears in *Physics* IV, 10–14, and here "when" (τὸ ποτέ) reappears. Hence we must ask the same question about "when" and "time" as we did about "where" and "place": what is the difference between them and why is it important?

"When" (τὸ ποτέ) raises difficulties from the outset. Aristotle's categories suggest that saying *where* a thing is and *when* an event occurs are regular forms of predication. But "when" does not always have this connotation; it is regularly, even in Plato, used to refer explicitly to the

---

11. Aristotle, *Physics* IV, 9, 217b20–28 gives a summary of the preceding arguments.

past. After Aristotle defines "time" (ὁ χρόνος) in *Physics* IV, he takes up a number of problems, including the meaning of ποτέ. He defines "when" as a determinate time either in the past or in the future. The crucial issue for Aristotle is not the reference to past or future but that the "length" of time must be determinate. His definition of "sometime" may be required by his definition of time (and beyond time by his larger account of motion and nature) and consequently may not reflect standard usage. But it must reflect the sense in which his account of time defines the meaning of the category τὸ ποτέ.

"Time" is taken up immediately after the void in *Physics* IV, 10–14. Much of Aristotle's argument about time (and consequently about "when" or "sometime") involves a third term, "the now" (τὸ νῦν) that is central to problems concerning both "time" and "sometime." All three terms seem to have very different relations to events found in the past, the present, and the future. Consequently, the problem of time—and however it involves "when"—concerns the character of these relations. Again, the problem is found clearly formulated in Plato, even if Aristotle ultimately rejects his solution.

As we saw in the account of "where" in Plato's dialogue *Parmenides*, the first hypothesis is, "if the one is" (*Parmenides*, 137c4–5). Parmenides quickly concludes that the one is not "in some time [ἔν τινι χρόνῳ]" (*Parmenides*, 141d5). He next distinguishes words used for past, present, and future, and here we find a clear distinction between time and sometime—a distinction in which "when" (τὸ ποτέ) clearly means "sometime in the past":

> [T]he words 'was,' and 'has become' and 'was becoming' seem to mean not participation in time but having become at some [past] time; . . . 'will be' and 'will be becoming' and 'will become' [seem to mean connection] with the hereafter; . . . 'is' and 'is becoming' with the present now.[12]

As the argument unfolds, the one in no way "participates in time [μετέχει χρόνου]," be it past, present, or future; but a thing can only have being in one of these ways; therefore the one in no way "participates in being [οὐσίας μετέχει]" (*Parmenides*, 141e2–9).

The relation of the one that is and time reappears when Parmenides seems to reach the opposite conclusion. He asserts that "'to be' is just participation in being with time of the present, just as 'was' and again

---

12. Plato, *Parmenides*, 141d7–e2: "τὸ ἦν καὶ τὸ γέγονε καὶ τὸ ἐγίγνετο οὐ χρόνου μέθεξιν δοκεῖ σημαίνειν τοῦ ποτὲ γεγονότος; . . . τὸ ἔσται καὶ τὸ γενήσεται καὶ τὸ γενηθήσεται οὐ τοῦ ἔπειτα [τοῦ μέλλοντος]; . . . τὸ δὲ δὴ ἔστι καὶ τὸ γίγνεται οὐ τοῦ νῦν παρόντος." It should be noted that there are various difficulties with the text in these lines. Cf. also *Timaeus*, 37d5ff, esp. 38a4.

'will be' is likewise participation with past or future ... if the one is, then it participates in time."[13] What Plato means by this argument has been debated since ancient times. My interest here lies in the important sense in which it sets the stage for Aristotle's account of time by identifying the problems involved in the notion of time.

When Aristotle opens his account of time, posing the problems central to this notion, he both raises the question of how time is past, present, and future and uses the expression "to participate in being [μετέχειν οὐσίας]": time seems to be composed of what has been and is not (now) and what is about to be but is not (yet); but it would seem impossible for what is composed from things that are not to participate in being.[14] Both the language of participation and the emphasis on the past, present, and future recall the *Parmenides*, although, of course, it is possible that both Plato and Aristotle reflect broader contemporary interests.

Again, my point here is not to pursue the details of Aristotle's argument—they are very difficult indeed—so much as to ask what his account reveals about the relation, as he construes it, between time (ὁ χρόνος), as a topic of physics, and when (τὸ ποτέ), as a category. Aristotle wishes to connect time with motion and, since motion can only occur in a magnitude, time too is linked with magnitude. In this respect, his entire account can be read as an implicit rejection of Plato's discussion of "if the one is" in the *Parmenides*—an account that seems to pose time entirely apart from any reference to body or magnitude. Time, as Aristotle defines it, is "the numbering of motion in respect to 'before' and 'after.'"[15]

Aristotle's analogy between time and motion allows him to define "the now" as the substratum of time, just as body, or magnitude, is the substratum of motion. All motion must be in or of a body; likewise, all time must have "the now" as its substratum. "The now" resembles a line, which has magnitude in one direction: each is continuous but potentially divisible at any given moment (or point). This definition of "the now"—it underlies all motion—produces, for Aristotle, an impor-

---

13. Plato, *Parmenides*, 151e7–152a2: "τὸ δὲ εἶναι ἄλλο τί ἐστιν ἢ μέθεξις οὐσίας μετὰ χρόνου τοῦ παρόντος, ὥσπερ τὸ ἦν μετὰ τοῦ παρεληλυθότος καὶ αὖ τὸ ἔσται μετὰ τοῦ μέλλοντος οὐσίας ἐστὶ κοινωνία; ... μετέχει μὲν ἄρα χρόνου, εἴπερ καὶ τοῦ εἶναι."

14. Aristotle, *Physics* IV, 10, 217b33–218a3: "τὸ μὲν γὰρ αὐτοῦ γέγονε καὶ οὐκ ἔστιν, τὸ δὲ μέλλει καὶ οὔπω ἔστιν. ἐκ δὲ τούτων καὶ ὁ ἄπειρος καὶ ὁ ἀεὶ λαμβανόμενος χρόνος σύγκειται. τὸ δ' ἐκ μὴ ὄντων συγκείμενον ἀδύνατον ἂν εἶναι δόξειε μετέχειν οὐσίας."

15. Ibid., 11, 219b1–2: "τοῦτο γάρ ἐστιν ὁ χρόνος, ἀριθμὸς κινήσεως κατὰ τὸ πρότερον καὶ ὕστερον."

tant and desirable conclusion about time: defined as the numbering of motion that has the now as its substratum, time must be continuous. As Aristotle makes clear in a moment, since time is continuous, there must be a determinate time between any two events.

Time is the numbering of motion in respect to "before" and "after." Aristotle turns immediately to "the before and after." All time is potentially divided at the now into past and future and in this sense the now is a limit of time (*Physics* IV, 13, 222a10–15). "The now," by underlying time, makes it continuous, and at any given moment marks the end of the past and the beginning of the future, i.e., divides time into "before" and "after." Consequently "the now" describes *both* a particular event that is "near," whether in the future or in the past, *and* the "on-going-ness" of time as continuous. In the first sense, we say, "he will come now because he will come today; he came now because he came today."[16]

But when an event is far removed we would not use "now" in respect to it. The time between "now" and the event is continuous—all time is continuous because "the now" is its substratum; our failure to describe remote events as "now" means that they are not near, but it does not mean not that the time between then and now is not continuous: "But the things in the *Iliad* have not happened now, nor is the flood now. The time toward these things is continuous, but it is not near."[17] In short, in one sense "the now" divides times, thereby defining past and future, and in another it unites all time into a single continuous whole.

By explaining how time is both continuous and divided, Aristotle prepares the way for his definition of "when" (τὸ ποτέ). "When" signals the sense in which time is always determinate, "e.g., at some time [when] Troy was taken and at some time [when] there will be a flood. For time must be determined in relation to the now. Therefore, there will be some determinate time from this to that and there was [some determinate time] in relation to what happened in the past."[18] Although Aristotle does not say so, the determinate character of time is often more obvious in relation to the past precisely because the events themselves are determinate; hence τὸ ποτέ would be more likely to appear with respect to past events. But—and here he seems to correct common usage—it could be used for any future event that is not near.

---

16. Ibid., 13, 222a20–22; for text, cf. Plato, *Parmenides*, 141d5ff.
17. Ibid., 13, 222a20–24: "τὸ μὲν οὖν οὕτω λέγεται τῶν νῦν, ἄλλο δ' ὅταν ὁ χρόνος ὁ τούτου ἐγγὺς ᾖ. ἥξει νῦν, ὅτι τήμερον ἥξει· ἥκει νῦν, ὅτι ἦλθε τήμερον. τὰ δ' ἐν Ἰλίῳ γέ-ο γονεν οὐ νῦν, οὐδύ ὁ κατακλυσμός [γέγονε] νῦν· καίτοι συνεχὴς ὁ χρόνος εἰς αὐτά, ἀλλ' ὅτι οὐκ ἐγγύς."
18. Ibid., 222a24–28: "τὸ δὲ ποτέ χρόνος ὡρισμένος . . . οἷον ποτὲ ἐλήφθη Τροία, καὶ ποτὲ ἔσται κατακλυσμός· δεῖ γὰρ πεπεράνθαι πρὸς τὸ νῦν. ἔσται ἄρα ποσός τις ἀπὸ τοῦδε χρόνος εἰς ἐκεῖνο, καὶ ἦν εἰς τὸ παρελθόν."

In this sense, "when" applies to any remote event, be it past or future.

What does this definition of τὸ ποτέ in the *Physics,* in Aristotle's account of time, tell us about τὸ ποτέ as a kind of predicate in the *Categories*? As in the case of τό που, this argument restricts the domain in which τὸ ποτέ is a meaningful predicate. It is only a meaningful predicate when a determinate time is being predicated. But a determinate time implies a relation to the now—a particular (not near) event that can be measured by continuous time—which is in its turn related to motion and magnitude. Since a predicate is always a predicate of something, this argument implies that the subject must be something that is by nature, i.e., a magnitude that possesses an intrinsic source of being moved and being at rest. Because of its relation to motion and nature, time is properly considered a topic of investigation within physics. Although Aristotle does not make the point explicit, we can see why "time" (like "place") does not belong to the investigation of substance found in *Metaphysics* XII. There we find an account of the first cause of motion, the unmoved mover; since the unmoved mover is outside nature (and hence has neither matter nor motion nor even the possibility of motion), god cannot take a predicate either in the category of τὸ ποτέ or in the category of τό που.

CONCLUSION

What then can be said of the categories "where" (or "place") and "when" (or "time")? The first point is, I hope, unambiguously clear: "place" (ὁ τόπος) is not the same as "where" (τό που), "time" (ὁ χρόνος) is not the same as "when" (τὸ ποτέ). "Place" and "time" are specific topics within the science of physics, the science of things that are by nature, and they must be examined in order to understand motion and ultimately nature. "Where" and "when," as they appear within Aristotle's *Categories,* are possible kinds of predicates; they are the kinds of things that might be said of substance.

But "where" and "when" also appear within the *Physics*—indeed, within the accounts of "place" and "time." What are we to make of their appearance there? First, their appearance in the *Physics* and the apparent relation of Aristotle's arguments to Plato's *Parmenides* (and the *Timaeus*) tells us something important both about Aristotle's language and about his definitions of the problems of philosophy: he works within the broader context of problems defined by Plato and even the pre-Socratics.

This point would not seem surprising except that Aristotle's language in formulating the categories is regularly challenged as somehow "unclassical," perhaps "Hellenistic" (in a derogatory sense). Philosophy as practiced by Aristotle (and Plato) was part of and contributed to the linguistic revolution (itself much more widespread than is generally recognized) that marks fifth-century Athens. And Aristotle's language both reflects and furthers that revolution. The linguistic revolution to which philosophy bears witness is part of an intellectual adventure that started at least as early as Parmenides (and perhaps other pre-Socratic philosophers as well) and in which Plato and finally Aristotle are enthusiastic participants. Consequently, Aristotle's language in the *Categories* does not represent a break with classical Greek so much as an extension of it that was very much a part of the contemporary scene.

This linguistic point brings me to my second point about Aristotle's categories of predication. Aristotle's *Categories* are often treated as logic, i.e., as a branch of philosophy that is quite separate from its other branches, such as metaphysics or epistemology. Indeed, the difficulty of Aristotle's work in some sense contributes to this impression. But although the language of Aristotle's categories is anticipated by earlier philosophers, the codification of philosophy as a discipline with branches that may be treated independently of one another *is* a break with traditions of classical philosophy as practiced by Plato and Aristotle. Indeed, the codification of philosophy into a discipline with clearly delineated branches is a feature of Hellenistic and not classical philosophy. In particular, the codification of the categories and problems in the *Categories* is regularly attributed to Porphyry, whose *Isagogue* "became a standard preface to work in Aristotle's logic."[19] And when we consider categories such as "where" and "when," it is not clear that such codification in fact reflects Aristotle's arguments.

Physics III, 1, tells us the topics that Aristotle takes to be necessary for an investigation by the physicist. The appearances of "where" and "when" in *Physics* IV tell us that topics in physics define the conditions under which these categories are (and are not) meaningful. A predicate, to be meaningful, must be attached to a subject. When we come to the specific sciences themselves, we see that not every subject is equally able to accept (in a meaningful way) every kind of predicate, i.e., every category. Hence the arguments of the *Physics* give us the actual subject that will be meaningful for two of the categories, the kinds of predicates, listed in the *Categories*. It also gives us, by implication, actual subjects for which these categories will not be meaningful. They will be meaningful neither for god nor for the world as a whole. In short, by

---

19. Porphyry, *Porphyry the Phoenician, Isagoge,* trans., introduction, and notes by E. W. Warren (Toronto: Pontifical Institute of Mediaeval Studies, 1975), 12.

keeping the language of Aristotle's categories clear of the topics of physics, we gain the categories and the relation of those categories to the real world and the concepts relevant to that world as defined by the physicist. Finally, we gain a sense of the project represented through Aristotle's arguments before they were taken up as the foundations of the different branches of philosophy as a discipline.

3 Aquinas's Metaphysics: Individuation and Constitution

ELEONORE STUMP

INTRODUCTION

This essay examines some features of what might be called "Aquinas's theory of things." This is not the same as his ontology or his theory of what there is in the world, since he supposed that being—what there *is*—is spread over all the ten Aristotelian categories and not just the category of substance, which includes things. It is not the same as his theory of substance either, however, since it is arguable that not everything Aquinas recognized as a thing counts for him as a substance.[1] For purposes of this essay, I will take things to include not only substances and artifacts but also at least some of the parts of which substances are constituted. By "parts," in this context, I mean both what Aquinas called "integral parts," such as the hand of a human being or the roof of a house, and also metaphysical parts, such as matter and form, which constitute material things in a way different from the way they are constituted by their integral parts.[2] In order to understand

---

1. By "thing" in this context I mean approximately—but perhaps only approximately—what Aquinas meant by the Latin expression *hoc aliquid*, which might be rendered into English roughly as "a *this*." I put this point in the text in a hedged way, because there is some lack of clarity regarding Aquinas's concept of a *hoc aliquid*. In *Sententia super Metaphysicam*, bk. 7, lect. 3, 1323, for example, Aquinas says that only a substance is a *hoc aliquid*, but elsewhere he says, for example, that parts of substances such as severed hands and the substantial soul also count as examples of a subsistent thing or a *hoc aliquid*. See, for example, Thomas Aquinas, *Quaestiones disputatae de anima*, q. 1, ad 3; and *Summa theologiae* (hereafter *ST*) I–II, q. 72, a. 2. Finally, by "thing," in this context, I do not mean what Aquinas meant by *res*, although that Latin word is often translated into English as "thing." For Aquinas, strictly speaking, *res* is found throughout the ten categories, and so it ranges much more broadly than "thing" or *hoc aliquid*, as that notion is used in this essay. It should perhaps be added that sometimes Aquinas uses *res* as broadly and loosely as "thing" is used in English. We say, for example, "That situation is the kind of thing that occurs only in bad dreams." Things in such a loose sense are not at issue here either.

2. Not everything that is appropriately designated the matter of something counts as a

Aquinas's basic worldview, it is important to understand his theory of things, and especially his view of what it is for something to be *one* thing. My focus in this essay is Aquinas's view of the individuation, identity, and constitution of things, and particularly of human beings.

INDIVIDUATION AND IDENTITY

For Aquinas, an angel, an immaterial intelligence, exists on its own, and it is differentiated from other immaterial intelligences just by the features of the substantial form of the angel.[3] That is, the properties that make up the nature or species of one angel, which the angel has in virtue of having the substantial form it does, are different from the properties that make up the nature or species of every other angel. According to Aquinas, there can be no more than one angel in any one species of angel. Consequently, an angel is individuated in virtue of its substantial form, which is unique to it.[4] And what is necessary and sufficient for something to be identical to *this* angel is that it have *this* substantial form.

For Aquinas, this view can be generalized to all substances. Any substance is individuated as *this* substance just in virtue of the fact that it has this particular substantial form. For example, a material substance such as Socrates is this human being in virtue of having *this* substantial form. And what is necessary and sufficient for something to be identical to Socrates is that its substantial form be identical to the substantial form of Socrates.[5]

MATTER AS THE PRINCIPLE OF INDIVIDUATION

But what makes something *this* substantial form rather than some other? Since on Aquinas's view there cannot be more than one individual for any species of immaterial things, in the case of an immaterial substance the substantial form is individuated just by the properties of that form itself; that very form cannot be shared by any other individual. For any species of material thing, however, there are many individuals

---

thing; similarly, not every form constituting a whole is a thing, in Aquinas's view. In general, the forms configuring immaterial substances and the form configuring human beings are things in his view; the forms of other material substances and the forms of artifacts are metaphysical parts of a thing but are not themselves things.

3. *ST* I, q. 50, aa. 1 and 5.
4. Ibid., a. 2.
5. Thomas Aquinas, *Expositio super librum Boethii De trinitate*, pars 2, q. 4, a. 2; cf. also *ST* I, q. 119, a.1; and Thomas Aquinas, *Quaestiones disputatae de potentia*, q. 9, a. 1.

within a species, and the species-specific properties conferred by the substantial form of each individual thing within the species will therefore be the same. Aquinas designates the collection of these species-specific properties with the Latin term translated "nature"; the nature of a thing is what is signified by the species name of the thing, and a thing's nature is given by its substantial form.[6] The species-specific properties conferred by the substantial form of Plato—that is, the nature of human beings—are the same as the species-specific properties conferred by the substantial form of Socrates. How, then, are the substantial forms of material objects such as human beings individuated?

We might be inclined to think that, on the contrary, such forms *cannot* be individuated. The configuration or the form of human beings is a universal, we might suppose. It is the same in every human being, which is why there is a human nature that is in every human being. One substantial form of a human being cannot be distinguished from that of another human being. *A fortiori*, a substantial form cannot be what individuates a human being.

Aquinas's response to this sort of objection is expressed succinctly in his well-known line that, for material substances, matter individuates.[7] It is easier, however, to repeat the line than to see what he meant by it. The difficulty has to do at least in part with the notion of matter at issue.

A substantial form of a material substance configures prime matter; but prime matter is matter devoid of any form, without any configuration, something that exists only potentially and not actually, since anything that actually exists is configured. Prime matter can thus hardly be what individuates one form from another.

On the other hand, any actually existing material substance has a determinate quantity of matter. At any given time it occupies a certain space; it is extended to a determinate degree in each of the three dimensions of space. If this particular chunk of matter were somehow responsible for individuating forms (or material things), then a form (or a material thing) would go out of existence when the quantity of matter in the material thing in question changed. Some metaphysicians might not mind such a conclusion, but Aquinas is not among them. The particular quantity of something is an accident, and an accident is a property that a thing can gain and lose while remaining one and the same, on Aquinas's view. The notion of matter at issue in Aquinas's account of

---

6. See, e.g., *Quaestio de unione verbi incarnati*, a.1, corpus; see also ibid., a. 2, ad 6, where Aquinas explains that the name of a species signifies a nature.

7. Perhaps the most detailed exposition of this view is found in his *Expositio super librum Boethii De trinitate*, pars 2, q. 4, a. 2.

the individuation of material things is thus neither prime matter nor matter configured as it is in an actually existing thing.

When Aquinas attempts to explain the concept of matter relevant to the individuation of material things, he tends to speaks of it as matter under indeterminate dimensions,[8] that is, matter that is extended in three dimensions but where the degree of extension in any dimension is not specified. Now, any actually existing matter has determinate dimensions. But the particular degree of extension in a dimension is one thing; the materiality, as it were, of matter is another thing. The determinate dimensions of a material thing have to do with exactly what space that thing occupies; the materiality of the matter is responsible for the space-occupying feature itself. Matter is the sort of thing that is *here now*, in a way that numbers, for example, are not. This feature of matter, however, can be considered without specifying the precise spatial locations that the matter occupies. When Aquinas talks of matter under indeterminate dimensions, he is calling attention to this feature of matter. It is not a feature that is ever had by any actually existing matter in isolation from that matter's having some determinate dimensions. Nonetheless, any actually existing matter with determinate dimensions has this space-occupying feature, which can be considered independently of that matter's determinate dimensions.

In his commentary on Boethius's *De trinitate*,[9] Aquinas raises the question whether form individuates. Given his oft-repeated line that matter individuates, one would expect him to answer the question in the negative; but in fact the answer is affirmative. Matter is *this* matter in virtue of having spatial extension; but spatial extension, even if the dimensions of that extension are indeterminate, is a quantity, and quantity is an accident. So there is at least a sense in which an accidental form individuates. Or, to put the same point in another way, prime matter, which lacks all form, is not matter under indeterminate dimensions and does not individuate.

On this way of understanding matter under indeterminate dimensions, *this* matter under indeterminate dimensions is distinguished from any other by spatial location and also, presumably, by spatial continuity.[10] Between this matter and that matter there will have to be

---

8. Ibid. Aquinas does not always describe his position on this score in the same way, and the variation in terminology suggests to some scholars either a development in his thought or a series of changes of mind. The issue is complicated, and so I am leaving it to one side here. Cf. *Sententia super Metaphysicam*, bk. 7, lect. 2, 1283, for a helpful discussion of matter and its dimensions.

9. *Expositio super librum Boethii De trinitate*, pars 2, q. 4, a. 2.

10. Although Aquinas doesn't focus on continuity in connection with matter under

a spatial discontinuity or gap. It also seems reasonable to assume that spatio-temporal continuity distinguishes this matter from that matter over time. A gap of either space or time thus entails that there is no longer the same matter.

No doubt one could wish for a great deal more clarity and precision with regard to the notion of matter Aquinas has in mind when he claims that matter individuates. But perhaps this is enough to point us roughly in the right direction for making sense of his concept of substantial forms that are individual rather than universal.

We can see Aquinas's point by taking a contemporary example. Consider, for instance, two molecules of water. Each one has the nature of water, the properties that make water water; and these are conferred by the water-specific configuration, the substantial form, of the molecule. But the form or configuration of water molecule A inheres in *this* matter, and the form or configuration of water molecule B inheres in *that* matter. Because matter has an irreducible space-occupying feature, we can distinguish one substantial form from another by its association with matter. This substantial form is the configuration of this matter, and that one is the configuration of that matter.[11]

In the case of human beings, Aquinas's idea is basically the same. What individuates Socrates? For Aquinas, it is not that Socrates has a set of essential properties unique to him, as an angel does. It is also not that, in addition to his having the usual set of properties essential to all human beings, a human nature, Socrates also has a collection of accidental properties such that the conjunction of them is not shareable by anything else. Rather, what individuates Socrates is *this* substantial form of a human being; and a substantial form of a material substance such as a human being is *this* substantial form in virtue of the fact that it configures *this* matter.[12]

Consequently, it is also clear why Aquinas thinks that properties other than those that are part of the nature of a thing are accidents. Only the nature is conferred by the substantial form, but since only *this* substantial form is necessary and sufficient for the existence of *this* thing, any other properties are such that the thing can gain or lose them and remain the same thing.[13] (On the other hand, it is also clear that any-

---

indeterminate dimensions, he does emphasize continuity as a basis for unity in certain circumstances. See, for example, *Sententia super Metaphysicam*, bk. 5, lect. 7, 849–58.

11. Cf., e.g., *ST* III, q. 3, a. 7, ad 1, where Aquinas says that a substantial form is multiplied in accordance with the division of matter.

12. Of course, *being configured by this matter* is a property of Socrates, and one that only he has; but it is a property that he has just in virtue of having *this* matter. And so the conclusion remains the same: Socrates is ultimately individuated by matter.

13. This is so even for the properties medieval logicians call "*propria*." A *proprium* is a

thing that has a substantial form necessarily has accidents, as a quick survey of the nine Aristotelian categories of accidents makes evident; nothing that has a substantial form can be without any accidents at all.)[14]

CONSTITUTION AND IDENTITY

A further conclusion from these views of Aquinas's is that constitution is not identity,[15] and a whole is something more than the sum of its parts.[16]

---

property that all and only the members of a species have and that they have always. The capacity for laughter, or risibility, is a *proprium* of human beings. *Propria* are classified by medieval logicians as a kind of accident just in virtue of the fact that, although the members of a species never lack the *propria* characteristic of that species, if a member of that species were to lack a *proprium* of the species, it would not be the case that it therefore ceased to be a member of the species in which the *proprium* is found.

14. God has no accidents, but it is also not true to say that God *has* a substantial form, because in the case of a simple God it is not possible to make a distinction between him and his nature.

15. See, for example, *Sententia super Metaphysicam*, bk. 7, lect. 17, 1672–74. There Aquinas says that in cases in which the composite is one thing, the composite is not identical with its components; rather the composite is something over and above its components. For interesting contemporary arguments against the reduction of wholes to their parts, see Mark Johnston, "Constitution Is Not Identity," *Mind* 101 (1992): 89–105; and Lynne Rudder Baker, "Why Constitution Is Not Identity," *Journal of Philosophy* 94 (1997): 599–621. For an excellent discussion of the constitution relation, see Lynne Rudder Baker, "Unity without Identity: A New Look at Material Constitution," *Midwest Studies in Philosophy* 23 (1999): 144–65.

16. Some confusion can arise in considering this claim because we can understand the parts and their properties in more than one way. In particular, we can be thinking of these properties either as (i) the properties the parts have when they are taken *singillatim* (as, for example, the properties including causal powers that the constituent atoms of a molecule have considered on their own, when they are not configured together into a molecule), or as (ii) the properties the parts in fact have when they are in the whole (as, for example, the properties the atoms of a molecule have when they are configured into the molecule). If we understand the properties of the parts in sense (i), it is true to say, as biochemists do, that the features of a whole such as a protein (its folded shape, for example) cannot always be derived from even perfect knowledge of the properties (including the causal powers) of the atoms that are constituents of the protein. This is so because large proteins achieve their biologically active form, including their folded shape, only with the help of certain enzymes acting on them; and so the properties of the whole are a function of something more than the properties of the parts taken *singillatim*. But if we understand the properties of the parts in sense (ii), then in effect we are smuggling the configuration, or the form, of the whole into the properties of the parts of the whole. In sense (ii), it would be very surprising if there were properties of the whole that were not a function of the properties of the parts of the whole. Nonetheless, in sense (ii), the properties of the whole are a function of the properties of the parts *in the configuration of the whole*. Consequently, in either sense (i) or sense (ii), the parts alone are not all there is to the whole; the configuration of the whole is also required. A whole is thus not identical to its constituents alone.

The general designation Aquinas uses for a thing that has a particular substantial form is the Latin term transliterated *supposit* or the Greek term transliterated into Latin as *hypostasis*.[17] Since he recognizes particulars in categories other than substance, he tends to use the Latin terms translated "particular," "singular," and "individual" more broadly than *supposit* or *hypostasis*. *This* redness, for example, is an individual or a particular in the category of quality. A *supposit* (or a *hypostasis*) is a particular or individual just in the category of substance.[18] The Latin term translated "person" is Aquinas's technical term for an individual substance of a rational nature.[19]

On Aquinas's view, although the existence of a particular substantial form is necessary and sufficient for the existence of a *supposit*, a *supposit* is not identical with its substantial form alone. A substantial form is only a constituent of a *supposit*.[20]

The reason for this view is that, first, any thing that has a substantial form necessarily also has accidents, even though it is not necessary that it have one accident rather than another. So a substantial form is not the only metaphysical constituent of a thing; any thing will also have accidental forms as metaphysical constituents. In addition, for material substances, the matter that makes the substantial form of a material *supposit* a particular is also a constituent of a *supposit*.[21] So any *supposit* has more metaphysical constituents than just a substantial form.

Second, it is also the case for Aquinas that a substantial form con-

---

17. These are not synonymous for him; although they pick out the same thing in reality (for this point, see, for example, Thomas Aquinas, *Summa Contra Gentiles* [hereafter *SCG*] IV, chap. 38 [3766]), they pick it out under slightly different designations, because *suppositum* is a term of second intention and *hypostasis* is a term of first intention. This complexity of medieval logic is one I will ignore here, for the sake of brevity. For the distinction, see, for example, Thomas Aquinas, *Quaestio de unione verbi incarnati*, a. 2, corpus.

18. Aquinas gives a helpful explanation of his use of these terms in *Quaestio de unione verbi incarnati*, a. 2; see also *Quaestiones quodlibetales* V, q. 2, a.1.

19. *ST* III, q. 2, a. 2.

20. Eric Olson argues that a human person is identical to a living organism but that the persistence of only a small, living biological part of the organism (a part of the brain) is necessary and sufficient for the existence of that organism. Aquinas's position can be thought of as the metaphysical analogue of Olson's: the persistence of a small, living metaphysical part of the whole human being is necessary and sufficient for the existence of that human being. See Olson, *The Human Animal* (Oxford: Oxford University Press, 1997).

21. See, for example, *Quaestio de unione verbi incarnati*, a. 1, where Aquinas says that a *suppositum* will not be the same as a nature in anything in which there is either accident or individual matter, because in that case the *suppositum* is related to the nature by means of an addition. See also *SCG* IV, chap. 40 (3781), where Aquinas explains the distinction between a singular and its *quiddity* or nature and goes on to explain that a *supposit* such as Socrates is not identical to his substantial form because in his normal or natural condition he is also constituted of designated matter.

figures prime matter, rather than integral parts that are themselves matter-form composites; and so a *supposit* is not identical to the collection of its integral parts either. A material substance, for example, is composed of elements but is not identical to the collection of elements that make it up. The integral components of a whole by themselves do not include the substantial form of the whole; and when one integral component is combined with others by the substantial form that conjoins the whole, the part loses whatever substantial form it may have had before merging into the composite. The particular bits of earth, air, fire, and water that compose a material substance on Aquinas's view are thus not identical to the substance they compose. A substantial form is also needed to conjoin the parts into a whole. And although we can decompose a whole substance into its integral components in such a way that they exist as actual substances in their own right, in the whole the substantial form configures prime matter, not the integral matter-form composites into which the whole can be decomposed.

Aquinas's views entail, then, that for substances constitution is not identity, for constituents of either a metaphysical or an integral sort.

CONSTITUTION AND IDENTITY: THE SPECIAL CASE OF THE SOUL

That constitution is not identity on Aquinas's view helps explain his claim that persons survive bodily death in virtue of the fact that a substantial form of a human being, a soul, can persist in a disembodied condition.

Since a material *supposit* is composed of matter and form as its constituents, if constitution were identity, then the loss of either matter or form would be enough to entail the loss of the whole *supposit*. In that case, any *supposit* would cease to exist when it lost either its substantial form or the matter configured by that form. But because constitution is not identity for Aquinas, it is possible for him to suppose that a *supposit* survives the loss of some of its constituents, provided that the remaining constituents can exist on their own and are sufficient for the existence of the *supposit*.

That for Aquinas constitution is not identity in the case of human beings is clear when it comes to integral parts, on either the macroscopic or the microscopic level. A human being can survive the loss of some of his elemental bits or even the loss of some of his larger integral parts, such as a hand. But Aquinas thinks the point about constitution and identity holds also for metaphysical parts in the special case of a human being, whose substantial form can exist on its own. Normally, the integral parts of a human being include two hands, but a human being can exist without being in the normal condition. Analogously, the metaphysical constituents of a human being normally include matter and substantial form, but Aquinas thinks that a human being can exist without being in the normal condition in this way either.

It is easy to become confused about Aquinas's position here. For example, in his commentary on 1 Corinthians,[22] Aquinas says,

Since a soul is part of a body of a human being, it is not the whole human being, and my soul is not me.[23]

Passages such as this one suggest to some scholars that for Aquinas a human person ceases to exist with the death of the body.

But these passages need to be read in the context of Aquinas's other views. So, for example, Aquinas thinks that after death a human soul either enjoys the rewards of heaven or suffers the pains of hell.[24] He maintains that the separated soul is capable of understanding and choosing (*ST* III, supp. q. 70, aa. 2–3). He also holds that after his death a human being can appear to the living; for example, speaking of the disembodied soul of a martyr, Felix, Aquinas says that Felix—not a simulacrum but the human being Felix—appeared to the people of Nola (*ST* III, supp. q. 69, a. 3). He thinks that the souls of deceased saints know the prayers of the living and respond to them (*ST* III, supp. q. 72, a. 2). He claims that the holy Fathers in hell—who existed there as separated souls—were waiting for Christ and were delivered by Christ's descent into hell (*ST* III, supp. q. 69, aa. 4–5). In these passages and many others, Aquinas attributes to separated souls properties that we take to be most characteristic of human persons, including intellectual understanding and love.

These passages are compatible with the passages in which Aquinas claims that a soul is not a human person if we give proper weight to the distinction between constitution and identity in his thought. A human person is not identical to his soul. Rather, a human person is identical to a particular in the species *rational animal*. A particular of that sort is ordinarily, naturally, constituted of an array of bodily parts and is composed of form and matter. Because constitution is not identity for Aquinas, however, a particular can exist with less than the natural complement of either integral or metaphysical parts. It can, for example, exist when it is constituted only by one of its main metaphysical parts,

---

22. I am grateful to Brian Leftow for calling this passage to my attention.
23. *Super I ad Corinthios*, chap. 15, l.2.
24. See, e.g., *ST* III, supp. q. 69, a. 2, hereafter cited parenthetically in the text.

namely, the soul. And so, although a human person is not identical to his soul, the existence of the soul is sufficient for the existence of a human person.

Analogously, some contemporary philosophers suppose that a human being is identical to a living biological organism; but it is also part of their view that, although this organism is ordinarily composed of a complete human body, it is capable of persisting even when the body has been reduced to nothing more than a living brain or a living part of a brain.[25] On this view, a human being is capable of existing when she is composed of nothing more than a living brain part, but she is not identical to the brain part that composes her in that unusual condition. In the same way, for Aquinas, a human person is capable of existing when she is composed of nothing more than a metaphysical part, without its being the case that she is identical to that metaphysical part.

A second, closely related objection that will occur to many readers at this point arises from Aquinas's insistence that the soul alone is not a human being.[26] On the interpretation I have been arguing for here, a substantial form is sufficient for the existence of the *suppositum* whose form it is, and so the existence of a human soul is sufficient for the existence of a human being. But if the existence of a soul is sufficient for the existence of a human being, then, since for Aquinas the soul (unlike any other substantial form of a material thing) sometimes exists in a disembodied condition, it seems that on my interpretation the soul in that condition must *be* a human being, contrary to Aquinas's own oft-repeated claim.

The solution here is the same as before. It is true that on Aquinas's account a soul is not *identical* to a human being; rather, as I said, a human being is identical to a particular in the species *rational animal*. But any particular in this species is such that, on Aquinas's account, it can exist when it is composed of nothing more than one of its metaphysical constituents, namely, its form or soul; for Aquinas, the persistence of one metaphysical part of the whole human *suppositum* is sufficient for the existence of that human being. Because constitution is not identity, however, it does not follow from this claim that a soul alone is identical to a human being.

Someone might also worry about the coherence of the position I am ascribing to Aquinas, since Aquinas clearly also holds that the substantial forms of material substances are individuated by matter. Separated

---

25. See, for example, Olson, *The Human Animal*.
26. See, for example, *SCG* II, chap. 57, where Aquinas argues at length against Plato's attempt to show that a human being is identical to a soul.

souls are substantial forms of material substances that no longer inform matter. So it might seem that, on Aquinas's view, either such souls are not individuals or matter does not after all individuate the substantial forms of human beings. But this objection is mistaken. It is possible for one separated soul to be distinguished from another on the basis of its *past* connection with matter, rather than on the basis of a present connection with matter. The disembodied soul of Socrates is the substantial human form that at some time in the past configured *this* matter, the matter that was part of Socrates in his embodied state. The disembodied soul of Plato is the substantial human form that at some time in the past configured the matter that was part of Plato in *his* embodied state. It remains the case, then, that matter individuates, even in the case of disembodied souls. Matter individuates a disembodied form in virtue of its past connection to matter. And, of course, it will also be true that this history carries with it other differences as well, including differences of memories, desires, understanding, and so on.

If this is right, then for Aquinas spatio-temporal continuity of material constituents isn't necessary for the existence of a human being. A human being can persist in a disembodied condition, so that there are spatio-temporal gaps in the existence of the material parts of a human person. On the other hand, temporal continuity of a substantial form is always necessary for the existence of a human being. If a human soul existed as a constituent in an embodied human being (say, Socrates) from t_1 to t_2, failed to exist at all from t_2 to t_3, and then existed again in a disembodied condition from t_3 to t_4, the explanation I gave for the individuation of disembodied souls by matter would fail. On what basis would one say that the disembodied soul that exists from t_3 to t_4 is the soul that from t_1 to t_2 configured the matter that was part of Socrates?

It is also worth noticing that if this interpretation of Aquinas's views were not correct, if Aquinas supposed a human being to be identical to her constituents so that she ceased to exist as a human being when she ceased to be embodied, then there would in fact be an incoherence in his position. That is because he could not hold such a view of a human being consistently with his view of the nature of change. On the Aristotelian understanding of change Aquinas inherits and accepts, a thing that gains or loses an accidental form undergoes change while remaining one and the same thing. Quantities, including quantity of matter, are accidents, however. So, on Aquinas's position, a human being who loses a quantity of matter, such as a hand or a leg, for instance, remains one and the same thing while undergoing change. If, however, constitution were identity for Aquinas, then a human being whose material constituents changed would cease to be the thing she was and become some other thing instead.[27] In that case, contrary to Aquinas's position, the gain or loss of an accident such as quantity of matter would not be a change in a human being; it would be the destruction of one thing and the generation of another. That Aquinas holds the view of change he does, then, supports the interpretation I have been arguing for here.

Finally, there is a concern about my interpretation of Aquinas's position that arises from Aquinas's definition of a person. As I explained above, Aquinas defines a person as an individual substance of a rational nature. Since a soul is not identical to a human being but is just a constituent of a human being, a soul is not a substance. Consequently, when the soul exists on its own, separate from the body, what exists does not meet Aquinas's definition of a person. How worrisome this conclusion is is not clear, however. It may be that Aquinas wants to reserve the term "person" as the designation for a human being in his normal condition. On the other hand, he inherits the definition from Boethius, who wanted it to be a general term useful also in discussions of the Trinity; and so it may be that "substance" in this definition is being used broadly, to cover anything subsisting on its own, whether it is a complete substance or not. The disembodied soul is a subsisting thing of a rational nature, and so it would fit the definition of *person* if "substance" in the definition were to be understood broadly. For one reason or another, then, this objection is not cogent.

In this brief exposition, I have only scratched the surface of Aquinas's account of the individuation and identity of things, including human beings; but even this quick exposition is enough to show that he has a complex and sophisticated account and that it is able to support his metaphysical and theological positions.[28]

---

27. Contemporary ways of harmonizing Leibniz's Law with change over time might offer Aquinas a way out here if they were compatible with the rest of Aquinas's metaphysics, but it is not clear that they are. See, e.g., David Lewis, "The Problem of Temporary Intrinsics," in David Lewis, *On the Plurality of Worlds* (Oxford: Blackwell, 1986), and Dean Zimmerman, "Temporary Intrinsics and Presentism," in *Metaphysics: The Big Questions,* ed. Peter van Inwagen and Dean Zimmerman (Malden, Mass.: Blackwell, 1998), 206–19.

28. I am grateful to Brian Davies, Brian Leftow, and Scott MacDonald for helpful comments on an earlier draft of this paper.

4 Reflections on Some Thirteenth- and Fourteenth-Century Views of the Categories

WILLIAM E. MCMAHON

For about fifteen hundred years the dominant categorial scheme in Western thought was that of Aristotle, and especially in the Middle Ages it was taken quite seriously. What I would like to focus on here is a period of roughly seventy-five years, from the mid-thirteenth century to the early fourteenth century, when there emerged challenges to what I call the "standard" medieval position on the categories.[1] The standard position numbered Thomas Aquinas and Albertus Magnus[2] among its advocates, and its tenets are: (1) there are ten and only ten categories; (2) they exhaust the sense of simple categorematic terms; (3) relations are distinctive intrinsic properties; and (4) the "six principles"[3] are extrinsic ones that are absolute and hence not reducible to relations. Figure 4.1 presents Thomas Aquinas's version of this point of view.[4]

---

1. William E. McMahon, "The Categories in Some Post-Medieval Spanish Philosophers," in *Medieval and Renaissance Logic in Spain, Acts of the 12th European Symposium on Medieval Logic and Semantics*, ed. Ignacio Angelelli and Paloma Perez-Ilzarbe (Hildesheim: Georg Olms, 2000), 355–70.

2. In his writings Albertus presents different formulations of the categories. One is quite similar to that of Aquinas, which leads one to believe that the teacher influenced the student here. Albertus Magnus, *De Praedicamentis*, in *Omnia Opera*, vol. 1, ed. August Borgnet (Paris: Ludovico Vives, 1890), bk. 6, chap. 1. However, another formulation in Albertus's *Categories* commentary has relation as an extrinsic category and the six principles as subspecies of it. Ibid., bk. 1, chap. 7. In addition, his commentary on the *Liber de Sex Principiis* appears to take a "modern" outlook: that relations are neither intrinsic nor extrinsic, but something else altogether. Albertus Magnus, *Liber de Sex Principiis*, in *Omnia Opera*, vol. 1, bk. 1, chap. 1.

3. The "six principles" are the six categories that are not given detailed treatment by Aristotle—action, passion, when, where, position, and *habitus*. A treatise on them (of unknown authorship), appeared in the twelfth century: Lorenzo Minio-Paluello, ed., *Anonymi fragmentum vulgo vocatum* Liber Sex Principiorum, in *Aristoteles Latinus*, vol. 1 (Bruges: Desclée de Brouwer, 1966), 6–7, 35–59 (hereafter LSP). It was seen as filling a gap in Aristotle and subsequently became an integral part of the logic curriculum, being the subject of many commentaries for a century or so.

4. See Thomas Aquinas, *Sententia super Metaphysicam*, bk. 5, lect. 9, 891–92. See also

By the late thirteenth century support for the Albertus/Thomas position on the categories was so strong that it became commonplace to attempt to demonstrate the sufficiency of the categories.[5] Challenges to the standard view were emerging, however, and they appear to have come primarily from two groups: (a) philosophers of an Augustinian bent, who were not inherently committed to Aristotle in the first place, and (b) the critical thinkers, whose philosophy manifested a strong logical orientation. The purpose of this essay is to consider the genesis of nonstandard views of the categories, which arose to challenge the position outlined above. These latter views included such features as removing relations from the set of intrinsic categories; reducing the number of categories by collapsing some into others; denial of the isomorphism of words, concepts, and things;[6] and ultimately questioning the sufficiency of the ten-category system. On these matters I shall consider the views of four philosophers—Henry of Ghent, John Duns Scotus, William of Ockham, and John Buridan.

We begin with Henry of Ghent, who was playing a prominent role in Paris shortly after the death of Thomas Aquinas. He can be considered a member of group (a), described above, being less committed to Aristotelianism than many of his contemporaries. Although keeping with the Boethian tradition, Henry alters the standard view of the categories.[7] The basic distinction regarding the categories in Henry is between *res* and *ratio*:[8] the *res* of a category is the specific things to which it applies, which are of that sort *(essentia et natura)*. The conception of that sort, of the mode of being proper to it, is the *ratio*. Hence the *ratio* of substance is *esse in se*, of accidents in general *esse in alio*.[9] Henry does not argue for the sufficiency of the categories per se but tends to assume that they constitute an adequate conceptual system for the description of reality. Nevertheless, not all the categories have *res* as such,

---

John F. Wippel, "Thomas Aquinas's Derivation of the Aristotelian Categories (Predicaments)" *Journal of the History of Philosophy* 25, no. 1 (1987): 13–34.

5. See William E. McMahon, "Radulphus Brito on the Sufficiency of the Categories," *Cahiers de l'Institut du Moyen-Age Grec et Latin* 39 (1981): 81–96.

6. Other discussions of the relations between ontological categories, on the one hand, and categories of thought and language, on the other, can be found in Chapters 7, 13, 14, and 15 of this volume.

7. Henry of Ghent, *Summa*, aa. 31–34, in *Opera Omnia*, vol. 27, ed. R. Macken (Leuven: Leuven University Press, 1991), a. 32, q. 5, 81–107.

8. "Res praedicamenti est quidquid per essentiam et naturam suam est contentum in ordine alicuius praedicamenti; ratio praedicamenti est proprius modus essendi eorum quae continentur in praedicamento. Ex quibus duobus, scilicet ex re praedicamenti et ratione essendi eius, quae est ratio praedicamenti, constituitur ipsum praedicamentum et diversificatur unum praedicamentum ab alio." Ibid., a. 32, q. 5, 79.

9. Ibid., a. 32, q. 5, 80.

FIGURE 1. Thomas Aquinas's Division of the Categories

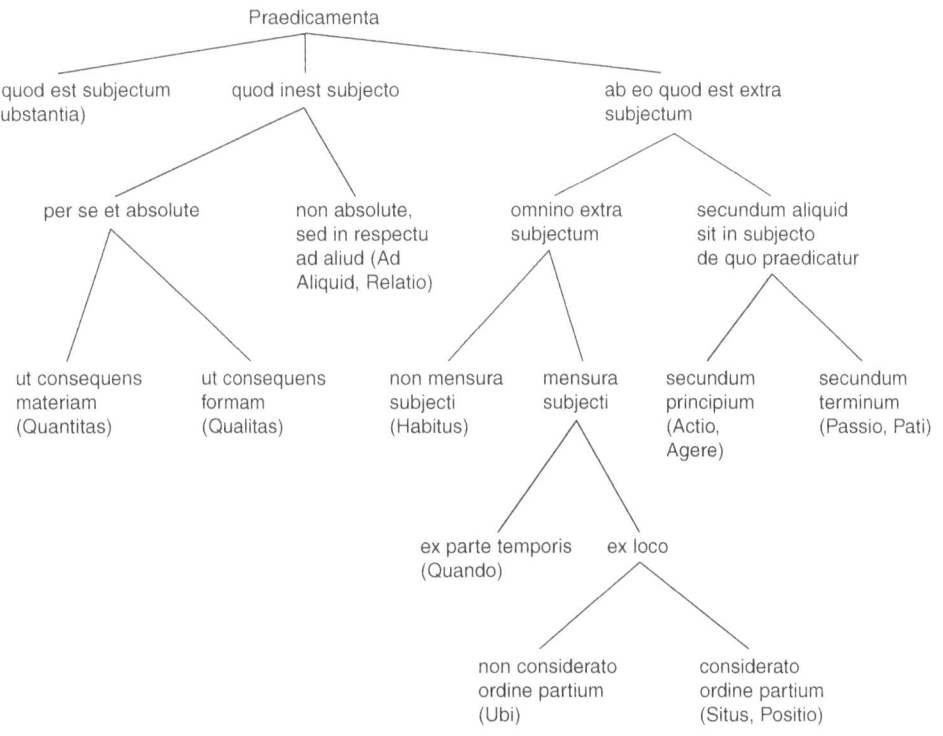

i.e., not all of them designate classes of real items. To put this in a contemporary idiom, Henry can be said to be separating the categories by means of the extension/intension distinction. That is, they all are distinct concepts *(rationes)*, but that does not entail that each category corresponds to a *res;* again, not all of these concepts designate.

Within earlier Aristotelianism there was a tendency to assume a parallelism of words, concepts, and things.[10] That would suggest, in accordance with the discussion of the "Aristotelian square" at the beginning of the *Categories*,[11] that the set of real items includes, in some sense or other, individual substances, their kinds, and their accidents. This idea

---

10. See, for example, Sten Ebbesen, "The Paris Arts Faculty: Siger of Brabant, Boethius of Dacia, Radulphus Brito," in *Medieval Philosophy*, vol. 3 of *Routledge History of Philosophy*, ed. John Marenbon (London: Routledge, 1998), 275–78.
11. Aristotle, *Categories*, in *The Basic Works of Aristotle*, ed. Richard McKeon (New York: Random House, 1941), 2, 1a20–b10, 7–8.

would then be qualified by saying, e.g., that kinds have derivative reality and accidents dependent reality.[12] Henry does not accept this formulation. For him the categories are divided into three groups.[13]

Created being *(esse participatum)* is first divided into *esse in se* (substance) and *esse in alio* (accident), into that which subsists and that which inheres. Then the accidents are further subdivided into those which are absolute and those which are relative. Here Henry does two things that are nonstandard:

1. He denies the distinction between "intrinsic" and "extrinsic" accidents, or reinterprets it as simply the absolute/relative distinction. The distinction dates back at least to the twelfth-century LSP,[14] and the idea is that intrinsic accidents are closely associated with the hylomorphic constitution of substance, while the extrinsic ones are superadded to that.[15] The difficulty with this picture concerns the category of relation. Since the LSP did not place it among the extrinsic six principles, there was a tendency to regard relation as an intrinsic accident—which of course created the problem of explaining how that could be so. Even Albertus Magnus recognized that relations are not as intimately associated with a substance as are the absolute properties of quantity and quality, and he noted that relations have "less being" than the absolute accidents.[16]

Henry goes a step further. He maintains that relations do not have *res* independently of their foundations, i.e., they are not real as such, so they can't be in the substance.[17] For example, two substances, a (Soc-

---

12. Jean Paulus suggests that Aristotle is able to maintain such a position because of his belief in the analogical character of being. Jean Paulus, *Henri de Gand, Essai sur des Tendances de sa Métaphysique*, in *Etudes de Philosophie Médiévale* (Paris: J. Vrin, 1938), 25:156n2, 165. Diverse items are real, but in different senses of "reality."

13. "Primo ergo esse participatum inquantum est ratio cuiuslibet praedicamenti generalis, dividit penes duas rationes speciales: quae distinguunt praedicamentum substantivae a praedicamentis accidentium. . . . Praedicamentum vero accidentis distinguit secundum duos modos participandi esse alteri inhaerendo, esse enim convenit alicui alteri inhaerendo: aut secundum se et absolute: aut in respectu ad aliud. Primo modo sunt duo praedicamenta accidentium: scilicet quantitas et qualitas. Secundo modo sunt alia septem praedicamenta relationis communiter dictae: quae ideo ad unum praedicamentum habent reduci. . . ." Henry of Ghent, *Quodlibeta* (Louvain: Bibliotheque S.J., 1961), 5, q. 2, 154vF–H.

14. Minio-Paluello, *Aristoteles Latinus* I, 6–7, 35–59. Some ascribe the distinction to Boethius. See Mark G. Henninger, *Relations, Medieval Theories, 1250–1325* (Oxford: Clarendon Press, 1989), 51; and Paulus, *Henri de Gand*, 149.

15. For my own formulation of the intrinsic/extrinsic distinction, see McMahon, "Categories in Some Post-Medieval Spanish Philosophers," 355–70.

16. Albertus Magnus, *De Praedicamentis*, bk. 4, chap. 1.

17. "In tota enim universitate creaturarum non sunt nisi tres res trium primorum praedicamentorum, substantiae scilicet, et quantitatis, et qualitatis: caetera autem omnia sunt rationes atque intentiones intellectus circa illas tres res, non habentes aliquid pro-

rates) and b (Plato), are white. The qualities are real determinations in the things. By virtue of them, aRb, where "R" designates similarity. The similarity is called a real relation in that the whitenesses on which it is founded are real. But it adds nothing to them and as such has no reality; its existence would thus be intensional. This does not, however, make it merely a conceptual relation, i.e., one between two concepts.[18]

2. The second alteration Henry makes is to eliminate some categories by collapsing the six principles into the category of relation (which, as we shall see, would also render them "unreal"). This is not a completely new idea; others had noted the ostensibly relational character of *actio, passio, quando, ubi, situs,* and *habitus*.[19] On the other hand, there were those who were emphatic about the absolute character of those categories, including Radulphus Brito, shortly after Henry.[20] But the relational view is more in step with contemporary metaphysics and semantics, as spatial, temporal, and causal notions are regarded as relational, and the means of expressing them, transitive verbs, prepositional phrases, etc., as Fregean dyadic relations.

But if the last six categories are subcategories of relation, why have ten categories instead of four or nine? In other words, what is the difference between *ad aliquid* and the other six categories? Again, it should be noted that only three categories pertain to what is *in re;* the others are *modi essendi* but not classes of beings. This point will be elaborated on below. Here the point is that Henry wants to say there are conceptual differences that warrant the retention of relation as an independent category, and his solution to this issue closely resembles one that can be found in Albertus Magnus.[21] Relation per se is founded on the absolute accidents of quantity and quality. This somehow makes it quasi-intrinsic, "being rooted in a completely absolute foundation."[22] Another way it is put is that relations are begotten *(nascitur)* through the intrinsic accidents.[23] The six principles, however, are founded on

---

priae realitatis nisi quia fundantur in rebus illorum praedicamentorum, ut dictum est. Propter quod, cum idea non est nisi rerum, idcirco relationum et respectuum dicimus non esse aliquas proprias ideas." Henry of Ghent, *Quodlibeta*, vol. 11, ed. G. A. Wilson (Leuven: Leuven University Press, 1991), 7, q. 2, 61–68. See also Henry of Ghent, *Summa*, a. 32, q. 5, 88–91, 94.

18. See, for example, Paulus, *Henri de Gand*, 164.

19. Ibid., 172–73; see also William E. McMahon, "Albert the Great on the Semantics of the Categories of Substance, Quantity, and Quality," *Historiographia Linguistica* 7 (1980): 145–57.

20. See McMahon, "Radulphus Brito," 81–96.

21. Henry of Ghent, *Summa*, a. 32, q. 5, 94–106; Albertus Magnus, *De Praedicamentis*, bk. 1, chap. 7. See also Paulus, *Henri de Gand*, 173–77.

22. Paulus, *Henri de Gand*, 175.

23. Albertus Magnus, *Liber de Sex Principiis*, bk. 1, chaps. 1, 6.

motion, and are either aspects of it *(actio, passio)* or result from it *(quando, ubi, situs, habitus)*.[24]

Let me take note of another suggestion by Henry that appears to have far-reaching consequences for the history of metaphysics. According to some commentators, Henry seems to be shifting the discussion from accidents to "modes of being."[25] An accident-ontology, such as what I have called the standard medieval theory of the categories, has been characterized as an ontology of layers.[26] Underneath everything there is the matter-form composite, on top of which we have the substantial form, the intrinsic accidental forms, and then the extrinsic ones. An alternative to this could be a "modal" interpretation of being. I shall return to discuss this point further at the conclusion of this paper, but here I would like to note that Henry of Ghent hints at a modal ontology.

Modes, i.e., *modi essendi* and their relationship to the *modi significandi*, had played a central role in grammatical theory.[27] But as Ebbesen puts it, "In works from the late thirteenth century there is an uneasy relationship between the properly grammatical modes of signifying (such as the substantive's *modus per se stantis*) and the so-called modes of category *(modi praedicamentorum,* such as the *modus substantiae* of 'whatever')."[28] There is no simple correlation of the parts of speech (as *modi significandi*) to the categories, and the *modi essendi* referred to by the grammarians have only a rough correspondence to the categories.[29]

But Henry of Ghent explicitly maintains that the *modi essendi* are the ten categories. "Modes of being," however, are not to be identified with classes of beings. The trick is that the substance-accident distinction, the one between independent and dependent things, is being transformed into a distinction between things and their modes, and modes need not be genuinely real. They are at least legitimate ways of thinking about things, and the categories, at least for the time being, will retain their honorific status in the description of reality. But what is being questioned is that there is a one-to-one correspondence between categorial terms and real items. This then opens the door to doubts about the validity of the categories. The progression, which appears to corre-

---

24. Henry of Ghent, *Summa,* a. 32, q. 5, 96–99.
25. See, for example, Paulus, *Henri de Gand,* 165–72.
26. See Marilyn McCord Adams, "Things versus 'Hows,' or Ockham on Predication and Ontology," in *How Things Are,* ed. James Bogen and James E. McGuire (Dordrecht: Reidel, 1985), 175.
27. See, for example, Ebbesen, "The Paris Arts Faculty," 273–78.
28. Ibid., 276.
29. See, G. L. Bursill-Hall, *Speculative Grammars of the Middle Ages: The Doctrine of the Partes orationis of the Modistae* (The Hague: Mouton, 1971), 88ff.

spond to the replacement of accidents by modes, is (1) to deny that all the categories are instantiated *in re*, (2) to eliminate or combine categories, and (3) ultimately, by the seventeenth century, to be completely skeptical about the validity of the Aristotelian conceptual system. It can be argued, then, that this originates with Henry of Ghent.[30]

I would like to treat the views of Duns Scotus briefly, noting especially a curious ambivalence toward the categories that may have originated with him and became more pronounced in his successors. Historians tend to focus on other aspects of Scotus's thought (the formal distinction, *haecceitas*, etc.), so his treatment of the categories is not well known. Actually, there are two views of the categories in Scotus, an overt one and a covert one, and they are ostensibly incompatible.

The overt one, which emerges from his commentaries, is a variant of the standard position. The ten categories are all classes of "real" things, i.e., the concepts designate extra-mental items.[31] Relations are real relative things;[32] in current parlance, Scotus has an ontology including relational tropes. Relations are beings *ad*, in one thing and toward another, i.e., immediately in the foundation, mediately in the other term.[33] A re-

---

30. Of course there is a straightforward historical explanation for Henry's adoption of the distinction of things and modes to delineate the categories: he got it from Boethius. That is: "Iamne patet quae sit differentia praedicationum? Quod aliae quidem quasi rem monstrant aliae vero quasi circumstantias rei; quodque illa quidem ita praedicantur, ut esse aliquid rem ostendant, illa vero ut non esse, sed potius extrinsecus aliquid quodam modo affigant. Illa igitur, quae aliquid esse designant, secundum rem praedicationes vocentur. Quae cum de rebus subjectis dicuntur, vocantur accidentia secundum rem; cum vero de deo qui subjectus non est, secundum substantiam rei praedicatio nuncupatur." Anicius Manlius Severinus Boethius, *"De Trinitate,"* in *The Theological Tractates*, trans. H. F. Stewart and E. K. Rand (London: William Heinemann, 1918), 24. And it seems clear that Henry thinks he is merely elaborating on Boethius's ideas here. Henry of Ghent, *Summa*, a. 32, q. 5, 87; see also Paulus, *Henri de Gand*, 149–52, 172–77. But since others disagreed with Boethius, or interpreted him differently, the hypothesis that there is something more here becomes quite tempting. See, for example, John Duns Scotus, *God and Creatures, the Quodlibetal Questions*, trans. Felix Alluntis, O.F.M., and Allan B Wolter, O.F.M. (Princeton: Princeton University Press, 1975), q. 3, a. 1, 62–63.

31. John Duns Scotus, *Quaestiones Super Praedicamenta Aristotelis*, in *Opera Philosophica*, vol. 1, ed. R. Andrews et al. (St. Bonaventure: Franciscan Institute, 1999), 1, 251; 11, 350–51.

32. "A relationship is real if, given real terms that are really distinct, it is there by the nature of things." Scotus, *God and Creatures*, q. 3, a. 1, 63. Scotus also writes: "For it is nonsense to speak of a relation being real unless its relationship to its opposite is real and as such it is really distinct from its opposite. Neither can it be really distinct from its opposite except as a real relation. And in this way it is a thing, insofar as to be a thing pertains to it. Therefore, of itself it is formally a thing, and of itself it is formally distinct from its opposite. But fundamentally and radically the relation gets both these characteristics from its foundation." Ibid., q. 3, a. 1, 66. Here I am using the translation by Alluntis and Wolter.

33. John Duns Scotus, *Quaestiones Super Libros Metaphysicorum Aristotelis*, bks. 1–5, in

lation *accidit* substance, having its proper *inesse* and proper accidentality.[34] Being a thing and being a mode or aspect are not incompatible; any property may be called a mode in a sense,[35] which does not preclude its having a distinctive reality. The six principles are also distinct genera, of absolute properties, hence not reducible to relation. "Being" is used equivocally in regard to the categories, so it is not their genus. The upshot of this overt view, then, is that there are ten distinct kinds of being, not reducible to one another, and ostensibly sufficient for describing the world.

The covert Scotist position on the categories has been unearthed recently by editors of his works such as Robert Andrews. They call attention to a note suggesting that Scotus did not accept the sufficiency of the categories. In a passage written later than the *Categories* commentary, Scotus says that there are various ways of dividing the categories and that they are flawed.[36] This is in keeping with the fact that Scotus doesn't provide a *sufficientia* in the place where it was customary to do so, in answer to the question *"Utrum Sint Tantum Decem Genera Generalissima."*[37] This line of interpretation suggests that Scotus ultimately was a skeptic about the categories, and according to Andrews (as noted in his edition of Scotus) this skepticism evidently came from Peter John Olivi.[38] But the note represents a puzzle in itself. It is not really congruous with the context, and it looks almost like a "throw-away comment." The explanation is that Scotus revised his works by means of additions, some of which come from Mauritius de Portu Hibernico.[39] The upshot

---

Opera Philosophica, vol. 3, ed. R. Andrews et al. (St. Bonaventure: Franciscan Institute, 1997), 5, 11, 583.

34. "It is a thing with its own accidentality which is not the accidentality of an absolute being but that of a relative being." Scotus, *God and Creatures*, q. 3, a. 3, 73; see also John Duns Scotus, *Ordinatio* II, 1, 5, 110, in *Omnia Opera*, vol. 7, ed. Carolo Baliæ et al. (Vatican City: Typis Polyglottis Vaticanis, 1973).

35. Scotus, *Ordinatio* II, 1, 5, 113–14.

36. "Nota: variae sunt viae divisivae ostendendi sufficientiam praedicamentorum, quae videntur dupliciter peccare. Primo, quia ostendunt oppositum propositi, scilicet quod divisio entis in haec decem non sit prima. Si enim prius fiat in ens per se et in ens non per se, et ultra unum membrum subdividatur vel ambo: aut quaelibet divisio erit tantum nominis aequivoci in aequivocata, quod nihil est probare—quia nomina sunt ad placitum; aut aliquo istorum decem erit conceptus communior immediatior enti, et ita ens non immediate dividitur in decem. Exemplum patet: ponendo quod per divisiones multas subordinatas in genere substantiae tandem deveniretur ad decem species specialissimas, illae non primo dividerent substantiam. Secundo, quia omnes illae viae divisivae non probant. Oporteret enim probare quod divisum sic dividitur, et praecise sic, et hoc ad propositum, scilicet quod dividentia constituant generalissima." Scotus, *Quaestiones Super Libros Metaphysicorum Aristotelis*, 5, 6, 464.

37. Scotus, *Quaestiones Super Praedicamenta Aristotelis*, 11, 343–54.

38. Scotus, *Quaestiones Super Libros Metaphysicorum Aristotelis*, p. xxxix, 5, 6, 464n73.

39. Ibid., pp. xxviii–xxix.

of all this is that more information about this point would be desirable.

And so, by the early fourteenth century there have emerged two models, both claiming to adhere to the Aristotelian tradition. One accepts the categories at face value and takes them as signifying various kinds of entities, albeit possessing different "degrees of being." The other accepts the categories as definitive within the conceptual order, as expressing the possible modes of signification, but challenges the connection between that order and what exists *in re*. There are fewer than ten real categories, and some of the *modi significandi* refer to the same real things.

This brings me to the final part of my story, the nominalist approach to the categories, as represented by the two greatest philosophers of the fourteenth century, William of Ockham and John Buridan. Painting with a broad brush, I shall group the two together. What is interesting about their attitude toward the categories is its ambivalence. On the one hand, skepticism about the categories may have originated with Buridan, who says:

And it should be known that Aristotle never posited a reason to show that there were not other predicaments beside these ten. Nor would it be unfitting to posit others, if there were found predicables having other modes of predication, neither reducible to nor contained under these modes according to which these ten predicaments are grasped.[40]

Also, Buridan speaks derisively about the constructors of *sufficientiae*, saying that they "labor in vain."[41] This, then, is the putative source for the view that the categorial distinctions are completely arbitrary, which is found in the Port Royal *Logic* and is subsequently repeated almost verbatim until the present.[42]

But, on the other hand, neither Buridan nor Ockham is really breaking from Aristotle. In fact, the way I read Ockham is that, in the sense

---

40. "Et sciendum est quod numquam Aristoteles posuit rationem ad ostendendum quod non esset alia praedicamenta praeter ista decem. Nec esset inconveniens ponere alia, si invenirentur praedicabilia habentia alios modos praedicandi, non reducibiles nec contentos sub istis modis secundum quos sumuntur haec decem praedicamenta." John Buridan, *Summulae in Praedicamenta,* Artistarium 10:3, ed. E.P. Bos (Nijmegen: Ingenium, 1994), 3, 1, 8.18. Translation mine—with thanks to Kevin Guilfoy.

41. John Buridan, *Quaestiones in Praedicamenta,* ed. Johannes Schneider (Munich: Verlag der Bayerischen Akademie der Wissenschaften, 1983), q. 3, p.19.

42. Antoine Arnauld and Pierre Nicole, *The Art of Thinking*, trans. James Dickoff and Patricia James (Indianapolis: Bobbs-Merrill, 1964), 42–45. See also Immanuel Kant, *Critique of Pure Reason*, 2d ed., trans. Friedrich Max Müller (New York: Macmillan, 1924), 67, B107; Adolf Trendelenburg, *Geschichte der Kategorienlehre* (Berlin: G. Bethge, 1846; reprint, Hildesheim: Georg Olms, 1979), 216–17; and Jerrold J. Katz, *The Philosophy of Language* (New York: Harper and Row, 1966), 224–27.

that someone is said to be more Catholic than the pope, Ockham is trying to be more Aristotelian than the Philosopher himself. In Strawsonian terms, Ockham is a descriptive metaphysician who believes his account to be more accurate descriptively than those of his adversaries. Buridan often takes a similar position, saying, e.g., that the LSP distorts Aristotle's ideas,[43] but he also appears to be more sympathetic to a "conventionalist" view of language and thought.[44]

Both Ockham and Buridan take the categories as belonging to the verbal/conceptual level, as semantical distinctions—classes of terms viewed with regard to their signification. At that level they do not challenge the ten-category system per se[45] and in that sense can be said to be conserving the tradition. Even Buridan, despite his disdain for what he regards as naive approaches, comes down in favor of the standard view:

> So if we should find some common predicables having other modes of predication beside the ten already stated, it seems to me above all that it ought not to be denied that there are more categories. . . . But nevertheless it appears to me certain that even if there were some others, these ten are more manifest and contain under themselves the greater number of predicates.[46]

Nevertheless, for both Ockham and Buridan only two of the categories, substance and quality, signify real things, while the others express ways of thinking about these things.[47] This entails that they question not only the reality of relations[48] but, curiously, also of quantity.[49] They did not, however, regard the categories as an arbitrary conceptual scheme that needed to be discarded. That move was yet to be made. In

---

43. Buridan, *Quaestiones in Praedicamenta*, q. 17, p.129.

44. See Alfonso Maierù, "Significatio et connotatio chez Buridan" in *The Logic of John Buridan*, ed. Jan Pinborg (Copenhagen: Museum Tusculanum, 1976), 101–4.

45. See William of Ockham, *Summa Logicae* I, 41.114–17, in *Opera Philosophica et Theologica*, vol. 1, ed. Philotheus Boehner, Gedeon Gál, and Stephen Brown. (St. Bonaventure: Franciscan Institute, 1974); and Buridan, *Quaestiones in Praedicamenta*, q. 3, pp.14–29.

46. "Unde si aliqua praedicabilia communia inveniamus habentia alios modos praedicandi praeter dictos decem, apparet mihi omnino, quod non esset negandum, quin essent plura praedicamenta. . . . Sed tamen mihi apparet pro certo, quod ista decem, si sint aliqua alia, sunt magis manifesta et continentia sub se maiorem pluralitatem praedicabilium." Buridan, *Quaestiones in Praedicamenta*, q. 3, pp. 19–20. My translation.

47. "The view is that nothing except substances and qualities exists either in act or in potency. Nevertheless, different names signify the same objects in different ways." William of Ockham, *Ockham's Theory of Terms: Part I of the Summa Logica*, trans. Michael J. Loux (Notre Dame: University of Notre Dame Press, 1974), 158. This is Michael Loux's translation of a passage from Ockham, *Summa Logicae* I, 49.154.

48. See, for example, Ockham, *Summa Logicae* I, 49.153–59; Buridan, *Quaestiones in Praedicamenta*, q. 10, pp. 70–74.

49. See, for example, Ockham, *Summa Logicae* I, 44–45, 132–45.

closing, then, I would like to make a few comments about these matters and also dispute the claim that the Aristotelian ten-category scheme is frivolous. First, Marilyn Adams notes that Ockham, having the model of Greek atomism, could have reduced quality to quantity.[50] However, as an Aristotelian descriptivist, Ockham never entertains that possibility, nor would he have opted for an event or process ontology over a thing ontology. For Ockham, the existence of quantity is more problematic than that of quality. His argument is that magnitudes (continuous quantities) and multitudes (discrete quantities) do not exist per se but rather are ways of expressing how substance may be measured. For example, points, lines, and surfaces are not entities but limiting concepts. The point is the limit of the line, the line of the surface, etc.[51] But Ockham and Buridan maintain that qualities are generally separable from the substance and, in the case of the Eucharist, can continue to exist where the substance has been changed.[52]

In order to make the ontological moves these philosophers wish to make, one must have a richer semantical theory than those that prevailed for most of the twentieth century. Thus, in addition to words and things there is posited another order, that of concepts (intentions). But whereas that is often thought of as proliferating entities, here it is for ontological parsimony. Categorial terms are divided into those which are *absolute* and those which are *connotative*.[53] Absolute terms signify what they designate (supposit for). Connotative terms appear to desig-

---

50. Marilyn McCord Adams, *William of Ockham*, 2 vols., Publications in Medieval Studies, Medieval Institute, University of Notre Dame, 26 (Notre Dame: University of Notre Dame Press, 1987), 1:283–84.

51. See also Ernest A. Moody, *The Logic of William of Ockham* (New York: Russell & Russell, 1965), 144–53.

52. See Ockham, *Summa Logicae* I, 55.179–82; see also Lambert M. de Rijk, "On Buridan's View of Accidental Being," in *John Buridan: A Master of Arts*, Artistarium Supplementa 8 (Nijmegen: Ingenium, 1993).

53. Moody gives a good explanation of this: "A connotative term is said to be one which signifies one kind of thing primarily, and a different kind of thing secondarily or obliquely. It stands for one kind of thing by connoting something distinct from it contingently connected with it, or by connoting a determinate part of it as if separated or separable from it. Thus the connotative term 'hot' stands for things in which heat can be present, by connoting the quality heat—but it does not stand for heat, nor can the word 'heat' stand for anything denoted by the term 'hot.' . . . All connotative terms have 'nominal definitions,' one of whose parts does not signify precisely the same things that the word defined is a sign of. It is by this character of the definition, that a connotative term can always be distinguished from an absolute term. Absolute terms have 'real definitions,' whose parts can stand for precisely the individual things for which the term can stand; thus 'man' is defined as 'rational animal,' and it is true to say that every man is an animal, and also that every man is rational. But the term 'father,' which is connotative, has only a nominal definition, one of whose parts cannot stand for that which is denoted by the term itself—for the thing that is said to be a father, is something which has a son or

nate properties, but this is illusory. Since on metaphysical grounds it has been determined that there are no such properties, the terms for quantity, relation, action, passion, etc., designate substances, while expressing various aspects of them. To explain this, let me return to a point raised earlier, concerning the ontological shift from accidents to modes. According to Gyula Klima, the modistic account of the categories came to be adopted by both nominalists and, later, realists because it allowed people to retain the categorial framework without positing all kinds of individual accidents.[54] Klima regards Buridan as the pivotal figure here. For Buridan the questionable categorial terms are not predicated essentially of their individual instances but rather connotatively or *per accidens*. Thus we need not treat these terms as referring to real properties, for what they designate (supposit for) are the substances themselves. What they connote are modes of substance. Although this enables us to retain the doctrine that the categories embody the semantics of ordinary language, one can readily change the semantics to reflect one's conception of reality, and even ultimately eliminate all distinct accidents, as occurs in "modern" philosophers such as Descartes.[55]

Finally, I would question the claim that there is no good reason for positing the ten Aristotelian categories. Actually, at a certain level the distinctions make a lot of sense. In support of that I would like to make two points. First, recent studies in lexical semantics are very Aristotelian.[56] That is, they take substantives, verbals, adjectivals, etc., as fundamental lexical categories, even across languages and language families, which undercuts the Whorfian outlook that influenced philosophers like the recently deceased W. V. Quine.[57]

---

daughter—it is not itself the son or daughter which it is said to have." Moody, *Logic of William of Ockham*, 55–56.

54. Gyula Klima, "Buridan's Logic and the Ontology of Modes," in *Medieval Analyses in Language and Cognition, Acts of the Symposium, "The Copenhagen School of Medieval Philosophy," January 10–13, 1996*, ed. Sten Ebbesen and Russell L. Friedman (Copenhagen: C. A. Reitzels, 1999), 473–95.

55. It should be noted that a modal interpretation of the categories does not entail that they are arbitrary. However, Klima makes the illuminating suggestion that it appears to be a step on the slippery slope. Although the history of it still needs to be unpacked, I think the idea is something like this: if x is a property, it would be per se "extra-mental." If it is a mode, it is primarily conceptual, which raises the further question of whether it corresponds to anything *in re*. As thought developed during the Middle Ages, especially among Augustinians, there was a retreat from Aristotelian naive realism, i.e., the mind becomes more and more constructive, rather than reflective, of reality.

56. See, for example, William Frawley, *Linguistic Semantics* (Hillsdale, N.J.: Lawrence Erlbaum, 1992).

57. Willard V. O. Quine, *Word and Object* (Cambridge: MIT Press, 1960).

Second, Buridan's substantive discussion of the different categories suggests a phrase-structure grammar (*cum* semantics) that is fairly comprehensive,[58] and I suspect that he was not unaware of that fact. I shall conclude with a sketch of that semantically based grammar: sentences are divisible into subjects and predicates. The subject role is played by nouns, which correspond to primary and secondary *substances*. The predicate role (as indicated by the categories) offers several possibilities: (1) "be" + noun (secondary *substance*), (2) "be" + adjective *(quality, quantity)*, (3) "be" + participle *(position, habitus)*, (4) "be" + prepositional phrase *(where, when)*, (5) "be" + adjective + prepositional phrase *(relation)*, (6) verb—active *(action)* or passive *(passion)*. Other grammatical devices include the construction of noun phrases from adjectives and nouns *(quality, quantity)*, adverbials *(where, when)*, and transitive verbs *(relation)*.

Thus the categories can be said to account for the major syntactic/semantic roles in language, and any term that can be taken as categorematic can in some sense be included within them. This of course does not establish their sufficiency, but it does show a *prima facie* plausibility. Although there are other ways to conceive of the world than in terms of things and their properties, a thing-ontology is probably the most common point of view, at least for speakers of Indo-European languages. And within that perspective the theory of the Aristotelian categories is a most valuable treatment of the semantics of ordinary language.

58. Buridan, *Summulae in Praedicamenta*, treatise 3, ch. 2–7, pp. 20–93.

5 Categories and Commensurability in Confucius and Aristotle: A Response to MacIntyre

MAY SIM

Alasdair MacIntyre argues, in "Incommensurability, Truth, and the Conversation between Confucians and Aristotelians about the Virtues," that despite certain agreements about the virtues, Confucian and Aristotelian traditions are ultimately incommensurable.[1] By this MacIntyre means that each of these systems "has its own standard and measures of interpretation, explanation, and justification internal to itself," so that when dealing with rival claims there are "no shared standards and measures, external to both systems and neutral between them, to which appeal might be made to adjudicate between" them.[2] For instance, a Confucian may notice that an act of giving fails to conform to *li* (ritual propriety) (for example, one might have neglected to use both hands and bow in the act), which lack prevents the act from being truly generous and the agent from being *ren* (the highest Confucian virtue—sometimes translated as benevolence, or humaneness, or authoritative conduct).[3] Such an omission, according to MacIntyre, is necessarily "invisible to the Aristotelian." The Aristotelian, who lacks even the words

---

1. Alasdair MacIntyre, "Incommensurability, Truth, and the Conversation between Confucians and Aristotelians about the Virtues," in *Culture and Modernity: East-West Philosophic Perspectives*, ed. Eliot Deutsch (Honolulu: University of Hawaii Press, 1991), 104–22. The literature against this particular view by MacIntyre is quite substantial. For instance, see David L. Hall and Roger T. Ames, prologue to *Thinking from the Han: Self, Truth and Transcendence in Chinese and Western Culture* (Albany: State University of New York Press, 1998), xiff.; James T. Brestzke, S.J., "The *Tao* of Confucian Virtue Ethics," *International Philosophical Quarterly* 35 (1995): 25–41; and Peter J. Mehl, "In the Twilight of Modernity: MacIntyre and Mitchell on Moral Traditions and Their Assessment," *Journal of Religious Ethics* 19 (1991): 21–54, to name just a few.

2. MacIntyre, "Incommensurability," 109, see also 110.

3. Aristotle may not understand the necessity of the Confucian standard of *li* (such as using both hands and bowing) in the act of giving. Nevertheless, even Aristotle would recognize that one who throws money at the beneficiary, instead of handing him the money,

to translate *li*, therefore would fail to see the moral shortcoming. By the same token, an Aristotelian may notice that an act fails to conform to the order of the ψυχή (soul) for a citizen of a πόλις (state), where both ψυχή and πόλις are understood in very specific teleological ways. The shortcoming is "invisible" to the Confucian because the standard is lacking—the Confucian lacks even the words for ψυχή or πόλις.

Aristotle's ten categories are of undeniable significance in all of his works. Confucius has no explicit list of categories.[4] But I shall argue that these categories—or ones sufficiently similar—are employed and play significant roles in Confucian thought. To show how these thinkers share a fundamental set of categories is also to show that there are grounds for a kind of commensurability and hence for the possibility of dialogue. Their actual, specific standards surely differ in important ways. But if the categories employed in their ethical thought are sufficiently similar (implicitly or explicitly), then it is possible for them to communicate their differences, and perhaps try to persuade each other on the specific points of contention. Lacking these more generic categorial grounds, such dialogue—even about disagreements—would be impossible.

Aristotle's ten categories consist of substance (οὐσίαν), quantity (ποσὸν), quality (ποιὸν), relation (πρός τι), place (ποῦ—literally "the where"), time (ποτέ—literally "the when"),[5] position (κεῖσθαι), state or condition (ἔχειν—literally "to have"), action (ποιεῖν), and affection (πάσχειν).[6] I will take each of these categories in turn and show how they are already employed in Confucius's ethics. Substance (οὐσία) will be discussed last because the greatest discrepancy between Aristotle and Confucius is found in this category. My claim is that Confucius uses these categories even when he does not mention them.[7] I focus in this short essay on showing how each of these ten categories is used in Con-

---

is not acting generously. Thus, even if *li* is not an explicit element in Aristotle's ethics, it does not follow that he cannot be made to understand that the manner in which an act is carried out has moral significance for Confucius. Nor does it follow that he would necessarily disagree with a lesser degree of such a standard.

4. A. C. Graham has examined in great detail how Aristotle's use of the ten categories in his inquiry is similar to what has been done in classical Chinese. Graham follows Benveniste's lead in focusing on the use of interrogatives in his investigation. Whether this is a productive way of examining Aristotle's categories is neither relevant to nor within the scope of this essay. A. C. Graham, "Relating Categories to Question Forms in Pre-Han Chinese Thought," in *Studies in Chinese Philosophy and Philosophical Literature,* ed. A. C. Graham (Albany: State University of New York Press, 1986), 360–411.

5. See Lang's essay on the categories "when" and "where" in Chapter 2 of this volume.

6. Aristotle, *Categories* 4, 1b25–26, hereafter cited parenthetically in the text.

7. One may object that I am merely imposing Aristotle's categories on Confucius. Such a criticism is especially likely to come from commentators like Chad Hansen, David Hall, and Roger Ames, who maintain that Confucius is not concerned with objectivity or

fucius's *Analects;* that they are used in Aristotle's thinking is a presupposition few if any Aristotelians dispute. A more elaborate comparison between these two philosophers' ethical employment of the categories must be undertaken elsewhere.

Quantities (ποσοί), with Aristotle, are discrete or continuous. Numbers like three and five are examples of discrete quantities, while lines and solids, places and times, are examples of continuous quantities (*Categories* 6, 4b20–5a13). The former are discrete because they do not have any common boundary (for example, three is not joined to five), while the latter do share common boundaries (for example, the past is joined to the present). Aristotle also maintains that the most unique feature of quantity is that equality (ἴσον) and inequality (ἄνισον) are predicated of it (*Categories* 6, 6a26). In its ethical contexts, quantity is a critical category—critical both because without it moral reason is too fluid, but also because an over-reliance on quantities leads to theoretical and practical troubles. Confucius invokes this category. He says that what worries the ruler of a state or the head of a household is not the people's poverty absolutely considered but "that wealth is inequitably distributed."[8] He goes on to recommend equitable distribution. Confucius speaks of quantity, that is, the amount, of wealth, which can be either equitably or inequitably distributed. Depending on its distribution, one either creates poverty or eliminates it, and thus is acting either correctly or not. Equity in the distribution of wealth is not merely arithmetical equality. It calls for Aristotle's notion of particular justice. Likewise, Confucius's view of the appropriate quantity is bound up with the circumstances and parties involved. For example, Ranyou supplies Zihua's mother with ten measures of grain; Confucius suggests two measures instead, because he can tell from Zihua's horses and fine furs that he is a rich man. Confucius says, "Exemplary persons help out the needy; they do not make the rich richer" (6.4). Hence equity in distributing wealth, for Confucius, is not simply a matter of giving everyone equal amounts of wealth. Rather, quantitative consideration is bound up with the relative wealth or poverty of the people involved and other situational factors. Nevertheless, Confucius uses the category

---

truth in his use of language but rather with conventional political or aesthetic phenomena. I argue against these commentators by showing that Confucius's use of language is intertwined with an objective nature and with heaven's mandate about the right *dao* of living. See May Sim, "Ritual and Realism in Early Chinese Science," *Journal of Chinese Philosophy*, 29 (Dec. 2002): 495–517.

8. Confucius, *The Analects of Confucius*, trans. R. Ames and H. Rosemont Jr. (New York: Ballantine Books, 1998), 16.1. Unless otherwise stated, all references to Confucius are to his *Analects*, hereafter cited in the text.

of quantity—and necessarily so—even if he does not dislodge it and hold it up for theoretical examination.

Relative things are for Aristotle explained by reference to something else (πρὸς ἕτερον) (*Categories* 7, 6a36–37). For example, both habit (ἕξις) and knowledge (ἐπιστήμη) are of something and hence are explained by reference to something else. Some relatives can have contraries. As Aristotle puts it, "for example, virtue [ἀρετὴ] is the contrary to vice [κακία] and knowledge [ἐπιστήμη] is the contrary to ignorance [ἀγνοία]" (*Categories* 7, 6b15–17, my translation). Some relatives can also admit of degree. For example, things can be more or less relative to each other. Finally, if properly defined, all relatives have correlatives; for example, master and slave, greater and less are correlatives. Confucius employs the category of relatives extensively. It is also important to note that the features of relatives described by Aristotle are also present in Confucius. For instance, Confucius talks about various virtues such as *ren* (17.6), courage (2.24, 9.92), acting appropriately (*yi*, 4.16, 17.23), living up to one's words, (*xin*, 1.6, 2.22) acting with loyalty and in accordance with the golden rule or reciprocity (*shu*, 4.15), to name just a few. So when one is said to have a virtue, he is said to have the virtue of courage or *ren* and so forth, and thus his virtue is defined with reference to the specific virtue he has. Such relatives as virtue and goodness vary in degree. For instance, he speaks of not befriending one who isn't as good as oneself (1.8). His constant contrasts between the *junzi* (exemplary individual) and *xiaoren* (petty or small person) (4.11, 15.21, 6.13, 4.25) also show that virtues and vices are contraries. Such relatives play a significant role in Confucius's ethics, for they allow him to identify the virtues and vices and note the variation of degrees in each virtue so that one could get clear about what to pursue and what to avoid and get clear about the degree of one's progress. Another highly significant Confucian use of this category lies in human relationships such as father and son, minister and sovereign, husband and wife. These are co-defining and correlative so that each has a well-defined role to play (1.4–1.7, 1.9, 2.5, 2.20–2.21, 3.19). Playing one's roles well, especially those beginning in the home, such as fulfilling one's filial and fraternal responsibilities, is the root of *ren* (1.2, 2.2). The category of relation cuts all the way down in Confucius. Aristotle makes quite a lot of human relations and the relativities of virtue,[9] but these are terminated in substances. Substance, the primary category for Aristotle, is not relative and hence is not defined by reference to something outside itself (*Categories* 7, 8a15ff.). I shall say

---

9. See Aristotle, *Nicomachean Ethics* VIII–IX, III, IV, and VII.

more about substance and relation with Aristotle and Confucius below.

Aristotle defines quality (ποιὸν) as that "in virtue of which people are said to be such and such" (*Categories* 8, 8b25). Habits (ἕξεις) such as knowledge and virtue are examples of quality, for it is in virtue of these that people are said to be knowledgeable and virtuous, respectively. Quality is also the category employed whenever Confucius marks out the abiding habits that qualify one as a person possessing a certain virtue. A condition for filial piety is: "A person who for three years refrains from reforming the ways of his late father can be called a filial son [*xiao*]" (1.11). Similarly, Confucius distinguishes bravery from *ren* by saying, "The one with *ren* is bound to have courage, but the courageous is not bound to have *ren*" (14.4, my translation). He also distinguishes loyal actions *(zhong)* from *ren* actions (5.19). Qualities like relations have contraries. For example, knowledge has as its contrary ignorance. Qualities also vary in degree; for example, some people are more or less virtuous than others. But most importantly for Aristotle, quality is the only category of which "like" (ὅμοια) and "unlike" (ἀνόμοια) can be predicated (*Categories* 8, 11a16–17). Confucius observes this characteristic in his use of quality. For example, he teaches that one should want to be like someone who is of "exceptional character" and not want to be like one who is the opposite, when he says, "When you meet persons of exceptional character think to stand shoulder to shoulder with them; meeting persons of little character, look inward and examine yourself" (4.17; see also 1.8). Quality is then a category that is significant to Confucius's ethical thinking, for implicitly he is constantly delineating the qualities of a certain virtue from those of another, and urging people to become like the exemplary character rather than the petty person. Quality, plainly, is important to Confucius both in reference to the variable qualities of habits and acts and the excellence of one's character. But more than this, Confucian thinking observes just those features of qualities that Aristotle highlights—their similarities and dissimilarities, variability and contrariety.

Both categories of action, (ποιεῖν) and affection (πάσχειν), also play prominent roles in Confucius's thinking. Consider his five attitudes needed to become *ren:* deference, tolerance, making good on one's word, diligence, and generosity (17.6). His insistence on *yi* (appropriate) acts (2.24, 7.16, 17.23), as well as *shu* (reciprocated/golden rule) acts (12.2, 15.24) also supports the prominence of action in his ethics. In conformity with Aristotle's discussion, we find that actions for Confucius admit of contraries (for example, inappropriate acts, *buyi*) and variation of degree (4.7). Again, that action is susceptible to both contraries, and variation of degree allows Confucius to encourage the virtuous act instead of its contrary, and the act with the greater degree of virtue instead of the lesser. Hence the usefulness and significance of this category in his ethics.

Confucius believes that an exemplary person should have certain affections and not others—should be vexed or glad in the *yi* situations. Affection therefore is also a commonly employed category in Confucius's work. He says, "The *ren* are not anxious; the wise are not in a quandary; the courageous are not timid" (14.28). Also, "Do not worry over not having an official position; worry about what it takes to have one. Do not worry that no one acknowledges you; seek to do what will earn you acknowledgment" (4.14). Affections and actions, then, are central to Confucius's ethics because certain affections, which accompany certain virtues, are to be cultivated, and others, which accompany vices, are to be avoided. If this point of comparison seems too obvious, remember that there are modes of ethical thought that do not make action and affection morally central. Think of Stoicism or (in at least one interpretation) Kantianism. To the extent that they use the category and use it similarly, Confucius's and Aristotle's ethics are to just that extent commensurable.[10]

That place (ποῦ—literally "the where") and time (ποτέ—literally "the when") are ethically relevant categories in Confucius's thinking is evident in that he distinguishes between places such as the home, the village, the court, the temple, and funeral sites, and discourses about the rituals proper to each of these places (1.6, 1.9, 3.6, 3.15, 9.16, 10.1). Likewise, time is essential to his ethics; Confucius insists that a three-year mourning period is necessary for one to be considered filial, for this somehow reciprocates the number of years that parents care for children (1.11, 17.21). He emphasizes both place and time when he insists on kowtowing immediately upon entering the hall (9.3). So place and time are relevant categories in Confucius's ethics.

That position (κεῖσθαι) and state or condition (ἔχειν—literally "to have") are also very visible in Confucius's highly ritualized system of ethics may be seen in his assertion that a silk rather than a hemp cap should be worn in observance of *li*. Similarly, the importance of position and state are emphasized in his instruction to stand up and walk quickly in the presence of those in mourning clothes (9.10). Such concerns might seem superficial to most twentieth-century observers, but for Aristotle, and even more for Confucius, they show two things. First,

---

10. It is not necessary for me to take sides on the issue of whether commensurability is necessarily determinate or indeterminate. Rather, whether two modes of thought are commensurable or not, and to what degree they are commensurable, is to be determined on a case-by-case basis.

they show that character is so pervasive that it is visible even in one's attire and position (which at least potentially exert an influence on others even prior to actions). Second, they show that matters of manners are ethical issues for both Aristotle[11] and Confucius. Manners and ceremony are on a continuum with other matters of ethical concern. Moral systems that recognize this, by according categories of *situs* (κεῖσθαι) and *habitus* (ἔχειν) moral pertinence, are again to that extent comparable.

Finally, substance (οὐσία) is the most important of all ten categories to Aristotle,[12] while Confucius gives priority to relations. But if we can identify something in Confucius that satisfies the criteria of substance, then dialogue between the two regarding their strongest difference will be all the more feasible. Aristotle defines primary substances as those which "underlie [ὑποκεῖσθαι] all other things and all other things will be either predicated of [κατηγορεῖσθαι] or present in [ἐν] them" (*Categories* 5, 2b15–18, my translation). The individual man and individual horse are examples (*Categories* 5, 2a13). But the most distinctive mark (ἴδιον) of substance is that it can change (μεταβολήν) to admit contrary qualities (e.g., virtue or vice) "while remaining one in number [ἓν ἀριθμῷ] and the same [ταὐτόν]" (*Categories* 5, 4b16–18, my translation).

Confucian commentators have often denied that there is any sense of a substantial self in Confucius.[13] Instead of focusing on the self that

11. Aristotle, *Nicomachean Ethics;* John Buridan, *Quaestiones in Praedicamenta*, ed. Johannes Schneider (Munich: Verlag der Bayerischen Akademie der Wissenschaften, 1983), 3, 1125a13–15.

12. In holding substance to be the most important of all ten categories, I agree with the traditional commentary on Aristotle's *Categories* and differ from Michael Frede's view that substance is not Aristotle's focus in the *Categories*. While Frede relies on the *Topics* to make his case, I disagree with his reading of the *Topics* on this issue. See May Sim, "Dialectical Communities: From the One to the Many and Back," in *From Puzzles to Principles?: Essays on Aristotle's Dialectic*, ed. May Sim (Lanham, Md.: Lexington Books, 1999), 183–214, for my position on the centrality of definition and hence the talk of substance in the *Topics;* and, subsequently, for the centrality of substance in Aristotle's *Categories*. See Michael Frede, "Categories in Aristotle," reprinted in Frede, *Essays in Ancient Philosophy* (Minneapolis: University of Minnesota Press, 1987), chap. 3. Cf. Jonathan Sanford's comments on substance in Chapter 1 of this volume.

13. Fingarette asserts that "Confucius teaches, as central to his way, that we must have no self and not impose our personal will." Herbert Fingarette, "The Problem of Self in the *Analects*," *Philosophy East & West* 29 (1979): 134. Fingarette's interpretation of the Confucian individual is that he is just a vehicle for realizing the *dao* (the way). The *dao* for Fingarette is like a concept in that it is totally independent of any particular individual (even though its realization depends on an individual). Ibid., 136. For Fingarette, the individual simply wills the *dao*. But the reason why or the end toward which the will is exercised is not determined by the individual. He says, "But the more deeply one explores the *junzi's* will, the more the personal dimensions are revealed as purely formal—the individual is the unique space-time bodily locus of that will; it is that which controls but it is nonsignificant regarding why, specifically, or in what specific direction, the control shall be

performs appropriate actions (for example, acting with *shu* or *zhong* in various circumstances), these Confucian commentators focus on the roles that dictate the *li* that is appropriate. These are really distinct issues. For even if one's roles do dictate how to act (with *shu* or *zhong* or *yi*) in various situations, an account of that which is capable of performing such actions is still needed. Confucius, without theorizing about it, does invoke a stronger sense of a self than commentators allow. Thus the Confucian self is minimally "substantial"; it persists through various changes, is the source of agency and can adopt various roles and perform them more or less well.[14]

Confucius's focus is sometimes the individual agent's personal commitment to an action. This requires an even stronger sense of self, since it involves an agent's care for her agency, a character's concern for her character. He stresses this personal investment in the performance of actions and quality of character—and he puts down the blind following of *li* when he says:

In referring time and again to observing ritual propriety [*li*], how could I just be talking about gifts of jade and silk? And in referring time and again to making music [*yue*], how could I just be talking about bells and drums? (17.11)

Confucius means by this that ritual ceremonies do not merely refer to the motions and materials. Contrariwise, appropriateness means that

---

exercised." Fingarette's *junzi* is so united with the *dao* that she will always will what *li* dictates for her role. Ibid., 135. One doesn't need a self, in Fingarette's view, because his role always tells him what is appropriate and this is all he needs to do. The "self" issue is so qualification-starved because, for many, "a space time bodily locus" and the "that which controls" is a "self."

Xinzhong Yao is another who denies a metaphysical self in Confucius, reasoning that a metaphysical self necessitates a substance that is fixed and unchangeable. Yao and other interpreters fail to recognize that Aristotle's substance is precisely that which changes (and becomes). Oddly, Yao also thinks that a substance is incapable of engaging in social relations or cultivating *ren* or sagehood. He says: "[T]he Confucian concept of the self is not a metaphysical nor an epistemological nor a psychological concept . . . it is an ethical concept and its significance for Confucian doctrine lies in a process of cultivating one's moral character that can be completed only in one's engagement in social and righteous causes." Xinzhong Yao, "Self Construction and Identity: The Confucian Self in Relation to Some Western Perceptions," *Asian Philosophy* 6 (1996): 186.

Roger Ames rejects Aristotle's view because of its teleology. He sees the movement from potentiality to actuality as a model with a fixed goal. Such a model is to be avoided, for it necessarily limits the flexibility and creativity in one's self-cultivation. Roger T. Ames, "The Focus Field Self," in *Self as Person in Asian Theory and Practice*, ed. Roger T. Ames, Wimal Dissanayake, and Thomas P. Kasulis (Albany: State University of New York Press, 1994), 201.

14. For a detailed discussion of such a minimal substantial self in Confucius, see May Sim, "The Moral Self in Confucius and Aristotle," *International Philosophical Quarterly* 43 (Dec. 2003): 439–62.

one must tune one's attitude to fit the situation (17.6). This means that one should participate in these rituals with one's entire being. As Confucius puts it, "The expression 'sacrifice as though present' is taken to mean 'sacrifice to the spirits as though the spirits are present' but 'If *I* myself do not participate in the sacrifice, it is as though *I* have not sacrificed at all'" (3.12, emphasis added). This *I* signifies the source of agency that persists through changes (and so is responsible) and is capable of filling roles. Similarly, Confucius condemns the "village worthy" as the thief of virtue, because even though he abides by the conventional standard of morality, his acts are motions that accord with his role without personal commitment (17.13). Mere role-playing, then, is not sufficient for Confucius. The distinction between one who fills her roles well and one who does not rests in an investment of the person. A substantial enough self must be presupposed for such an investment. Without such a minimal self, we can have neither personal investment nor ownership of the action, let alone a creative addition to the tradition.[15]

A role tells one what a father does, but a role cannot act. A role needs a bearer who can take responsibility for his acts. Commentators who propose a selfless view or a self-as-social-roles view frequently deny the notion of personal responsibility.[16] To support the stronger sense of self in Confucius, a self that is an agent or a source of choice and responsibility is required.[17] Similarly, while he focuses on relations, Confucius does not at all deny that relations need something to relate to—

---

15. This emphasis on a self that is sincere and true to himself is the ultimate virtue in *The Doctrine of the Mean*. See Confucius, *Confucian Analects, the Great Learning and the Doctrine of the Mean*, trans. J. Legge (Oxford: Clarendon Press, 1893; reprint, New York: Dover Publications, 1971). As he puts it, "It is only he who is possessed of the most complete sincerity that can exist under heaven, who can give its full development in his nature. Able to give its full development to his own nature, he can do the same for the nature of other men. Able to give its full development to the nature of other men, he can give their full development to the nature of animals and things" (22; cf. 25.2). For a detailed comparison between Confucius and Aristotle on the mean, see May Sim, "Harmony and the Mean in the *Nicomachean Ethics* and the *Zhongyong*," *Dao: A Journal of Comparative Philosophy* (Summer 2004): 253–80.

16. This is clear when Fingarette points out the incompatibility of such views and personal responsibility. He says: "[T]he Confucian viewpoint, seeing 'person' as a complex abstraction from the concrete social nexus, does not require or even permit use of our concept of personal responsibility for an act or consequence thereof." Herbert Fingarette, "Comment and Response," in *Rules, Rituals, and Responsibility: Essays Dedicated to H. Fingarette*, ed. Mary I. Bockover (La Salle, Ill.: Open Court, 1991), 200.

17. That a more substantial self is already there in Confucian literature is apparent in Confucius's statement that filial piety consists in refraining from reforming a father's way for three years after a father's death (1.11). Such talk of refrain or restraint presupposes that there is some figment of a self that is to be restrained beyond that of a son whose role is to adhere to the father's wishes—for what of the years following the mourning?

such as particular mothers and children. The same is true for the other non-substance categories. My argument is that Confucian texts point to a minimally substantial self—a self that persists through change, terminates relations, bears roles, initiates acts, suffers, and owns qualities—a "minimal" sense of substance. A substance in the minimal sense is an article that terminates recognized accidents—for instance, whatever else it is, it is that which bears qualities, acts and receives action, stands in relations, occupies positions, fills out roles, spaces, and times, and so on. A more maximal sense of substance is a further theory of what this is: for instance, a hylomorphic theory, an account of teleology, and so on. The texts of Confucius provide ample evidence for not only the nine accidental categories but also for the substance category—but only in a minimal sense (because of his heavy emphasis on the categories of relation and quality). Aristotle not only proffers a maximal sense of substance, he leans on features of this theory of substance in his ethics. That is a prime source of the differences between Aristotle and Confucius.

I began this essay with MacIntyre's view that Aristotle lacks the words to translate *li* and hence would fail to see any shortcoming from violating the *li* in action. Similarly, MacIntyre holds that Confucius lacks the words for ψυχή and πόλις, so that he would fail to see the moral shortcoming of actions that violate the order of the ψυχή and πόλις. Having shown that Confucius has an implicit understanding of Aristotle's ten categories, which means that therefore Confucius and Aristotle can communicate with each other, let me illustrate how Aristotle would be able to explain the concepts of ψυχή and πόλις to Confucius, and how Confucius in turn would be able to explain the concept of *li* to Aristotle.

Even though no single term in Confucius's vocabulary translates πόλις, Confucius could understand Aristotle's concept of πόλις because he could grasp that human beings come together to form associations to secure their survival and pursue other goods. He also understands that such human associations necessarily occupy certain places, last for a certain period of time, and vary in character and style depending on how people are related. Hence, even if they were to disagree about which kind of human association is best, Confucius and Aristotle could understand each other in the main.

Starting from his own discourses about rulers relating effectively to their subjects, we can explain to Confucius that the πόλις consists of relations between rulers and ruled. Given his own convictions about how rulers and ministers should conduct themselves, Confucius could understand Aristotle's further claim that good rulers need certain qualities. Confucius wrote that "Rulers should employ their ministers by observing ritual propriety, and ministers should serve their lord by doing their utmost [*zhong*]" (3.19), and "The ruler must rule, the minister minister" (12.11; see also 12.14) can be used to show that the citizens of the πόλις are the ones who undertake the ruling for Aristotle.[18] Furthermore, given that Confucius also prescribes a hierarchy between the rulers and the ministers, where the ministers are the same in rank, one could also explain to him how Aristotle's ideal πόλις is made up of many rulers who are the same in rank. He need not agree that it is good that the rulers should be the same in rank to be able to understand that it is a possible mode of government. On the other hand, that the ruled are to be governed (*Politics* VII, 8–9) can be communicated to Confucius by pointing to his own claims that "common people do not debate affairs of the state" (16.2) and how they are to be ordered (2.3, 2.19).

More importantly, according to Aristotle the purpose of the πόλις is to satisfy the needs of the ruler and ruled so that all citizens can pursue the good life (that is, the life of virtue) (*Politics* I, 1–2). This may be explained to Confucius by showing that he too believes that the ruler's job is to be concerned with having enough food for the people: one of Confucius's proposals for effective government is to "[m]ake sure there is sufficient food to eat" (12.7; cf. 12.9). Aristotle's claim, obscure or scandalous to the modern West, that beyond necessity the point of the πόλις—its final cause—is moral education, would be perfectly intelligible to Confucius. For he maintains that once the necessities are met, the next order of business is to "teach them" (13.9). The ultimate goal of ruling is to make the people virtuous—this is evident in Confucius's constant interest in the effects that exemplary rulers can have on the people:

> The excellence [*de*] of the exemplary person [*junzi*] is the wind, while that of the petty person is the grass. As the wind blows, the grass is sure to bend. (12.19)

> Lead them with excellence [*de*] and keep them orderly through observing ritual propriety [*li*] and they will develop a sense of shame, and moreover, will order themselves. (2.3; cf. 2.1)

Given his interest in developing the virtues of the people, Confucius would also understand how there should be a certain quantity of people in the πόλις—not so few that it cannot be self-sufficient, and not so

---

18. Aristotle, *Politics*, 1275a22–23, hereafter cited parenthetically in the text.

many that it cannot be governed properly (*Politics* VII, 4; see also *Analects*, 13.9). The size of the territory is also a quantitative consideration relevant to the well-being of the πόλις (*Politics* VII, 4–5). Confucius asks, "How can one speak of a territory of sixty or seventy—or even fifty or sixty—*li* square, and not be referring to a state?" (11.26). Aristotle and Confucius would be mutually intelligible on such quantitative considerations of place. Finally, Confucius could also understand why Aristotle would also make recommendations for the best kind of place for his ideal πόλις (*Politics* VII, 11), if he considers his own view that states are related to each other, which relations are affected by one's location (13.3, 9.14, 3.5, 1.10).

MacIntyre would assert that this does not yet show that Confucius would understand Aristotle's concept of the πόλις.[19] The reason is that MacIntyre has a very different conception of the preconditions for understanding and explaining a concept. He believes that his strict contextualist conception of concept is "stronger" than my more Aristotelian category- and topic-based conception.[20] Since Confucius lacks experience with the precise forms of social life that are the matrix for the concept of πόλις, MacIntyre maintains that Confucius will altogether lack the ability to grasp the concept.

I don't deny that one's understanding and use of concepts are bound up with the context within which they have application and are understood. But I want to argue that it is sometimes possible to communicate enough about a context to make an alien term intelligible. The precondition is that there be enough affinity between the two traditions. My argument is that Confucius's narrower understanding of political government can be expanded to accommodate Aristotle's concept of πόλις because of the proximity of their views about the good of practical life and how political and social institutions are to serve this good. Moreover, Confucius's implicit use of categories sufficiently similar to Aristotle's categories also paves the way for an explanation of Aristotle's concepts. I do not believe that all thinkers or all traditions share categories, but when they do—even when the categories are used but not mentioned—it is an important bridge to mutual understanding.

Plainly Confucius cannot understand an alien political system by simply being given its name. For instance, to say that a particular society has an "aristocratic" or "timocratic" or "oligarchic" form of govern-

---

19. And he asserted this in a letter dated February 4, 2002.
20. For details of my Aristotelian, topic-based conception of concepts, see Sim, "Dialectical Communities."

ment would make no sense to Confucius. MacIntyre rightly points out that Confucius wasn't exposed to the practices and contexts within which these concepts developed, and therefore that they could not mean to him what they do to others who have had such an exposure—if they mean anything to him at all. MacIntyre believes that concepts develop in a history to which they remain internal; if people do not share a history, they cannot share concepts. I believe that concepts develop in contexts but (once developed) need not remain internal. Some concepts are more strongly "contextual" or "internal" than others. Concepts with objective content are not so internal. My argument is that Confucius and Aristotle happen to share some concepts with objective content. Since these aren't strongly internal to a history, shared understanding does not require shared history. In these cases, since the pertinent categories are already implied by Confucius's own discourse, explanations that are couched in them may also make sense to him. So, while I agree with MacIntyre that a concept like πόλις can't be understood without a sense of its context and associated practices, I disagree that it must therefore remain inaccessible to Confucius. Confucius already understands such a form of political government as monarchy. Such a context, though seemingly narrow when compared to Aristotle's grasp of a variety of constitutions, can, *by using the relevant categories*, be expanded to enable him to grasp Aristotle's concept of πόλις. Such an expansion of Confucius's context is even more likely in light of how both share so many views regarding the family and the significance of the state for the well-being of the people. In fact, I think that a Confucian could more readily understand Aristotle's concept—and may be better equipped to evaluate it—than a modern Western contractarian individualist. That is true despite the lack of a shared history in the Confucian case.

To say that Confucius can understand Aristotle's πόλις is not to say that he needs to agree with Aristotle's specific recommendations about it, or with Aristotle's analyses of what features might affect it. My thesis is that the basic dimensions of intelligibility are the pertinent categories: place and time, quantity and quality, and so on. Once mutual understanding is achieved on the basis of such categories, disagreement will be rife. For instance, for Confucius, neither the size of the territory nor the number of people nor its location could affect the well-being of the inhabitants of the state. Confucius makes this clear in his emphasis on the significance of the rulers' virtues in affecting the people (13.4, 13.11, 13.13, 12.17), so that ultimately it is not such things as wealth or location or population size that affect a state's well-being but the quality of the rulers and how they handle these factors.

Confucius's ideal ruler "does not worry that his people are poor, but that wealth is inequitably distributed; [d]oes not worry that his people are too few in number, but that they are disharmonious" (16.1). Consequently, one could imagine Confucius's de-emphasizing those same factors that Aristotle recommends for his ideal πόλις, and his replacing these considerations with the importance of having exemplary rulers. Again, the fact that Confucius could disagree with Aristotle about whether and to what extent features such as number of people, place, and prosperity are relevant to the people's well-being is a sign that he could understand Aristotle's position on these features (explicable through the categories of quantity, place and quality, etc.). It is because Confucius also employs these same categories—even if he neither mentions nor reflects philosophically upon them—that he could understand Aristotle's claims about the πόλις.

The category of substance is supposed to be the greatest stumbling block to mutual understanding between these two traditions. But what does substantiality amount to in Aristotle's discussion of the πόλις? The substantiality of the πόλις is by no means beyond Confucius's comprehension: it is the independence and self-sufficiency, the wholeness and unity, the endurance and stability of the organized political body. Using the minimal sense of substance implicit in his thinking, Confucius could see that Aristotle's ideal πόλις has a high degree of self-sufficiency, independence, and wholeness, and that it remains one and the same πόλις through various changes. It consists of parts (people) who cannot satisfy their needs or develop their virtues without belonging to this whole. These parts/people are related to each other, act and are acted upon, make up a certain number (quantity), are located in a certain place of a certain size, and pursue certain actions in order to reach their goal. Consequently, even though Confucius lacks the words to translate Aristotle's πόλις, he could still understand what it is by using the relevant categories, most of which are already employed in his own claims about the state and government, even if they go unremarked.

Aristotle's concept of ψυχή (soul) could be explained to Confucius in much the same way, insofar as Confucius has experience of individual persons, how they live, die, eat, grow, think, act, are virtuous or vicious, become better or worse, possess knowledge or not, and are identifiable as the same persons over time. Aristotle could explain that the ψυχή is the single source of the several functions and the cause of the several capacities. Confucius recognizes the difference between a living body and a dead body. Aristotle would say that the difference between the living and dead body is the presence of a ψυχή in the former. The ψυχή is an internal source of life and motion, without which a body cannot carry out its functions like eating, perceiving, thinking, and acting. I not only suggest that Confucius could make sense of this claim; I would wager that he would find Aristotle's claim of a single internal source of life and thought *more* intelligible than would post-Cartesian dualists in the West. Aristotle's soul is closer to Confucius's heart-and-mind *(xin)* than it is to modern ideas of consciousness or the cognitive mind. In addition to being one, the ψυχή remains one through various changes. Confucius's description of his own evolution expresses his understanding that one can change over time and yet remain essentially the same:

From fifteen, my heart-and-mind was set upon learning; from thirty I took my stance; from forty I was no longer doubtful; from fifty I realized the propensities of *tian* [*tianming*]; from sixty my ear was attuned; from seventy I could give my heart-and-mind free rein without overstepping the boundaries. (2.4; cf. 1.11, 19.5)

Were Confucius inclined to metaphysical speculation, he might argue with Aristotle over such questions as whether the form that accounts for the individual's unity is identical with the species-form. But again, such disagreements presume sufficient common ground for argument, and the categories provide this ground.

Confucius could understand Aristotle's πόλις and ψυχή because of his implicit use of the categories through which these concepts may be explained. Aristotle, likewise, can understand Confucius's *li* even though he lacks the words to translate this term.

Confucian *li* prescribes the appropriate actions and manners for one in various roles. One could explain *li* to Aristotle by invoking the categories of relation, action, quantity, quality, place, time, position, suffering, *habitus*, and substance. One could say that in relation to his father, a son's obedience is necessary to his moral training. Since Aristotle already believes that the moral virtues are attained by repeating the same appropriate actions in the situations that call for them, he would be able to understand why a prescribed set of actions between, say, father and son will help in cultivating the son and in letting the father exercise his role of nurturing, educating, and ruling over his son.[21] Apart from obedience, deference and respect are also appropriate ways of comporting oneself toward one's parents for Confucius. So acts that show honor toward parents, such as children's "contributing their energies when there is work to be done, and deferring to their elders when

---

21. Aristotle, *Nicomachean Ethics*, 1161a16–18, hereafter cited parenthetically in the text.

there is wine and food to be had" (2.8) can again be explained to Aristotle as the appropriate acts children should accord their parents, and hence are acts that are to be repeatedly performed in such relations to cultivate the proper way of honoring parents. One could explain, using Aristotelian categories, that *li* is a set of normative actions—patterns, habits of social history, something like ethics writ large. Aristotle could understand Confucius's *li* because he already shares with Confucius the understanding that the quality of honor is to be accorded one's superior and already agrees that habituation is key. All Aristotle lacks is a concept for the large-scale cultural pattern. This concept, though lacking, can be encroached along the lines laid down by the pertinent categories. Aristotle would have little trouble understanding the intertwining in *li* of the deepest moral matters with details of manners, dress, posture, and so on—far less trouble, it seems to me, than most ethicists in the modern West. Aristotle, after all, describes the parent-child relation as a friendship of superiority and says, "that is why parents are also honored" (*Nicomachean Ethics* VIII, 11, 1161a20–21). But it is also crucial that this honor be manifested by "standing up, [and] giving up seats and so on" (*Nicomachean Ethics* IX, 2, 1165a28). He would then understand Confucius's *li* as the social pattern of habits and acts that exemplify the universal virtue of honor.

Li, for Confucius, is not just a set of motions one performs in various situations. He says:

Those today who are filial are considered so because they are able to provide for their parents. But even dogs and horses are given that much care. If you do not respect your parents, what is the difference? (2.7)

And also:

It all lies in showing the proper countenance. As for the young contributing their energies when there is work to be done, and deferring to their elders when there is wine and food to be had—how can merely doing this be considered being filial? (2.8)

Confucius could explain to Aristotle that the *li* is not simply a set of behaviors to be mindlessly imitated; he, like Aristotle, maintains that there are internal conditions that make one truly virtuous. These conditions include knowing that it is a virtuous act that one is carrying out, deciding on the act for its own sake rather than for the sake of some gain to oneself, not regretting one's action, and taking pleasure in the act (*Nicomachean Ethics* II, 4, 1105a30–35, II, 4, 1104b3–9). Because of these qualities of mind (decisions and states) that must accompany an act in order for the actor to be considered virtuous, Aristotle would understand easily why Confucius would put down one who adheres to all the moral acts required of him and yet is totally devoid of any personal investment in carrying out those acts. Such a person is exemplified in Confucius's discussion of the "village worthy." Recall Confucius's judgment of the "village worthy," whose "excellence *(de)* [is] under false pretense" (17.13). The "village worthy," for Confucius, is one who appears to be outwardly excellent in that he abides by all the laws or moral acts expected of him but is inwardly bankrupt in that he lacks the appropriate attitudes and motives that should accompany those acts.

Li dictates that one is to act in such and such a manner (exhibiting the qualities of the right attitude and virtue, attributing the right quantity of honor or respect, giving the right quantity of gifts) in relation to particular persons (one's relatives, or sovereign, or subordinates—where each of these persons is understood through a minimal sense of substance that makes them remain who they are), at such and such a place (in the court, or home, or at the graveyard), and at such and such a time (of ritual sacrifice, wedding, or funeral). The concept of *li* would be accessible to Aristotle because he shares with Confucius the categories of quality, relation, place, time, quantity, and even action and passion; and *li* can be explained in terms of those categories. Once again, I urge that explainability, not translatability, is the pivotal issue for mutual understanding.

A final objection to my argument for the possibility of mutual understanding is the Confucian idea that *li* is the last appeal for matters of proper behavior and attitude. But Confucius would want to explain that *li* is not a set of arbitrary prescriptions for ritual propriety but is rooted in a *dao* (way) that has been transmitted through tradition. That the *li* exemplifying the proper *dao* will always be captured by people's way of life is evident in the response of Confucius's student, Zigong, to the question, "With whom did Confucius study?"

> The way [*dao*] of Kings Wen and Wu has not collapsed utterly—it lives in the people. Those of superior character [*xian*] have grasped the greater part, while those of lesser quality have grasped a bit of it. Everyone has something of Wen and Wu's way in them. Who then does the Master not learn from? Again, how could there be a single constant teacher for him? (19.22)

Although it may have been modified over time, *li* is preserved not only in the people's way of life but also in written works. In response to a question about what the *li* would look like in ten generations, Confucius says:

> The Yin dynasty adapted the observances of ritual propriety [*li*] of the Xia dynasty, and how they altered them can be known. The Zhou adapted the obser-

vances of ritual propriety of the Yin, and how they altered them can be known. If there is a dynasty that succeeds the Zhou, even if it happens a hundred generations from now, the continuities and changes can be known. (2.23)

That we rely on written works to know the *li* of a particular dynasty is clear when Confucius says:

I am able to speak on ritual propriety [*li*] during the Xia dynasty, but its descendent state, Qi, does not provide adequate evidence. I am able to speak on ritual propriety during the Yin dynasty, but its descendent state, Song, does not provide adequate evidence. It is because these states have inadequate documentation and few men of letters. (3.9; see also 17.9 on how the *Songs* can transmit the proper *li*)

Aristotle would understand the variations of *li* in various dynasties because of his attunement to how variations in the types of people who make up the ruling and the ruled, and their characteristics (wealth, virtue, occupations, etc.) all contribute to making their constitutions quite different from others. There are even variations within the same type of constitution, and these differences typically reflect variations in the customs and manners of the respective groups. For instance, he discusses five types of democracy and four types of oligarchy (*Politics* IV, 4–5, 1291b14–93b22). So there could be one kind of democracy where the poor count as much as the rich, and another kind where only the propertied can participate but where the property qualification is so low that the many may qualify, and yet another where birth determines one's share in office, and another where birth does not count. Apart from these considerations, the occupations of the ruler and ruled will determine whether a democracy is primarily agricultural or primarily trade oriented, and thus whether law or the will of the rulers is sovereign. Because of Aristotle's understanding of the variety of constitutions and how each may require a different kind of rule or way to govern and habituate the people, he would also understand Confucius's view that a different set of *li* might better suit a different set of people precisely for the purpose of moral training toward a set of virtues.

Aristotle says, "For law [νόμος] has no power to persuade [πείσθεσθαι] beside custom [ἔθος], but this will not come to be [οὐ γίνεται] if not through [διὰ] a great length of time [χρόνου]" (*Politics* II, 8, 1269a20–23, my translation). To the extent that the laws, for Aristotle, constitute the content of cultivation, he would understand that Confucius's *li* serves a similar function. Confucius's understanding of law is different from Aristotle's, however, for Confucius doesn't conceive of laws as forming the content of cultivation but rather as external and without the kind of impact that *li* has on character formation. As Confucius puts it:

> Lead the people with administrative injunctions [*zheng*] and keep them orderly with penal law [*xing*], and they will avoid punishments but will be without a sense of shame. Lead them with excellence [*de*] and keep them orderly through observing ritual propriety [*li*] and they will develop a sense of shame, and moreover, will order themselves. (2.3)

Even better than written law for understanding Confucius's *li* is Aristotle's view of unwritten law or "custom." This is more sovereign in Aristotle's view because it not only encompasses more, and more significant issues, than written law but is also safer than written law because it is immune to the tendency toward tyranny from the rule of a man. As Aristotle puts it:

> But laws resting on unwritten custom are even more sovereign, and concerned with issues of still more sovereign importance, than written laws; and this suggests that, even if the rule of a man be safer than the rule of written law, it need not therefore be safer than the rule of unwritten law. (*Politics* III, 16, 1287b5–8)

We see again that even without the words to translate Confucius's *li*, Aristotle could understand the concept because it is explicable by the qualities to be cultivated, the significance of differences in place and time, the focal importance of relations (especially relations between the rulers and ruled), the shaping of actions and passions by ongoing customs, and so on. Again, my claim is that the pivotal issue for mutual understanding is not the translation of terms, but the explanation of concepts. Explanation is made possible, in this case at least, because of an underlying similarity in categorical structure.

MacIntyre has argued that in spite of their agreements about the virtues, the Confucian and Aristotelian traditions are ultimately incommensurable because they have no shared standard or measure of interpretation, explanation, and justification through which to adjudicate their differences. These differences, MacIntyre maintains, are radical enough that each lacks the words for the other's key concepts. He maintains that they necessarily fail even to recognize the other's problems and moral shortcomings. I have shown how Confucius's text provides ample evidence for the nine Aristotelian accidental categories, and even for the substance category in a minimal sense. Even supposing that these two ethical systems do not share common standards and measures in every respect, it does not follow that they are so radically disparate as to lack kindred concepts, or that they must necessarily find utterly unintelligible what the other advocates or repudiates. My point is that given the significant role of these categories in both views, MacIntyre exaggerates the distance between them. Those ten basic concepts Aristotle presents as our basic modes of predication are used by both thinkers, and so can help us to investigate the similarities and differences between them. Thanks to the ten categories, dialogue between these two great and culturally diverse traditions of thought looks not only possible but fruitful.[22]

22. I am grateful to Wes DeMarco for our endless discussions on this essay. As always, they were invaluable in helping me crystallize my position. I am also indebted to Professor MacIntyre for his comments, which clarified our differences and spurred me on to explain in more detail my understanding of concepts. Special thanks are also owed to P. J. Ivanhoe for his most helpful commentary at the Central division American Philosophical Association meeting, Chicago, 24–26 April 2002, and to the participants of the Metaphysical Society of America meeting at SUNY–Buffalo, 9–11 March 2001, for their provocative questions.

PART II
MODERN APPROACHES

6   Kant: The Practical Categories
TIMOTHY SEAN QUINN

INTRODUCTION

Perhaps no thinker since Aristotle devoted as much attention to the concept and use of categories than did Immanuel Kant. For Aristotle, the categories stand at the nexus of our knowledge of the world and the being of the world; they represent the primary predicates according to which a being is said to be what it is in itself.[1] Although Kant would seem to owe elements of his basic list of categories to Aristotle, his intentions in the employment of that list is, if anything, anti-Aristotelian. The relevance of Kantian categories is not metaphysical but solely epistemological and moral. Thus, in the *Critique of Pure Reason*, the categories stand at the center of Kant's claims concerning knowledge, its conditions, its systematicity, and its restriction to the phenomenal world. In the *Critique of Practical Reason*, another account of the categories plays a role in establishing Kant's well-known categorical morality.[2] This second, moral application of the categories has garnered significantly less attention than has the account of the theoretical categories and their notoriously thorny deduction. This neglect is due in part to the relatively few pages Kant devotes to explaining the practical categories, compared to the rather lengthy exegesis, substantially modified between the first and second editions of the first *Critique*, which he devotes to the theoretical categories. As well, the practical categories seem to play no central or formative role in the argument of the second *Critique*; by the time Kant introduces them, he has already formulated the core of his moral doctrine, the celebrated categorical imperative. There thus seems to be an odd disconnection between assent to the categoriality of morality and those moral cate-

---

1. See Sanford's, Lang's, Sim's, and Garver's essays, Chapters 1, 2, 5, and 9 of this volume.

2. References to Kant's works are from the Prussian Academy of the Sciences edition of *Gesammelte Schriften*, 13 vols. (Berlin, 1902–10), here abbreviated AK. References to the *Critique of Pure Reason* (AK. vol. 3–4) cite the pagination in both A and B editions of the text (where appropriate). References to the *Critique of Practical Reason* (AK. vol. 5) appear in the text, followed by the page number. Translations of the first *Critique* are based on Werner Pluhar's translation of the *Critique of Pure Reason* (Indianapolis: Hackett, 1996). Translations of the second *Critique* are based on Lewis White Beck's translation of the *Critique of Practical Reason*, 3d edition (New York: Macmillan, 1993).

gories whose role, one anticipates, would be to secure this very categoriality. The impression with which one is left is that the practical categories are derivative notions, interesting but inessential to the principal claims of the second *Critique*. Nevertheless, Kant remarks of the practical categories that "they have a manifest advantage" over the theoretical categories; this advantage, as it plays out in Kant's moral philosophy, consists in their revelation of a power of reason to realize its end—the highest good—in all of its uses. The goal of this essay is to explain Kant's notion of the practical categories with an eye to what it reveals about reason's activity in the world, as Kant understands that activity. After a cursory account of the theoretical categories, I will explain the doctrine of the practical categories as it emerges in the second *Critique*. The third section of the essay will compare theoretical and practical categories. The final section will attempt some broad conclusions about the role played by categories in Kant's thought.

I

In the first *Critique* Kant treats of the categories in two phases. The first phase, in what the second edition (B159) names a "Metaphysical Deduction," offers an account of what categories are, meant explicitly to contrast with the Aristotelian understanding of the categories as the primary predicates of being. This initial account therefore renders the concept of categories "metaphysically neutral," that is, it silences their traditional metaphysical or ontological relevance by associating them with forms of thought about objects rather than with forms of objects. In the second phase of his argument Kant names a "Transcendental Deduction." Its goal is to establish, as Kant puts it, our "right" to use the categories on behalf of our cognition of the phenomenal world, given that these categories are entirely *a priori*, underived from experience, and wholly intelligible independent of any appeal to experience. The ensuing deduction is not syllogistic in character but juridical, concerning, as it were, the right of ownership of a certain intellectual property.[3] This discussion results in Kant's assigning the "birthplace" of the categories to an "epigenesis of reason" (§27). The relationship between these two phases of Kant's discussion is thus that between a *quaestio facti* and a *quaestio juris*, the former indicating those categorical "functions" (as Kant calls them) that require justification by the latter.

3. See Dieter Henrich's essay, "Kant's Notion of a Deduction and the Methodological Background of the First *Critique*," in *Kant's Transcendental Deductions: The Three Critiques and Opus Postumum*, ed. Eckart Förster (Stanford: Stanford University Press, 1989).

According to the argument of the "Metaphysical Deduction" (§10–12), categories are "pure concepts of the understanding." Their purpose is to explain the possibility of a coherent, systematic knowledge of experience by revealing the conditions necessary for any possible experience.[4] Although they are responsible for our knowledge of objects, the categories themselves do not constitute such knowledge: knowing the categories in light of which an object becomes "possible" is not identical with knowing that object.[5] Kant therefore refers to them variously as concepts, rules, principles, functions—terms meant to designate their purely formal character. What they are functions or rules for is the creation of unity within the manifold of what is given to us in intuition, in space and time. They therefore allow us to "think" an object given in intuition, making it possible for that object to become an object of knowledge. The categories come to light for Kant whenever we are engaged in an act of judgment, that is, whenever we are synthesizing representations under "higher" representations (A69/B94), which Kant takes to be the fundamental activity of understanding. There are, therefore, as many categories as there are logical functions of judgment, or forms of unity (A79/B105; A95/B128). Unlike Aristotle, who, "having no principle, snatched them up as he came upon them," Kant's table of categories is (in his view) not "rhapsodic," since all categories, as well as their interrelationships, stem from a common principle: the basic synthetic activity of understanding as it is exhibited in the power of judgment (A80/B106).

According to Kant, the understanding "contains" these "original pure concepts of synthesis" *a priori*. They are the very forms of thought. However, the sense of the word "contains" *(enthalten)* is not immediately evident. In particular, it becomes necessary for Kant to show in what way the category-rules for unifying representations are in fact objective, and not merely a set of subjective dispositions indicating the ways we happen to think about our experience. He therefore turns in the

---

4. It is tempting, although erroneous, to understand Kant's term "possible experience" to mean "universal experience." As the Transcendental Deduction makes plain, our knowledge of the phenomenal world always depends upon the manifold present to us in intuition. Even though the categories are *a priori* and (as Kant argues) objective, their objectivity is ensured finally only by being tied to the particular intuitions before us.

5. Note Kant's insistence on this point, for example, in his letter to Reinhold (12 May 1789), in response to Eberhard's criticism that Kant has failed to account for the principle of synthetic judgments: the principle is the synthesis of category and intuition; once we see this, Kant writes, "we shall be convinced that they [the categories] do not by themselves provide genuine knowledge, and that, when supplied with intuitions, they do not give us any supersensible theoretical knowledge." He adds, however, this interesting qualification: " . . . though they can be used for practical ideas without stepping outside their proper sphere" (AK. 11. #359 [337]).

"Transcendental Deduction" to an attempt to establish our right to use there "original pure concepts" as a way of judging appearances and the empirical world, given that that world always makes immediate and confusing demands upon our attention. Kant puts the problem this way. On the one hand, purely empirical evidence only explains how concepts can be acquired through experience or through reflection upon experience. Empirical, "physiological" deductions (as Kant calls them) at best concern *quaestio facti;* they are not, therefore, deductions at all (given the juridical sense in which Kant is using the term). On the other hand, the categories of understanding "do not at all present to us the conditions under which objects are given in intuition" (A89/B122). Objects can appear without a necessary reference to our understanding and its categorial functions. Given the curious discordance between "subjective conditions of thought" and "objective validity," it becomes all the more important for Kant to "display a birth certificate" for the categories (A86/B119). Given the complexity of the ensuing argument, I wish to confine myself to a few observations for the sake of indicating Kant's basic themes.[6]

1. The basis for the synthetic activity of the categories is not a category of unity, but the unity of an "original" self-consciousness, or transcendental unity of apperception. The germ of Kant's argument is that "we cannot present anything as combined in an object without ourselves having combined it beforehand" (B130). This sense of combination, more basic than that performed by the categories themselves, is a result of the consciousness that "I think" accompanies all representations, if they are in fact one's own (B132). The basis of the synthetic unity of understanding in its use of the categories to order the manifold of intuitions is therefore the unity of an ego conscious of its transcendental (rather than empirical and episodic) self-identity (B139/40).[7]

2. The transcendental unity of apperception is therefore the basis of Kant's claim for the objective validity of the categories. While the unity of a given manifold is subject to the original synthetic unity of apper-

---

6. My remarks will be based on the Deduction as it is presented in the second edition of Kant's first *Critique,* given that the issues raised in this version of the Deduction speak most directly to the account of the categories in the second *Critique.* For a discussion of the differences between the two versions of the Deduction, see Dieter Henrich, "The Proof-Structure of Kant's Transcendental Deduction," in *Kant on Pure Reason,* ed. R. C. S. Walker (Oxford: Oxford University Press, 1982), 66–81.

7. For a more complete development of the way in which the identity of ego is responsible for the synthetic activity of the categories, see Dieter Henrich, "Identity and Objectivity," in *The Unity of Reason,* ed. and with an introduction by Richard Velkley (Cambridge: Harvard University Press, 1994): 123–208.

ception, the act of understanding that brings a manifold under one apperception is the work of the categories (B143). As Kant puts it: "Through the synthesis of understanding, the manifold contained in an intuition that I call mine is presented as belonging to the *necessary* unity of self-consciousness, and this presenting is done by means of the category" (B144). A category therefore represents an instance of a particular synthesis of the manifold; categories are but "rules" that determine the way in which understanding brings the synthesis of the manifold to the unity of apperception (B145). There are two important consequences of this thought. First, understanding knows, strictly speaking, nothing; it consists only in an activity of synthesis. Knowledge involves not only the use of a category (Kant now renames them "concepts," B146) through which an object can be thought, but also an intuition through which the object is given. Kant is emphatic, here and elsewhere, that the categories do not in and of themselves represent knowledge of anything: "We cannot *think* an object except through the categories; we cannot know an object . . . except through intuitions corresponding to those concepts . . . no cognition is possible for us a priori except of objects of possible experience" (B165–66). Categories are merely the conditions for the possibility of knowledge. The second important consequence is a result of this conclusion: that understanding, as a result of the pure formality of the categories, is wholly restricted to its attempts at knowing the phenomenal world (B148). Only sense and intuition provide the categories with "meaning and significance" (B149). The categories therefore represent the supreme limiting condition of all possible knowledge; nothing "supersensible" can become an object of cognition.

3. Even so, within their sphere of operation, the categories enjoy central responsibility for explaining our knowledge of nature, in particular its law—governedness. Since the categories "prescribe laws a priori to appearances" in their ordering of intuitions, and since nature is given originally as appearances conforming to no intrinsic order, the very possibility of something we call "nature" depends, according to Kant, upon the categories. The categories are, in short, the basis of the mechanical ordering of nature, the silencing of (Aristotelian) notions of final causes.

4. While the transcendental unity of apperception accounts for the synthetic functions of the categories, it does not account for their origin. Kant traces their birth certificate back to an "epigenesis" of reason. Given the *a priori* character of the categories, their origin cannot be found in experience; on the other hand, the categories necessarily agree with experience. In order to explain why such an agreement

should exist at all, a question of the generation of pure concepts becomes all the more salient. If experience itself were to be the ultimate source of the agreement between categories and intuition, the result would not be an explanation but a *generatio aequivoca*—a production of offspring by parents of an entirely different species. The only alternative, Kant writes, is to hold that the categories make experience possible through "a system of epigenesis, as it were, of pure reason" (B167). The rival to this alternative would be a "preformation system" of pure reason, wherein the categories amount to "subjective predispositions" implanted in our nature and mysteriously harmonizing with the laws of nature. Kant seems to have in mind here a pre-established harmony doctrine of a Leibnizian sort, whose only basis would be the supposition of a divine guarantor or harmonious interaction. In that case, Kant writes, the categories and their application to experience would lack necessity; lacking necessity, they could become the basis for any sort of intellectual "illusion," and thus arm the skeptic with a potent weapon against reason. In so saying, Kant reveals what is in fact at stake for him in his defense of the categories—not metaphysically or epistemologically, but morally: the attempt to negotiate a path between the Scylla of a "physiologizing" of reason (of which Aristotle, as "physiologist" of reason, is the paramount example), and the Charybdis of illusion and (religious) fanaticism. The doctrine of epigenesis, by contrast, is the source of the greatest intellectual sobriety.[8]

In all, then, Kant's doctrine of the theoretical categories is central to his most important claims concerning knowledge: its restriction to the phenomenal realm, and rejection of the possibility of supersensible knowledge. When Kant turns, in the second *Critique*, to a discussion of practical categories, however, these restrictions and rejections will be modified: the status of the phenomenal realm comes to be rendered more contingent, and the supersensible becomes the very agency of the practical categories.[9]

---

8. In reflection #4851 (AK. 28:8–10), Kant indicates that the difference between his own account and fanaticism lies in the difference between a notion of conceptual epigenesis and a doctrine of innate ideas. See also #4275 (7:492) and #4859 (8:12). In the *Critique of Judgment* (AK. 5:423–24), Kant offers his most sustained remarks on the notion of epigenesis and its role in biological explanation. Finally, see the discussions of the issue of epigenesis by Judith Wubnig, "The Epigenesis of Reason," *Kant-Studien* 60 (1969): 147–52, and C. A. Genova, "Kant's Epigenesis of Reason," *Kant-Studien* 65 (1974): 259–73. For Aristotle as "physiologist," see first *Critique*, "The History of Pure Reason" (A852–56/B880–84).

9. See Thalos's essay, Chapter 12 of this volume, for further reflection on the relationship between theoretical and practical categories. See Gorman's and Weissman's essays, Chapters 10 and 11 of this volume, for more on normative categories.

11

In the *Critique of Practical Reason*, Kant introduces the practical categories in the second chapter of the "Analytic," titled "The Concept of an Object of Pure Practical Reason" (AK. 57). Already one notes the parallelism between the account of the theoretical categories in the first *Critique* and this account of the practical categories: in both instances, the categories come to light when Kant considers how an object comes to be regarded as "possible." There is, too, a similar division into two parts in Kant's analysis. In the first part, Kant establishes the nature and activity of the practical categories, culminating in a table of categories resembling in its main divisions the table of the first *Critique*. In place of a Transcendental Deduction, however, Kant addresses what he names the "Typic of the Pure Practical Faculty of Judgment" (AK. 67), whose theme echoes that of the Schematism in the first *Critique*, that is, to determine the conditions under which (moral) concepts can be shown to be actual. Apparently, there is no need to justify our right to use the practical categories; in fact, Kant allows that their justification lies in "the fact of reason" itself.[10]

To begin, the concept of an object of pure practical reason is a representation of an object "as an effect possible through freedom" (AK. 57). Kant's accent falls on the word "possible": deciding whether something is an object of *pure* practical reason (Kant's emphasis) involves knowing the possibility or impossibility of willing the action that will produce this object. Possibility is therefore not physical possibility or force; the issue is not whether the action willed ever comes to be but whether we should will an action that would generate "the existence of an object if it were within our power" (AK. 58). Physical possibility is only an issue to the extent to which we regard the object itself as determining our desires. For an object to be *morally* possible, by contrast, the "law of the will" and not the object itself must be the basis for our desires. The "law of the will" is the categorical imperative; the "objects" in question, good and evil. Hence the problem whose solution requires an account of new, practical categories: how to determine the relationship between the good or moral "object" and the law of the will, which prescribes those actions intended to make actual this good? Kant develops

---

10. In the second *Critique*, the Deduction of the moral law precedes the exposition of the categories. The question of the right to use the practical categories has in effect been resolved indirectly and in advance of their exposition by Kant's conclusion in the Deduction, that moral obligation is established only by "the fact of pure reason." In the event, the practical categories do not establish the moral law, the way the theoretical categories establish the laws of nature, but presuppose its operation.

the problem in this manner. If the good were to be the source of the moral-practical law, and not derived from it, it would have to be some good object, a discrete object of our desire, and therefore reducible to the pleasant. Kant, of course, strenuously objects to this possibility. Pleasure and its converse, pain, are consequences of an object or action; they are known only by experience. While pursuing pleasure and avoiding pain might yet be crucial for securing our well-being, they would fail to secure moral worth.

Indeed, it is not self-evident why a subordination of the moral law to some notion of the good would inevitably reduce the good to the gratifying. Kant's premise seems to be: by subordinating the moral law to something we consider good, reason itself is subordinated to that good. Bereft of determination by anything except our private inclinations, the good becomes equal to the gratifying and, together with the moral law itself, merely a means of securing gratification. The moral law, in short, ceases to be moral: it becomes what Kant elsewhere calls a "technical" imperative, or an imperative of prudence.[11] Kant thus confronts us with two ways of understanding the objects of pure practical reason. Either there exists a rational principle that determines the will without reference to possible objects of desire—that is, reason itself determines the nature of the good—or some "determining ground" precedes the practical law and becomes the basis for our volitions—the moral law, determined by the "world of sense" (AK. 62). In the first instance, the one Kant clearly wishes to adopt, the principle in question would be an *a priori* practical law that would require us to understand reason as intrinsically practical, to the extent to which its activity was identical with that law. In the second instance, the "determining ground" would be an object of pleasure or displeasure, attraction or aversion. The goodness of actions performed on this basis would depend utterly on the attainment of the end, on some instance of gratification. Kant's problem, then, is to discover what are precisely the *a priori* practical principles of reason. These principles will be what Kant calls the practical categories, or "categories of freedom."

Kant acknowledges the paradoxical nature of his proposal here: that the concepts of good and evil defined by the moral law seem to be presupposed in order to frame the moral law in the first place (AK. 62–63). His solution to this paradox requires, he explains, an analysis of pure practical reason, that is, the discovery of the aforementioned identity between pure practical reason and the moral law. Such an

---

11. See, for example, Kant's remarks in the *Grundlegung zur Metaphysik der Sitten* concerning the division of imperatives into technical and practical (AK. 4:416ff.).

analysis would lead us to the inescapable conclusion that the moral law not only defines the good but "makes it possible" (AK. 64). The alternative would be to fall into the errors of both "ancients" and "moderns" (AK. 64), that is, either searching in vain for the highest good among notions of perfection, happiness, or the will of God, or rejecting the very possibility of a highest good (for example, Hobbes's celebrated denial of the existence of a *summum bonum*). Kant conceives of his own project, by contrast, as an attempt to secure the autonomy of morality by showing how the concept of the highest good follows from the internal relations between pure practical reason and the moral law, rather than serving as their basis. He has as his goal equally to establish the goodness of reason and the rationality of goodness.

These internal relations within pure practical reason are mediated by the practical categories. The ensuing argument takes its bearings in part from the account of the theoretical categories. Since good and evil are consequences of the *a priori* determination of the will, they presuppose a "pure practical principle"; this principle is a causality of reason to produce morally good objects. In that event, two points follow. First, unlike the theoretical categories that determine the synthetic unity of the manifold in a single act of consciousness, good and evil do not refer "originally" to objects as they are in given in intuition and experience. Instead, Kant writes, "they presuppose these objects as given," that is, their possibility as objects has already been established by the theoretical categories. Practical categories, unlike theoretical categories, are not constitutive of experience but presuppose its constitution by theoretical acts of reason. Hence Kant's second point: good and evil so construed are "modes" of a single category, causality, "so far as its determining ground consists in reason's representation of a law of causality which, as the law of freedom, reason gives itself, thereby showing itself to be practical" (AK. 65). To understand this argument, it is necessary to advert briefly to Kant's treatment of causality in the first *Critique*. Initially, Kant classifies the category of causality as a "derivative" category of the "root" category of relation. The function of the category of causality is to bring order to experience by assigning a necessary, determinate relation between successive appearances; for example, when we say that y necessarily follows x, or that with the appearance of x, y will necessarily follow. Since perception registers only the temporal succession of appearances itself, causality must not be a property of objects but a pure concept brought to the appearances by the activity of understanding. In no case does causality reveal anything about what Kant calls the "supersensible" noumenal realm of the thing-in-itself, which lies beyond the perceptual succession of appearances and is inaccessible from it. Within the ambit of pure practical reason, however, causality functions differently. Its basis is not the understanding but a law of freedom given by reason itself; this law of freedom, since it represents a will to bring about some object or action, entails within itself the concept of causality. Practical reason produces the category of causality simultaneously with its production of a law of freedom. Good and evil, as "effects possible through freedom," Kant now calls "modes" of causality in so far as they do not name objects that already exist but "possible" moral actions produced by free acts of the will. Unlike the theoretical category of causation that synthesizes two objects of intuition into a causal sequence, the practical version of this category sets an object given in intuition into a determinate relationship with something that exceeds intuition, free rational will. Thus Kant:

> On the one side the actions are under a law which is a law of freedom instead of a natural law and thus belong to the conduct of intelligible beings, and on the other side as events in the world of sense they belong to appearances; so that the rules of practical reason are possible only with respect to events in the world of sense and consequently in accordance with the categories of the understanding. (AK. 65)

Practical and theoretical categories stand in contrast to one another, as the intelligible realm of freedom stands in contrast to the world of sense—a familiar contrast in Kantian thought. They are related in as much as human actions are events occurring in both realms. In this respect Kant seems to imply that the theoretical categories restrict the scope of the causality of free will, since the "rules" or maxims willed by practical reason must be possible in light of the world of sense, and thus in light of that world as it is ordered by the theoretical categories (try as one might, one will never be able to will a denial of the law of noncontradiction). Practical possibility presupposes theoretical possibility. However, pure practical reason can decide upon its objects independently of whether one can actually produce them as objects in the phenomenal world—a point upon which Kant insists, since, failing such independence, morality would become a function of the world of sense, the very possibility he is attempting to foreswear. As Kant later puts the matter in his discussion of the Typic of practical judgment, "The subsumption under a pure practical law of an action which is possible to me in the world of sense does not concern the possibility of the action as an event in the world of sense" (AK. 68). As Kant earlier emphasized, it is not the physical possibility but the moral possibility of an action that is at issue. Thus moral actions belong under a law of freedom rather than a natural law, even though as real events they belong at the same time to the world of sense and are thus subject to theoretical categories. The distinction between theoretical and practical functions of causality echoes that between *questio facti* and *quaestio juris:* the former concerns only the existence of objects, the latter, their significance or value to us.

Thus Kant's judgment that the practical categories contribute nothing to our theoretical understanding of nature. On the other hand, Kant indicates that their function is analogous to that of theoretical categories. Whereas theoretical categories bring the manifold of intuition under a single consciousness, practical categories subject the manifold of desires to a single will. Just as the consciousness that "I think" must accompany all of one's representations, the consciousness that "I will" accompanies the representation of all objects deemed good. As Kant argued earlier, objects deemed good must display a necessary, "categorical" relation to the will and pure practical reason; they are deemed morally good only by virtue of this necessary relationship. The possibility of a coherent moral experience of the world, like the possibility of a coherent phenomenal world, depends upon the consciousness of the willing self that accompanies practical reason's causal activity.

Thus far Kant has identified good and evil as modes of a practical category of causality; he has indicated in general terms the relationship between this category and the rational will; and he has distinguished between practical and theoretical categories. This distinction is premised upon the irreducibility of freedom to nature; thus practical and theoretical categories, while enjoying parallel functions, appear to reign over separate realms.[12] Nonetheless, Kant indicates that the practical categories, or "categories of freedom," "have a manifest advantage" over the theoretical categories. The latter are only forms of thought, the basis of whose activity—"the form of intuition"—lies outside of reason, in sensibility. The basis of the practical categories, by contrast, is "the form of a pure will given in reason and thus in the faculty of thought itself" (AK. 66). Their manifest advantage is therefore their autonomy, their identity with the activity of practical reason and their freedom from intuition, which allows pure practical reason to determine its objects without reference to the phenomenal world. Practical concepts "immediately become cognitions," independent of media-

---

12. Freedom is reducible to nature; but as the third *Critique* indicates, nature is not inevitably irreducible to freedom. In his discussion of fine art (§ 45) Kant argues that fine art should resemble "the products of nature." This resemblance consists, however, not in their law-governedness but in their freedom and spontaneity. This aesthetic sense of nature is the result of a silencing of the activity of theoretical understanding, the abstention of aesthetic judgment from all cognitive interest.

tion by intuition and sensibility. This independence and immediacy in the intelligibility of practical categories results, according to Kant, from the fact that "they themselves produce the reality of that to which they refer (the disposition of the will)—an achievement which is in no way the business of theoretical concepts" (AK. 66). It is impossible to overstate the significance of this assertion, namely, that practical reason has the power to generate its own objects directly, in accordance with its operation as a law of freedom. For, Kant states, "freedom is regarded as a kind of causality (not subject to empirical grounds of determination)" (AK. 67), because reason freely asserts this freedom as its principle. As a result, the activity of freedom can be understood according to categories of causality that determine what sort of actions are (morally) possible for us without ever having recourse to intuition.

These causal acts are explicated in Kant's table of categories. Like the table in the first *Critique*, the table in the second *Critique* is divided according to the logical functions of judgment: quantity, quality, relation, modality. As in the first *Critique*, Kant parses each "root" concept into three "derivative" forms wherein the first two are intended to generate the third. Unlike the categories in the first *Critique*, however, the practical categories are not merely "forms of thought" but are possessed of a particular content, causality, whose various modes they represent. Rather than attempt an explication of the table, I wish to confine myself to a few remarks concerning its significance for an understanding of practical categories in general. First, as forms for determining the ways in which freedom of the will brings about its objects, the categories serve as rules or concepts for producing a given action. They are each of them modes of practical causality. As a result, the term "practical reason" does not invariably intend a moral use of reason, or *pure* practical reason; the list of categories under each root concept display a threefold transition from subjective acts of inclination to acts wherein the rule of law comes to be determinative. Kant in fact cautions that we understand the categories to refer to "practical reason in general"; his table will henceforth proceed, he states, from "morally undetermined, sensuously conditioned" categories and arrive at "sensuously unconditioned, morally determined" categories. Thus the final transition to a specifically moral causality emerges only in the fourth root category, the category of modality. In this light we can understand Kant's remark that it is not until we arrive at the categories of modality that a transition is initiated from (general) practical principles—principles for any sort of human doing—to explicitly moral principles. These aspects of the table, while puzzling, are also inevitable if Kant is to preserve, so to speak, the "freedom" of free will equally to produce moral or immoral actions: were the practical categories to necessitate the production of a certain action, the way the theoretical categories necessitate our knowledge of nature, freedom of the will—and therewith the ability to judge the goodness or badness of an action—would be obviated. In the end, the practical categories are not merely logical categories, useful for our interpretation of moral experience. They are generative of that experience, subjecting our desires to the order of a rational will, and in this way allowing pure practical reason to realize itself even in the domain of intuition.

III

Kant's account of the categories ends with the claim that his table of practical categories is "sufficiently understandable in itself" and, apparently, not in need of further elucidation—a claim not accepted even by his most fervent students.[13] Nonetheless, we are in a position to consider whether there exists a unity within Kant's thought concerning categories, theoretical and practical. In fact, as Kant's literary remains attest, as early as 1765 Kant sought for a way of deriving moral obligation from transcendental apperception and the unity of ego. The same synthetic function of the theoretical categories in understanding would evolve in the realm of human action, with the same effect. Thus Kant: "The reason for the necessity of a first action that forms the basis of all that is accidental is to be found in reason . . .; for the self proves to be the ultimate end of all reasons for our actions" (AK 17. #4338). In later formulations, Kant attempts to understand moral error as the equivalent of a logical contradiction (AK 17. #6853), thus blurring the lines between theoretical and practical categories. That Kant conceived of the attempt at a deduction of moral categories from the theoretical exercise of understanding is revealing of his overarching goal: an account of the unity of reason, and therewith the goodness of reason, in all its uses.[14] The doctrine of the categories certainly lends itself to this sort of expectation. The theme of both sorts of categories is unity: both theoretical and practical categories unify a manifold in accordance with concepts that are themselves produced by the mind in its acts of judgment. In particular, the primacy of the "I," in both its theoretical and practical versions—"I think" or "I will"—is the postulate shared by both theoretical and practical categories. In this light, (as Dieter Henrich

---

13. See Schutz's letter to Kant, 23 June 1788 (AK. 10. #330 [309]).
14. For a treatment of the unity of reason in light of the highest good, see Richard Velkley, *Freedom and the End of Reason* (Chicago: University of Chicago Press, 1989).

has expressed it), the categorical imperative seems to be but one way in which this demand for a comprehensive unity of reason under a transcendental ego is realized. By the time of the second *Critique,* however, the transcendental ego has disappeared: the "I will" is irreducible to the "I think." In place of a transcendental justification of practical categories Kant offers what he calls "the fact of pure reason."[15] Kant speaks variously of the fact of reason as the consciousness of the fundamental law of moral obligation (AK. 31), its givenness (AK. 47), and its autonomy (AK. 42). If moral obligation cannot be derived from the self, the way the unity of experience can be so derived, then it must be an irreducible fact; our consciousness of this fact is the source of the moral law itself. The ultimate justification for the use of the practical categories must be this same fact of pure reason; in this manner, we can understand Kant's insistence upon the separateness of theoretical and practical concepts. We can understand, as well, Kant's identification of all practical categories as modes of causality. If pure reason is a fact, and if the moral law is given in the fact of reason, then moral law is an aspect of the same causal act by means of which reason gives rise to itself. Pure reason must cause itself to be itself, since it is irreducible to the mechanism of nature; it must therefore be free.[16] The practical categories emerge then as special ways in which the freedom of reason's essential causality displays itself in the assertion of moral laws. By means of the practical categories, the willing self comes to be related to its supersensible ground; the practical categories thus "exhibit" the supersensible givenness of reason in the entire ambit of human action and desire—an achievement impossible for theoretical categories.

In spite of Kant's having abandoned an attempt to deduce morality from theoretical categories, he does posit what amounts to a parallelism between theoretical and practical categories. In the "Typic of the Pure Practical Faculty of Judgment," Kant argues that while theoretical categories can be schematized, that is, exhibited through their relationship with intuitions, practical categories cannot be schematized, because their supersensible causality exceeds anything given in intuition. On the other hand, theoretical judgments about laws of nature can serve as the type of moral judgments; the form of moral-practical law is

15. For an account of the "pre-history" of this concept within Kant's literary remains, see Dieter Henrich, "The Concept of Moral Insight and Kant's Doctrine of the Fact of Reason," in Velkley, *Unity of Reason,* 55–87.

16. In this respect, Kant's doctrine of the fact of reason receives support from the historical account Kant offers of reason's self-creation, its irruption in nature; see his *Idea of a Universal History from a Cosmopolitan Standpoint* (AK. 8), third thesis; also, *Conjectural Beginnings of Human History* (ibid.). See as well the discussion of reason's self-creation in Emil Fackenheim's "Kant's Concept of History," *Kant-Studien* 48 (1956): 381–98.

modeled upon that of natural law. Thus, Kant writes, "if the maxim of action is not so constituted as to stand the test of being made the form of a natural law in general, it is morally impossible (although it may still be possible in nature)" (AK. 70–71). Moral judgments must display the universality, necessity, and coherence of a law of nature, since the actions they produce are intended to become events in the natural world. The coherence of the natural order is henceforth a model for the coherence of the moral order, even though each is irreducible to the other.

We must note, however, that in this arrangement the theoretical categories are implicitly setting the standard for the synthetic activity of the practical categories. As Kant explained in his first *Critique*, nature comes to be regarded as a mechanical system precisely owing to the activity of the theoretical categories in ordering our experience of natural events. The account of nature resulting from the work of the theoretical categories is, therefore, "metaphysically neutral"; the extent to which, as Kant claims, the theoretical categories make not only the ordering but even the *existence* of nature possible is the extent to which the meaning of nature is restricted to appearances. In this way the theoretical categories, establishing the type of the moral law, supply the necessary negative sanction against the importation of any natural or supernatural causality in our understanding of the phenomenal world; they clear a space, as it were, to be filled by the moral law and its causal activity. Thus the "manifest advantage" of the practical over the theoretical categories, which Kant had remarked earlier, depends upon the specific ways the theoretical categories neutralize traditional theological or metaphysical alternatives to the "fact of pure reason."

This symbiosis of theoretical with practical uses of reason is indicated by the way Kant chooses to conclude his discussion of the Typic. The value of the Typic, that is, of modeling moral upon natural law, is that it "guards also against the mysticism of practical reason" that would seek "to supply real yet non-sensible intuitions (of an invisible kingdom of God) for the application of the moral law" (AK. 70–71). It guards as well against the other extreme, of rooting moral obligation in an empiricism that would reduce all moral dispositions to the condition of physical inclinations and interests. The type of the moral law would, Kant argues, clearly secure the rationality of morality, and therefore militate against the human tendency either to sublimity or bestiality. Interestingly, Kant introduced his Deduction of the theoretical categories with a similar admonition, against fanaticism and skepticism (A94–95/B127–28). The former, represented by the Lockean application of "pure concepts . . . for cognitions that go far beyond the boundary of experience," is an immoderacy of reason: once reason has acquired its "rights," it attempts to ply them even where it has no authority. The latter, represented by Hume, represents a rejection of reason's rights in favor of a strict empiricism. The categories, by contrast, are to steer us between these "two cliffs" by allowing theoretical reason sway in its own proper sphere, keeping it within strict boundaries. Both practical and theoretical categories guard against a common opponent, whose tendencies toward either excess or deficiency, as it were, threaten both the rationality of moral obligation and the rationality of human experience.

The categories are the guardians of our intellectual and moral sanity—a sanity threatened by Aristotle, among others.

IV

In all, then, the categories establish the unity of our experience. But since human experience is twofold, of a physical world and of a moral world, the categories are correspondingly of two kinds. But of the two, Kant gives the hand to the practical categories. The theoretical categories, by unifying the manifold of intuition, make objects and experience possible, that is, intelligible and rational; these acts of unity or synthesis illuminate the centrality of the "I," its givenness with all acts of understanding. The practical categories, on the other hand, by unifying the manifold of desires under the "I will," display the causal power of pure reason to transform the experience given to it by the theoretical categories into a moral whole. In their independence from intuition, the practical categories are free to regard all possible objects as objects of moral judgment. In this way they illuminate the supersensible freedom that stands behind the self, that is, in short, coincident with "the fact of pure reason."

But both sets of categories stop at the threshold of knowledge of the self, and of its supersensible freedom. They thus point to, without achieving, the final unity of reason they imply by their synthetic activity. Kant was fully aware of this limit when, in his last reflections in the *Opus Postumum*, he speculates on the possibility of a single power that would unify in one self the physical with the moral.[17] Kant's speculation, and his exegesis of the categories that underscore it, point to a fundamental *aporia* it has remained the goal of philosophy to obtain. Confronting this *aporia*—the unity of reason—is perhaps what remains of lasting value in Kant's account of the categories.

17. See Kant's surprising aphorism in his *Opus Postumum* (AK. 21:4, 6): "Zoroaster: the ideal of physical, and at the same time moral-practical reason unified in a single sense object."

7   Charles Peirce's Categories, Phenomenological and Ontological

CARL R. HAUSMAN

Philosophical categories are necessary conditions of intelligibility. Charles Peirce proposes three such conditions—a short list when compared with the long lists proposed by Aristotle and Kant. The short list applies to the most fundamental, pervasive, or universal features identifiable in any phenomenon, whether the phenomenon is regarded as real, actual, fictitious, or as any kind of subjective experience.

In addition to his so-called pragmatism, Peirce's three categories are probably relatively familiar. If they are known by name, they are usually known as Firstness, Secondness, and Thirdness, or the monad, the dyad, and the triad. These terms reflect his mature account. They are based on two methods or approaches, logical and what he calls phenomenological. Both methods yield categories that have ontological significance.[1]

The ontological significance of the logically derived categories presupposes that logical structures somehow reflect reality. Peirce's general reason for adopting this presupposition is that he considers perception and thought our only initial access to what is real, and he assumes that thinking is attuned to reality. The logical and phenomenological versions are counterparts to each other. One of my aims is to suggest several ways in which the categories approached phenomenologically are integral to Peirce's ontology and cosmology, which I take to be a unique evolutionary realism. I want also to raise the question whether the three categories are sufficient to account for Peirce's view of evolution. I shall begin by offering a brief review of the origin and evolution of Peirce's mature versions. I shall then consider how the categories have ontological import. Finally, I shall address the question of whether

---

1. Other discussions of the relationship between ontology, on the one hand, and logic or phenomenology, on the other, can be found in this volume; see especially Chapters 4, 13, 14, and 15.

the three categories account for Peirce's view of evolution and propose that they need the annexation of a special condition that is in part responsible for evolution.

TWO APPROACHES TO DETERMINING THE CATEGORIES AND THEIR ANTICIPATION IN EARLY WRITINGS

Peirce bases his mature account of the categories on two approaches or methods, the first being logic, specifically the logic of relations, and the second phenomenology. Peirce anticipates the later categories in several early works, notably in "On a New List of Categories."[2] In this essay he intermingles logical and phenomenological, or descriptive, methods. Assuming a classical logic, in which a proposition consists of a predicate applied to a subject, he distinguished what he called universal conceptions. The proposition unifies experience and is composed of the three components—a subject or object, and a predicate or quality, which are joined by a copula. Each of these components exemplifies universal conceptions or categories that render experience intelligible and serve as the basis of the later categories.

The three conceptions in the new list, then, are quality, which becomes Firstness, the object, which, with qualification, becomes Secondness, and the unifying copula, which becomes Thirdness. As his thinking evolved, Peirce shifted from subject-predicate logic to the logic of relations as well as to his phenomenology. In the logic of relations, the classical form of the proposition was transformed into relational considerations that govern the form of the proposition and the terms that enter it. Attention to these led Peirce to say that the structure of a proposition is constituted by, and must be reducible to, three terms in relation. One term mediates the other two terms through the copula. Thus the completed proposition is a triad—for example, "John gives a flower to Mary." The act of giving constitutes a relation between John, the flower, and Mary. There are other relations of lower order than the triad. A subject term and predicate term may interact without the mediation of a copula. This two-term relation is dyadic; it has no mediating third term—smoke results from and signifies fire, for example. And a

---

2. "On a New List of Categories" was first published in *Proceedings of the American Academy of Arts and Sciences* 7 (1867): 287–98. It also appears in Charles Sanders Peirce, *Collected Papers,* ed. Charles Hartshorne and Paul Weiss, vols. 7–8 ed. A. W. Burks (Cambridge: Belknap Press of Harvard University Press, 1958–66), 1:545–59. *Collected Papers* cited hereafter parenthetically in the text using the standard form of citing volume number and paragraph number(s).

monad is a single quality that might be but is not attributed to an object. An example is black, apprehended as an abstraction, which could be embodied in coal. The categories, then, are the triad, the dyad, and the monad, which for Peirce are exhaustive of all relations of higher complexity, such relations being reducible to triads.

Before turning to the phenomenological approach to the categories, I want to make three points, which, I hope, will provide a framework for the exposition and the extrapolations I shall add later.

The first point is that, as phenomenological, the categories are universal and provisionally exhaustive. The qualification "provisionally" is Peirce's addition. He invited the reader to join him in examining any possible experience and, if seemingly appropriate, to correct or modify the categories that he discovered. The second preliminary point is that although all the categories are present in each domain of experience, one or two generally will be predominant in any distinguishable experience. The third point is that Peirce's categories underlie and provide a basis for interconnections between all the other main components of his philosophy. They constitute a network with an architectural structure, which is applicable to his classification of the sciences (including philosophy), to his semeiotic, to his view of the function of thought and the evolutionary movement of inquiry, to understanding the universe, and to the universe itself.

The idea that the categories play a fundamental role in Peirce's thought is borne out in his classification of the sciences. Thus phenomenology is placed along with mathematics as foundational. The special sciences (physical, biological, social, and psychological) presuppose metaphysics, which presupposes the normative sciences of logic, ethics, and aesthetics, while the normative sciences presuppose or depend on phenomenology and mathematics. Each science has principles that distinguish it from the science on which it depends. The categories comprehend the phenomena that become data for all the sciences. What, then, are the characteristics of the categories?

The phenomenological examination, also called phaneroscopy, is an examination of any phenomenon, any complex of items experienced, without consideration of its relation to reality or to conditions that are or might be independent of what is experienced. Thus phenomenology is not concerned with whether a phenomenon is subjectively conditioned. "Phaneroscopy is the description of the *phaneron;* and by *phaneron* I mean the collective total of all that is in any way or in any sense present to the mind, quite regardless of whether it corresponds to any real thing or not" (1.284). Thus phenomenology "sedulously avoids . . . hypothetical explanations of any sort" (1.287). This avoidance, I think, is a kind of bracketing or exclusion of epistemological and metaphysical interpretations of the experiences it describes. Further, the categories are "inextricably mixed together" and "no one can be isolated" (1.286). Let me add here that although Peirce knew Husserl as a logician, I know of no evidence that Peirce had Husserl in mind when developing his own phenomenological examinations.

As noted above, Peirce identifies his categories as Firstness, Secondness, and Thirdness. He also uses the ordinals First, Second, and Third, without adding the suffix "ness," in order, I believe, to refer to instances of the categories. Sometimes, however, the two meanings merge verbally, as when he uses the terms "category the First, category the Second," and so on.

Each category can be identified and described in its own terms by virtue of prescinding. Prescinding is a kind of abstraction in which a reasoner abstracts a class or character that is more general and more fundamental than the class or character from which it is abstracted. The abstracted component, then, is presupposed. Color, for example, can be prescinded from red and blue, but neither red nor blue can be prescinded from color. (The statement "if there is color, then there is red" is not necessarily true; being a color does not depend on being red.) Space can be prescinded from color, but not color from space.

In brief, Firstness is the aspect or tone of qualitatively, immediately felt experience. Secondness is the aspect of otherness and contrast or resistance in experience. Thirdness is the aspect of interpreted regularity and the anticipation of future experience.

The first category is probably the most difficult to understand and appreciate. The main reason for this difficulty, as Peirce himself insists, is that once Firstness is identified and described, it is past and gone in the sense that it vanishes in its immediacy, that is, in its status as uninterpreted, immediate experience. For, in being singled out, it has been specified or characterized and thus has been subjected to an initial stage of interpretation. Yet it is possible indirectly to point the listener or reader toward the aspect of immediate experience at issue. This is attempted through a kind of bombarding of the reader, often in figurative language, with a multiplicity of suggestions about what is immediately felt.

Peirce claims that every thing experienced, including subjective moments, has a qualitative tint or tone, an aspect of something present to consciousness. Further, he says, "The idea of First is predominant in the ideas of freshness, life, freedom" (1.301). It becomes predominant in the ideas of "measureless variety and multiplicity" (ibid.). What is crucial to Firstness, however, is its autonomy, its independence from anything other than itself, relation to which would change its status to a second. Another way to put it is that Firstness is a suchness that is *sui generis* (1.303) and that appears without parts. It is the qualitative aspect of any phenomenon, it is that phenomenon's very presence.

Peirce illustrates this description. "Among phanerons," he says, "there are certain qualities of feeling, such as the color of magenta, the odor of attar, the sound of a railway whistle" (1.304). These phenomena, it should be emphasized, are *what* is sensed; they are not the sensation in the mind. The examples cited and others like them are what prompt me to distinguish the first category from what Peirce refers to as Firsts. I interpret Firsts as instances of Firstness, whereas Firstness is the general category. Firsts, such as colors, odors, and sounds, are determinate and discriminable and can be distinguished from one another and, when identified, are outcomes of interpretation or classifications. They are not pure, as is Firstness, which is indeterminate. They are not perfectly autonomous, because they require discrimination and differentiation to be identified.

There are no pure Firsts in actual experience. Pure Firsts are abstractions, the outcome of prescinding. Thus there are no immediately experienced events that can be described as they are given. Yet even as instances, the Firsts, such as specific qualities, are abstractions from more general impressions, and they are attended to as if they were detached from those impressions. Ideally, a pure quality such as red would not be embodied, for if it were embodied, it would be dependent in part on the embodying thing. A pure red would be a "mere maybe," as Peirce puts it. Its only being consists in the fact that there might be such a peculiar, positive suchness embodied in a phaneron (1.304). A quality as such is a may-be without being occasioned in actuality. If it were a general, in the sense of a regularly experienced thing, or a kind of rule for instantiation, it would be a possibility in the sense of a potentiality rather than a may-be possibility. And this would be a Third, an interpretive mediation and rule of instantiation in particulars. However, a single actualized quality must be embodied, and thus it is not a mere possibility or an immediate, uninterpreted, qualitative aspect of a phenomenon. Thus Peirce points out that quality as such does not inhere in a subject (1.304). By this I take him to mean that consciousness of redness or color in general is consciousness of a prescinded instance of a category, namely, of Firstness. The self-relation of quality as such, in any case, is monadic. But the reference to instantiations of Firstness points toward the second category.

Peirce argues that every experience and every thing experienced includes a degree of struggle, even if only slight, in which there is a component of resistance or otherness. "By struggle," Peirce says, "I must explain that I mean mutual action between two things regardless of any sort of third or medium, and in particular regardless of any law of action" (1.322). "This is present even in such a rudimentary fragment of experience as a simple feeling. For such a feeling always has a degree of vividness, high or low; and this vividness is a sense of commotion, an action and reaction, between our soul and the stimulus" (ibid.). For Peirce, then, every phenomenon presents polarity, which occurs in two ways. One way is in the relation between that which apprehends the phenomenon and the phenomenon itself. Simply being conscious of anything is, in itself, a dyadic relation. There must thus be two components in the experience that appear as self (as awareness) and not-self (as an object of awareness), even if these are not present reflectively to consciousness at the moment. Peirce points out that awareness of something other than the self prompts the realization of the self. "We become aware of ourself in becoming aware of the not-self" (1.324).

The other way polarity is present is in the phenomena themselves. When the thing is recognized as something here or there, now or then, this rather than that, it is other than something else. It has a second or is a second in relation to some other thing that can be discriminated.

Secondness is typically exemplified when the thing and its other appear as causally related. "The idea of second is predominant in the ideas of causation and of statical force. For cause and effect are two; and statical forces always occur between pairs" (1.325). This is not a final causality, for which the effect acts as a cause in the future. It is not a relation involving a mediating third, added to the initial first, the causal thing, and the last, the final end. A Secondness is more like efficient causality. It is a brute, unmediated, compelling resistance to unification between a first thing and another, between a First and a Second, and it can thus be regarded as a struggle. Peirce says, "By struggle I must explain that I mean mutual action between two things regardless of any sort of third or medium and in particular regardless of any law of action" (1.322). The relation, then, is dyadic.

Further, as suggested a moment ago, there is a resistance in what is experienced. What is experienced in some degree forces itself on the experiencer. "We are continually bumping up against hard fact. We expected one thing, . . . but experience forces that idea into the background, and compels us to think quite differently." In contrast to Firstness, which is the category of immediacy, Secondness concerns what comes to experience as something already there, in the past, and resisting the will of the experiencer. Peirce, of course, has more to say about Secondness, but let us move on to Thirdness.

Peirce's third category is found in the experience of futurity, and it is felt as anticipation. Peirce says that "we constantly predict what is to be" (1.343). Thus there is a thread of continuity, of generality, which suggests interpretation and meaningfulness. The phenomenon calls for interpretation. What is crucial at this point for Peirce's account is that interpretation requires three things in relation. In the order of determining things experienced, first, there is the thing prompting interpretation (which Peirce sometimes refers to as the Dynamical Object), second, there is the thing that is the sign of the first thing, and, third, there is the meaning that the sign assigns to the object. This point can be seen in light of terminology in Peirce's semeiotic. The relation that is constitutive of Thirdness is triadic, and the triad just referred to, now in the semeiotic order, or order in which interpretation is structured, consists of the sign, the object, and the interpreter, or more generally in Peirce's semeiotic, the interpretant. (Peirce introduced the term "interpretant" in order to show that interpretation of the sign is not restricted to the subjective action of an individual human intelligence and is productive of interpretations continued into the future.)

The triadic process of interpretation manifests itself phenomenologically in continuity, for the relation of a sign to its object is in one way dependent on and continuous with an interpretant. Just as the sign is prompted by and in that sense determined by the object, so the sign is interactive in prompting, and in part determining, the interpretant, which itself contributes to the meaning of the sign. The interpretant in turn becomes a sign for further interpretation, which continues to enhance the process with reinstitutions of the triadic process. A continuum is thus suggested in the sense of anticipation and the predictability, summed up in Peirce's statement that "Continuity represents Thirdness almost to perfection" (1.337).

Because experience is rendered intelligible under the category of Thirdness, another aspect of Thirdness is included in the recognition of continuity through anticipation of the future: the category of Thirdness as law. Laws are instantiated in regularities of repeatable particulars that function in triadic relations among the phenomena experienced under Thirdness. But laws are not exhausted by or reducible to their repeated instantiations. This is perhaps most evident in laws of human behavior, in which, for conscious beings, regularities are habits. Habits are dispositions rather than the actions carried out through habits. Peirce broadens the term "habit" to apply to nature: laws are nature's habits. As exemplifications of Thirdness, laws are aspects of phenomena that show why Peirce insisted that the category of Thirdness is the category of fully intelligible experience. For Peirce, such laws are not rigid, invariable conditions of regularities. They are subject to evolutionary change and to departures that make room for new laws.

One obvious bit of evidence for the view that laws evolve is present in some of the features that Peirce assigns to Firstness, which, it should be emphasized, is prescinded from Secondness and Thirdness. This means that if there is a Third, there must be a Second and a First. No Third escapes the functioning of the two lower categories, Secondness and Firstness. Laws are unintelligible without Seconds and Firsts. They are possibilities and potentialities of Seconds and Firsts. Thus evidence of the evolution of habits is found in the attribution of originality to Firsts, which are present with Thirds. It is with respect to Firstness that spontaneity may be introduced into a regularity or law. At that point the law is modified or a new law breaks off from the law in which the intrusion occurred. In discussing what is an actual occurrence that may be present in an instant in a continuum, Peirce refers to accidental coincidences to which things following regularities are subject. He says, "there are cases, as in qualities of feeling, self-consciousness, etc., in which such isolated flashes come to the front. Originality, or Firstness, is another of my categories" (2.85). Peirce's more extensive considerations of originality and spontaneity as they function in evolution unpack this thesis that originality has a place in continuity. Before developing this aspect of Peirce's philosophy, however, let me say something about the transition from the categories as phenomenological to their function in metaphysics and to their pervasiveness in other aspects of Peirce's thought.

THE TRANSITION TO METAPHYSICS

This transition, I think, has been taken for granted by Peirce from the beginning. He seems to have assumed that examining phenomena phenomenologically was consistent with and simply preparatory to viewing the categories as having ontological status. I think Sandra Rosenthal regards the transition this way, too. She points out that Peirce views the categories as metaphysically understood in the sense that, being metaphysical, they "go beyond" phenomenology.[3] To go beyond phenomenology is to show how the categories are real constituents of the world. Three overlapping considerations support this idea.

First, it should be observed that if universal features of phenomena

---

3. Sandra B. Rosenthal, *Charles Peirce's Pragmatic Pluralism* (Albany: State University of New York Press, 1994), 86.

were not constrained by something at least partially independent of finite interpretive actions, one would be assuming a metaphysics of pure phenomenalism, or a view that all there is, is created completely by perceptions. Peirce does not accept phenomenalism in this sense that all reality is only the product of perceptions. The categories Peirce claims to have discovered do contain the signs of an independent reality, or at least of an independent condition constraining mental action. Secondness reveals something that constrains attention and opposes will and intention on the part of the examiner; thus there is something other than what is immediately interpreted. In his semeiotic, Peirce distinguished the Immediate Object, which is the initial outcome of interpretation, and the Dynamical Object, which is an extra-conceptual external constraining condition. The Dynamical Object presumably is felt under the category of Secondness. However, it must be emphasized that although ontological reality for Peirce functions in relation to mind and includes mental and physical processes, it is reducible neither to mental action nor to physical process. Thus, as may be obvious, the categories ontologically embrace both subjective and objective phenomena. However, although related to mind, the Dynamical Object constrains both subjective and objective interpretations of reality. The reality of the Dynamical Object is not reducible to that to which it is related. These points are important for the application of the categories to evolutionary processes and evolutionary theory.

Second, the assumption that phenomenology has ontological significance and is continuous with metaphysical thinking is explicit in at least one of Peirce's descriptions of the categories. He calls them modes of being. "My view," he says, "is that there are three modes of being. I hold that *we can directly observe them in elements of whatever is at any time before the mind in any way.* They are the being of positive qualitative possibility, the being of actual fact, and the being of law that will govern facts in the future" (1.23, emphasis added). Clearly, in introducing the categories as modes of being, Peirce has in mind what he elsewhere derives from phenomenological examinations. It is important also that Thirdness or law can be directly experienced in the anticipation and suggestion of interpretation and continuity or law. Ontological conclusions are not then based only on presupposing, rather than empirically finding, that human intelligence is at least to some extent in tune with nature.

A third reason for the transition is that the idea that laws can be directly experienced is also an entry into one aspect of Peirce's ontological realism: his scholastic realism, which is the kind that views universals as real, in nature, and as reducible neither to their instances nor to abstract ideas that have being only in the mind. Nominalism was anathema to Peirce, at least in the later stages of his thought. But there is a crucial turn to his scholastic realism that lies in his view of the reality of universals. As pointed out earlier, Peirce's universals are subject to change, to evolution, and, in Peirce's terminology, are better thought of as generals. The idea that generals can grow also distinguishes his view from the Platonism according to which forms are eternal or unvarying realities that make particular things intelligible. Thus Peirce says that even the forms can grow. He says, "The evolutionary process is, therefore, not a mere evolution of the existing universe, but rather a process by which the very Platonic forms themselves have become or are becoming developed" (1.194).

Peirce's consideration of the categories as having metaphysical import is simply a continuation of the accounts he offers in his phenomenological examination. To consider them metaphysical is to add descriptions of their relations to what is considered to be in the world—to what is real or existential. Thus, when Peirce referred to his categories as modes of being, he called them "the being of positive qualitative possibility, the being of actual fact, and the being of law that will govern facts in the future" (1.23). Firstness is the category of the pure possibility of any quality that is instanced in an actual fact, in which case it becomes potentially repeatable and is subject to regularization as law, that is, as a Third. Secondness is the category of fact as an instance of actuality. I should note that Peirce sometimes uses the word "fact" to refer to specific referents of true propositions. Thirdness is the category of law in the sense of Thirds, or regularities that are characterized by continua of their instances in Seconds and thus also of Firsts, the qualitative aspect of each instance.

In one passage Peirce describes the metaphysical import of his categories as the phenomenological categories considered with respect to the ways the experiences that fall under each category relate to "the universe of existents" (1.24). Firstness is not necessarily related to the world except as possibility. Secondness relates to the world as actuality. Thirdness relates to the world in terms of the potentialities of its laws for that which could be instanced. This last characterization of Thirdness raises a crucial issue for Peirce's metaphysical perspective on the nature of the cosmos, which I cautiously take to be his cosmology. The reality of the generals or laws, which render the world intelligible through interpretation, is dynamic. Peirce suggests this in part in his insistence on the evidence of the reality of laws. Laws must be operative in nature, and the evidence for this lies in the predictability of their instances. Predictability depends on what would happen in the future if certain circumstances prevailed. Such predictability is a property of laws that reflect "a tendency to be fulfilled" in future events. These tendencies provide continuities or patterns by which one can predict, for instance, that a stone will fall if there are no upward forces to oppose it (1.95). The reality of law is a reality of process. The dynamic of laws, however, requires more than a repetition and regularity of events for Peirce. To reiterate, lawful processes change, and although the changes are outcomes of spontaneous moments, they are usually not arbitrary; the change is a condition for a new direction, a new law. This point is crucial for the discussion of evolution to which I shall turn after briefly considering how the categories provide a framework for all dimensions of Peirce's thought.

Fundamental to the exemplification of the categories throughout Peirce's philosophy is his semeiotic, which is integral to the way all of experience is interpretable from the perspectives of the categories.

The most widely known aspects of Peirce's semeiotic are his three classes of signs: icons, indexes, and symbols. Icons are things that function as signs constituting their meanings through the qualities of the things themselves. The quality resembles the quality of the thing meant by the icon. A gray swatch may be used as an iconic sign of the cloth used in a garment. A portrait is an iconic sign of the person painted. In contrast, an index is a referential sign that points to what it signifies. The index may bear a causal relation to its referent, as does a bullet hole to a bullet. Or "the index, which like a pronoun demonstrative or relative, forces the attention to the particular object intended without describing it" (1.369) "[T]he third [or symbol] is the general name or description which signifies its object by means of an association of ideas or habitual connection between the name and the character signified" (ibid.).

Icons have no referents in the sense of pointing an interpreter to them. A portrait exhibits certain qualities also found in the sitter. An icon's meaning lies in the sheer physical or perceptual quality of the sign. I should note that what Peirce calls hypoicons, or icons whose meanings depend on something else, function figuratively as analogies or as metaphors.[4] Hypoicons, however, are not pure icons. Pure icons are autonomous and monadic. Further, even an analogy or a metaphor that is interpreted either analogically or metaphorically depends on the presence of the intrinsic character of the sign itself. An index is related directly to what it signifies and depends on a dyadic relation. It

---

4. The point that an icon may function figuratively is based on a brief account of three kinds of icons, or, more accurately, what Peirce calls hypoicons, impure icons or icons functioning in contexts that involve other kinds of signs (2.277).

refers beyond itself. A symbol relates triadically to its object through a mediating interpretant and through association or through a lawful, repeated, and repeatable reference—a continuity. It is obvious, then, that the three classes of sign parallel, or, more accurately, exemplify, the three categories. The first is monadic and exhibits Firstness, the second is dyadic and exhibits Secondness, and the third is triadic and exhibits Thirdness. Thus each class of signs falls under its respective category.

The universality and supportive framework of the categories is also evident in Peirce's descriptions of human personality and, in turn, of semeiotic communities. A self and its growth is a miniature cosmologically understood as an agency in development. This point may be illustrated by a brief summary of one of Peirce's views of personality, which also will help in approaching his ideas about evolution. In his paper "The Law of Mind," Peirce identifies personality as a coordination of ideas or habits. Tracing the law of mind to its instancing in persons, he says, "personality is some kind of coordination or connection of ideas" (6.155). He adds that a connection between ideas is a general ideal, which is a "living feeling" and is in process. The process is teleological, "and in the case of personality this teleology is more than mere purposive pursuit of predeterminate ends; it is a developmental teleology" (6.156). This kind of teleology might also be called emergent teleology, to highlight the idea that new purposes and new habits are unprecedented in developmental teleology. Peirce insists on opposing a mechanical conception of teleology, a teleology of predetermined purposes. Changes in a personality may be dramatic, but more often they occur in minute departures from the complex of habits. Some of the more dramatic ones are acts of creation. It is of utmost importance, then, that the teleology here is not traditional, the main example of which is Hegelian teleology as Peirce understood it. This is a teleology according to which a dialectical process of growth follows an implicit logic. For Peirce, such growth is a kind of necessitarianism, a point to be considered later. The result is that Peirce affirms a tychism, or a view of uncaused departure from established laws or habits. This aspect of his view of evolution is similar to Darwinism, but it is Peirce's view goes much further than this.

Peirce proposes that there are three kinds of persons: the artist, the man of action, and the scientific inquirer, each of which is dominated by one of the three categories. Of course this does not mean each actual person is an ideal embodiment of one of these types; obviously each person is a composite and there is plenty of overlap and mixing. But in Peirce's view each person is dominated by one of these three types. This is most important for the third class, because the scientific inquirer, or intellectual, cannot help but be sensitive to quality and, although in a cerebral way, must act decisively in forming hypotheses and reasoning to conclusions.

What appears as miniature cosmic evolution is present in the maturation that takes place from childhood to adulthood. That the first type of person, the artist, lives by feeling and immediacy is consistent with some theories of childhood imagination and the origin of creativity, and therefore corresponds to the child. The man of action corresponds to the adolescent, who is prone to act without regard for the consequences. And the mature adult is, ideally, thoughtful and capable of living an intellectually governed life.

COSMOLOGY: SPONTANEITY AND THE ORIGIN OF NEW LAWS

Peirce's conception of evolution can be summarized in terms of two phases. The first phase is negative in that it rejects determinism. The second phase is positive in that it posits that a special creative agency participates in evolution.

In the 1890s Peirce wrote a series of papers for *The Monist* explaining his view of evolution. The first of these, "The Doctrine of Necessity Examined," sets out his anti-necessitarianism, or his opposition to determinism.[5] Peirce says that the premise of necessitarianism is that

> The state of things existing at any time, together with certain immutable laws, completely determine the state of things at every other time (for a limitation to *future* time is indefensible). Thus, given the state of the universe in the original nebula, and given the laws of mechanics, a sufficiently powerful mind could deduce from these data the precise form of every curlicue of every letter I am now writing. (6.37)

Although he is chiefly concerned with mechanical explanations, or explanations that trace the thing to be explained to antecedent causes, I want to emphasize that his argument also applies to teleological explanation of the kind traditional in his day. One reason suggested by Peirce appears in his second kind of theory of evolution, anancasm, another name for necessitarianism. He finds it insufficient as a theory of evolution, because it regards evolution as a result of necessity, that is, of causal factors "external to the mind, . . . or *internal* to the mind as logical developments of ideas already accepted" (6.307, emphasis added). I think he suggests here a teleological component in the form of necessi-

---

5. "The Doctrine of Necessity Examined," *Collected Papers* 6:35–65, originally published in *The Monist* 2 (1892): 321–37.

tarian causal factors internal to the mind. Even if this were not the case, a closed teleological system in which change renders explicit what was implicit is surely a form of necessitarianism.

Peirce's fundamental reason for challenging necessitarianism is that its justification lies in what he calls a postulate. The postulate is that every event and thing in the universe, past, present, and future, will be shown to be necessitated. Every thing and event, then, will in the future be found to be predictable. According to Peirce, a postulate is an assumption that is not justified by observation. Necessitarianism holds that predictability is necessary and universal, while Peirce saw this prediction as no more than a hope, and it is contradicted by past and present observation. Observation shows that the more precisely one measures predicted instances in which continuities or regularities are actualized, the more imprecision, deviation, and irregularity creep in. Thus, in order to account for diversity and irregularity, the determinist needs to claim that undiscovered laws, which connect all the diversity and variety in the world, must have been present from the beginning of the universe. Peirce believes that this necessitarian hypothesis is less plausible than his own proposal that diversity and variety are inevitable aspects of reality. It is less plausible because it leads to inexplicable ultimate laws. And these laws have not yet been confirmed in what experience shows us.

The second stage of Peirce's defense of his view of evolution follows directly from the negative charge against necessitarianism. He points out that departure from law is observed throughout nature. Not only are standard deviations common, but occasionally more dramatic deviations occur. Spontaneity, deviation, and random events are to be expected. They are inevitable—more fundamental (in one sense) than lawful processes. Peirce even says that law, rather than chance, needs explaining. With Peirce's rejection of that rigorous necessitarianism in mind, let us turn to his positive view of evolution.

What I have reviewed in describing Peirce's three categories suggests the necessary, but not sufficient, ingredients of his account of evolution. Spontaneity in evolution has its locus under the category of Firstness, which includes autonomy, freedom, and indeterminacy. Being autonomous, Firstness is independent, not dependent on other categories or other aspects of experience. Prior to contributing to the other categories, the freedom of Firstness provides the possibility of spontaneity. When spontaneity occurs, however, it is actualized in an event and in the departure from the law in which the spontaneous moment occurs. The event exhibits Secondness. The new law exhibits Thirdness. Firstness with its spontaneity, then, is crucial to evolution. It is the basis of what Peirce calls tychasm, which is the first stage of three modes of evolution. The other modes and the other categories are integral to these three kinds of evolution. Peirce says,

> Three modes of evolution have thus been brought before us: evolution by fortuitous variation, evolution by mechanical necessity, and evolution by creative love. We may term them tychastic evolution, or tychasm, anancastic evolution, or anancasm, and agapastic evolution, or agapasm. The doctrines which represent these as severally of principal importance we may term tychasticism, anancasticism, and agapasticism. On the other hand the mere propositions that absolute chance, mechanical necessity, and the law of love are severally operative in the cosmos may receive the names of tychism, anancism, and agapism. (6.302)

I shall simplify the terminology by using throughout the terms "tychism," "anancism," and "agapism" to refer to the theories, and I shall use "tychasm" or "tychastic," "anancasm" or anancastic," and "agapasm" or "agapastic" to refer to the modes of evolution.

Thus, there are three kinds of evolution, tychasm, anancasm, and agapasm, which exemplify the three categories. Tychasm, as suggested, exemplifies Firstness, and it includes what, in accordance with Darwinism, may be called mutations. In the passage quoted above, it should be noted, Peirce referred to absolute chance as the condition of tychasm. It is important to recognize that absolute chance is not simply unexpected connections among specific relations. Absolute chance is not relative, as in cases of a coincidence or accident. Rather, absolute chance is a feature of reality and is an effect of chaos, which has no relations that can be traced completely and unerringly to antecedents. Peirce's insistence on its reality is, obviously, a metaphysical claim.

The second mode of evolution is anancasm, which is evolution that proceeds by necessity through governing antecedent and/or future conditions for development. In short, anancasm is either mechanistic or deterministically teleological in the traditional sense that every thing and event is necessitated by invariant causal connections.

The third mode, agapasm, is the process Peirce affirms. It is evolution that develops through the activity of an agency, agape, or what Peirce also refers to as evolutionary love, and that permits spontaneous departures from law to evolve into new laws. Thus Peirce repudiates those who would charge him with tychism. Agapasm is a developmental teleology according to which purposes and laws emerge. Agapasm, then, is exemplified not only in Firstness and Secondness but, most important, in Thirdness—or what may be an enhanced Thirdness, as I shall suggest a bit later.

I must now elaborate briefly with a few comments about the interplay of the three modes of evolution. Peirce's own view, as we have seen, is that real chance, or spontaneity, inheres in the very constitution of the cosmos. He grants that this view, like determinism, is not demonstrated. Both his and the determinist's views are hypotheses that must be subjected to both scientific experience and critical common sense. Moreover, a hypothesis implying a postulate that affirms inexplicable ultimates must be rejected. Thus Peirce insists that observations show and have shown that diversification and variety continuously occur. Irregularity, departures from law, variety, and growth are givens and have been recognized since observation and inquiry began. Variety and growth have also persisted throughout time, which prompts Peirce's hypothesis of spontaneity and the law of growth.

This hypothesis, he admits, does not explain specific instances of divergence and growth, but it does explain irregularity that is natural and to be expected. We do not try to explain it away. We accept it and limit explanation to identifying antecedents and laws that are necessary but not sufficient conditions for new developments.

Furthermore, what is crucial to evolution is agapasm. Peirce suggests, on his hypothesis, "that there is probably in nature some agency by which the complexity and diversity can be increased" (6.58). His hypothesis "does explain irregularity," he says, "that is, it explains the general fact of irregularity, though not, of course what each lawless event is to be. . . . it gives room for the influence of another kind of causation, such as seems to be operative in the mind in the formation of associations" (6.60). This other kind of causation, I think, means purposive or teleological development. Further, the agency that is probably in nature must be what he calls agape, a term he introduces in a paper entitled "Evolutionary Love." Evolutionary love emanates from the agency of spontaneity, diversity, and variety in nature. It is thus the occasion for the emergence of law.

This idea of agape arises in Christian doctrine, but its significance need not be equated with the Christian conception of divinity. Agape can be described quite independently of its probable religious origins and associations. It is a mistake, I think, for some Peirce enthusiasts to scoff at Peirce's daring proposals concerning evolution because they are metaphysical and are couched in the language of Christianity. Peirce admittedly does become speculative and figurative in his treatment of evolution. But I admire his honest approach to an issue that still challenges those who seek explanations for what Peirce thought was an intractable phenomenon.

In regarding this agency as agape, Peirce rejects both mechanistic and traditional teleological determinism. It may be helpful to make this point in the context of a comparison of agape with eros. The idea of eros is consistent with deterministic teleology because Eros is an agent aimed at a pre-formed end. Eros's purposes are prescribed, in the sense that it seeks to unite with the perfection of the beloved. Agape, by contrast, does not aim at an end that is desired because it is a lure for the lover. Agape is a dynamic tendency that is open to new possibilities. Its way of aiming or of giving direction to evolution is to be open to its own and its creatures' emerging ends and to a final emergent end that evolves toward an ideal reached only in an ideal future. Such an end is problematic, it should be added, because Peirce refers to the progress of inquiry, and to evolution itself, as inevitably faced with instances of Secondness, or departures that grow into future continuities or laws, no matter how minute these departures may be. If this were not so, the first two categories would collapse into Thirdness, which is an outcome that Peirce found objectionable in Hegel. Thus evolution is inevitable as it moves toward the infinite future.

Peirce's three categories are intended to fit all phenomena. It is the third category, however, that exhibits what is or could be intelligible. To be intelligible is to be general or lawful. What concerns me is whether the agape hypothesis fits the requirement for intelligibility as framed in accordance with Thirdness. That is, does the concept of agape exhibit a phenomenon that is not evident in Peirce's phenomenological description of Thirdness? Does Agapasm require acknowledgment of an annexation or, better, an enhancement of all that is or could be understood in terms of the categories?

In the past I have proposed that the three categories alone are not enough to necessitate the introduction of agape. Intelligibility depends on continuity. Evolution introduces discontinuity or, presumably, a break in intelligibility. This is not to suggest that agape requires the admission of a fourth category. One reason it does not is that it is not universally present as a condition in all phenomena. It is only a condition of intelligibility for evolutionary processes. But when Peirce turns to his account of evolution, his hypothesis points to an additional condition not otherwise evident in, and not reducible to, the three categories. It is thus integral to his developmental teleology. The agape hypothesis, then, commits Peirce to enhancing, if not adding (numerically) to his three categories.

There are four reasons for my claim: (1) the introduction of an agency as a source of emergence extends, enriches, or enhances Thirdness, because agape arises once discontinuity, inherent in Firstness, has disrupted lawful process; (2) the counterargument that the interaction of the three categories is sufficient to account for the emergence of law and of agape can be answered; (3) the introduction of an agency that is also agapastic adds a normative dimension to the categories, for agape advances beyond sheer spontaneity and discontinuity; (4) the idea of normative action implies accountability on the part of the agency of evolution, and accountability is not a feature of the categories as phenomenologically described.

The first reason depends on a point already suggested: there is a paradoxical tension between the view that new laws can emerge and the criterion of intelligibility as law or continuity. On the one hand, what is intelligible is dependent on law or continuity. As Peirce says, Thirdness is the category of continuity: "Continuity represents Thirdness almost to perfection" (1.337).

Now for Thirdness. Five minutes of our waking life will hardly pass without our making some kind of prediction [which] is essentially of a general nature [and] has a decided tendency to be fulfilled, [and this] is to say that the future events are in a measure really governed by a law. This mode of being [the tendency to conform to law] . . . consists in the fact that future facts of Secondness will take on a determinate general character. (1.26)

On the other hand, the discontinuity that occurs when new laws emerge injects a moment of unintelligibility. The recovery of intelligibility depends on an additional condition, and this condition is the agency of agape. By virtue of agape, there is a reinstitution, a creation, of new law. Thus there is a law of growth, a law of evolution, which is made possible because of the addition of the ingression of agape.

It is important to emphasize that emergent laws are not necessitated by past laws. Emergent laws are not reversible. They cannot, in principle, be traced to or reduced to other laws. Furthermore, the law of growth itself is emergent. There is no law that serves as an explanation of it; it is a hypothesis, and a hypothesis to which Peirce adds the hypothesis that there is an agency, agape, an energetic source, that functions to nudge forward the initiation of the emergent laws. In short, the law of growth introduces a special feature that enhances the category of spontaneity and in turn enhances the basic aspect of Thirdness, to be law abiding.

My claim, then, is that the possibility of emergence from law-abiding processes and the addition of an active agency as a condition of emergence is evidence of an enhancement of what Peirce attributed to the manifestation of spontaneity, forcefulness, and the predictable character of Thirdness.

The second reason for my claim already has been suggested. The view that emergence is not an addition or an enhancement of continuity might be defended on the grounds that the third category is built on the other two, which are immanent in Thirdness. Thirdness is continuity that renders intelligible the spontaneity of Firstness and the forceful pressure or constraining action of Secondness. We might conclude that Firstness and Secondness are not left behind—*aufgehoben*, as for Hegel—but are integral to Thirdness.

I believe that Sandra Rosenthal must have assumed this when she challenged the idea that the emergence of new laws and of agape are not additions to the categories. As I understand her, she believes that agape is accounted for by virtue of the interrelation of the categories: "[E]mergence or creativity is itself an emergent feature of the interrelation of the three Peircean categories."[6] She objects that agape is not "a process that is required in addition to the interrelation of the categories."[7] But there seem to be two points that she overlooks. The first is that agape is not "a process," but rather, as Peirce himself proposes, the *agency* of the process. The second point she overlooks is that the very idea of emergence is an enhancement. If "[E]mergence or creativity is itself an emergent feature of the interrelation of the three Peircean categories," then the three categories in interrelation are, at the very least, enhanced. Agapastic evolution, as emergent, could not be reduced to that from which it emerges, that is, categories in interrelation. But this is precisely the claim I have been trying to make. The interaction of the categories with themselves yields creativity and evolution, which, as Peirce puts it, implies the probability of an agapastic agency. Something irreducible has been added, and what has been added, or serves as an enhancement, is the possibility of emergence itself.

To put it another way, if emergence of new law is injected into the account of evolution, and if the law of growth or emergence is built into the categories, then there is no need for adding it, because it has already been added. However, the addition builds into the categories a tension between the idea of intelligibility that is dependent on lawfulness and the idea that there is conflict within continuity, and thus with intelligibility, at any given point in time. The alternative, I think, is what Rosenthal seems to admit: if something emerges from the interaction of the categories, then there is an enhancement of the categories that is not necessitated (anancastically) and that is not simply an instance of tychastic spontaneity.

It seems to me that the first reason that I have just offered for my

---

6. Rosenthal, *Charles Peirce's Pragmatic Pluralism*, 125.
7. Ibid., 125–26.

claim should be sufficient to make it plausible. However, there are two final reasons that follow from what I have just argued, which, I think, add strength to the first reason.

Just as agapastic evolution emerges from the categories, so also does a normative dimension of agapasm. Spontaneity, resistance or forcefulness, and continuity, do not *themselves* imply a norm. Peirce regarded evolution as growth toward *better* laws, that is, laws that contribute to future intelligibility. Knowledge is headed somewhere; it has a tendency to approach and eventually reach ideal harmony manifest in concrete reasonableness, what Peirce sometimes calls the *summum bonum*. The inclusion of an ideal limit in a final Good in Peirce's cosmos is surely an enhancement of the categories as they were phenomenologically described. Indeed, the view that agape enhances the categories is supported by Peirce's own avowed addition of a fourth grade of clearness in light of his reference to a final Good as justification for saying that pragmaticism required purposive action (conduct) directed toward what is meaningful.

Moreover, if normative conditions and the possibility of emerging new laws and values are assumed for evolution, then still another condition is implied: responsibility for achieving outcomes with stages on the way toward that which evolution progresses. I use the term "responsibility" to refer to efficient and final causality with the added association of a normative outcome—that is, the agent's being responsible in the sense of being accountable for that which occurs in consequence of its action. Without such responsibility, we would not have directed change and teleological progress; that is, we would not have the creativity that is the core of evolution. The agency of evolution, agape, then, is the source of valuable diversity and new intelligibility, and the outcome of its action as well as its appearance as a condition of evolution are emergent enhancements to the categories.

I should add that for Peirce the responsibility of agapastic action is not limited to agape, for the office of agape is to give freedom and responsibility to what evolves. The efficient and final causal action of agape is neither predetermined nor predetermining. When an instance of spontaneity occurs, it is not an occurrence with a fixed direction or with predetermined or necessitated law. Thus a responsible agapastic source serves to nudge, but leaves open the specific direction of, the development of the new outcome. Agape is an outflowing love (to incorporate its figurative formulation) that agapastically surrenders control to other individual created sources of evolution. It surrenders— that is, limits its causal efficacy—to the local instances of emergence so that these originations develop on their own, just as the artist in creating new styles does so by surrendering an increment of control, letting the work develop and thereby discovering what emerges. I make this point because I want to emphasize that Peirce did not regress to necessitarianism in hypothesizing agape as the principle of evolution. Peirce's view makes room for emergence rather than either sheer chance occurrences or necessary consequences following from spontaneous occurrence.

The claim I have made concerning the enhancement of the categories needs to be developed through the further suggestion that the idea of agape that Peirce introduces implies that agape is not a single source. Its energy flows outward to other agapastic occasions, that is, to those finite creatures—individual agents—or localized sources of growth engaged in creative activity. For instance, the creatures that evolved into animals capable of flying expressed such localized energy. Development of this point, however, would lead to another essay.[8]

In conclusion, let me reiterate what has been crucial in this discussion. The three categories or conditions of intelligibility embrace three fundamental aspects of experience. First, there is qualitative presence, including spontaneity or absolute chance; second, there is resistance or constraint that accompanies the limits and brute action that is exemplified with the qualitative and the spontaneous; and third, there is continuity and tendency toward ends. The continuities of Thirdness can change or progress so that new tendencies are introduced and new norms enter the progress. However, because of this evolutionary feature, I think that the three categories require one more condition, not a universal condition or a fourth category but a condition present in those moments of process that are creative or productive of emerging, potentially valuable outcomes. This fourth condition is the power of emergence focused in an agency, agape. Thus it has been my contention that the Peircean view of cosmic evolution shows that the phenomenological and the logical presentations of the categories have been enhanced by Peirce's principle of evolution, "evolutionary love," or agape.

I hope that with these final comments I can offer this essay as one way of understanding Peirce's categories.

---

8. I considered this point about the multiplicity of agapastic actions in Carl R. Hausman, "Eros and Agape in Creative Evolution: A Peircean Insight," *Process Studies* 4 (1975): 11–25.

8 Husserl and the Categories

DAGFINN FØLLESDAL

In Chapter 5 of this volume, May Sim explains that whereas Aristotle gives us a complete list of ten categories, Confucius provides no such list. Husserl does not give us any complete list of categories, either, but we can draw together from his various writings a long list of *kinds* of categories.

noematic	pure	grammatical
noetic	analytic	syntactical
eidetic	logical	signification-
ontological	formal analytic	categories
ontic	formal logical	object-categories
material	formal ontological	apprehensional
regional	formal objectual	categories

This list is not complete, but it is already quite long and may appear utterly confusing. It may remind one of a "certain Chinese encyclopedia" that has been reported by Jorge Louis Borges and that you may have encountered in Foucault's writings:[1]

Animals are divided into: a) animals belonging to the Emperor, b) embalmed, c) tame, d) sucking pigs, e) sirens, f) fabulous, g) stray dogs, h) included in the present classification, i) frenzied, j) innumerable k) drawn with a very fine camel hair brush, l) *et cetera*, m) having just broken the water pitcher, n) that from a long way off look like flies.

When confronted with the list of categories in Husserl, we are baffled. It is unclear what many of them are supposed to be, and where we

---

1. Gracia's essay, Chapter 16 in this volume, deals at length with Foucault's view of categories. See also Jorge Luis Borges, "The Analytical Language of John Wilkins," trans. Ruth L. C. Simms, in Jorge Luis Borges, *Other Inquisitions, 1937–1952* (Austin: University of Texas Press, 1993), quoted in Michel Foucault, *The Order of Things: An Archeology of the Human Sciences* (New York: Random House, 1970), xv.

think we understand what some of them are, we seem to have no unified basis for classifying the categories; many of them appear to intersect and overlap. But things are not so unsystematic as they might seem. My primary task in this essay is to familiarize readers with the main outlines of Husserl's phenomenology, so that they may see some order in this list of categories and get some insight into how Husserl conceived of the categories.[2]

TRANSCENDENTAL VERSUS TRANSCENDENT

Husserl states clearly that any theory of categories must reflect the fundamental ontological distinctions that he endeavors to establish in his phenomenology. The first of these is the distinction between the transcendental and the transcendent:

The theory of categories must start entirely from this most radical of all ontological distinctions—being *as consciousness* and being as something that becomes "*manifested*" in consciousness, "transcendent" being—which, as we see, can be attained in its purity and appreciated only by the method of the phenomenological reduction. In the essential relationship between *transcendental* and *transcendent* being are rooted all the relationships already touched on by us repeatedly but later to be explored more profoundly, between phenomenology and all other sciences.[3]

What, then, is this distinction between transcendental and transcendent? In order to understand it, we have to look at Husserl's idea of intentionality, which is the central theme of phenomenology, its *Generalthema*, Husserl tells us in the *Ideas* (§ 84). All of phenomenology can be regarded as an unfolding of the idea of intentionality.

It is well known that Husserl's interest in intentionality was inspired by his teacher, Franz Brentano, but there are many differences between Husserl's and Brentano's treatment of this idea. Let us look first at these differences and then at the features of Husserl's notion of intentionality that go beyond Brentano.

---

2. See Sokolowski's essay, Chapter 13 of this volume, which explores some of Husserl's categories.

3. Edmund Husserl, *Ideen zu einer Phänomenologie und phänomenologischen Philosophie*, § 76, Husserliana III, ed. Walter Biemel, 141–42 (The Hague: Martinus Nijhoff, 1952), 1, 159.5–15. See also Fred Kersten's translation, *Ideas Pertaining to a Pure Phenomenology and to a Phenomenological Philosophy* (The Hague: Kluwer, 1983), 171.

INTENTIONALITY AS DIRECTEDNESS

Husserl retains Brentano's basic idea that "We understand by intentionality the peculiarity of experiences to be 'consciousness *of* something'" (*Ideas*, 188.20). Husserl's formulation comes close to Brentano's oft-quoted passage from *Psychology from an Empirical Point of View*:

> Every mental phenomenon is characterized by what the scholastics in the Middle Ages called the intentional (and also mental) inexistence of an object, and what we could also call, although in not entirely unambiguous terms, the reference to a content, a direction upon an object.[4]

Already at this starting point, however, there is an important difference between Brentano and Husserl. While Brentano says straightforwardly that for every act there is an object toward which it is directed, Husserl focuses on the "of-ness" of the act. There are two reasons for this difference. First, Husserl wants to get around the difficulties connected with acts that lack an object. Second, Husserl aims to throw light on what it means for an act to be "of" or "about" something. Let us examine these two differences between Husserl and Brentano.

ACTS THAT LACK AN OBJECT

First, acts that lack an object. Brentano's thesis may seem unproblematic in the examples he considers: just as when we love there is somebody or something that we love, so there is something that we sense when we sense, something we think of when we think, and so on. However, what is the object of our consciousness when we hallucinate, or when we think of a centaur?

Brentano insists that even in such cases our mental activity, our sensing or thinking, is directed toward some object. The directedness has nothing to do with the reality of the object; the object is "intentionally" contained in our mental activity. And Brentano defined mental phenomena as "phenomena, which contain an object intentionally."

Not all of Brentano's students found this formulation satisfactory, and the problem continued to disturb both them and Brentano. Brentano struggled with it for the rest of his life and suggested, among other things, a translation theory, giving Leibniz credit for the idea:

---

4. Franz Brentano, *Psychology from an Empirical Point of View*, vol. 1, bk. 2, chap. 1 (Leipzig: Duncker und Humblot, 1874), 85; reprinted in *Philosophische Bibliothek* (1924; reprint Hamburg: Felix Meiner, 1955), 124. Quotation from D. B. Terrell's English translation of this chapter in *Realism and the Background of Phenomenology*, ed. Roderick M. Chisholm (Glencoe, Ill: Free Press, 1960), 50.

when we describe an act of hallucination, or of thinking of a centaur, we are only apparently referring to an object. The apparent reference to an object can be translated away in such a way that in the full, unabbreviated description of the act there is no reference to any problematic object. Brentano's proposal has two weaknesses. First, unlike Russell later, Brentano does not specify in detail how the translation is to be carried out. Second, if such a translation can be carried out in the case of hallucinations, etc., then why not carry it out everywhere, also in cases of normal perception? What then happens to the doctrine of intentionality as directedness upon an object?

One of Brentano's students, Meinong, suggested a simple way out. In his *Gegenstandstheorie* Meinong maintained that there are two kinds of objects, those that exist and those that do not exist. Hallucinations, like normal perception, are directed toward objects, but these objects do not exist. Brentano was not happy with this proposal. He objected that he, like Kant, could not make sense of existence as a property that some objects have and others lack.

Husserl's solution was, as we noted, to emphasize the "of." Consciousness is always consciousness *of* something. Or better, consciousness is always *as if of* an object. What matters is not whether or not there is an object but what the features are of consciousness that make it always be as if of an object. These three words, "as if of," are the key to Husserl's notion of intentionality. To account for the directedness of consciousness by saying only that it is directed toward an object and leaving it at that leaves us in the dark about what that directedness is. This leads us to the second reason why Husserl diverged from Brentano. Husserl wanted to throw light on just this issue: what does the directedness of consciousness consist in? He made it a theme for a new discipline, the discipline of phenomenology.

WHAT IS DIRECTEDNESS?

To get a grip on what the directedness of consciousness consists in, that is, to understand better the word "of," which was emphasized by Husserl, let us note that for Husserl intentionality does not simply consist in consciousness directing itself toward objects that are already there. Intentionality for Husserl means that consciousness in a certain way "brings it about" that there are objects. Consciousness "constitutes" objects, Husserl says, borrowing a word from the German idealists but using it in a different sense. I put the phrase "bringing about" in quotation marks to indicate that Husserl does not mean that we create or cause the world and its objects. "Intentionality" means merely that the various components of our consciousness are interconnected in such a way that we have an experience as of one object. To quote Husserl, "the object is 'constituted'—'whether or not it is actual'—in certain concatenations of consciousness that in themselves bear a discernible unity in so far as they, by virtue of their essence, carry with themselves the consciousness of an identical X."⁵ Husserl's use, here and in many other places, of the reflexive form "an object constitutes itself," reflects his view that he did not regard the object as being produced by consciousness. Husserl considered phenomenology as the first strictly scientific version of transcendental idealism, but he also held that phenomenology transcends the traditional idealism-realism distinction, and in 1934 he wrote in a letter to Abbé Baudin: "No ordinary 'realist' has ever been as realistic and concrete as I, the phenomenological 'idealist' (a word which by the way I no longer use)."⁶

In the Preface to the first English edition of the *Ideas* (1931), Husserl states:

Phenomenological idealism does not deny the factual [*wirklich*] existence of the real [*real*] world (and in the first instance nature) as if it deemed it an illusion.... Its only task and accomplishment is to clarify the sense [*Sinn*] of this world, just that sense in which we all regard it as really existing and as really valid. That the world exists... is quite indubitable. Another matter is to understand this indubitability which is the basis for life and science and clarify the basis for its claim.⁷

INTENTIONALITY, THE NOEMA

According to Husserl, our consciousness structures what we experience. Our experience in a given situation can always in principle be structured in different ways; what reaches our senses is never sufficient to uniquely determine what we experience. How it is structured depends on our previous experiences, the whole setting of our present experience, and a number of other factors. If we had grown up surrounded by ducks but had never even heard of rabbits, we would be more likely to see a duck than a rabbit when confronted with Jastrow's duck/rabbit picture that became famous through Wittgenstein; the

---

5. Husserl, *Ideen,* § 135, Husserliana III, 1, 313.16–20. See also Kersten, *Ideas,* 325.
6. Letter quoted in Iso Kern, *Husserl und Kant. Eine Untersuchung über Husserls Verhältnis zu Kant und zum Neukantianismus,* Phenomenologica 16 (The Hague: Martinus Nijhoff, 1964), 276n.
7. Edmund Husserl, preface to W. R. Boyce Gibson's translation of *Ideas Pertaining to a Pure Phenomenology and to a Phenomenological Philosophy* (London: Allen & Unwin, 1931). Taken here from the German version in Husserliana V, 152.32–53.5, my translation.

idea of a rabbit would probably not even have occurred to us.[8] In a few rare cases, such as in the duck/rabbit example, we can go back and forth at will between different ways of structuring our experience. Usually we are not even aware of any structuring going on; we simply experience objects as having a structure.

The structuring always takes place in such a way that the many different features of the object are experienced as connected with one another, as features of one and the same object. When, for example, we see a rabbit, we do not see a collection of colored patches, various shades of brown spread out over our field of vision (incidentally, even seeing colored patches involves intentionality; a patch is also a kind of object, but different from a rabbit). We see a rabbit, with a determinate shape and a determinate color, with the ability to eat, jump, etc. It has a side that is turned toward us and one that is turned away from us. We do not see the other side from where we are, but we see something that has another side.

It is this peculiarity of our consciousness that Husserl labels *intentionality*, or directedness. That seeing is intentional, or object-directed, means just this, that the near side of the object we have in front of us is regarded as a side of a thing, and that the thing we see has other sides and features that are co-intended, in the sense that the thing is regarded as more than just this one side. This structure that makes up the directedness of consciousness Husserl calls the *noema*. The noema is the comprehensive system of determinations that gives unity to this manifold of features and makes them aspects of one and the same object.

It is important at this point to note that the various sides, appearances, or perspectives of the object are constituted together with the object. There are no sides and perspectives floating around before we start perceiving, which are then synthesized into objects when intentionality sets in. There are no objects of any kind, whether they be physical objects, sides of objects, appearances of objects, or perspectives of objects without intentionality. And intentionality does not work in steps. We do not start by constituting six sides and then synthesize these into a die; we constitute the die and the six sides of it in one step.

The word "object," obviously, must be taken in a very broad sense. It comprises not only inanimate objects but also animals, persons, events, actions, and processes, and sides, aspects, and appearances of such entities.

When we experience a person, we do not experience a physical object, a body, and then infer that a person is there; we experience a full-

---

8. On this point, see Garver's essay, Chapter 9 of this volume.

fledged person. We encounter somebody who structures the world, experiences it from his or her own perspective. Our noema is a noema of a person, and no inference is involved. Seeing persons is no more mysterious than seeing physical objects; no inference is involved in either case. When we see a physical object we do not see sense data and then infer that there is a physical object there; our noema is the noema of a physical object. Similarly, when we see an action, what we see is a full-fledged action, not a bodily movement from which we infer that there is an action.

FILLING, THE 'HYLE'

In the case of an act of perception, its noema can also be characterized as a very complex set of expectations or anticipations concerning what kind of experiences we will have when we move around the object and perceive it, using our various senses. We anticipate different further experiences when we see a duck and when we see a rabbit. In the first case we anticipate, for example, that we will feel feathers when we touch the object, in the latter case we expect to find fur. When we get the experiences we anticipate, the corresponding component of the noema is said to be *filled*. In all perception there will be some filling: the components of the noema that correspond to what presently "meets the eye" are filled, similarly for the other senses.

Such anticipation and filling is what distinguishes perception from other modes of consciousness, for example, imagination or remembering. If we merely imagine things, our noema can be of anything whatsoever, an elephant or a locomotive standing here beside me. In perception, however, my sensory experiences are involved; the noema has to fit in with my sensory experiences. This eliminates a number of noemata that I could have had if I were just imagining. In my present situation I cannot have a noema corresponding to the perception of an elephant. This does not reduce the number of perceptual noemata I can have just now to one, for example, of you if you were sitting in front of me.

As noted earlier, a central point in Husserl's phenomenology is that I can have a variety of different perceptual noemata that are compatible with the present impingements upon my sensory surfaces. In the duck/rabbit case this was obvious; we could go back and forth at will between having the noema of a duck and having the noema of a rabbit. In most cases, however, we are not aware of this possibility. Only when something untoward happens, when I encounter "recalcitrant" experience that does not fit in with the anticipations in my noema, do I start seeing a different object from the one I thought I saw earlier. My noema "explodes," to use Husserl's phrase, and I come to have a noema quite different from the previous one, with new anticipations. This is always possible, says Husserl. Perception always involves anticipations that go beyond what presently "meets the eye," and there is always a risk that we may go wrong, regardless of how confident and certain we might feel. Misperception is always possible.

The experiences I typically have when my sensory organs are affected, and that constrain my acts of perception, Husserl calls *hyle*, using the Greek word for matter. He regards his view on perception as a variant of hylomorphism; the hyle, my sensory experiences, constrain and are informed by the noema, the "form." Note that the hyle, for Husserl, are experiences; they are not objects of acts, they are components of acts. We can turn them into objects by reflecting on them, but in the normal acts of perception they are not perceived but rather constrain our acts of perception. For Husserl there is not something "given" in perception, no intermediaries of the kind appealed to by sense datum theorists.

THE WORLD AND THE PAST

We constitute not only the different properties of things but also the relation of the thing to other objects. If, for example, I see a tree, the tree is conceived of as something that is in front of me, as perhaps situated among other trees, as seen by other people than myself, etc. It is also conceived of as something that has a history: it was there before I saw it, it will remain after I have left, perhaps it will eventually be cut down and transported to some other place. However, like all material things, it does not simply disappear from the world.

My consciousness of the tree is in this way also a consciousness of the world in space and time in which the tree is located. My consciousness constitutes the tree, but at the same time it constitutes the world in which the tree and I are living. If my further experience makes me give up the belief that I have a tree ahead of me because, for example, I do not find a tree-like far side or because some of my other expectations prove false, this affects not only my conception of what there is but also my conception of what has been and what will be. Thus, in this case, I reconstitute not just the present but also the past and the future. To illustrate how changes in my present perception lead me to reconstitute not just the present but also the past, Husserl uses an example of a ball that I initially take to be red all over and spherical. As it turns, I discover that the ball is green on the other side and has a dent:

[T]he sense of the perception is not only changed in the momentary new stretch of perception; the noematic modification streams back in the form of a retroactive cancellation in the retentional sphere and modifies the production of sense stemming from earlier phases of the perception. The earlier apperception, which was attuned to the harmonious development of the "red and uniformly round," is implicitly "reinterpreted" to "green on one side and dented."[9]

VALUES, PRACTICAL FUNCTION

So far I have mentioned only the factual properties of things. Things also have value properties, however, and these properties are constituted in a corresponding manner, Husserl says. The world within which we live is experienced as a world in which certain things and actions have a positive value, others a negative. Our norms and values, too, are subject to change. Changes in our views on matters of fact are often accompanied by changes in our evaluations.

Husserl emphasizes that our perspectives and anticipations are not predominantly factual. Nor are we living a purely theoretical life. According to Husserl, we encounter the world around us primarily "in the attitude of the natural pursuit of life," as "living functioning subjects involved in the circle of other functioning subjects." Husserl says this in a 1917 manuscript, but he has similar ideas about the practical both earlier and later. Thus in the *Ideas* (1913) he says, "this world is there for me not only as a world of mere things, but also with the same immediacy as a world of values, a world of goods, a practical world."[10]

Just as Husserl never held that we first perceive bodies and bodily movements and then infer that there are persons and actions, or that we first perceive sense data that are then synthesized into physical objects, so it would be a grave misunderstanding of Husserl to attribute to him the view that we first perceive objects that have merely physical properties and then assign to them a value or a practical function. We experience things directly as having the features, functional and evaluational as well as factual, that are of concern for us in our natural pursuit of life.[11]

---

9. Edmund Husserl, *Erfahrung und Urteil* (Hamburg: F. Meiner, 1972), § 21a, p. 96. See also James S. Churchill and Karl Ameriks's English translation, *Experience and Judgment* (Evanston: Northwestern University Press, 1973), 89.

10. Husserl, *Ideen*, § 27, Husserliana III, 1, 58.13–19. See also Kersten, *Ideas*, 53; I have changed his translation slightly.

11. See Gorman's essay, Chapter 10 of this volume, for further reflection on this point.

HORIZON

When we are experiencing an object, our consciousness is focused on this object. The rest of the world and its various objects are there in the background as something we "believe in" but are not paying attention to at present. The same holds for most of the many features of the object itself. All these further features of the object, together with the world in which it is set, make up what Husserl calls the *horizon* of that experience. The various features of the object, which are co-intended, or also-meant, but not at the focus of our attention, Husserl calls the *inner horizon*, while the realm of other objects and the world to which they all belong he calls the *outer horizon:*

> Thus every experience of a particular thing has its *internal horizon*, and by "horizon" is meant here the *induction* which belongs essentially to every experience and is inseparable from it, being in the experience itself. The term "induction" is useful because it suggests [*vordeutet*] (itself an "induction") induction in the ordinary sense of a mode of inference and also because it implies that the latter, for its elucidation to be completely intelligible, must refer back to the original, basic anticipation.... However, this aiming-beyond [*Hinausmeinen*] is not only the anticipation of determinations which, insofar as they pertain to this object of experience, are now expected; in another respect it is also an aiming-beyond the thing itself ... to other objects of which we are aware at the same time, although at first they are merely in the background. This means that everything given in experience has not only an internal horizon but also an infinite, open, *external horizon of objects cogiven* .... These are objects toward which I am not now actually turned but toward which I can turn at any time.... all real things which at any given time are anticipated together or cogiven only in the background as an external horizon are known as real objects (or properties, relations, etc.) *from* the world, are known as existing within the one spatiotemporal horizon.[12]

To take a simple example of an item belonging to this outer horizon, if I ask people who are entering a lecture hall what their expectations are, they may mention something about friends they expect to meet, the lecture they expect to hear, and so on. It is highly unlikely that they would mention that they expect there to be a floor in the room. Yet, seeing them confidently stepping in, I would have every reason to believe that they expect there to be a floor. They do not think about it, their attention is directed to other things, but they have a disposition that they act on. Also, if I ask them whether they expect there to be a

---

12. Husserl, *Erfahrung und Urteil*, § 8, pp. 28–29; Churchill and Ameriks, *Experience and Judgment*, 32–33. The emphasis is Husserl's.

floor in the room, they might wonder why I would ask such an odd question, but they would probably answer yes.

Expectations and beliefs are dispositional notions. We count as beliefs not only thoughts that we are actively entertaining but also things that we rarely think about, for example, that two plus two equal four. We do have a problem when we try to delimit exactly what beliefs we have. The method of questioning is not reliable. On the one hand, it gives too much. Remember how in the *Menon* a skilled questioner uncovers that the slave boy has the most unexpected geometrical beliefs. Plato took this as evidence for his theory of *anamnesis*. On the other, it yields too little. As Freud and others have taught us, we often sincerely deny that we have beliefs that seem all too apparently to underlie our actions.

The most reliable criterion, one we often fall back on, is the assumption that people have those beliefs that best explain their actions, including their verbal activities. But the states we appeal to in order to explain people's actions are not exclusively cognitive states. Various physical states are needed as well, and skills of various kinds that are often hard to classify as mental. Thus, while our arithmetical skills are presumably mental, our skills in swimming or walking can hardly be classified as mental. Then we have tricky intermediate cases, such as one's keeping a standard distance from partners in a conversation, where the standard may vary from culture to culture. Is keeping this distance a matter of a tacit belief that it is the proper distance? Or is it a matter of a bodily skill that is gradually acquired as one grows up in this culture? And what about the way we sign our name?[13] Obviously, cognitive activities are involved in the process that brought us to sign it the way we do; we had to learn the alphabet, we had to learn our name, and so on. But also, in our semi-automatic way of signing it, bodily skills are involved to a great extent. Various personality traits play a role, as do certain general traits of our culture.

Opinions on activities such as these may vary, and we have no clear-cut way to settle such matters, lacking a precise definition of what is to count as mental, what as physical. But there is obviously an interplay here, both in the process that leads to the skill and in the skill itself, and any satisfactory theory of intentionality must take this interplay into account. The noema may still be defined as a structure, but the anticipations that are related through this structure are not merely the anticipations involved in seeing, hearing, and the like, but also the an-

---

13. The conversation example is Sam Todes's; the signing-one's-name example came up in conversations with David Wellbery.

ticipations involved in kinesthesis and bodily movement, which we become aware of when something "goes wrong." We are familiar with this experience of "going wrong" from cases of misperception: we cannot always tell exactly what went wrong, but we are aware that something did.

Husserl states already in the *Ideas* that we encounter the world "not only as a world of mere things, but also with the same immediacy as a world of values, a world of goods, a practical world." In later manuscripts, particularly after 1917, he focuses more and more on the role of the practical and the body in our constitution of the world. We have seen one aspect of this, namely, that we experience objects as having practical, or functional, and not just factual, properties. Husserl is very explicit about this. What I am now concerned with is a different and more difficult issue, namely, in what way the various features of the world, be they factual, valuational, or practical, are reflected in the noema. Here Husserl is less explicit and more tentative.

In an earlier paper[14] I have tried to show that Husserl would consider our anticipations not merely beliefs—about factual properties, value properties, and functional features—but also bodily settings, which are involved in kinesthesis and also play an important role in perception and in the movements of our body. In numerous passages, some of which I quoted in that paper, Husserl talks about practical anticipations and the role of kinesthesis in perception and bodily activity.

INTERSUBJECTIVITY

Husserl emphasizes that the world we intend and thereby constitute is not our own private world but an intersubjective world, common to and accessible to all of us. Thus in the *Ideas* he writes: "As what confronts me, I continually find at hand a spatio-temporal actuality [*Wirklichkeit*] to which I belong like all other human beings who are to be found in it and who are related to it as I am."[15] Husserl stresses the shared, intersubjective nature of the world particularly in § 29 of the *Ideas*, which he entitles "The 'Other' Ego-subjects and the Intersubjective Natural Surrounding World." He there says:

---

14. Dagfinn Føllesdal, "Husserl and Heidegger on the Role of Actions in the Constitution of the World," in *Essays in Honour of Jaakko Hintikka*, ed. E. Saarinen et al. (Dordrecht: Reidel, 1979), 365–78.

15. Husserl, *Ideen*, § 30, Husserliana III, 1, 61.15–18; Kersten, *Ideas*, 56–57, slightly modified by me.

I take their surrounding world and mine Objectively as one and the same world of which we are conscious, only in different ways [*Weise*].... For all that, we come to an understanding with our fellow human beings and together with them posit an Objective spatiotemporal reality.[16]

In the later works one finds similar ideas, particularly in the many texts that have been collected by Iso Kern in the three volumes of the Husserliana devoted to intersubjectivity (volumes 8, 14, and 15), but also in many other works, for example in the *Crisis:* "Thus in general the world exists not only for isolated men but for the community of men; and this is due to the fact that even what is straightforwardly perceptual is communal."[17]

THE PHENOMENOLOGICAL REDUCTION

In our daily life and also in the sciences we are normally concerned with objects in the world and their various properties. According to Husserl, in order to do phenomenology we have to carry out *two* modifications of this "natural attitude."

I. The Eidetic Reduction

The first of these modifications is one with which we are familiar from mathematics: instead of focusing on the individual physical object in front of us, we focus on what Husserl calls an essence *(Wesen)*, or *eidos*, instantiated by this object. Many philosophers would deny that there are such things as essences. Given Husserl's theory of intentionality, however, the notion of essences and experiences of essences comes naturally. I mentioned that a central point in Husserl's phenomenology is that I can have a variety of different noemata that are compatible with the present impingements upon my sensory surfaces. These noemata need not be of a physical object. For example, when I am looking at a triangle that has been drawn on a blackboard, I need not focus on this particular physical triangle, with all its irregularities. I can instead focus on the essence triangularity, which is exemplified by this particular material triangle but can also be exemplified by many other material objects. The essence is an object in its own right. It is not a temporal

---

16. Husserl, *Ideen*, § 29, Husserliana III, 1, 60.16–26; Kersten, *Ideas*, 55–56.
17. Husserl, *Die Krisis der europäischen Wissenschaften und die transzendentale Phänomenologie*, § 47, Husserliana VI, ed. Walter Biemel (The Hague: Martinus Nijhoff, 1976), 166.19–22. See also David Carr's translation, *The Crisis of European Sciences and Transcendental Phenomenology* (Evanston: Northwestern University Press, 1984), 163.

object that will disappear when the triangle on the blackboard is erased but has various properties that have long been studied in mathematics. Mathematics is the most highly developed study of essences, but Husserl holds that there can be systematic studies of other kinds of essences, for example, those that later came to be studied in topology. A special case of this is the essence of one-holed-ness that is exemplified by cups and donuts but not by no-hole objects, like glasses, or by two-hole objects, like pretzels. The change of attitude that leads from experience of individual physical objects to experience of essences Husserl calls the *eidetic reduction*. He calls it a reduction because it leaves out many of the specific anticipations that are involved in experiencing physical objects. And he calls it eidetic because it leads us to an *eidos*.

II. The Transcendental Reduction

The most important change in our attitude when we do phenomenology is that we reflect on our own consciousness rather than on the objects in the world around us. Husserl called this reflection a "reduction," too, since we are disregarding something that we focused on before the reflection, namely, the objects in the world around us. This brings us to the distinction that I mentioned at the outset, the distinction between the transcendent and the transcendental. Husserl calls the ordinary objects in the world around us *transcendent:* they are not part of our consciousness but are experienced as independent of our consciousness. Further, they are experienced as having more to them that what we are presently aware of; they have a wealth of properties that lie there waiting to be explored. Their richness of further features is inexhaustible; as we go on exploring them, new expectations of further features arise. These two features, not being part of our consciousness and being inexhaustible, can be regarded as defining of the transcendent.

The *transcendental* is that which we become aware of through the reflection. It could be defined as that which is crucial to our experience of the world, but which we do not notice in our ordinary natural attitude. In spite of the similarity of the two words, the transcendent and the transcendental are therefore radically different. The transcendental comprises the noema, which we have discussed above, and also the hyle. In addition, it comprises two further kinds of elements, what Husserl calls the *noesis* (plural *noeses*), and what he calls the *transcendental ego*. I am not going to discuss these here, but will only note briefly that the noeses are experiences that correspond to the noemata. As Husserl puts it, the noeses are the meaning-giving experiences in our acts, while the noemata are the meanings given in the acts. Just as the noemata, as we noted, is a structure, a comprehensive system of determinations, the noeses are the experiences thanks to which our consciousness has this structure. A parallel is the distinction between a judgment in the sense of an act of judging, and a judgment in the sense of the proposition that is the outcome of the act.

Each act will have a noesis, and corresponding to this noesis will be a noema. However, since the noema is nontemporal, two acts could, in principle, have the same noema, but never the same noesis, since the noeses are experiences, temporal events, that can be similar but not the same from one act to the next.

The transcendental ego is the transcendental, meaning-giving aspect of the ego, as opposed to the transcendent, empirical aspect, which we notice, for example, when we see ourselves in a mirror. Husserl often opposes the transcendental to the empirical ego, but he does mean that we have two egos. Rather, his view is that we each have one ego, but that this ego has two aspects, one empirical and one transcendental. This emphasis on aspects is typical of Husserl. We always experience things from a point of view, under a certain aspect. The things we experience are not themselves these aspects; they are full-fledged things that have many more aspects, aspects that can be experienced from other points of view, at other times or by other persons.

The *phenomenological* reduction, for Husserl, is the combination of the eidetic reduction and the transcendental reduction. Husserl does not require that the two reductions be performed in a specific order. Usually he starts with an eidetic reduction: he starts from an act that is focused on an individual physical object and then carries out an eidetic reduction, focusing on an eidos. Then he performs a transcendental reduction, focusing on the structures of our consciousness when we are experiencing this eidos. Alternatively, we may perform the transcendental reduction first: we start from an act that is focused on an individual physical object and carry out a transcendental reduction, where we focus on what our consciousness is like in such an act. Then we perform an eidetic reduction, where we single out some essential features of that consciousness. The objects we end up studying will not be the same in the two cases but will depend on the order in which we carry out the reductions. However, the study we carry out after we have performed the two reductions will in both cases be what Husserl called phenomenology.

THE DIFFERENT KINDS OF OBJECTS AND THE SCIENCES ABOUT THEM

With these distinctions in mind we can better map out Husserl's ontology and understand his rich and complicated list of kinds of categories. Figure 8.1 may help to clarify his various distinctions.

According to Husserl, there are four groups of objects, each group being explored by one particular science. The exact description of the contents of the quadrangles on the right side depends on the order in which the reductions are performed. Here we have assumed that the eidetic reduction is performed first, followed by the transcendental reduction. As just noted, this is the order Husserl most often used.

Note how the realm of ontology is divided into material and formal ontologies. In the material ontologies, one studies essences that can be instantiated only by physical objects, such as weight, physical shape, etc. The formal ontologies focus on essences that can be instantiated by any

FIGURE 8.1

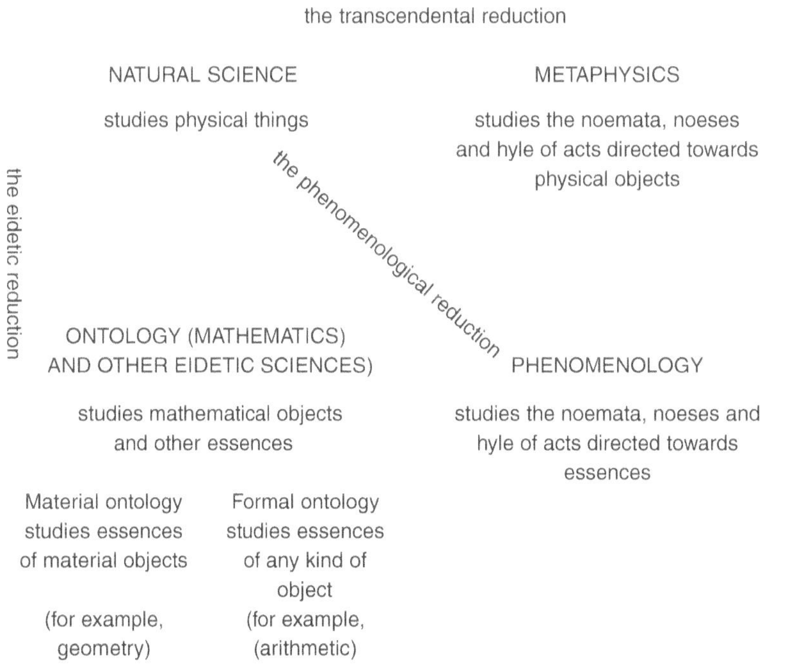

the transcendental reduction

NATURAL SCIENCE

studies physical things

METAPHYSICS

studies the noemata, noeses and hyle of acts directed towards physical objects

the eidetic reduction

the phenomenological reduction

ONTOLOGY (MATHEMATICS) AND OTHER EIDETIC SCIENCES)

studies mathematical objects and other essences

PHENOMENOLOGY

studies the noemata, noeses and hyle of acts directed towards essences

Material ontology studies essences of material objects

(for example, geometry)

Formal ontology studies essences of any kind of object

(for example, (arithmetic))

kind of object, including abstract ones. All objects can be counted, and numbers therefore belong to the formal ontologies.

For each of these basic realms of objects there will now be a kind of category. There are the noematic and noetic ones (the categories of the various sorts of noemata and noeses, respectively), eidetic categories, and so on for the other rubrics in the diagram. Although Husserl never gives a list of categories, there will be a set of categories for each basic kind of objects. Thus, going back to our list of kinds of categories at the beginning of the article, there will be a set of *object-categories* corresponding to the normal objects of acts:

| physical things | numbers | properties | relations | etc. |

Corresponding to these categories, there will be a set of *noematic categories:*

| noemata of physical things | noemata of numbers | noemata of properties | noemata of relations | etc. |

Likewise there will be a corresponding set of *noetic categories:*

| noeses of physical things | noeses of numbers | noeses of properties | noeses of relations | etc. |

The *eidetic categories,* to take the second item in the list given at the beginning of the essay, will be the various categories of eidos, such as numbers, geometrical shapes, and other general features that can be instantiated by various objects. The eidetic categories will therefore be a subclass of the object categories, namely, the categories of objects that are general features of other objects.

The *ontological categories* are just another label for the categories of objects that one studies in ontology, that is, the eidetic categories. Similarly for the other kinds of categories that were listed at the outset. It would be somewhat tedious to go through them all, but we can note that not all the kinds of categories on that list are specific to Husserl. Thus, for example, the logical, grammatical, and syntactical categories are standard categories that he takes over from Bolzano and uses in his analysis of language. Husserl distinguishes, as does Bolzano, logical form from grammatical form. Expressions belong to the same syntactical, or grammatical, category when they can be substituted for one another everywhere without turning a grammatical expression into a nongrammatical one. The logical categories are less refined; expressions belong to the same logical category when they can be substituted for one another without changing the logical form of expressions that contain them. General terms, singular terms, and sentences would be examples of logical categories. Husserl also includes among the logical categories the fundamental notions that are studied in logic, such as ground *(Grund)* and consequence *(Folge)*.

Husserl nowhere presents us with an organized list or table of categories. However, reflection on some of the crucial distinctions in his philosophy can enable us to understand his views on categories. The aim of this essay has been to contribute to that project.

9 Language-Games as Categories: An Aristotelian Theme in Wittgenstein's Later Thought

NEWTON GARVER

1. PREDICATES AND PREDICATIONS

Aristotle and Kant agree that the species of predicates (or concepts) go hand in hand with the species of predications (or judgments). Why these two classifications go hand in hand is not, in either case, a matter of empirical discovery but has to do instead with the very nature of the project. The project, in Aristotle's terms, in one of making sense of "things that are said."[1] In Kant's terms it is how judgments are possible, a judgment being in the first instance the determination that an object falls under a concept, that is, how a concept can be true of an object.[2] In these general terms the two projects are very much alike, and Kant says that he is clarifying what Aristotle did. Both Aristotle and Kant proceed in terms of subject-predicate logic, and the project is one of specifying at least some of the ways in which predicates can be true of subjects. The two classifications have to go hand in hand because they are both aimed at classifying things that are said. There are not in practice separate criteria for classifying predicates and for classifying predications.

They also largely agree that parts, logically and metaphysically, come before wholes: that one focuses on the classification of predicates or concepts in order to achieve a classification of predications or judgments. It is true that Kant first presents a table of judgments that is derived, he claims, from the logically possible forms of judgments, and then derives his table of categories from the table of judgments. But the table of judgments is hardly convincing, and the general line of his

---

[1]. For other reflections on Aristotle's categories, see the essays by Sanford, Lang, and Sim, Chapters 1, 2, and 5 of this volume.

[2]. For further reflection on Kant's categories, and on his practical categories in particular, see Quinn's essay, Chapter 6 of this volume.

argument is that different sorts of concepts (different categories) synthesize our intuitions and perceptions in different ways. He does not begin by differentiating the different sorts of synthesis.

The theoretical reasons for beginning with parts rather than wholes are complex and I will return to them toward the end of this essay. The issue is partly dependent on one's conception of the nature of logic, and especially on what one takes to be the most elementary logical forms. Aristotle's logic is a logic of terms, especially of subjects and predicates. These are parts of statements, the statements being constructed out of them, and so Aristotle naturally focuses on terms. Kant accepts Aristotelian logic and therefore follows him in this regard, although Kant's presentation of the possible forms of subject-predicate judgment is somewhat idiosyncratic. The main point is that a term logic, focusing on subjects and predicates, differs significantly from truth-functional logic, like that of Frege and Russell. Truth and falsity apply to judgments or predications rather than to their parts. A main shift in the philosophy of logic and the philosophy of language occurred with Frege's focus on propositions *(Gedanken)* as the primary or primitive elements of language and logic. In spite of this shift in the philosophy of language, there remains an attractiveness to starting with words, since we are conscious of building our sentences out of words, and it seems natural (metaphysically speaking) to derive sentences from words rather than the other way around.

The consequence of starting with kinds of words (predicates or concepts) rather than with kinds of statements (predications or judgments) is that the categories one derives are bound to be semantic categories. They are semantic in the sense that they derive from and apply to the meanings of words. Jerrold Katz, who accepts Frege's logic, has presented a sophisticated exposition of Aristotle's categories as semantic categories, making use of linguistic methods—he is indebted to Chomsky—that are thoroughly alive to modern logic. Katz begins with words, understood as signs together with their meaning, and explicates meaning in terms of abstract entities called "semantic markers." Logical relations hold among semantic markers, which are therefore the most basic logical forms as well as elements of meaning. Categories are the ultimate semantic markers, that is, those that do not entail any further semantic markers.[3] They are therefore the building blocks for lexical meaning and hence for the sense of "things that are said."

---

3. See Jerrold J. Katz, *The Philosophy of Language* (New York: Harper and Row, 1966). For discussion, see Newton Garver and S. C. Lee, *Derrida and Wittgenstein* (Philadelphia: Temple University Press, 1994), 160–68.

On the other side of the theoretical issue we find two considerations, one having to do with the nature of logic and the other with the relation of language and logic. Modern logic, beginning with Frege, regards the logic of propositions (truth-functions) as providing the most elementary logical forms and therefore tends to regard propositions (judgments, predications) as more basic than concepts. Frege insisted on this priority, not just as a matter of logic but quite generally:

> But we ought always to keep in mind a complete proposition. Only in a proposition do the words really have a meaning. The mental pictures that may pass before us need not correspond to the logical components of the judgement. It is enough if the proposition as a whole has a sense; its parts thereby also obtain their content. (Austin, 71; Beaney, 108)[4]

If we adopt a methodology based on Frege, our categories will not be semantic, since semantic meaning attaches to words. Instead our categories will distinguish different ways of saying things, or different things that are said, just as Aristotle initially put the matter, and will take its grip from the give-and-take of discourse rather than from abstract semantic markers. In the next section I will show that Aristotle made reference to the give-and-take of discourse in distinguishing categories. The perspective that categories distinguish different kinds of contribution to discourse, and hence precede rather than follow from logical form, gives deeper insight into Aristotle's naturalism, opens the way for conceiving of Wittgenstein's language-games as categories, and enables us to see logic as arising from natural language rather than the other way around.

2. ARISTOTLE'S NATURALISTIC CATEGORIES

Aristotle's *Categories* is powerful, cryptic, and puzzling. Placed at the beginning of the *Organon*, it forms an introduction to everything else, even to matters of logic and metaphysics. Because of this priority, it is perhaps no surprise that the work and its subject matter are difficult to focus. One can report and describe its features, but it is not easy to see how they fit together. Its features include a mixture of language and reality, a characteristic naturalism, a deference to ordinary ways of speaking, an equal deference to genus and difference (scientific classifica-

---

4. The first page reference is to J. L. Austin's translation of G. Frege, *The Foundations of Arithmetic* (Oxford: Blackwell, 1950), which retains the pagination of the original edition of 1884. The second reference is to Michael Beaney's more recent translation, in Beaney, *The Frege Reader* (Oxford: Blackwell, 1997).

tion), and an open-endedness both about what categories are and about how many there might be.

Aristotle begins talking about "things that are said" (*Categories*, 1a17) but then quickly talks about "things that are" (1a20) and about genera and their differentiae (1b16–24). The enigma of the first pages of Aristotle's work is the uncertainty about whether he is talking about speech-acts or about the world itself. Because of a greater philosophical interest in metaphysics, and Aristotle's reiteration (and modification) of points about categories in his *Metaphysics*, philosophers have generally looked at his views from the perspective of his metaphysics. While this is certainly an important perspective, more attention needs to be focused on the relation of categories to matters of language and logic. From this perspective Aristotle's views are more interesting and than is generally acknowledged.

Our word "category" comes from the Greek word meaning "statement" or "accusation," and the Latin translation of this word is *predicamentum*. The very word, therefore, makes reference to speech. Aristotle, however, is selective here: he has nothing to say in these pages about speech-acts such as greetings or warnings or exclamations or apologies. (He says some things elsewhere; tropes, for example, are discussed in the *Poetics*.) The "things that are said" are not all the things that are *uttered* in the course of human intercourse but are among things that are said in the sense of being *predicated*. Since predications, unlike some other speech-acts, have both a subject and a predicate, Aristotle has a category for expressions that serve only as subjects, as well as various categories for expressions that serve as predicates.

Differentiating categories, in the *Categories*, is not concerned with "carving up reality" but rather with carving up our discussion of reality. The main metaphysical issue involved, its principal metaphysical underpinning, is the preservation of reality from the corruption that derives from fudging of language and linguistic patterns. If being human is a category of *substance*, then something is either human or not; one thing cannot (in this category) be more human than another. Of course we can *say* that one person is more human than another, but by admitting a more or a less we shift from the category of substance to the category of quality. Separating the categories in this way is a way of preserving not only the integrity of speech but also, so to speak, the reality of reality. In this rejection of both naive realism and wholesale idealism, there lies wholesome commonsense caution rather than any grand scheme. And it is with such caution in mind that we should read Aristotle on categories.

Ackrill implicitly ascribes categories to the realm of discourse rather than to lexical meaning when he notes that "one way he [Aristotle] reached categorical classification was by observing that different types of answers are appropriate to different questions."[5] Answering a question about "What?" tends to identify a substance. Answering a question about "How much?" or "How many?" identifies a quantity. And so forth through the categories. Each of the categories Aristotle discusses can be seen as a way of talking or predicating that responds to a distinctive question. In this way of approaching the categories we are clearly treating them as a matter of discourse rather than as mere semantics.

A problem with going too far along this line is that it presupposes some way of distinguishing the questions used as the basis for the process. This is easy enough to do for Aristotle's categories, but it is by no means easy either to see how far this intuitive process could be carried out or to give an account of just what differentiates one type of question from another (for we seem clearly to be dealing with types of questions rather than with individual queries). Another problem is that this informal approach appears inappropriate for constructing a theory, since it would require treating questions as more basic than statements, which is questionable from either a philosophical or a linguistic point of view. Even if Ackrill is right that this is in part the way that Aristotle proceeds, we need to look deeper by examining more closely what he said about the individual categories. As we do so we see that the converse of Ackrill's remark also holds: each of the categories supports different follow-up questions, and also different follow-up comments. Let us look at an example.

Substance. "Substance, it seems, does not admit of a more or a less" (*Categories*, 3b33). Whether or not a predicate "admits of a more or a less" has to do with the discourse possibilities that are opened or closed by the use of that predicate in a predication. If X admits of a more or a less, I can ask whether a is more X than b, or whether a is less X today than it was yesterday. Aristotle's remark entails that such questions are ruled out if X has occurred in a substantial predication, and this is surely correct. If something is a sugar maple, then it makes no sense to suggest that it is more of one than the neighboring tree, or that it was less of one yesterday. Aristotle does not rule out the form of *words* but rather presents us with a criterion to determine to which category the words belong. I can indeed say, "This sugar maple is more of a sugar maple than that one," meaning that it produces more sap or better sap. Aristotle's point here is that the entry of "more" here shows that the predication is one of *quality* rather than *substance*.

---

5. J. L. Ackrill, *Aristotle's "Categories" and "De Interpretatione"* (Oxford: Clarendon Press, 1963), 79.

Note that it is clearly discourse features rather than semantic features that come into play in the use of this criterion. The same words with the same lexical meaning can occur in different kinds of predication.

Aristotle also says that a substantial predication involves not only *predicating* X of *a* but also *saying* X of *a*. The latter, but not the former, carries with it a commitment to predicate the definition of X of *a*. That is, both the genus of X and also the differentiae of it are also implicitly predicated of *a* when X is *said* of *a*. This obviously shapes the subsequent discourse possibilities. For example, when I am visiting a zoo and say that something is a penguin or a camel, I readily agree to predicate of that same thing the definition (genus and differentiae) of "penguin" or "camel." I intend to identify the substance, the kind of thing at hand. On the other hand, when e. e. cummings says, "a poet is a penguin; his wings are to swim with," he will refuse to predicate of the poet the genus or differentiae of penguins. We already know what poets are, and cummings is describing or characterizing them—making a qualitative rather than a substantive predication. Cummings *predicated* "penguin" of "poet" but did not *say* of poets that they are penguins. The distinction between *predicating* and *saying* is no doubt subtle, but Aristotle got it right.

Conversely, the discourse possibilities also determine the category. It is the failure of the discourse possibilities associated with the category of substance that show definitively that the remark of cummings about poets does not belong in the category of things that are said as predications about substance.

Admitting of a more or a less and *saying* as well as *predicating* are just two of several features—all of them discourse features—that Aristotle uses to distinguish categories. The list includes whether or not something is in a subject; whether or not something is said of a subject; whether or not something can have contraries; whether or not something can be called equal and unequal; whether or not something has a correlative that reciprocates. Aristotle makes repeated use of these features in distinguishing the categories from one another. In his discussion of each category at least two or three of the features are mentioned. Admitting a more and a less and admitting contraries are those most frequently cited, but there is no reason to think that they have a higher rank than other features. Nor is there any reason to think that one could not note further features, not mentioned by Aristotle, in attempting to extend Aristotle's discussion beyond where he left it off.

One important thing about the distinctive features Aristotle uses to identify the categories is that their affirmation connotes subsequent discourse possibilities, and their negation connotes subsequent discourse impossibilities, or in other words nonsense. The categories are therefore not *a priori*, for they cannot be determined except by looking at how we actually do speak. Nor are they scientific, for they have to do with the way we speak rather than with the world we speak about, and there is no empirical discipline, not even the cutting edge of linguistics, with a methodology competent to determine categories. Categories seem to be open-ended: certainly Aristotle did not pretend that his list was exhaustive, and it is unclear what sort of achievement ever could bring closure to the sort of investigation his work initiates.

3. KANT'S TRANSCENDENTAL CATEGORIES

In his *Critique of Pure Reason*, Kant found these uncertainties intolerable and he therefore changed the topic, though he says that his primary purpose is the same as Aristotle's (B105).

Kant does not begin with a discussion of categories. He begins instead by discussing how thinking is possible at all, noting that it presupposes two sorts of input: the passive input of the impressions (sensations) that are given to us and the active input of our spontaneous synthesis of these impressions so as to make them intelligible. While there may be other forms of synthesis (e.g., in fantasies or fairy tales), Kant focuses on the sort of synthesis that results in empirical predications or judgments. No particular impression or empirical judgment is necessary, but each and every impression or synthesis requires a framework within which to occur. Such a framework—and this is the core of Kant's transcendental idealism—has a necessity derived from the operation of our minds rather than from the external world. Kant takes space and time, which he calls the "forms of intuition," to be the transcendentally necessary framework of impressions, and he takes the categories to be *a priori* concepts that supply the transcendentally necessary framework for judgment.

Besides being transcendental rather than empirical, there are two other ways in which Kant's categories differ from Aristotle's. One is that they depend on rather than precede logic, and the other is that they constitute a closed rather than an open set.

Kant takes logic as a given, and he takes it for granted that Aristotle had presented in all essentials an adequate formulation of logic. He presents a "Table of Judgments" that contains, as he supposes, all twelve logically possible forms of judgment (B95). The forms are arrangements in four modes—Quantity, Quality, Modality, and Relation—with three variations within each of the modes. Any given proposition will combine several of these forms, with words that connote a certain modality, a certain quantity, and so on. This table is entitled "The Clue to the Discovery of All Pure Concepts of the Understanding." The categories are the "Pure Concepts of the Understanding," and Kant derives his twelve categories, also arranged in four groups of three, from this table. They are presented in the "Table of Categories" (B106).

Separate from the particular way in which Kant derives his categories is his idea that categories are a transcendental requirement of thought. Such a requirement is a conditional rather than an absolute or metaphysical requirement. It could be thought of as a new way of stating what Aristotle recognized, combined with the recognition (due to Hume) that any kind of necessity must be something other than empirical.

Immediately following his presentation of the "Table of Categories" Kant says that the table is "systematically generated from a common principle, namely the faculty for judging" (B106), and he claims that it is this principled derivation that makes the table complete, assuring his readers that it contains just the concepts of pure understanding and no others. He gives credit to Aristotle for the idea of categories but then says that, "since he had no principle, he rounded them up as he stumbled on them" (B107). Kant therefore takes the open-endedness of Aristotle's list as a fault, and thereby misses, or dismisses, the distinctive naturalism that marks Aristotle's work. Kant may have thought he was simply tidying up the loose ends of Aristotle's doctrine, but he completely changed the topic, as Ryle noted.[6] Kant's categories *follow* from logical principles rather than precede them, his method is transcendental rather than naturalistic, his divisions are therefore subject to weakness from the fallibility of Aristotelian logic, and he has completely severed the connections with language and linguistics.

4. TRANSCENDENTAL NECESSITIES GROUNDED IN LANGUAGE

There are four main areas of tension between Aristotle and Kant with respect to categories. The first is whether the list of categories is and ought to be closed or open-ended. The second, which perhaps depends in part on the first, is whether categories precede or follow from logical principles. The third is whether categories are a natural fact or a transcendental requirement. And the fourth, which is connected to the third and perhaps to all the others, has to do with the relation of categories to ordinary discourse and to linguistics.

---

6. Gilbert Ryle, "Categories," in *Collected Papers*, vol. 2, *Collected Essays, 1929–1968* (London: Hutchinson, 1971): 170–84.

Categories are not just facts. In spite of possible variability, they are necessary. Conceiving them as necessary features of reality rather than of our understanding is one form of transcendental illusion. Kant saw this because of Hume's insistence that there is no valid inference from an *is* to an *ought* or a *must*. His great contribution was his "Copernican Revolution," which leads to the recognition of transcendental illusion: that some of what we experience is grounded in our ways of perceiving and understanding rather than in the nature of what we perceive and understand.

5. LANGUAGE-GAMES AS CATEGORIES

In his "Notes on Logic" of 1913, Wittgenstein wrote,

Philosophy gives no pictures of reality.
Philosophy can neither confirm nor confute scientific investigations.
Philosophy consists of logic and metaphysics: logic is its basis.[7]

These cryptic remarks, each of which is given a separate paragraph, sketch the framework within which Wittgenstein fashioned his subsequent decades of philosophical work. He made continual refinements, so that many have supposed that even his framework changed. From beginning to end, however, it is left to science to describe life and the world. Wittgenstein never lets the framework become part of reality, and characterizing the framework is the work of philosophy. Logic, conceived broadly as the rules and principles of meaning and inference, gets to be called "grammar" and continues to supply the framework—but only the framework—for both descriptions and prescriptions. Confusing the framework with reality is likely to lead either to naive realism or to skeptical or relativistic idealism, and such confusion is characterized perspicuously as a kind of philosophical sin in *Philosophical Investigations* § 104: "We predicate of the thing what lies in the method of representing it. Impressed by the possibility of a comparison, we think we are perceiving a state of affairs of the highest generality." The idea expressed here is the essential core of Kant's "Copernican Revolution." The commonsense naturalism involved in it marks a point of accord among the three philosophers.

The framework is all-embracing. One cannot employ or invoke just one small corner of it, for any corner of it presupposes our whole language. In the *Tractatus* Wittgenstein expressed this by saying: "Although

---

7. Ludwig Wittgenstein, *Notebooks, 1914–1916*, 2d ed., ed. G. E. M Anscombe and G. H. von Wright, trans. G. E. M Anscombe (Oxford: Basil Blackwell, 1979), 106.

a proposition determines only one place in logical space, the whole of logical space must be given by it."[8] In the *Philosophical Investigations* it is perhaps § 199 that best expresses his continuing commitment to the need for an all-embracing framework, if one is to employ the rules that make it possible to understand anything at all:

> Is what we call 'obeying a rule' something that it would be possible for only *one* man to do only *once* in his life? —This is of course a note on the grammar of the expression 'to obey a rule.'
>
> It is not possible that there should have been only one occasion on which someone obeyed a rule. It is not possible that there should have been only one occasion on which a report was made, an order given or understood; and so on. — To obey a rule, to make a report, to give an order, to play a game of chess, are *customs* (uses, institutions).
>
> To understand a sentence means to understand a language. To understand a language means to be master of a technique.

In this passage Wittgenstein adapts both the pragmatism and the holism of Kant: concepts are not intellectual abstractions but the ability to do something, and they do not come isolated or piecemeal but bound up in a comprehensive system.

Wittgenstein introduces language-games and explains what they are without mentioning Aristotle or Kant. Knowingly or not, he incorporates main points from both of them. He parallels Aristotle both in the assumption that the categories/language-games are to be identified in the context of human activity and in the methodology by which they are distinguished from one another. His organization of the *Philosophical Investigations*, which begins with the introduction of language-games (§ 1–37), also parallels the organization of Aristotle's *Organon*, which begins with the discussion of categories. He parallels Kant in holding that no utterance can be understood without recognizing what language-game (category) it belongs to: nothing can be understood in isolation all by itself; for example, "one forgets that a great deal of stage-setting in language is presupposed if the mere act of naming is to make sense" (§ 257). That there must be language-games is therefore not an absolute necessity but a requirement of language (Kant's point), and what language-games are is therefore not fixed absolutely but is to be determined by noticing categorical differences in ways people use language (Aristotle's point).

---

8. Ludwig Wittgenstein, *Tractatus Logico-Philosophicus*, trans. David F. Pears and Brian McGuinness (London: Routledge and Kegan Paul, 1961), § 3.42.

6. RESTORATION OF ARISTOTELIAN NATURALISM

Consideration of categories confronts naturalism with its greatest challenge: what is the status of necessities?[9] Categories are necessities of a sort. We cannot get along without them, for individual utterances depend for their sense on their being understood as moves in one language-game or another. An individual utterance could no more be understood on its own than putting a circle or a cross in a square could be understood apart from the game of tic-tac-toe. What can the nature of this necessity be?

Since Hume, at least, it has been unsatisfactory to suppose that necessities are matters of fact. Wittgenstein says in the *Tractatus* (6.37) that there is only logical necessity, agreeing with Hume and apparently challenging both Aristotle and Kant. This point about necessity is not connected with the ideas about simple objects or independent elementary propositions that Wittgenstein rejected in his later work. It is part of the worldview he retained and refined. In the *Investigations* we find an echo of this remark about necessity in PI 104: "We predicate of the things what lies in the method of representing it," and again in PI 372: "Consider: 'The only correlate in language to an intrinsic necessity is an arbitrary rule. It is the only thing which one can milk out of this necessity into a proposition.'" In the first of these passages Wittgenstein reiterates his sense, in agreement with Kant, that metaphysics confuses talking about the framework with talking about the world. Elsewhere, in the same vein, he says that metaphysics—obviously in a pejorative sense—consists in blurring the distinction between grammatical and empirical propositions. These various remarks hang together with *Tractatus* 6.37 as crisscrossings of the same area, making and iterating in different words the same point Kant made in his "Copernican Revolution," namely, that we will not understand our experience of the world rightly until we firmly distinguish between what is due to the world and what is due to our ways of representing the world. Wittgenstein is perhaps firmer than Kant in insisting that modalities depend on our representations, since the world itself consists of plain fact.

Very well. But what is the status of our representations? Is it not just a plain fact that we do represent facts in the ways in which we do? Kant's answer seems to be that it is not just a plain fact but a transcendental necessity: we could not possibly make judgments any other way. Wittgenstein can be read as following Kant in this regard in his early

---

9. See Thalos's reflections on naturalism in Chapter 12 of this volume.

work, as Stenius, for example, suggests.[10] But however much Wittgenstein was inclined to ask a Kantian question in the *Tractatus*, it is clear that at the end of the work he erased the Kantian answer by throwing away the ladder. Coming back to the same area and crisscrossing it from another starting point in his later work, Wittgenstein gives an entirely Aristotelian answer. Language-games and the human mastery of the use of a language are just plain facts of human natural history—there is nothing transcendental there at all. The necessities and other modalities arise in the rules through which we describe and individuate the various uses of language. These rules are arbitrary in that they are not grounded in empirical fact (in some fact external to the language-game itself), and there is no necessity that we should engage in the language-game. If he wishes for a new slogan, Wittgenstein might then have said: "There are only grammatical necessities." The point is that the necessities we experience in our lives are not absolute metaphysical necessities but contingent necessities. They are, or arise in, features of our language-games, and these exist as just plain facts.[11] The language-games distinguish different types of "things that are said" and they therefore represent a revival and generalization of Aristotle's categories.

Categories are necessities that precede rather than follow from science; they remain stable as science changes. They also precede rather than follow from logic.[12] It is from the necessities inherent in language-games of assertion and reporting and other forms of truth-claims that we can abstract the forms of truth-functional logic, for which nothing further is required beyond the semantic contrasts that are inherent in such language-games. So logic as well as categories are determined naturalistically, the naturalism involved (natural history) being firmly distinguished from scientism.[13] Wittgenstein in this way revitalizes a kind of Aristotelian naturalism without denying the great insight of Hume.

---

10. Erik Stenius, *Wittgenstein's "Tractatus"* (Ithaca: Cornell University Press, 1960), esp. chap. 11.

11. Cf. essays by Sokolowski, Smith, and Gracia, Chapters 13, 14, and 16 of this volume.

12. See DeMarco's reflections on a similar idea in Chapter 15 of this volume.

13. See Peter F. Strawson, *Scepticism and Naturalism: Some Varieties* (New York: Columbia University Press, 1985). Strawson makes it clear that naturalism need not be identified with scientism, as is done in the article "Naturalism" by Arthur Danto in *The Encyclopedia of Philosophy* (New York, Macmillan, 1967), 4:448–50.

PART III
NORMATIVE CONSIDERATIONS

10 Categories and Normativity
MICHAEL GORMAN

Anyone who tries to understand categories soon runs into the problem of giving an account of the unity of a category. Call this the "unity problem." In this essay I describe a distinctive and under-studied version of the unity problem and discuss how it might be solved.

First, I describe various versions of the unity problem. Second, I focus on one version and argue that it is best dealt with by thinking of at least some categories as "norm-constituted," in a sense that I try to make clear. Third, I discuss some objections to my proposal. Fourth, I compare norm-constituted categories to categories that are normative in a different sense. Fifth, I briefly discuss the possibility of grounding the normativity of norm-constituted categories. Finally, I raise a few questions for further research.

Let me make two preliminary points. When I say "category" in this paper I am talking very generally about kinds or classes and not, in the specifically Aristotelian sense, about *highest* kinds or classes. And I am restricting my discussion to genuine categories as opposed to spurious ones; by "spurious" I mean categories like "games played in 1997 by red-headed boys." The restriction presupposes that there is such a distinction, but I cannot provide an account of it here.

VERSIONS OF THE UNITY PROBLEM

To think in terms of categories is to suppose that things belong in groups and that such groups have something to do with common traits of the individuals so grouped. What I am calling the "unity problem" is the problem of accounting for the unity of a group or category, that is to say, the problem of understanding what sort of commonality gives rise to a category's unity. And one reason why the unity problem is particularly problematic is that, typically, members of a category have not only commonality but also differences. We must explain how the commonality is not undermined by the differences. There are variations within categories, and we need to understand the unity that categories have in a way that is consistent with those variations.

There is no good reason to suppose ahead of time that there is a single unity problem or a single solution to it; perhaps there are several types of categories, each of which has a different type of unity. Hence it makes sense to speak of "versions" of the unity problem. A convenient way of uncovering two versions of the unity problem at once is by reflecting on a famous passage from Wittgenstein's *Philosophical Investigations*:

> Consider, for example, the proceedings that we call "games." I mean board-games, card-games, ball-games, competitive games, and so on. What is common to all of them?—Don't say: "There must be something common to them, or else they would not be called 'games'"—but look and see whether there is anything common to them all. For if you look at them you will not see something that is common to them *all*. . . . Are they all "amusing"? . . . [I]s there everywhere winning and losing, or competition between the players? . . . Look at the roles played by skill and luck. And how different skill in chess and skill in tennis are.[1]

Here Wittgenstein takes aim at the idea that categories have to have their unity in virtue of features shared by all their members. This suggests a distinction between categories that do have their unity in that way and categories that do not. Let us consider them in turn.

First, there are what we can call "rigid categories." Good examples of such categories come from geometry. Consider the category *triangle* and consider three figures: a triangle of area ten, a triangle of area twenty, and a square (of any area). These figures have various features. One is a feature that all the figures share, namely, that of being closed; another is a feature that only the first two share, namely, that of being three-sided; still another is a feature that the first has but that the second does not, namely, that of being of area ten. Now, the category *triangle* contains only figures that are closed and three-sided. Being both closed and three-sided is *non-optional* for being a triangle. This means that the third figure, the square, cannot be a triangle, whereas the first two, because they have the two stated non-optional features, can be triangles (one would have to be sure that there were no further requirements). No variation is permitted, then, with regard to having or not having non-optional features. Figures that lack them fail to be triangles. Note, however, that having this or that area is optional as far as membership in the category of triangles is concerned. This is what allows the

---

1. Ludwig Wittgenstein, *Philosophische Untersuchungen*, ed. Joachim Schulte (Frankfurt am Main: Suhrkamp Verlag, 2003), para. 66; 56–57. My translation.

first two figures both to belong to the category of triangles, despite the fact that they differ in area.

This gives us the following way of thinking about the unity of a category. For certain categories, the "rigid" ones, there is a distinction between non-optional and optional features. Whatever lacks a non-optional feature is not a member of the category in question; having the non-optional features is necessary for membership. For this kind of category, the unity problem is solved by insisting on unity in non-optional features and allowing for diversity in optional features.

This way of solving the unity problem does seem to work for some categories. As we have just seen, however, Wittgenstein points us to cases in which it seems *not* to work. He calls our attention to variations within the category "game," and he seems to be saying that there is nothing common to all the things we call games.[2] Using the terminology introduced above, he is saying that there are no non-optional features of games. This gives rise to a different kind of unity problem, the problem of accounting for the unity of categories whose members need not have features in common. Assuming that there really are categories of this sort, there are two basic responses. One is to take rigid categories as the only type of category and to conclude that games and the like are "not real categories." Another is to find a way of dealing with the unity problem different from that embodied in rigid categories. As is well known, this is the approach that Wittgenstein points us toward with what has come to be known as the "family resemblance" theory. Roughly, the idea is that relationships of similarity can bind members into a sufficiently strong unity, even if there are no distinguishing marks that all the members have. Wittgenstein's remarks have given rise to a fair amount of discussion. Just what is a family resemblance category?[3] Could all categories be of this sort?[4] Are family resemblance categories categories for which we can state necessary and sufficient con-

---

2. As Keith Campbell points out, this is wrong in a way that is easily set right. Of course there are features that all games share—for example, they all take place in time. The point is, rather, that games have "nothing in common sufficient for the predicate's use"; see Keith Campbell, "Family Resemblance Predicates," *American Philosophical Quarterly* 2 (1965): 241.

3. For just four of the many articles devoted to clarifying the notion of family resemblance, see Renford Bambrough, "Universals and Family Resemblances," *Proceedings of the Aristotelian Society* 61 (1960–61): 207–22; Campbell, "Family Resemblance Predicates"; Kathryn Pyne Parsons, "Three Concepts of Clusters," *Philosophy and Phenomenological Research* 33 (1973): 514–23; David Pears, "Universals," *Philosophical Quarterly* 1 (1951): 218–27.

4. For an argument in favor of a negative answer to this question, see Campbell, "Family Resemblance Predicates," 243; for an argument that a positive answer is not required, see Parsons, "Three Concepts of Clusters," 515–16.

ditions?[5] The issues are many and complicated. I do not intend here to add to this literature. Instead I would like to think about a third kind of category.

A good way of introducing this third kind of category is by reflecting further on the Wittgenstein text quoted above. When we encounter a game that does not involve competition, we might say, "Oh, it's a noncompetitive game," but we do not say, "There's something wrong with this game!" The variations that Wittgenstein is pointing to are not of a normative sort. Parallel variations could be found within the category *waterfowl*.[6] We can imagine Wittgenstein saying, "Consider the animals we call waterfowl. I mean whistling swans, wood ducks, hooded mergansers, and so on. What is common to them all? Do they all have long necks? Do they all perch in trees? Do they all dive under the water?" The answer in each case would be "no," and in none of these cases would we say that waterfowl that lack the traits mentioned have something wrong with them as waterfowl—lacking those traits would not make them defective waterfowl. Unlike wood ducks, hooded mergansers do not perch in trees, but that does not mean that there is something wrong with them as waterfowl.

But suppose our ornithological Wittgenstein were to proceed differently. "Consider the animals we call waterfowl. What is common to them all? Can they all fly? Do they all have working circulatory systems? Do they all have vision?" The answer would again be "no" to each of these questions. Some waterfowl have broken wings; some are about to die of heart failure; some have been blinded. Again we have variation, but this time with an important difference. Lacking features such as these means that there is a defect. There is something wrong with a waterfowl that cannot fly.

What sort of unity problem do we have with a category of this sort, a category, that is, that exhibits normative variations? We have the problem of explaining how a category can have both defective and nondefective members. Can this problem be solved by the rigid or the loose approach? It is not as easy as it might seem. Consider the rigid approach, which rests on the distinction between optional and non-

---

5. M. W. Beal argues that the question of whether members of a category have something in common is not the same as the question whether we can state necessary and sufficient conditions for that category; see M. W. Beal, "Essentialism and Closed Concepts," *Ratio* 16 (1974): 190–205.

6. I am following the nomenclature of Roger Tory Peterson, who uses the informal name "waterfowl" to refer to the family *Anatidae*, encompassing swans, geese, and ducks; other birds that we might be tempted to call "waterfowl," such as cormorants (family *Phalacrocoracidae*), are thus excluded by the term as I use it here. See *A Field Guide to the Birds of Eastern and Central North America*, 4th ed. (Boston: Houghton Mifflin, 1980), 42.

optional features. If we treat flying as a non-optional feature of waterfowl, then crippled waterfowl will be excluded from the category, which seems clearly to be wrong. If, on the other hand, we try to keep them in the category, it seems we will be able to do this only by thinking of flying as an optional feature of waterfowl. Two problems then arise. First, if features like flying turn out to be optional, then the range of what is optional expands enormously. Flying, seeing, having a working circulatory system, being feathered, and many other features all turn out to be optional. There are hardly any non-optional features left, and that is a problem, because the non-optional features are crucial for defining the borders of the category. How then could waterfowl be distinguished from cormorants, or squirrels, or stones? Second, although in one sense flying and the others are "optional" features, it seems clear that in another sense they are not. Diving and non-diving are different ways of being a waterfowl, but flying and non-flying are not. This suggests that there is another sense of "optional" that we need to take into consideration. I follow up on this suggestion in the next section of this essay.[7]

What about the family resemblance theory? Can it explain the unity of a category that exhibits normative variation? Couldn't we say that some non-flying birds are waterfowl because of their family resemblance to flying waterfowl? There are two problems with this approach. First, it leaves all features together in the same class. As was just pointed out, even if in one sense flying and diving are both optional, in another sense only one of them is, and a theory of the category's unity that does not respect this difference is inadequate. In other words, it is a mistake to buy the unity of the category at the price of due attention to the diversity within it. Second, in practice, it seems unlikely that the family resemblance approach would do the job. A waterfowl that lacked a sufficient number of the features it should have might be indistinguishable from a bird of another category that lacked a sufficient number of the features it should have; at least in principle, a defective swan and a defective cormorant could have more family resemblances to each other than to the members of the families they do in fact belong to. So, whatever its merit might be in handling the unity problem for certain kinds of classes, the family resemblance theory seems inadequate to the task of solving the unity problem for categories with normative variations.

One of the arguments just given against using the family resemblance approach to solve the normative version of the unity problem is

---

7. An Aristotelian-minded philosopher might object that a biological category could be treated rigidly by saying that *having a certain kind of soul* was what unified the category. This will be discussed in the next-to-last section of the paper.

that it treats normative and nonnormative differences in the same way, i.e., that it solves the unity problem by ignoring a difference that ought not to be ignored. Other possible solutions are inadequate for the same reason. Consider the idea that one might appeal to *ceteris paribus* laws by saying that the *Anatidae* are governed by laws of the form "*Anatidae* can fly, all other things being equal." The best theory of what *ceteris paribus* laws mean seems to be the one that says that they express (overrideable) tendencies. That approach, however, does not help us here; the point is not just that *Anatidae* have a tendency to fly, a tendency that can be overridden, but also that it is normal and good for them to be able to do so, a point that is invisible to the *ceteris paribus* approach.[8]

Other approaches that do not work for much the same reason can be drawn specifically from biology; since biological categories are the main examples under consideration here, that restriction hardly makes them irrelevant. If it seems difficult to explain how something can belong to a category while lacking what would appear to be an important characteristic, perhaps one should define the borders of the category by reference to something other than what would normally be thought of as "characteristics." For example, one can think of the unity of a biological species in terms of evolutionary descent, so that individuals are conspecific if they are descended from a single population group having its own evolutionary role, or one can think of the unity of a biological species in terms of reproductive isolation. Either of these ways of thinking includes abnormal instances within their classes, which is desirable, but it does so by making invisible the difference between normal instances (which possess the relevant characteristic) and abnormal instances (which lack it).[9]

This point about non-characterological approaches to categories brings out a further important issue. The normative version of the unity problem arises only when we think of a category in terms of the characteristics that its members have.[10] This does not mean that other ways

---

8. For *ceteris paribus* laws understood as expressing tendencies, see Terence Horgan and John Tienson, "Soft Laws," in *Midwest Studies in Philosophy* 15 (1990): 256–79; Peter Lipton, "All Else Being Equal," *Philosophy* 74 (1999): 155–68; Harold Kincaid, "Defending Laws in the Social Sciences," *Philosophy of the Social Sciences* 20 (1990): 56–83.

9. For these and other ways of thinking of biological species, see Michael Ruse, "Biological Species: Natural Kinds, Individuals, or What?" *British Journal of the Philosophy of Science* 38 (1987): 225–42. For confirmation that the genealogical approach does not account for normativity, see David L. Hull, *The Metaphysics of Evolution* (Albany: State University of New York Press, 1989), 12, 17–22.

10. For biological examples, this means thinking in phenotypic or genotypic terms, but it does not matter which.

of thinking about the very same categories should be ruled out. But neither should we abandon a characterological approach. Even if we accept for the sake of argument that non-characterological approaches solve the normativity problem, albeit by being blind to it, still it is important to show how the normativity problem can be solved from within a characterological approach. Otherwise there will be too large a gap between prescientific intuitions, which are characterological, and non-characterological approaches. In the long run, it would be better to show how the various approaches converge.[11]

In light of all these difficulties and failed attempts, one might be tempted to say that the fact that categories such as the *Anatidae* exhibit normative variations proves that they are not really categories, or at any rate only second-rate categories.[12] But perhaps it is better to think in terms of a third kind of category and a third kind of unity problem. In this third kind of category, there can be variation within "non-optional" features, where "non-optional" means something different from what it means in the rigid and loose theories. In the next section, I will propose a solution to the unity problem for this kind of category by explaining this different sense of the optional/non-optional distinction, showing how it can be related to the other sense of the distinction, and showing how it can be used to solve the normative version of the unity problem.

NORM-CONSTITUTED CATEGORIES

In this section I propose a solution to the unity problem for categories exhibiting normative variation. Recall that this is the problem of figuring out how to draw the borders of a category in a way that includes defective members, without saying that features like flying are purely optional. So the first step is to work out the alternative sense of the optional/non-optional distinction. An optional feature, in this new sense, is a feature such that lacking it does not constitute being defec-

---

11. In "Biological Species," Ruse describes not only a species-concept framed in terms of descent and a species-concept framed in terms of reproductive isolation, but also a species-concept framed in terms of morphology and a species-concept framed in terms of genetics. But these, he argues, reinforce rather than compete with one another.
12. Evan Fales says, "The fact is that there can be and sometimes are monstrous genotypes as well as phenotypic freaks, of greater and lesser degrees. This militates against the existence of strict classification-producing *de re* necessities regarding biological species and individual organisms." Evan Fales, "Natural Kinds and Freaks of Nature," *Philosophy of Science* 49 (1982): 85. For Fales, although there are strict kinds at the level of "fundamental entities"—e.g., basic particles—only a weak and exception-ridden system of classification holds at the level of "derivative entities," among them biological organisms.

tive. Non-optional features, by contrast, are features such that lacking them does constitute having a defect. A waterfowl that cannot fly is a waterfowl, but it is a defective waterfowl. Flying is thus a "non-optional" feature of waterfowl in what we can call the "normative" sense of the optional/non-optional distinction. And let us call the earlier sense of the distinction, the one that worked so well for triangles, the "nonnormative" sense.

As we have seen, flying is optional for waterfowl in the nonnormative sense of the "optional/non-optional" distinction, the sense that was inadequate to the task of solving this version of the unity problem. That sense was tailor-made for categories that do not exhibit normative variation, categories of which there are no defective members. There are no defective triangles—a figure that one might be tempted to call a defective triangle is in fact not a triangle at all, but some other figure. Now, however, we have a sense of the optional/non-optional distinction that is more appropriate to the kind of category we are dealing with, a sense that allows us to say that flying is non-optional for waterfowl. But how can we put it to use to solve the unity problem?

The way to proceed is by reflecting further on what is presupposed by this whole line of thinking. To speak in terms of normative variation is to presuppose that, for some categories of things, there is such a thing as the way something should be. A waterfowl, for example, *should* be able to fly. This is something that is true of every waterfowl. We can speak of this by saying that there is a norm, a norm that states that waterfowl should be able to fly, and that every waterfowl is subservient to this norm.[13]

The "should" involved here is not in any way a moral sort of "should." To say that a non-flying waterfowl is "not what it should be" is to say not that it is being wicked but only that it is imperfect or defective in a completely non-moral way. If someone were to reply that words like "norm," "should," and so on apply only in the realm of human action, I would reply in two ways. First, I would deny that we do actually use the words only in that way. Second, I would give the objector the use of those words and find different ones. In other words, if someone wants to argue that it isn't right to say that a wingless waterfowl "is not what it should be" but grants that such a bird is "imperfect" or "abnormal," then I can agree for the sake of argument but then dismiss the point as merely terminological.

---

13. For further discussion of the notion of norm-subservience, see my "Subjectivism about Normativity and the Normativity of Intentional States," *International Philosophical Quarterly* 43 (2003): 5–14.

Now then, if it is true of every waterfowl that it ought to be able to fly, then we can say that every waterfowl has the property or feature of *being such that it ought to be able to fly*. This allows us to solve the unity problem for this kind of category. Just for the sake of having a handy phrase, let us say that everything that should be able to fly is "subject to the norm of flying." Then we can put it like this: although some waterfowl can fly and some cannot, all are subject to the norm of flying, all have the feature of being subject to the norm of flying. Having this feature is a necessary condition of being a waterfowl, so something that didn't have it would not be one—even if it had wings, feathers, and all the rest.

The move that I am making can be made clearer as follows. In the normative sense, it is optional for waterfowl that they be, for example, of a certain color, and non-optional that they be able to fly. Seeing that color falls on one side of this distinction while flying falls on the other is an important insight into the nature of waterfowl. And my proposal is to exploit this insight by taking normatively non-optional features as clues or pointers to nonnormatively non-optional features. The feature *being able to fly* is normatively non-optional, and this fact points us to the nonnormatively non-optional feature *being subject to the norm of flying*. While the category waterfowl admits of both flying and non-flying members, it does not admit of both members that are subject to the norm of flying and members that are not. It is a necessary condition of being a waterfowl that one be subject to the norm of flying. Thus we have, in a way, figured out how to reduce normative categories to a kind of rigid category. Nonetheless, we have done this only by making the important move of appealing to normative features, features the having of which consists in being subservient or subject to a certain norm. For this reason, it is appropriate to distinguish this kind of rigid category from the ordinary kind by calling it a "norm-constituted" category. The normative requirement is constitutive of the category in the sense that membership in the category is determined by whether or not something is subject to the norm.

One way of clarifying the interplay between the two senses of the optional/non-optional distinction is by reflecting on something once said by Hilary Putnam. In "The Analytic and the Synthetic" he writes, "We are no longer so happy with the Aristotelian idea that a necessary truth can have exceptions."[14] It seems right to say that a necessary truth can-

---

14. Hilary Putnam, "The Analytic and the Synthetic," in Hilary Putnam, *Mind, Language, and Reality: Philosophical Papers*, vol. 2 (Cambridge: Cambridge University Press, 1975), 52.

not have exceptions, but the insight behind this Aristotelian idea can be saved by making a distinction. Suppose someone were to say that, necessarily, waterfowl can fly. What would this actually mean? Interpreted one way, it would mean that every waterfowl is subject to the norm of flying; this claim would be necessary and would admit of no exceptions. Interpreted another way, it would mean that every waterfowl could in fact fly; this claim would admit of exceptions and would not be necessary. So the "Aristotelian idea" is not really that a necessary truth can have exceptions. There is a non-necessary reading, the one that doesn't rest on normative features, and this reading admits of exceptions. There is also a necessary reading, the one that rests on normative features, and this one admits of no exceptions.

Putting things in a way that is easy to grasp but not perfectly accurate, then, we can say that a norm-constituted category is one whose members belong to it not in virtue of what they are but rather in virtue of what they should be. Putting it more accurately, we can say that a norm-constituted category is one whose members belong to it in virtue of what they are, but what they are is this: subject to a norm or set of norms. They *are* such that they *should be* such-and-such.[15]

Still more accuracy can be gained by noting that the normatively non-optional features one would point to in defining normative features are not all of the same sort. To begin with, some are such that lacking them results in more or less immediate death; having a working circulatory system is, for waterfowl, a feature of this type. Others, by contrast, are such that lacking them results only in a failure to flourish; having the right number of legs would be a good example. (Probably the line between these two sorts of features is not perfectly sharp.) Further, some features are such that lacking them makes it impossible for an individual of the kind in question to exist in any way at all, even for a short time; animals, for example, absolutely must be physical objects. Now, it would perhaps sound strange to call it a "defect" in an animal not to be a physical object, and this suggests that this feature is not the basis of a normative feature. It would follow that there could be norm-

---

15. Richard Mohr appears to propose a theory of this type when he argues that universals are best thought of as "standards"; however, the way he develops his theory makes it clear that he does not mean "standard" in a normative way but only as something to which other things are compared. See Richard Mohr, "Family Resemblance, Platonism, Universals," *Canadian Journal of Philosophy* 7 (1977): 593–600. David Weissman grounds certain kinds of general truths in what he calls kinds that have "normative force," but he does not mean what I mean when talking about normativity and kinds; he means to speak of kinds that involve immanent, observer-independent necessities of form. See David Weissman, *Truth's Debt to Value* (New Haven: Yale University Press, 1993), chap. 5, esp. 235–38, 244–45, 255–58, 261–63, 277–79.

constituted categories that were not wholly norm-constituted but instead were hybrids.

This last remark points to the fact that what I have done is only to show how the normative variations within a category can be handled in a way that does not destroy the category's unity. There might be other variations within the very same category that would have to be handled differently—by a more straightforward, nonnormative use of the rigid approach, or by an appeal to family resemblance, or in some other way.

Thus we have an outline for a solution to the unity problem for categories with normative variations. It is only an outline because in each particular case—waterfowl, mallard, squirrel, oak, and so on—the details would have to be worked out on the basis of actual knowledge of the category in question. In other words, for any given category, what counts as normative and what does not cannot be settled solely through armchair analysis. Fieldwork is required.

Before moving on, let us look at some other approaches that attempt to take the normative issues seriously. Two authors who have developed ideas somewhat similar to these are Ruth Garrett Millikan and Nicholas Wolterstorff. Discussing things that are defined in terms of function, Millikan states the issue well: it is possible for something to be a failed or defective can opener or mating display; the question is what makes it a can opener or mating display. Her answer is similar to mine in that she sees being subject to a norm as crucial. However, my account of norm-constituted categories is more general, being aimed not only at function-categories but also at substance-categories, such as *Anatida;* further, I would treat the metaphysical grounding of norms quite differently from Millikan, as will become apparent below.[16] Wolterstorff's "norm-kinds" are similar to my "norm-constituted categories." However, my interest in the unity problem leads me to draw out a point that Wolterstorff does not, namely, that it is crucial to every instance of a norm-constituted kind that it be subject to the norms governing that kind. Further, because Wolterstorff is discussing art, which relies on human intention, his account of the basis of the normativity involved in kinds is quite different from the account that I give concerning kinds found in nature (see below).[17]

A different approach to the problem of defective instances can be found in the work of E. J. Lowe and Stephen Mumford. Despite their

---

16. For "function-categories," see Ruth Garrett Millikan, *White Queen Psychology and Other Essays for Alice* (Cambridge: MIT Press, 1993), 21ff.

17. See Nicholas Wolterstorff, *Works and Worlds of Art* (Oxford: Clarendon Press, 1980), 45–84, esp. 56–57.

disagreements, they both approach the issue from the standpoint of laws of nature, instead of from the standpoint of categories. Instead of asking how a defective instance of a category can still be a member of that category, they ask how there can be laws of nature that admit of exceptions. To use their example, they ask how it can be a law that all ravens are black, given that there are albino ravens. Both hold that the answer is in construing laws of nature as "disposition ascriptions to sorts or kinds";[18] in other words, when we say that all ravens are black, we don't mean "$\forall x$ (x is a raven $\supset$ x is black)," which admits of no exceptions; instead we mean that instances of the kind "raven" have a disposition to blackness in a way that makes non-black ravens both possible and abnormal.

Mumford and Lowe disagree over whether natural laws should be thought of as "normative." For Lowe, they should, while for Mumford this ought to be resisted, both because the proper grounding of normativity is hard to find and because the differences between laws of nature and paradigm cases of normative laws make the label "normative" suspicious. But both Lowe's and Mumford's accounts are "normative" in the sense I am concerned with, because both want to acknowledge the reality of abnormal cases and nonetheless include them together with the normal cases. So the question for us here is: can thinking of laws of nature as attributions of dispositions to sorts or kinds be a good solution to the normative version of the unity problem? I believe the answer is no. The disposition-ascription approach to laws is a way of making sense of laws of nature, but any application of such laws presupposes (quite legitimately) that we know which things are subject to which laws. For example, suppose we find a white bird; should we treat it as an abnormal raven or as a normal bird of some other species? The thought that ravens are dispositionally (normatively) black is not relevant until we know whether the bird in question is in fact a raven. So the disposition-ascription approach to laws of nature, whatever its merits, does not solve the unity problem but rather presupposes that it has a solution. (Nor, it should be added, is that approach to laws of nature intended to solve the unity problem; I am not attacking that theory but only pointing out one thing it does not do.)

---

18. Stephen Mumford, "Normative and Natural Laws," *Philosophy* 75 (2000): 278. For Lowe's position, see E. J. Lowe, "Sortal Terms and Natural Laws," *American Philosophical Quarterly* 17 (1980): 253–60; "Laws, Dispositions, and Sortal Logic," *American Philosophical Quarterly* 19 (1982): 41–51; and *Kinds of Being* (Oxford: Blackwell, 1989), chaps. 8–10.

SOME OBJECTIONS

Now I turn to five objections to the proposal I have been making. The first calls into question the entire project, as follows. There is no solution to the unity problem for categories exhibiting normative variation, according to this objection, because there are no norms (except perhaps those imposed by observers). Believing in norms is part of failing to accept the naturalistic worldview, a worldview according to which no states of affairs are better than any others, there is no difference between normal and abnormal, and so forth.[19] On this basis, one could argue that there is no special kind of category definable on the basis of variation in normative properties.

A full-scale reply to this objection would be an essay in itself. It goes without saying that I myself think that there are norms and normative features, but I cannot argue for it here.[20] Those who accept norms can think of this essay as an exploration of their kind of philosophy. Those who do not can think of it as a kind of thought experiment: assuming there were normative features, and assuming there were categories that exhibited normative variations, this is how one could solve the unity problem for such categories.

The next three objections all share the aim of casting doubt on the idea that biological species are normatively constituted categories. For different reasons, these objections say that modern, post-Darwinian biology has shown that biological species are not properly thought of as norm-constituted categories. Before dealing with them individually, I would like to discuss a certain way of responding to them collectively. I could simply point out that my argument concerns the nature of norm-constituted categories in general and does not depend on any particular example's being a good one. In other words, I could grant that biological examples are not good ones but insist that my analysis holds for whatever other examples there might be. The weakness of this reply, however, is that biological categories appear to be the best examples of norm-constituted categories. If normality is not found in biology, it is hard to imagine how it could be found anywhere. For this reason, it is

---

19. As Barry Stroud puts it, "Naturalism is widely understood to imply that no evaluative states of affairs or properties are part of the world of nature"; see Barry Stroud, "The Charm of Naturalism," *Proceedings and Addresses of the American Philosophical Association* 70 (1996): 50; see also 53–54. For another example, see John Searle, *The Construction of Social Reality* (New York: Free Press, 1995), 13–16. For complications concerning Searle, see my "Intentionality, Normativity, and a Problem for Searle," *Dialogue: Canadian Philosophical Review* 41 (2002): 703–13.

20. For an argument, see Gorman, "Subjectivism about Normativity and the Normativity of Intentional States."

wise not to rely too much on this reply and instead to deal with each of the objections head-on.

The second objection, then, points out that modern biology does very well without normativity[21] and goes on to say that this shows that biological categories are not norm-constituted. In reply, it should first be noted that the pre-philosophical attitude includes the idea that there is a difference between the normal and the abnormal in the living world; this is a very strong intuition that should not be cast aside lightly. Now, has modern biology really shown that normativity has no place? Modern biology could instead be understood as abstracting from such considerations to focus on natural selection and other such nonnormative causes. That taking this approach brings a lot of success is not open to doubt, but it does not follow that it is the only possible way of looking at the living world, or the final and most complete way. There might well be a bigger picture that includes norms, a picture into which the nonnormative aspect fits as a crucial part but a part nonetheless. (Analogously, the fact that it is helpful to abstract from the difference between people and luggage when calculating how much fuel to put into an airplane doesn't mean that there is no difference between people and luggage.) Working out how the whole fits together would be a great philosophical task; for present purposes the point is merely that the fact that a particular approach works well does not prove that it is comprehensive or that all other approaches are no good at all. And that is enough to let us go on with our current discussion of normative categories, using biological categories as the most likely examples.

The third objection points out that, according to modern biology, species are not clearly distinguishable from one another. Whether we think in phenotypic or genotypic terms, there are enough interspecific similarities and intraspecific differences to force us to reconceive species as peaks on a continuous characterological graph, rather than as discrete groupings of organisms.[22] Kinds of warblers, for example,

21. Cf., for example, Hull, *Metaphysics of Evolution*, 17–22, who argues that notions of normality have little significance in biology.

22. "A traditional assumption that dates back at least to Aristotle is that organisms could be unambiguously sorted into discrete kinds on the basis of overt morphological characteristics. Since the theory of evolution undermined the belief in the fixity of species, this assumption has become increasingly untenable. It is now widely agreed that gross morphological properties are not sufficient for the unambiguous and exhaustive partition of individuals into species. Crudely, this is because there is considerable intraspecific variation with respect to any such property, and the range of variation of a property within a species will often overlap the range of variation of the same property within other species. . . . [I]t may be thought that some description of the genetic material could capture a genuinely essential, or at least privileged, property. . . . But it is equally

shade over into other kinds. If this is so, then the idea that species represent natural kinds appears highly questionable. Perhaps species are conventional groupings, formed when biologists draw lines where nature has none. And then, *a fortiori*, this would undermine the idea that biological species are norm-constituted categories. If we cannot clearly mark off one species from another in terms of its traits, then *a fortiori* we cannot mark off one species from another in terms of its normative traits, and therefore we cannot appeal to such traits to solve the unity problem.

There are two replies to this objection. First, it mistakes the purpose of my account. I do not need to give a complete theory of what makes for the unity of a biological species, but only to show how defective instances can be fitted in. The question of what, for instance, settles whether or not the Bullock's Oriole and the Baltimore Oriole are conspecific is distinct from the question of how we may include a defective Baltimore Oriole in its species. This leads to the second reply. Even if there can be fuzzy borders between species, and thus features for which there is no clear answer to the question "Is this a proper characteristic of the species?" nonetheless there are many features, including many normative features, that are unquestionably characteristic of their species. Even if there is some unclarity about how many species of Oriole there are, it is altogether clear that it is normal for Orioles to have wings, feathers, and legs, be able to fly, and so on. The lack of clear breaks between species, then, does not mean that we are unable to talk about them as norm-constituted categories.

A fourth objection concerns evolution. Modern biology has taught us not only to think of species as having fuzzy borders but also as being subject to change over time; the borders are not only fuzzy but also in motion. This could be taken as another reason for worrying about the fixity of features and therefore, *a fortiori*, of normative features. Even if it is clearly the case that a given feature is normatively non-optional today, it might not be a few million years from now, when a new species has emerged. Now, the case of an established new species might not be a problem, because such a case is precisely a case in which we would expect there to be differences in normative traits; but what about in the interim, the transitional time during which a group of organisms originally belonging to one species is evolving into another? Wouldn't it be

---

possible that there should be as much or more genetic variability as morphological variability. That is, intraspecific genetic variability may overlap interspecific variation as much as, or more than, morphological variability does. In fact, there are good reasons for supposing this to be the case." John Dupré, "Natural Kinds and Biological Taxa," *Philosophical Review* 90 (1981): 84.

unclear whether the organisms had a certain normative trait, in which case we wouldn't be able to use it to solve the unity problem?

A reply can be constructed on the basis of what has been said to the previous objection. Suppose that a population belonging to a certain species of warbler is in the process of evolving into a new species. This new species, presumably, is still going to be fairly similar to the original species; it is not, for example, going to be a species of seagoing mammals. So there is going to be a great deal of continuity between the old and the new species, and in the continuity zone there will be clear cases of normative features, even though there will also be a range of features whose status is unclear. Thus, just as in the previous case, the normative version of the unity problem can be raised and addressed without needing to hold that species boundaries are precisely fixed in every respect. Variation at the edges can coexist with stability at the center, even through changes across the species barrier.

A fifth objection concerns the particular solution I have proposed. Thinking of categories as norm-constituted, one might say, makes them mysterious and even mystical. If a waterfowl is something that actually has certain nonnormative features, then we have tolerably clear grounds for saying what is and is not a waterfowl. But when we start saying that a waterfowl is something that *should* have certain features, we cannot tell by investigation what is a waterfowl and what is not. "Being subject to the norm of flying" doesn't sound like a property that someone could investigate; putting it differently, it sounds like a property someone could have and never know it. For all I know, I myself am only a very strange bird.

In response to this objection, I would first point out that it is very "theoretical" in the pejorative sense of that term. There is no reason to suspect that I am a duck or a swan and not a human. Second, we can in fact tell—almost always, at any rate—what is a waterfowl and what is not. For one thing, many waterfowl that lack important normatively non-optional traits still have other traits that suggest strongly that they are waterfowl. For another, suppose there is some animal that lacks a given anatidian trait, and suppose that makes us doubt whether it is a waterfowl at all. We can ask the following question: "If it were to gain the anatidian trait it lacks, would its existence or flourishing be enhanced?" If it would, then we have reason to think that, despite its lacking that trait, it is a waterfowl; if it wouldn't, then we don't. Now, actually, this response requires a fair bit of refinement. The question to ask should really be something like, "If it were to gain the trait it lacks without undergoing a major anatomical and physiological overhaul, would its existence or flourishing be enhanced?" The point of speaking about a "major overhaul" is this. It might seem that humans would be better off with feathered wings, but just adding wings would not help. More and bigger muscles, lighter bones, and so on would all have to be added, and this would require the elimination of some, perhaps many, of our current (human) features. The fact that a wide-ranging restructuring would be needed counts against the suggestion that we ought to have wings; we are just not "designed" to have them. But this is not the place to work out such details. Third, the mere fact that we can make mistakes about the category that something belongs to does not mean that the categories are not real. The theory I am proposing is compatible with a thoroughgoing modesty about our epistemic powers.

NORM-CONSTITUTED CATEGORIES AND EVALUATIVE CATEGORIES

I have been calling certain categories "norm-constituted." The reason I have not been calling them by the simpler name "normative" is that there is more than one way for categories to be involved with norms. So let us turn to a discussion of what I will call "evaluative categories." An evaluative category is a category like "good" or "justified." The first thing to note about evaluative categories is that they are not norm-constituted. Recall that a norm-constituted category is a category that something is in only if it ought to have such and such a feature. If an evaluative category were norm-constituted, then we would be saying something like this: a belief is justified only if it *should* be such and such. But that is not what it is for a belief to be justified. A belief is not justified by virtue of the fact that it should be something; instead, it is justified by virtue of the fact that it actually is one of the things it should be. A belief is justified only if it actually fulfills certain requirements. So an evaluative category is not norm-constituted; it is instead a category that things belong to when (a) they are themselves members of a norm-constituted category and (b) they actually adhere (or fail to adhere—there are negative evaluative categories too) to the requirements constituting that norm-constituted category. Some evaluative categories are rather general, specifying only that norms have (or have not) been adhered to—"good" is close to a fully generic evaluation. Other evaluative categories are domain-specific—"justified" is a good example.

GROUNDING NORMATIVE FEATURES

The main goal of this essay, to set forth the normative version of the unity problem and explain how appealing to normative features can solve it, has been accomplished. Now I would like to discuss, briefly, a question one might raise about grounding normative features. Perhaps it is the case, one might say, that normativity isn't mystical in the sense that it can only be divined through some magical means; perhaps, in other words, it's true enough that, at least most of the time, we can tell which norms a given being is subject to. But to grant this is only to grant an epistemic point, i.e., a point about whether we can know about normativity. There is another point that still needs to be addressed, a properly metaphysical one: how are the norms grounded? *In virtue of what* is it the case that a waterfowl should be able to fly, a dog should be able to bark, and so on? This is a question about the metaphysical grounding of norms, not a question about the epistemic accessibility of norms.

Someone who asks this question is not looking for an answer such as the following: a waterfowl should be able to fly in virtue of the fact that it has the feature of being subject to the norm of flying. The questioner wants to know what *causes* waterfowl to have the feature of being subject to the norm of flying. And since it is the normativity that is the difficult point, he wants an answer that does not appeal to normativity. So what he really wants to know is: what are the non-norm-constituted features of waterfowl that make them have their norm-constituted features?

That waterfowl are subject to the norm of flying will not be because they have a certain shape, or because they have wings, or because they have a certain genome; as we have seen, these are all nonnormatively optional, while being subject to the norm of flying is not nonnormatively optional for waterfowl. Indeed, it seems unlikely that appealing to *any* ordinary feature or structure is going to provide a satisfactory answer. So we have to face the possibility that normativity goes all the way down, that it is basic and irreducible. This cannot be ruled out *a priori;* after all, *something* has to be basic, on pain of problematic regress.

But what about the soul (in the Aristotelian, not the Cartesian, sense), which was mentioned earlier in a note, only to be deferred? Maybe souls, unlike wings or genomes, can never be defective, and maybe the explanation of why waterfowl are subject to norms has to do with their souls.

There are good reasons for talking about souls, but doing so will not, it seems, enable us to dispense with talk of normativity. Suppose someone wants to know why waterfowl are subject to the norms to which they are subject. It will not be enough to say: because they have souls. We are, after all, dealing with the question of categorization, and in particular with what makes waterfowl belong to the category of waterfowl. So instead we would have to say: because they have *this kind* of soul. But which kind? The answer "anatidian souls" will be true but uninformative; the soul has to be specified. But unfortunately, we cannot (so to speak) look under the hood to see what kind of soul it is. To specify a soul, we must describe it in terms of what it does for the organism, namely, cause it to live and grow and act in certain ways. In other words, we explain the soul in terms of its powers.[23] But, if there is any point to the normative version of the unity problem, it can happen that a soul is unable to fully exercise its powers—the thing grows wrong, or is handicapped, for example. So we cannot characterize souls in terms of what powers they actually do exercise; if we did, we would have to say that a very handicapped human didn't have a human soul. Instead, we have to characterize souls in terms of what powers they are *supposed* to exercise. In other words, we are back to normativity. So even if a thing's normative features turn out to be secondary characteristics, less fundamental than its having a certain kind of soul, still in practice the most basic characterization we will be able to give of an organism will be one that (in part) describes it as subject to some norms; even much of what we say of the soul itself has to be put like this. Even if we decide to qualify some of the strong language used earlier in this paper, according to which norm-subservience "constitutes" categories, in practice norm-subservience will be our only access to those categories.[24]

CONCLUSION

I have discussed a version of the unity problem that has not received much attention in recent philosophy. I have argued that the unity of such categories is best accounted for by construing some categories as norm-constituted, and, more provisionally, I have cast doubt on any hope of reducing their normativity to something nonnormative. I do not, to be sure, claim to have solved all problems. I conclude by very briefly mentioning some issues that future research on this topic might take up.

First, although there are clearly norm-constituted categories of a hu-

---

23. Cf. Aristotle, *De anima* II, 2, 413b10–13: "[S]oul is the source of these phenomena and is characterized by them viz., by the powers of self-nutrition, sensation, thinking, and motivity." Aristotle, *De anima*, trans. J. A. Smith, in *The Basic Works of Aristotle*, ed. Richard McKeon (New York: Random House, 1941), 557–58. See also Thomas Aquinas, who holds that the soul's essence is distinct from its powers but also that our way of specifying souls is in terms of their powers and not in terms of their essences. Thomas Aquinas, *Summa theologiae* I, q. 77, a.1, corpus, and ad 7.

24. The claim that we cannot in practice reduce the normative to the nonnormative should not be confused with the highly problematic idea that the normative and the nonnormative are two entirely separate realms.

manly constructed variety (like Millikan's favorite example of the can opener), biological categories seem to be the best and possibly the only examples of natural norm-constituted categories. Is this really the case? If so, why?[25]

Second, if biological categories are norm-constituted, how is this fact to be understood together with the norm-neutral approach usually taken in modern biology? I have indicated some of the questions associated with this when dealing with objections above.

Third, in all of this, it would be helpful to investigate the work of philosophers who give a greater role to normativity than contemporary philosophy typically does. Such investigations would most probably begin with Aristotle and the medieval scholastics.[26] How far their views would have to be modified in order to square them with the findings of modern science is, of course, a crucial question.

If what I have said here is correct, normativity is more bound up with our thinking than we might have suspected. It is intimately involved with some of our most important categories. To go beyond this, however, and to determine its consequences for other matters, will require another occasion.[27]

---

25. For discussion of the "problematic dualism" of the living and nonliving, see Richard F. Hassing, "Modern Natural Science and the Intelligibility of Human Experience," in *Final Causality in Nature and Human Affairs*, ed. Richard F. Hassing (Washington, D.C.: Catholic University of America Press, 1997), 211–56.

26. See, for example, Aristotle, *Metaphysics* V, 22, 1022b22–23a6; Thomas Aquinas, *ST* I, q. 48, a.1; and Thomas Aquinas, *Quaestiones disputatae de malo*, q. 1, a. 1.

27. In writing this essay I have benefited from discussions with Jean DeGroot, Anne-Marie Gorman, Jorge Gracia, Richard Hassing, Brian Shanley, Barry Smith, and John Wippel.

11   Categorial Form

DAVID WEISSMAN

    Philosophic inquiry was once dominated by two linked questions: What are the categorial features of reality? What moral difference do they make? Plato, Aristotle, Spinoza, Marx, and social Darwinists answered that human character, actions, laws, and virtues are properly sensitive to our nature and circumstances. Skeptics challenged this link: what do we know of the external world and its constraining effects? Idealism (the skeptics' heir) shrinks the ambient world to the luminous space where individual minds create thinkable experiences. It says that freedom from material constraints entails our power to choose the rules that limit action. This response is familiar but indefensible if mind is the activity of body. For mind's materiality entails that we humans are everywhere constrained by physical laws or social rules we do not make. The rules are sometimes changeable, the laws are not. Either way, the character of our bodies and circumstances makes a considerable difference to the things we should do or cannot resist doing.

    This chapter invokes *categorial form* to reaffirm that physics and metaphysics have consequences for morals. It argues that what and where we are constrains what we ought to do or be. If categories are the generic features of being, categorial form is its design. Think of the architect's plan realized in a building. Discount the designer, and suppose that reality too embodies a plan. This plan—the system of categories—is categorial form. There are seven points to consider: (i) the evidence of categorial form; (ii) the method for discovering it; (iii) Kantian objections to the realist, essentialist implications of categorial form; (iv) a sketch of plausible candidates; (v) antecedent formulations; (vi) some practical implications; and (vii) a question: which hypothesis about categorial form is best?

1. THE EVIDENCE OF CATEGORIAL FORM

No one lives through a waking day without engaging some or all of the principal features of categorial form. But interests are initially practical and parochial: our understanding of bodies, space, time, and motion is calibrated to the scale of middle-sized things moving at relatively low velocities. Hypotheses about categorial form would be crippled were we to stop with these first approximations. We embellish, revise, and sometimes replace them with the hypotheses of empirical science. They have the scope, economy, and depth appropriate to our inquiry. Yet science is not the last world about categorial form. Aristotle's remark—that sciences invoke causality without explaining it—is still pertinent. Scientists are careful to explicate some features of categorial form—mass and space-time, for example—but casual but others. The status of laws may be the signature example of our time: scientists discover and cite them without specifying their place in nature. Philosophers of science gloss the issue by identifying natural laws with sentences or equations, but laws have a regulative force that is unexplained by any feature of these inscriptions.

Who worries about the ontological status of laws? Who formulates and tests notions of categorial form when science and practical reflection decline the responsibility? Only philosophers, and especially metaphysicians. This is our defining task, though we often disqualify ourselves in three ways: (i) we ignore the work for the good reason that it is difficult; (ii) we are too often apriorists who don't know how to use the empirical information supplied by practical life and science; (iii) we have largely devoted ourselves, for 2,500 years, to two sterile projects, one theological, the other mentalistic. Rational theology proposes that God is the capstone, necessary ground, or container for all Being. It usually ignores the natural world, while adducing no evidence or compelling argument to justify its claims about God's character or existence. The other failed project is mentalism. Making *nous* or the *cogito* the fundament for Being, it says that nothing is better known to mind than mind itself (including mind's structure and ideas). Nature is ignored, because these apriorists suppose that natural phenomena derive all their character from ideas they instantiate, ideas that originate within thought. Thinkers since Democritus have objected to this claim, but it was engineers and physiologists—not philosophers—who confirmed that being cannot be located altogether in thought, because mind is the activity of a physical system.

Theological and mentalist metaphors have been squeezed for every useful nuance. Metaphysicians who reject them look for categorial form in the material world. Our evidentiary bases are the two mentioned above: practical experience and empirical science. Both expose us to things that embody categorial form, and both provoke inferences that specify additional categorial features—universals and modalities, for example. Our aim is a theory of categorial form. Having one would be evidence that metaphysics generalizes and extrapolates from information supplied by practical life and science.

2. THE METHOD FOR DISCOVERING CATEGORIAL FORM

We learn the shape of things by engaging them. Like people moving without light in a strange house, we go slowly at first, learning as much from mistakes as successes. Evolution averts egregious errors by supplying a good if partial map of our world's categorial form. But the map is generic, not particular: it prefigures an unbounded space, not the chair that trips us in the dark. Our information about categorial form is appropriate to the scale of our activities but warped by perspective. Inherited instincts are calibrated to the aims of middle-sized creatures that survive by engaging things of similar scale. Our assumptions about the world's categorial features need revision in the light of inferences that generalize, analogize, and extrapolate from findings germane to this scale and perspective.

The inferences that power inquiry are, principally, inductive and abductive. Induction generalizes: we infer from the bits we know to generalities about a domain or the whole. Abduction is conceptual exploration. Starting from an effect, we infer its possible condition or conditions. Sometimes these conditions are necessary, as space and time are necessary conditions for motion. More often, the inferences are probabilistic: we infer from an effect to one or more alternative sufficient conditions, each contrary to the others (different explanations for global warming, for example).

The possibility that the same effect may have either of two or more mutually exclusive conditions is an obstacle to theories about categorial form, because a preference for one contrary or the other is provisional and fallible. It is also troubling that suspected aspects of categorial form may be integrated in either of several ways. Is matter distinguishable from space-time, or only the effect (mass) of motion in space-time? Even the target is speculative: the idea of categorial form—the integrated assembly of categorial features—signifies a possibility that may not obtain. These difficulties guarantee that the inquiry is piecemeal and dialectical, not linear and sure. Still, this idea dominates metaphysical thinking. Discovering any particular categorial feature, we locate it, however tacitly, within the hypothesized network of categorial features.

3. KANTIAN OBJECTIONS

Should we agree that categorial form is a regulative idea (a schema used to organize experience), not the immanent design of things whose existence and character are independent of ways we think about them? Is the dialectic of categorial hypotheses a political struggle, one whose winner prescribes the idea used to organize our understanding of the "world"? These Kantian objections scorn the realist, essentialist bias of my suggestion that reality has a particular categorial form, one having normative effect on every feature of being, irrespective of what and how we think of it. Here are some realist answers to three Kantian questions:

1. Kant supposed that character and relations are projected into experience by the rules used to make it thinkable. Is this so? *Is every candidate for categorial form merely a schema used to organize experience?*

Suppose that a circle, a square, and a triangle are set before us on a flat plane. Could we perceive each of the figures in one of the three ways? Remember the Whorf hypothesis: it says that a tribe's language determines the character and relations of phenomena perceived, varieties of snow or sand, for example. Empirical studies—of the sort my example invites—refute Whorf's claim. People see many differences not prefigured in their languages: we distinguish shapes—faces, for example—while having no words for them. A culture or language might emphasize two of the figures while saying nothing of the third. Or we might see one as an oddly distorted version of the other two. Still, we would see it as different from them.

2. *Is categorial form merely a regulative idea?* It may be. There is likely to be no *a priori* proof that there are generic and pervasive—categorial—features of things, or that categorial features are integrated as a single categorial design. This is a question for empirical inquiry: can we establish that one or another integrative design does obtain? Establishing this would require two steps: formulate a theory that specifies the categorial features of things; then adduce evidence that the theory applies. We may fail to confirm that candidate theories do apply, but this would not prove that reality has no categorial form: not finding what we look for doesn't prove that it isn't there. Kant would demur. We are chasing our tail: experience—the only reality we know—must shadow the conceptualization used to think it. Its coherence is an effect of the integrated conceptual system used to schematize sensory data; or experience is

fragmentary because the schematizing conceptual system is unintegrated.

What is the point of inquiry—implying theories revised under the press of experiment—if this is so? Why not contrive whatever consistent theories we can, showing that each can be used throughout experience? Let fiction and fantasies of every sort replace empirically testable hypotheses. We demur, because the experiments of practical life and science confirm that most conceptual systems are false: reality has a character and edge we discover but do not make. Let Chicago's street plan supply a counterexample. State and Madison are point zero in a Cartesian coordinate system. Numbers in the four quadrants progress from there. Do I impose order on otherwise chaotic data when I go to particular Chicago addresses, or is it true instead that I navigate within an order I have learned, one that limits and directs me?

The paradoxes of quantum theory challenge this claim without refuting it. Phenomena that sometimes look like waves, other times like particles, are not concurrently waves and particles. This perplexity is sometimes construed as evidence of an equivocation in nature, though all the history of thought, practice, and experiment suggests that our inability to comprehend quantum effects under a single rubric—one that may differ from any currently available—is evidence that we don't yet understand them. It is too early to affirm that nature does not have a single, decided categorial form.

3. *Is the dialectic of categorial form a struggle for the power to impose society's organizing theory or myth?* We fear truths that would restrict our freedom to do or be as we choose. We resent the idea of categorial form because it implies restriction. Never mind that we are already confined by layers of restraint, including age, gender, size, intelligence, custom, citizenship, gravity, the shape of space, the laws of motion. Categorial form is one more insult to our freedom. Anyone proposing it must have hegemonic aims. But I do not. Categorial form is merely the last step in a hierarchy of limits. No human freedom is gained or lost if it obtains. It obtains or not, irrespective of our fears. Discerning it would illumine our situation, better enabling us to master it and ourselves.

4. SOME POSSIBLE CATEGORIAL FORMS

Here are three hypotheses about categorial form. Each exhibits the generality and explanatory power required of such hypotheses, though each is the fragment of a more comprehensive theory. These theories—individualism, communitarianism, and holism—may be represented graphically as follows:

FIGURE 11

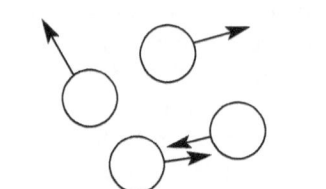

Atomism / Individualism

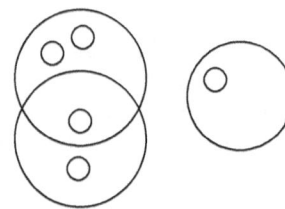

Communitarianism

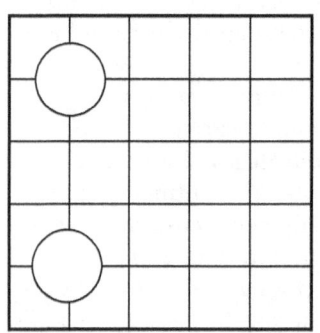

Holism

*Individualism—atomism—*affirms that reality comprises self-sufficient particulars. There is, presumably, a medium in which particulars are distributed: space or God's sensorium, for example. Some variations suppose that particulars are self-activating; others say that things do not move unless pushed or pulled. All agree that relations, whether dynamic or static, are incidental to the character of the things related. Individualist theories have illustrious support and an ancient history. Democritean atomism and Aristotelian primary substances are its materialist formulations. Luther's souls and Cartesian minds are spiritualist and mentalist versions. *Holism* affirms that there is a single particular—the whole—and that every "thing" is an aspect or part. It acknowledges that parts are distinguishable within the whole but denies they are separable. Its preferred metaphors are organic or political and social: separating body parts kills them or the body; people separated from states or societies suffer civic or cultural death.

Communitarianism shares some of its claims with individualism and holism, but this is the third point of a triangle, not an eclectic stew. It alleges that "things" are systems, each created by the causal reciprocity of its proper parts. Let molecules be our example. Their proper parts are ions, meaning atoms that have more or less than the standard complement of electrons. Ions join when one gives and the other receives one or more electrons. The molecule thereby formed is stabilized by the balance of forces that bind electrons to the nuclei of its atoms. This is the causal reciprocity of the molecule's proper parts: each of the causes binds the other to itself.

Systems are modules. Their individuality derives from the relations of their parts, not (as in Aristotle) from the portion of matter that supports each one's properties. Systems also behave holistically: each is sustained by the complementary roles of its proper parts. There is, however, no single totalizing system (with one exception). For systems relate to one another in any of four ways. They are mutually independent, reciprocally bound, overlapping, or nested. Reality is an array of systems, some that are more or less densely nested or overlapping, others that are mutually independent. The one totalizing exception is space-time. Every system falls within the light cone of its successors, either directly or by way of intermediaries, and each is affected gravitationally by everything in its light cone. Communitarianism is not otherwise holistic.

How do these hypotheses fare when compared to one another in respect to a feature or features for which each must provide? Let the modalities—possibility and necessity—be our example.

Atomism emphasizes the individual's freedom of motion, hence the many possible directions it may go. Necessity is minimized but not eliminated, because space-time is a necessary condition for motion where particulars are material: motion is a trajectory through space-time. Souls exhibit possibility in their freedom to will good or evil, and symmetrically in the necessity that they be rewarded in kind. Minds are free to reflect upon ideas of their choice, with the proviso that possibilities for thought are subject to necessities of two sorts: mind is necessarily conscious of itself, whatever ideas it entertains; and necessities—invariances—are discerned in the structures of ideas (circles or squares, for example). Holism reduces the play of possibility while emphasizing a kind of necessity. Each node within the whole has restricted possibilities, because its role is tightly constrained by its relations to other nodes. The range of choices reduces to two: each node fulfills its nature as determined by its role, or it thwarts itself by renouncing its role. The first is necessary if the second is self-extinguishing (hence, implicitly, a contradiction). Communitarianism avers that possibility and necessity are the complementary aspects of a thing's roles in systems: a system's proper parts may participate in systems other than the one that engages them—they will likely establish other systems when this one dissolves, or merely when their roles within it are satisfied—but the parts are made for and shaped by the systems in which they participate. All the necessities just cited are situational: they are conditions that must obtain if a particular result is to be achieved. Necessities of this sort compare to the unconditional necessities that apply universally within possible worlds of every sort: namely, the requirements that nothing occurring should violate the principles of noncontradiction, identity, or excluded middle. Modern thinking locates these principles of least order within thought or language only. But this is odd, because thought is the only domain where they are often violated.

Theories of categorial form would embellish these interpretations of the modalities with claims about additional categorial features, including properties, space-time, mass, energy, motion, efficacy and relation, the hierarchical relations of systems and their emergent properties, dispositions, and laws. This is more than a laundry list of traditional issues. Some are apparent within practical experience. Others have refined scientific descriptions. A few are considerations to which metaphysics extrapolates. All are topics for a comprehensive metaphysics of nature.

Is this project sabotaged by the simple objection that it implies ontological essentialism, the claim that reality has a distinct, constitutive categorial form? I suggest that disparate categorial forms are contraries: nature embodies one while excluding every other. There is nothing odd about this: one chooses the design of a new house from an array of designs that are mutually exclusive. The categorial profile of space, time, matter, causality, and motion may be equally singular and exclusive.

5. ANTECEDENT FORMULATIONS

There are affinities between the idea of categorial form and Stephen Pepper's *World Hypotheses*.[1] Pepper's candidates were atomism, mechanism, organicism, and contextualism, each defended by its proponents as comprehensive and self-sufficient. Pepper believed that the history of philosophy is the dialectic of these opposed conceptions, each belittling the others while justifying itself. Richard McKeon made similar claims about the sixty-four possible theories generated by joining the four expressions of his three rubrics: ideas, methods, and principles.[2] Or McKeon argued that there are four rubrics—the other three and interpretation, each with four expressions—so that there are 256 possible philosophic views. Pepper and McKeon may have been inspired by Kant's antinomies. They agreed that we can use any consistent conceptual system—any consistent regulative idea—to think about reality. Yet thought's plasticity doesn't entail that reality is formless or endlessly determinable. It may have a decided form, one theory (and translational equivalents) being true, while its contraries are false. The essentialism of categorial form is no more objectionable than that of chess or this

---

1. Stephen Pepper, *World Hypotheses: A Study in Evidence* (Berkeley and Los Angeles: University of California Press, 1970).
2. Richard McKeon's views are presented systematically (with neologisms by the author) in Walter Watson's *The Architectonics of Meaning: Foundations of the New Pluralism* (Chicago: University of Chicago Press, 1993).

building. Each of them has an essential form. Why shouldn't reality have one too?

6. PRACTICAL APPLICATIONS

Metaphysical theories, like practical beliefs and natural science, should be empirically testable. Testability looks two ways: to the empirical evidence for truth, and to cogency. We want empirical data for our claims, because we cannot know without it that hypotheses are true. We want hypotheses that are cogent, because metaphysics serves human aims: it is one of the inquiries that tell what we are, what the world is, and what place we have within it. Kantian world-making doesn't do as much. It directs that we think of the world "as if" it has a particular form. But fantasies don't appease us: we need and want to know what and where we are. Only truths can tell us.

A true theory of categorial form would be cogent in this way: it would enable us to locate ourselves in the world. We are well located already, in the respect that our bodies have position. But this is not the sense of *location* relevant here. Location of the other sort is a demand we make of self-understanding. Motivated by a combination of wonder and insecurity, we want to know our place in the world. A comprehensive, empirically and dialectically validated theory of categorial form would temper our hopes, appease some fears, and justify others. One anticipates the mix of satisfaction, terror, and awe this theory would promote. Wanting such knowledge is a first cousin to religious aims, with the difference that resolution comes with inquiry, not dogma.

Categorial form is also cogent because of its implications for moral life, though the demand for acuity is reduced. Wonder about our place in the world deepens with precise information about its age, structure, and scale: think of the pictures of dust clouds trillions of miles high, newly formed stars blazing at the crests. Moral issues also want categorial direction, but they are insensitive to many such details. Is the cosmos huge? Einstein and the astronomers amplified Newton's claim without altering its moral implication: the universe is stable and vast; we are small and ephemeral. Knowing the fine structure of space-time adds little or nothing to this sober appraisal of our place and significance.

Each of the hypotheses summarized above—individualism, holism, and communitarianism—is morally germane though mute about such details. Individualism affirms our self-sufficiency and freedoms, both freedom to and freedom from. It says that responsibilities are assumed rather than primary: they don't constrain us until we acquire duties to other people (as when contracts are made). Holism inverts the priorities. It emphasizes duty, saying that freedom is the opportunity to satisfy one's place in the whole. Communitarianism objects that freedom and duty are not contraries. It agrees with holism that we are inevitably located within networks of obligation; but it adds that some are freely chosen, and that selfhood emerges as we learn to fill and choose our roles. The moral quality of selfhood varies accordingly. Individualism affirms that each of us is self-concerned. Holism entails that the moral vector points beyond us to a corporate reality. Communitarianism acknowledges the moral conflicts that occur when persons located in several systems—work and family, for example—choose the order and degree of their commitments.

The moral determinism of categorial form is somewhat relieved, because each form may be expressed in several or many different ways. Individualism affirms that bodies are separable and self-sufficient; it doesn't specify the number of bodies or the dimensions of the spaces they occupy. Holism doesn't detail the complexity of the system it postulates: there may be many nodes or few; each node may be connected to several others or to all. Communitarianism alleges that reality is an array of systems; it doesn't prescribe how many systems there shall be, the depth of nesting and overlap among them, or the number of mutually independent hierarchies.

Each of the categorial forms is determinable. Contingencies—scarcity and crowding, for example—determine its lower-order expressions, hence their distinctive moral imperatives. So Locke writes of the time when "all the world was America," a wilderness where individuals did as they pleased without affecting others. Hobbes assumes that freedom is everywhere impeded by those with whom one competes for scarce resources. One implies tolerance for people rarely or never met; the other describes the perpetual war of each with all. Accordingly, we qualify the principle affirmed above: categorial form doesn't determine moral imperatives until contingencies realizing the form are also given.

7. WHICH IS THE BETTER HYPOTHESIS?

Each of the three hypotheses has supporting evidence. All agree that what we can and ought to do is determined by what and where we are. Each implies moral directives that are appropriate to its version of our nature and circumstances. So young people behave atomistically in the void between systems they have outgrown and those they will make or join. They confirm a theory that encourages us to behave as if we were freer than we are, until these same people subordinate their individual identities to the demands of clubs, cults, or gangs that enforce duties and roles. We bend either way, accommodating ourselves successively to one theory, then the other. But how is this possible? Shouldn't we be incapable of satisfying directives from two or more of the hypotheses, if only one of the three contraries is true? I suggest this solution. Each of the hypotheses can be used effectively as a regulative idea, because humans are adaptable: our behavior is determinable within limits.

Does this variability disqualify human behavior as evidence for or against hypotheses about categorial form? Could we adapt to each of the three forms, like people who twist their feet into shoes more stylish than comfortable? Human malleability confuses the issue without altogether obscuring it. For behavior is distorted when hypotheses about categorial form are used as recipes to remake the underlying structures of social life. Organizations and associations of every sort—including families, teams, businesses, and states—may be misconstrued as aggregates bound by nothing but mutual advantage or fear. Or we may care only about the integrity of the whole, annihilating every lesser system, stifling the interests and initiatives of the people who join to create them. Both effects cripple personal development and vital social interests because they disrupt or ignore basic social systems.

Communitarianism is a better hypothesis about reality, human life and society included, because it predicts and explains the empirically justified aspects of atomism and holism, though they are incapable of providing for its claims. Systems are modular, and they behave sometimes as individuals. Systems are holistic, because they are comprehensive and totalizing, as businesses, states, or religious sects may be. Yet atomism has no way of describing either the systems established by the reciprocal causal relations of their members or the hierarchies of nested, overlapping systems. Holism ignores both modularity, hence the individualism it promotes, and mutually independent hierarchies of systems (California and New York, for example).

Atomism and holism are, historically, the two principal ontological alternatives, because their theorists have hidden the evidence for communitarianism. Let Mill and Rousseau be our examples. One emphasizes autonomy but ignores the families, schools, workplaces, and states where it emerges. The other would force us to be free, requiring that we defer to the general will. Communitarianism is more accurate: it describes the emergence of moral selves in contexts where autonomy and responsibility are acquired by infants, children, and adults engaged reciprocally to parents, friends, teachers, workmates, and fellow citizens. Atomism and holism are off-setting distortions of this more ample account. We may satisfy atomist or holist demands, but we are mutilated if they exceed the tolerances of our communitarian reality.

Moral implications such as these may trump every other motive for wanting to know reality's categorial form. What and where are we? What should we do and be? What is optional or required where *is* constrains *ought*? Hume's dictum—*is* doesn't entail *ought*—is true of particular circumstances (unhappiness or abuse, for example), but not of categorial form. If fish could speak, we might reproach them: "Why not live on land and breathe good air, as we do. You ought to try." "But we oughtn't, because we can't," the fish would say. "Can't precludes ought. Such things as we ought to do fall within the circle of things we can do because of what we are. *Is* limits *ought*." Categorial form comprises the most general features of all that is. Anything that exceeds these limits, anything contrary to them, violates us. Kant, the master deontologist, agreed. Morality, he said, is the imperative of our rational nature. We want maxims that are consistent if universalized, because universality and consistency are to reason as water is to fish.

The regulative implications for law and morality are clear, though complex. Categorial form constrains what we are and do. Yet specific constraints are often determinable: there is variability within limits. No society survives without children, though the rules and customs for marriage and childrearing vary. Any of several considerations may justify a variation, but each assembly of family members satisfies the relevant feature of communitarian categorial form: each is a system; each system is a module, nested within or overlapping others.

Hence this finding: variability is restricted; categorial form is its limit.

PART IV

EPISTEMOLOGICAL AND METAPHYSICAL CONSIDERATIONS

12 Distinction, Judgment, and Discipline
MARIAM THALOS

Philosophers in the analytic tradition insist upon a distinction between knowledge and fact, normally as follows: knowledge is something held by a subject of some sort, and fact is—well, it stands on its own feet, without a fact-finder, subject, or "observer" to thank for its existence. Thus facts owe no ontological debt to second parties whose movements bring about the existence of facts. Whilst knowledge comes out as fundamentally a relation—one that holds between a knower and an object of knowledge. So, first in time we (in the West) distinguish—we say that this is not that: "knowledge is not mere fact." To distinguish is, first of all, to make a statement of nonidentity, and thereby to invite others to see two things, where before they might—for want of reflection or training or some other route to insight—have seen only one.

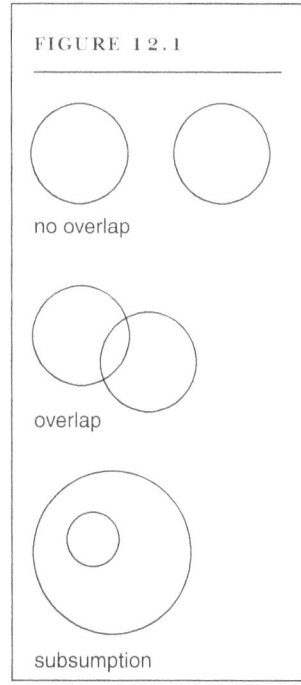

FIGURE 12.1

no overlap

overlap

subsumption

A distinction suggests one of three relations between the terms of the distinction (see Figure 12.1): (1) no overlap—a situation in which the categories are disjoint; (2) simple overlap—a situation in which the intersection between the categories is smaller than either of the overlapping categories; or (3) subsumption—a situation in which one category is related to the other as genus to species. At the same time, then, a distinction prompts the further question of just how the "distinguands" differ, since the distinction claims that the terms name nonidentical things. A distinction is a device that prompts immediately for a definition. It is a move in the enterprise for analysis that calls immediately for an allied move. (This suggests that there are impulses in judgment toward maximal systematicity—toward a maximal system of interlocking or bridging connections.)

The distinction between fact and knowledge is the foundation for the division, in classical and Anglo-American philosophy, between the disciplines of epistemology, on the one hand, and the discipline of metaphysics, on the other. Thus the distinction founds a division between two philosophical enterprises, while at the same time prompting the question of whether, and to what extent, they overlap. (This is the normal way of founding disciplines.) And the standard Anglo-American way of articulating the *definition* that goes along with the distinction is to say that metaphysics is concerned with how things stand in the world, while epistemology is concerned with how subjects get to be mindful of these standings-in-the-world-of-things. This articulation of the difference between fact and knowledge privileges the fact over the knowledge of it: it puts the fact (and hence metaphysics) in the independent position and defines knowledge (and hence epistemology) in terms of it. This way of proceeding in analytical philosophy causes two distinct problems.

The first is that it suggests, quite baselessly, that a definition or analysis can be found—and indeed should be sought—of the dependent term of the distinction in terms of the independent one (among other things, to be sure). This might, for all we know, be just false. Bertrand Russell begins, in the 1912 *Problems of Philosophy*, with a distinction between fact and knowledge in the spirit outlined above, adding: "The question as to what we mean by truth and falsehood . . . is of much less interest than the question as to how we can know what is true and what is false."[1] Then, immediately, he—no less handily than, for example, Edmund Gettier, and considerably earlier—generates the problem of the analysis of knowledge as follows. First, he wonders how knowledge might be related to the fact it purports to know. Is knowledge merely true belief?

If a man believes that the late Prime Minister's name begins with the letter B, he believes what is true, since the late Prime Minister was Sir Henry Campbell Bannerman. But if he believes [we can add: for good reason] that Mr. Balfour was the late Prime Minister, he will still believe that the late Prime Minister's name began with the letter B, yet this belief, though true, would not be thought to constitute knowledge. . . . Thus it is clear that a true belief is not knowledge, when it is derived from a false belief [we can add: however well justified].[2]

So the first problem caused by the routine way of distinguishing between fact and knowledge is the problem of the analysis of knowledge,

---

1. Bertrand Russell, *Problems of Philosophy* (New York: H. Holt & Co., 1912), 131.
2. Ibid., 131–32.

which *might*—just as well as not—be a genuine problem. The second problem is dialogical rather than doctrinal.

There is a school of thought, today largely associated with certain philosophers of the European continent, that insists there is no such creature as the independent fact of which we can simply attain knowledge (in due time, to be sure, and with the right balance of patience, luck, modesty, and self-application). Proponents of this view insist that somehow the activity of investigation has something not so trivial to contribute to the fact, which thus turns out not to be independent of the knower. These thinkers clearly have no use for a distinction between fact and knowledge that puts the fact in the independent position. And without a distinction between fact and knowledge, acceptable to both these thinkers and their critics, there can be little fruitful commerce between the two camps, as perhaps we are all too well aware.

By the end of this essay I hope to have offered, if not an acceptable recipe, then at least a *strategy* for seeking a distinction that does not put one of the distinguands in a privileged position. This will illustrate (among other things) how disciplines can be reinvented. Indeed, this essay is fundamentally about disciplines—sciences—and their relations to practical life. It is therefore a meta-disciplinary piece. It is concerned with the relations amongst the practices of distinction making, defining, judgment, and decision making, and above all with how these things contribute to the founding of academic disciplines. I shall put forward an Aristotelian account of the disciplines and their relations to the practical exercise of reason.[3]

1. DISTINCTION BEFORE JUDGMENT?

Distinctions are close to a philosopher's heart for good reasons. Robert Sokolowski, in his article "Making Distinctions," says why. Indeed, he says that philosophy itself is not established as a "distinctive" enterprise until a crucial distinction is made, and until that distinction is made philosophy remains confused with psychology or myth or natural science or ideology. Sokolowski says that judgment, which according to him amounts to the placement of something (individual or class) under a predicate, must be preceded by one or more distinctions:

Only because a predicate has been distinguished from other kinds or features is it definite enough for us to say explicitly that this or that is a case of the pred-

---

3. For another discussion of categories in light of the relations between the theoretical and the practical, see Chapter 6 of this volume.

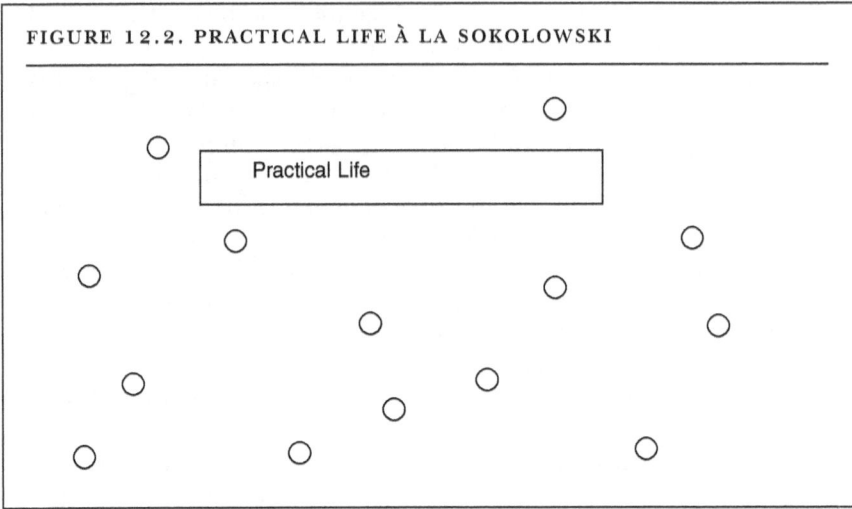

FIGURE 12.2. PRACTICAL LIFE À LA SOKOLOWSKI

icate. This reliance of judgments on distinctions comes out neatly in sentences that both place an instance under a category and, at the same time, display a distinction: "He could practice abstinence, but not temperance"; "We had talk enough, but no conversation"; "I have found you an argument; but I am not obliged to find you an understanding." Behind such judgments, and also showing through them, are the distinctions "Abstinence is not temperance," "Talk is not conversation," and "Argument is not understanding." And if the judgments were simple, devoid of the contrasting element—"He could abstain," "We talked," "You have the argument"—the distinction would still be behind them but would no longer show through.[4]

Immediately he proceeds to claim that the definition that naturally accompanies logically presupposes the distinction, but is not itself part of the activity of distinguishing. By contrast, I said at the outset that the companion definition is preceded in time by the distinction between fact and knowledge, but suggested that definition and distinction are logically coeval, since distinction immediately prompts for definition, and can do so in a leading way. So here is where my account begins to diverge from that of Sokolowski, in spite of my enormous admiration.[5]

Sokolowski writes, "Distinctions push against an obscurity that needs the distinction in question."[6] The word "needs" here suggests—and

4. Robert Sokolowski, "Making Distinctions," in *Pictures, Quotations, and Distinctions: Fourteen Essays in Phenomenology* (Notre Dame: Notre Dame Press, 1992), 59.
5. In fairness to Sokolowski, I should say that his account of distinction making is put to a very different use from what I have in mind here. And it is the beauty and right-headedness of his account that drives me to cannibalize it for my own ends.
6. Sokolowski, *Pictures, Quotations, and Distinctions*, 55.

Sokolowski takes the point up explicitly in due time—that there is a *practical* end to be gained by making the distinction in question, which precedes the distinction making itself and arises out of the practical affairs of human life. The need for a distinction, according to Sokolowski, is activated in situations that call for practical action. (A favorite story is that of Jack, who is attended by a very careful physician. Jack learns that stress electrocardiograms are to be had for a good price at a local clinic. Taking the test in the name of saving on medical expenses, Jack reports to his physician with results in hand. The physician tells him: "Well, I will put these results in your file. But we do distinguish between medical data and medical care.") So this is one side of Sokolowski's picture: distinctions emerge in the regular course of personal affairs (see Figure 12.2).

On the other hand, Sokolowski says: "The distinction is achieved in a contemplative act. It is a simple recognition of how things are and how they have to be. Even if it is uttered in an intensively active situation, the making of the distinction is a detached acknowledgment of necessity, not a further step in the course of action."[7]

But can we have it both ways? Can it be both that distinctions are always and everywhere born in acts of pure contemplation, and also that distinctions sometimes occur in situations in which we struggle against an obscurity for the sake not simply of removing that obscurity but also of achieving some further practical end as well? This tension requires some assessment and treatment. I shall urge a more nuanced account of distinction making, as a friendly amendment to Sokolowski's account. For it, we shall (naturally) require a new distinction.

Let us distinguish between distinctions of a practical origin, which are just as Sokolowski says they are, and distinctions of a theoretical or disciplinary or scientific origin, which arise in situations where distinction is sought for its own sake—or, to put it in an equivalent way, where distinction is sought purely for the sake of furthering the discipline itself. Let us call the latter the *clinical* or *disciplinary* setting.

Sokolowski's picture (Figure 12.2), intended or not, suggests moments of transcendent detachment in practical life. It suggests that the clinical (the philosophical or scientific) breaks into the everyday, as from above. It suggests that disciplinary life—the life of contemplation for the sake of truth, for the sake of an intellectual discipline—is transcendent, and only anomolously present (when it is) in practical life. Just as there is, on some ontologies, no room for the universal alongside the particular except where absolutely unavoidable, there is on this

7. Ibid., 60–61.

picture no room for disciplinary activity in the ontology of the everyday, except where absolutely unavoidable.

Ironically, the picture is reminiscent of another painted by (of all people) Rudolf Carnap, who in later years espoused a certain pragmatism. Carnap held, as Kant did before him, that while our experiences do not put us in direct contact with the realities that bring them about, even so experience evokes descriptions or theories that get cast in what he called *linguistic frameworks*. About these frameworks Carnap would recognize only two sorts of questions as legitimate. The first he called an *internal* question: a question framed in the vocabulary of the framework, asking about what appears to be a straightforward factual matter in the subject for which that vocabulary was designed. (For example, What is the first prime number in the language of number?) The second sort of legitimate question he called an *external* question, which (as he held) calls upon us to evaluate—on non-epistemic grounds, please note well—the framework's very presuppositions. (For example, should we adopt this framework for handling our talk of numbers, or that contrasting one?) And he dismissed all other questions as either ill formulated or ill defined. (Such questions, for example, as: Do numbers exist? What are numbers? And so on.) He held that, once a framework is adopted, framework presuppositions themselves dictate which questions are ill defined, as well as how to go about answering those that are legitimate.

Sokolowski's picture puts me in mind of Carnap's for the following reason. Carnap thought that an external question is a purely practical one, concerned purely with instrumental reasons for or against adoption of a framework. And that all other legitimate questions are matter-of-fact questions, to be answered in a prescribed fashion once the framework issues themselves have been duly sorted out. He thus painted a picture of scientific life in which moments of transcendent *non-*detachment are interspersed amongst the mundane moments in which detachment is the rule. On Carnap's picture (see Figure 12.3), the *practical* is transcendent, whereas detachment is the ordinary business of the day. And of course this is just the reverse—the negative—of Sokolowski's picture.

Now these pictures (as I am calling them, and drawing them too) are founded on substantive epistemological doctrines. Sokolowski's is founded on the doctrine that the overriding imperatives in human life are practical. For him moments of detachment, while philosophically significant, are the transcendent and anomalous ones. And for that reason Sokolowski's picture (which I dare say is the better subscribed to these days) invites the question: Why be disciplinary? On Carnap's pic-

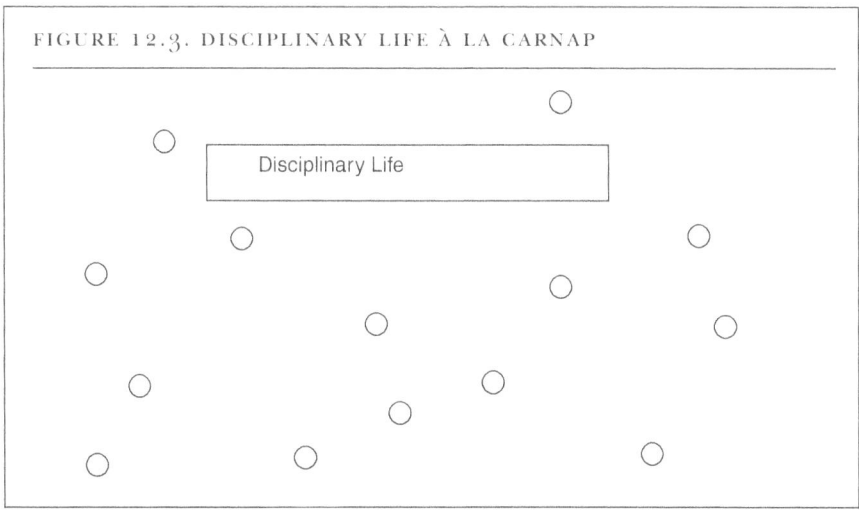

FIGURE 12.3. DISCIPLINARY LIFE À LA CARNAP

ture, by contrast—a picture drawn in a more optimistic era of human history—the overriding imperatives in human life are the disciplinary ones that draw their authority from their status as "rules of the game." (And these are accepted on grounds that Reason, with a capital T for "theoretical," cannot itself pronounce judgment upon, because the practical lies outside its domain of sovereignty.) For Carnap, moments of non-detachment, while again philosophically significant, are isolated and transcendent. *They* are the anomalous ones.

Now, I think that both pictures are similarly incorrect, because they are similarly (indeed, symmetrically) incomplete: each leaves out the other's daily business as anomalous. The scope of each is insufficiently wide. There is today a school of thought in the philosophy of science that would bring these two pictures together: it is called *Bayesianism*. Bayesianism is an uneasy marriage between eighteenth-century empiricism, on the one side, and modern decision theory, on the other. Bayesianism, like many of its rivals, divides reasoning into two kinds: theoretical (or disciplinary) reasoning, and practical reasoning. Practical reasoning has the function of controlling action or decision: its point is to figure out what to do. This is contrasted with disciplinary reasoning, whose aim is to figure out how things stand in the world, rather than what to do about them. Bayesians hold, moreover, that disciplinary and practical reasoning are architecturally and functionally separate, and so operate in complete procedural independence. This (if true) preserves the impartiality of the disciplines, by way of ensuring that the opinions we hold as to how things stand in the world are not influenced by how we might wish things stood. And this, of course, guarantees that science and other theoretical acts performed in clinical settings are never tainted by wishful thinking.

Bayesians also believe that all reasoning, even clinical reasoning, is at bottom a form of decision making, to which a cost-benefit calculus applies at the ground floor. Thus, while the Bayesian marriage between theoretical reason and practical reason is supposed to be a marriage of equals, it really is not. And so the contemporary Bayesian doctrine sides with Sokolowski, against Carnap, by acquiescing in the idea that the fundamental imperatives for all of human life are practical. I shall agitate for a true marriage between equals. Such a marriage will involve tensions that cannot be eliminated in advance by establishment of a system of domains of sovereignty. This is the price one pays for true equality.

Bayesianism, as a theory of empirical science, is attempting to solve a certain problem—one that anyone who would offer an alternative must also handle in some way. Bayesianism is answering Hume. Hume, like his empiricist contemporaries and against his rationalist foes, believed that theoretical reasoning vis-à-vis contingent matters of fact (like, for example, whether the sun shall rise tomorrow, or whether bread nourishes), must proceed from the instances (of the sun having risen in the past, or of bread having nourished in the past) to the sort of universal generalizations that would license inference to future such events. Thus he sought something that deserves to be called a *logic of induction* for the purposes of science. But Hume, unlike Carnap, despaired of such a logic, and at least on one reading resigned himself to skepticism. Carnap and his party, for their part, would do battle with generations of anti-empiricists who, like Henri Poincaré, shared Hume's pessimism about a logic of induction while advancing various forms of conventionalism instead. Conventionalists hold that certain matters (the famous example being the choice between Euclidean and non-Euclidean geometry) cannot be handled by appeal to observation—indeed, that such choices cannot be made by appeal to how things stand in the world at all. Choices of this sort are purely matters of convention—matters of discretion, and of utter indifference for the purposes of advancing science.

The conventionalist position introduces the idea of decision as something narrower or more specialized than reasoning as such, but nonetheless something performed in the course of reasoning. Decision making, according to the conventionalists, is conducted in *both* practical *and* theoretical reasoning. Thus the logic of science, on this view, is partly—that is, in parts—a logic of decision.

Karl Popper short-circuited the conventionalist program—insisting in effect that one cannot go only part way in the direction of a logic of decision for science. One has to go all the way: the logic of science is a logic of decision, through and through. And thus Popper laid the foundation for the idea that science—that is to say, all of theoretical reasoning—is practical all the way down. This idea converges, as I will explain, with classical pragmatism, to which I shall offer an alternative.

2. SCIENCE AND DECISION

Although an empiricist, Popper nonetheless insisted that observation *alone* could never advance one hypothesis ahead of its competitors, since any given body of observations will be consistent with numerous and mutually incompatible bodies of theory. In place of a logic he sought a decision procedure that accounts for how an idea, however initially outrageous, over time becomes something that takes a rightful place in the ranks of dignified scientific theories, to the point of overthrowing older and initially better-regarded theories. This can happen, according to Popper, if there exists a (unique) scientific method for deciding objectively between theories—of testing one theory against another. That method, said Popper, is the method of conjectures and refutations (by authoritative empirical evidence), which method also marks the difference between science and other academic endeavors. A theory is scientific, according to Popper, to the extent that it *excludes* or *prohibits* certain possibilities that are in principle observable (and is *ipso facto* falsifiable). And it is corroborated to the extent that it survives tests aimed at refuting it.

Now this position would appear to commit Popper to the doctrine that observation is in some sense primary or fundamental—at least that it is independently distinguishable from scientific theory as such. But Popper does not seem happy with such a commitment. Like those of his time on the conventionalist side, Popper repudiated the view that observation is either infallible or foundational, in the sense of purely "given," and argued that observation is not mere report of sensations passively registered but is instead description of what is observed *as interpreted in the light of a theoretical framework*—that observation is therefore theory laden. Accordingly he asserted that statements of observation are open-ended hypotheses: they are not functions of experience alone, nor can they be verified by experience as such. But if this is true, then how can a scientific theory be refuted in the objective sense? For if it is always a matter of judgment and not a matter of simple fact whether an observation sentence is true, where is the objectivity?[8] Pop-

---

8. William James might have replied here, in defense of Popper, that objectivity lies in the consequences that the world imposes on our decisions. But of course the retort will

per's resolution of the matter is to view observation statements as "prompted" by experience but not determined by them. Therefore observation statements "are accepted as the result of a decision or agreement, and to that extent they are conventions. The decisions are reached in accordance with a procedure governed by rules."[9]

Popper is well aware of the move he is making: he is saying that scientific reasoning—which is the very model of all disciplinary reasoning—is decision making all the way down. Even the method of conjectures and refutations, while distinguishing the scientific from the nonscientific, still involves a form of decision making. Does this obliterate the distinction between practical and theoretical decision making? And where, in the end, is there room for the objective testing of hypotheses against evidence that Popper so venerated? Popper had no satisfactory answer.

The Bayesian answers that practical and disciplinary reasoning must come together, and that the marriage must be responsive to new evidence, but like Popper the Bayesian admits that all such responses are conditioned in part by considerations of utility. Therefore the Bayesian answer does not afford the objectivity Popper sought. And in the process of so answering the Bayesian commits a reduction of disciplinary reason to practical reason. I want to suggest a different approach to Popper's dilemma. I will advise that we give up the ideal of harmony and insist—at all costs in economy—upon equality between the practical and the disciplinary, just as Aristotle did.

3. THE CITIZENRY

I shall defend the (Aristotelian) view that practical life and disciplinary life are in tension, and that individuals move between practical and disciplinary life as they move between rooms in a house. On my picture, neither practical life nor disciplinary life is fundamental (see Figure 12.4). Neither overrides the other. Each has its sphere or domain; neither arrogates to itself territory to which it is not entitled. And with each sphere comes a distinctive and defining set of imperatives. Human reasoning transpires within both spheres, sometimes at the same time, just as an individual can sit in one room of a house and look into an adjoining one. It is a complex tension between the personal

---

be: just as there are no unchallengeable observations, so too there are no unchallengeable consequences—they are subject to challenge in precisely the same way all hypotheses are.

9. Karl Popper, *The Logic of Scientific Discovery* (London: Hutchinson, 1959), 106. (This is a translation of *Logik der Forschung*, 1934.)

FIGURE 12.4. THE ARISTOTELIAN PICTURE

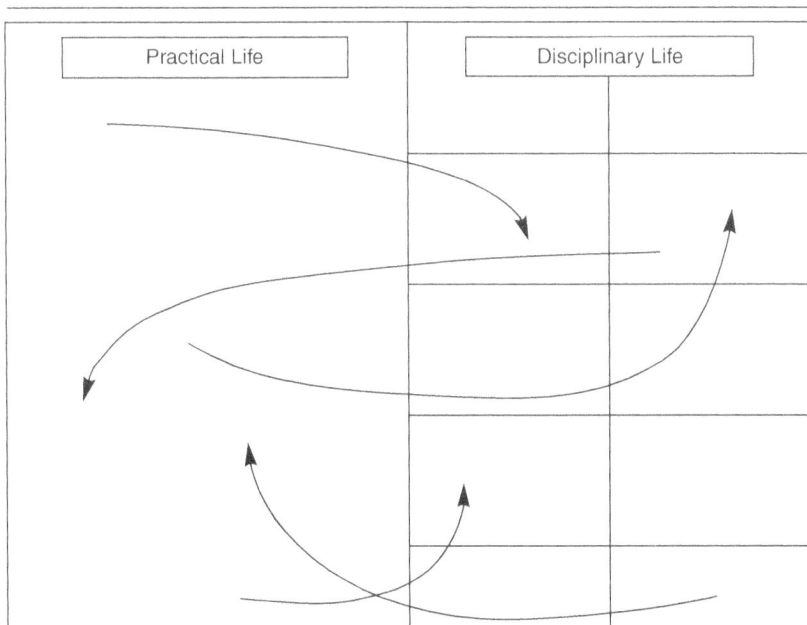

and the disciplinary, between individual life and cultural or corporate life, which cannot be resolved once and for all by establishment of spheres of authority. (The existence of these spheres is a matter of the different functions the spheres have served in the economy of our species: each sphere has grown up because of the evolutionary advantages it has rendered in the natural history of our species.)[10]

In saying this I do not mean simply that one moves freely between deciding on where to have lunch, on the one hand, and which of several theories to adopt in relation to black body radiation, on the other hand. I have in mind also that one moves between making the decision amongst theories of black body radiation on purely (as we might say) disinterested grounds, on the one hand, and making the decision on grounds that might also pertain to where one has lunch—grounds of personal utility. An account of the epistemic plural subject position, and how it gets occupied by someone who is *also* an occupant of the

---

10. I discuss this matter at some length in "The Natural History of Knowledge," in progress.

practical singular subject position, will afford us an account of how individuals can come to view certain matters impartially, without themselves—as individuals—occupying an impartial position.[11]

The empiricists sought a foundationalist epistemology when they went in search of a logic of induction. The conventionalists replaced logic by decision—for a certain class of theoretical questions—thereby answering Hume by rejecting foundationalism piecemeal. Popper sought the wholesale replacement of logic by decision, and on this course Bayesians remain intransigent. Their project is coherentist through and through. But it leaves no room for the objective criticism of theory by (independently acquired) evidence, because it leaves no room for a distinction between clinical and practical. This is not true of Popper's stance. Popper's stance can be saved, as I shall argue, but the Bayesians' cannot, because Popper, but not the Bayesians, can make room for a distinction between clinical and practical.

Let us refer to the view that a decision as to what theory to accept is just another practical matter as *pragmatism*. It is the view that the imperatives of science fall under the imperatives of practical life as a special category. Classical philosophical pragmatism was an American phenomenon, originating in the scholarship of the triumvirate of C. S. Peirce, William James, and John Dewey, and focusing upon science as the paradigm of knowledge. Fundamental to classical pragmatism is its commitment to Darwinism, in the form of a doctrine to the effect that the favorable designation of "knowledge" should fall to beliefs in human history that happen to have been recruited (or simply to be recruitable) in the service of overcoming obstacles to the satisfaction of human needs or wants. "Science," therefore, refers to those beliefs or attitudes that serve to confer upon certain organisms in the lineage of *homo sapiens* an evolutionary advantage. It emphatically does *not* refer to beliefs purporting to portray the world "as it really is."[12] For how could a species have acquired the ability to *represent* the universe—especially the universe as it really is, as opposed to how it is usefully described, relative to the particular needs of members of that species? Pragmatism today subdivides into a number of species, but uniting

---

11. We might take as our model for such an account Margaret Gilbert's plural subject theory as outlined in Margaret Gilbert, *On Social Facts* (Princeton: Princeton University Press, 1992), and *Living Together: Rationality, Sociality, and Obligation* (Lanham, Md.: Rowman & Littlefield, 1996).

12. Of course here I am separating pragmatist epistemology from pragmatist theories of truth, as does the foremost pragmatist of our present era, Richard Rorty; see his "Pragmatism," in *Routledge Encyclopedia of Philosophy*, ed. Edward Craig, (http://www.rep.routledge.com). Theorists who marry the two will of course object that there is no independent conception of the world "as it really is."

them all is the idea that science, such as it is, is "natural" in the sense that it is continuous with practical reasoning—that science serves each human organism in the way that a bat's wing serves the bat. And thus pragmatism is a pole against which my multidimensional picture of reasoning strives, in two substantive ways.

First and most obviously, pragmatism does not demarcate between practical and theoretical reasoning, because it collapses the latter into the former, whereas my picture maintains them in tension. Second, and less obviously, pragmatism fails to demarcate between the decisions of a collective and the decisions of individuals. Popper, by acquiescing in the idea that experiment and observation in science are just more individual decision making, inclines toward pragmatism in both these ways, and thus becomes vulnerable to the no-objectivity charge. But Popper need not have acquiesced in either way: for example, he could have maintained the idea that observation *by individuals* is an ordinary matter of personal decision, and thus subject to every kind of bias, while at the same time insisting that decisions vis-à-vis a body of evidence, assembled and preserved by citizens acting not with personal aims for personal gain, but rather as faithful public officers, are not at all like personal matters of decision. Popper could have insisted that decisions of collectivities are subject to higher standards that transcend those that apply to personal decision. Thus Popper could have made effective use of a distinction between individual and collective reasoning, in support of his bid for preserving objectivity, as follows.

Social life is a network of strategic interactions. It is also a stage on which strategies, like everything else that is subject to transmission from one generation to the next, vie for survival and reproduction.[13] Strategies need not be individual- or organism-bound, for their transmission is not restricted (as biological transmission is) to the vertical transmission from parent to offspring. Because strategies can be transmitted through imitative learning, they can float freely in a culture (they are not bound to bodies as are organs and other strictly physiological traits). When related strategies coalesce, we may call the resulting package a *practice*.

With these ideas in mind we can ask: what are disciplinary enterprises good for, as social rather than individual practices, in the economy of human life? Here we are after a natural history of the sciences, in the Darwinian sense we have come to esteem. A natural history of a prac-

---

13. Ever since the appearance of John Maynard-Smith's *Evolution and the Theory of Games* (New York: Cambridge University Press, 1982), this characterization of the social has been very influential.

tice records not only the function of the practice but also the competitors against which it won the day, as well as the circumstances or evolutionary pressures that rendered it more likely to reproduce itself (to flourish in adherents) in relation to its competitors. So what were the competitors to our many and diverse knowledge practices? And what sorts of circumstances rendered their adoption more advantageous, so that they were better smiled upon by selection forces? Why is knowledge, thought of as a community's repository of carefully crafted theories and hard-won evidence for them, worth having? What practices has it had to compete with or displace, and how has it won renewed and redoubled investment? While the specifics may never be known for certain, we can certainly conceive of the possibility that, while some practices serve individual goals, others serve the goals of communities. And that disciplinary enterprises—the sciences—are better regarded in the latter category than in the former.

My picture of reasoning is another way of offering the proposal, the polar opposite to pragmatism, that the knowledge enterprise is not continuous with practical reasoning or even with common sense. This picture can be defended through the idea that disciplinary practices are group adaptations, along the lines sketched above—not individual adaptations, as the pragmatists would insist.[14] It is a position that Popper could have defended to some advantage, in support of a strong demarcation between collective and individual reasoning.

4. WHEN DISTINCTIONS GO WRONG

Consider now the following distinctions:

- Biology is not psychology.
- Knowledge is not fact.
- Distinctions of a practical origin are not distinctions of a theoretical origin.

---

14. This is (roughly) because we cannot give an account of common sense as aimed at truth, or as functioning to provide the believer with true belief as such. Precious resources go into the fixation of each belief. And apportioning belief according to the evidence would be an evolutionary disaster for the *individual organism,* when an organism's beliefs could be apportioned instead so as to maximize evolutionary advantage for that organism. In this world an organism's beliefs are one more means to sustaining that organism's being; so that aiming at truth for its own sake is a luxury that no *individual* can afford. So long as there is no independent payoff to apportioning belief in a way that makes it count as knowledge, there can be no natural history of knowledge. If there is to be such a payoff, it must be instituted within culture, for it is not found in nature. Knowledge and common sense are consequently not continuous with one another.

What are the identifying features of these distinctions?

1. The terms name things that are themselves distant from household concerns.
2. In fact, they typically name disciplines, or genera of disciplines, or concepts that are universal to disciplinary life.
3. They involve no overlap.
4. Point 3 explains a further feature of these distinctions: they require some sort of definition at the same time. For it will not do just to make a separation—the obscurity remains unless a positive characterization of each term in the distinction is offered.
5. Most important, they require judgment, because giving a definition always involves a judgment as to whether one of the terms is dependent upon the other and, if so, which is the dependent and which the independent. Judgments of this sort are fundamentally important. Disciplines are founded upon them. And their maintenance serves to separate one discipline from another.

Sokolowski writes there are only two ways in which we can go wrong vis-à-vis distinction: (a) we may fail to make a distinction that we ought to make, and (b) we may make a distinction that does not really exist. In (a) we under-distinguish and in (b) we over-distinguish. This would follow if (as Sokolowski supposes) distinction comes logically before judgment and presupposes nothing. But if, as I am suggesting, distinction prompts for definition and can do so in leading ways, then distinction making can go wrong in a third way. A distinction can—through the prompt for definition—make an erroneous or at least a contentious claim as to the independence of one of its terms in relation to the other. In this third way, the standard distinction between fact and knowledge causes unnecessary trouble. For that particular distinction can be drawn another, less contentious way. The secret is to seek a third term or object, in terms of which both terms of the distinction can be defined. I shall illustrate this strategy by handling the distinction between fact and knowledge, through defining both in relation to a third term: the notion of an activity.

Consider the activity of writing a bank check. It can be said to have two dimensions: (1) *form*, and (2) *content*. The form is the internal structure or logic of the activity—in this case, the form involves how and where the name of a recipient is inscribed, the amount, the signature, the exchange of slips of paper, and the recording of figures in independent ledgers. The content lies in how the activity affects or makes contact with other realities—in the case of writing a check, the content is transfer of funds, and all that this implies. Characteristically, small children are as keenly attuned to the form of writing checks as they are profoundly blind to the content. With adults it is often just the reverse. Thus the subject of an experience is not always attuned to both dimensions of an activity at the same time.

The content of an activity is, in Aristotelian language, its *telos*—its end—whether the agent acknowledges an end in it or not. The form of an experience is something that deserves calling a *logic*.

Mature experience, as a species of activity, is thus a kind of imaging or picturing—a term I am borrowing from Sokolowski too[15]—with two aspects, the capacities for which do not always arrive simultaneously: (1) the *activity* of picturing itself—which involves a logic or grammar, and so has the quality of compositionality (it can be broken down into parts that are themselves individually meaningful or self-contained or complete, and combinable in other ways), and (2) the object or objective of the image *as* an image, *as* presented. An experience is a biological-*cum*-psychological happening, which in the more mature members of our species is directed at something in the world in ways that admit of systematic categorization. Experience is thus a kind of illumination or disclosure, involving the disclosed as disclosed and the disclosing as an activity or enterprise with a logic or grammar, which allows combination and recombination of the basic parts or elements. An episode in the enterprise of disclosing can be subjected to numerous forms of evaluation, as much as it can be subject to failure as an episode of disclosing a target object. And the different forms of evaluation are the basis of the contrast I think we should be drawing between epistemology on the one side and metaphysics on the other.

5. EPISTEMOLOGY AND METAPHYSICS

Epistemology, I suggest we say, is concerned with assessment of the *logic* of a form of disclosure, as to (in cases of knowledge by acquaintance) how well or effectively the form in question discloses the intended object as it is in itself, or alternatively (in the other cases) as to how effective at bringing forward objects (and I am thinking now of propositions or axioms) that deserve an allegiance. Metaphysics, by contrast, is concerned with (among other things) the *process* of disclosure as process, as well as with the dependence relations in which the discloser stands to the disclosed, as players in the drama of disclosure.

This way of handling the contrast between fact and knowledge leaves entirely open the question of whether there are dependence relations

---

15. Sokolowski, *Pictures, Quotations, and Distinctions*, 3–26.

between the process of disclosure—in which the fact plays whatever role it does—and the form of disclosure under which we apprehend it. Thus it leaves room for disagreement. So disagreement on the question of independence need not foreclose dialogue prematurely.

I do not intend this suggestion as a final statement of the distinction between metaphysics and epistemology. There is still some question whether the distinction so posed does not put epistemology, for once, in the independent position. For there is some question whether the ideas involving *disclosure* are as neutral between the two camps as I am (at least for the moment) making out. These questions require detailed treatment, which I cannot give them here. My suggestion is intended simply to illustrate the strategy of finding a third term, in relation to which the objects to be contrasted can be related. It is intended to illustrate a certain attempt to redraw a boundary, and thereby to reinvent the disciplines that depend upon that boundary.

Neither is my stratagem intended to heal the division in our discipline between analytic and continental philosophy or to effect rapprochement. It is intended exclusively as a means to productive conversation about that division and about potential rapprochement. But the distinction between metaphysics and epistemology is, at least in this instance, itself intended as a distinction of a clinical or disciplinary, rather than practical origin. It is a distinction sought for its own sake—or, equivalently, for the sake of the disciplines whose boundaries are in question.

6. DISCIPLINES

The strategy we have devised illustrates a method by which we can deliberately keep certain questions open, in the interests of not foreclosing dialogue precipitously. What good is such a strategy? Apart from keeping dialogue genuine—live—and productive, it helps us to focus upon the boundaries of disciplines, and to illuminate the fact that such boundaries are fixed at least partly by the interactive play among distinction making, definition, and judgment as to the relative dependence or independence of certain questions or terms upon others. It sends a message of caution vis-à-vis the suggestions sent by distinctions, especially as to dependence relations amongst terms or categories. And it reminds us that there are important relations amongst the activities of distinction making, judgment, and definition. To summarize, distinction making, judgment, and definition are, to be sure, different activities. But they overlap. Distinction making prompts for definition, and definition presupposes judgment as to the dependence relations amongst the terms or categories thereby defined. And any of the steps taken in an episode of definition or distinction can unwittingly presuppose—and therefore foreclose—open discussion and debate about its corollaries.

7. CONSTRUCTION AND DE-CONSTRUCTION

Our continental colleagues have noticed something that analytic philosophers have failed to take seriously. They have noticed that distinction making is an act, and that many such acts are of such a pedigree as to play a founding role in a good deal of high intellectual activity. Many of our continental colleagues have assumed—too hastily, to be sure—that what can be achieved one way can be achieved any way one likes, and have thereupon concluded that there is no such thing as objectivity. And, contrariwise, many of those on the other side of this question simply assume that there is only one way to make a distinction. Like Sokolowski, they hold that "A distinction is immediate, and shows its necessity on its face."[16] And this too is entirely too hasty, for many a proposed distinction can be refused, as well as amended, for good reasons. This fact suggests that our vision can be cloudy, so that distinctions, even if they show their necessities on their cherubic faces, are not apprehended with the clarity we may wish. But the original point is not to be missed: a distinction is a dynamic and ongoing achievement, performed in a specific historical venue, and standing in need of continued maintenance. It is not something static, fixed, a matter merely for the discipline of logic to take account of.

This being the case, there is important philosophical work in addressing the following questions, in light of the fact that distinctions are achievements:

What does objectivity amount to?

What does it mean to say that something is true, either partly or wholly, in virtue of meaning? For if we take seriously the idea that the foundation of linguistic meaning is distinction making, then we are founding meaning on a range of human acts and achievements, unequal in caliber. And this raises the further question of just how such a ragtag bunch of very specific achievements can bear that burden. (So Sokolowski, Quine, and Davidson are all justified in seeking, each in his own very distinctive way, to exorcise meanings as objects in the head.)

What is the relationship of logic to truth, on the one hand, and judgment, on the other?

---

16. Ibid., 86.

In light of all this, what is knowledge? (Not simply as contrasted with fact, now, but what is its definition?) The former answer—"justified, true belief"—is more than ever painfully inadequate. The traditional questions in epistemology take on new depth in light of the realization that distinctions are achievements.

8. THE UNDOING OF DISTINCTION

And with this new depth a new and fascinating range of questions about disciplines comes to light. We have already attended to some of these, namely those that concern the *founding* of disciplines. Others that we have not yet touched upon—for example, as to the evolution of disciplines that may be at the end of their lives—are illustrated by focusing on claims made by naturalizers of epistemology. In light of what we've said about distinctions, and particularly about discipline-founding distinctions, what does the claim of the naturalizer of epistemology—to the effect that epistemology must look to psychology for its answers—amount to? Logically speaking, it's a distinction in reverse. It is saying that where we used to see two things (two disciplines), we should henceforth see only one. It is, in Sokolowski's terminology, a claim to the effect that we have in the past over-distinguished. But what does this amount to? Does it amount to saying that there can be no genuine difference between an epistemological imperative (vis-à-vis inference, for example) and the simple description of universal or near-universal inclinations to associate or infer? If it does—as it seems to do—then those who still manage to retain the distinction are not entitled to a place in the naturalist roll of honor. But who of us is now unable to sustain the distinction, even in light of what Quine and the other apostles of naturalization have said? Who among us is truly seeing only one set of issues vis-à-vis passages amongst judgments, where before they were seeing two? What picture do we achieve of the discipline of metaphysics, vis-à-vis *psychology*, if the distinction is erased? What do we get in place of the distinction, if we should let it go? Do we get once again the felt obscurity against which the original distinction pushed? Or do we attain instead a new sort of clarity that before we did not possess, and which is such as to justify having made the error of over-distinguishing in the first place? Can over-distinguishing serve a purpose?

Note that we can raise all these questions even if we think that the naturalizers are wrong in their claims. It is purely a set of questions to do with the logic of distinction and its proposed retraction, not with the naturalizer's position in particular. And it is a fascinating set of questions, for which, at the moment, I have no answers.

13   Categorial Intentions and Objects
ROBERT SOKOLOWSKI

Some kinds of intentionality are rather colorful and concrete, for example, imagination, picturing, and memory. Here we will discuss a kind of intentionality that is more austere and more purely rational. We will examine what phenomenology calls *categorial* intentionality. This is the kind of intending that articulates states of affairs and propositions, the kind that functions when we predicate, relate, collect, and introduce logical operations into what we experience. We will examine the difference, for example, between simply intending an object and making a judgment about that object.

We recall that the word "categorial" is related to the Greek term *katagoreuō*, which originally meant the act of denouncing or accusing someone, of stating publicly that some feature belongs to him, that he is a murderer or a thief. In philosophy, the term came to mean the act of saying something about something. The phenomenological term "categorial" draws on this etymology. It refers to the kind of intending that articulates an object, the kind that introduces syntax into what we experience. A house is a simple object, but the fact that the house is white is a categorial object. The meaning of the term "Fido" or "dog" is a simple meaning, but the sense of "Fido is hungry" or "dogs are domesticated" is categorial. When we move to the categorial domain, we move from simple, "one-rayed" intentions to complex, "many-rayed" intentions. How do we move from the simple to the categorial? How do we infuse the things we experience with syntax? How do we move from perception to intellection?

The issue we are about to study is a development of signitive intentions. Signitive intentions, those associated with words, practically always put us into syntax and categorial form. We almost never just say a single word, and when we do, the word usually serves more as an exclamation or expletive ("Harry!" "Trouble!" "Hurry!") than as a fully operative linguistic unit. We exercise our humanity most fully, we act as rational animals most intensely when we use words, and our achievement of truth and thinking is implicated in our use of language; the discussion of categorial intentionality is, therefore, of great importance in phenomenology, in our study of what it is to be human and what it is to be a dative of manifestation. Furthermore, it is especially in its treatment of categorial intending that phenomenology provides resources to escape the egocentric predicament of modern philosophy. Some of phenomenology's most original and valuable contributions to philosophy are found in its doctrines about categorial intentions.

THE GENESIS OF JUDGMENTS FROM EXPERIENCE

Before we examine the importance of categorial intentions, let us try to convey a more complete idea of what they are. How do categorial intentions arise from the experience of simple objects? To spell out the process, we must distinguish three stages.

Suppose we are perceiving an object; suppose we are looking at a car:

1. At first, we just look at it in a rather passive way. Our gaze moves from one part to another, we go through the manifolds of sides, aspects, and profiles, we go through the color, the smoothness, the shine of the surface, its feel of hardness or softness. All this is a continuous perception, all carried out on one level. No particular thinking is engaged as we continue to perceive. Furthermore, as we go through the various manifolds of presentation, one and the same car is continuously given to us as the identity in the manifold.

2. Now, suppose that some abrasions on the surface of the car catch our attention. We zero in on them. We highlight this part of the car; not just this spatial part, but this feature, this abrasiveness, in the spatial part. This focus is not just more of the dawdling perception that preceded it; this highlighting is qualitatively different from what had been going on continuously before. However, it is not yet the establishment of a categorial object. So far, we are at an in-between point: we continue to experience the appearances of the car, and we continue to recognize one and the same car in all the appearances, but we have now spotlighted one of the appearances and brought it to center stage; it stands out from all the rest. A part comes into the foreground against the general background of the whole.

3. One more step is needed to establish a categorial object. We interrupt the continuous flow of perception; we go back to the whole (the car) and we now take it precisely as being the whole, and simultaneously we take the part we had highlighted (the abrasion) as being a part in that whole. We now register the whole as containing the part. A relation between whole and part is articulated and registered. At this point

we can declare, "This car is damaged." This achievement is a *categorial intuition*, because the categorial object, the thing in its articulation, is made actually present to us. We do not just have *the car* present to us; rather, *the car's being damaged* is made present.

What happens in this third stage is that the whole (the car) is presented specifically as the whole, and the part (damaged) is presented specifically as a part. The whole and its part are explicitly distinguished. A relation between them is distinctly registered. An articulation is achieved. A state of affairs clicks into place. We have moved from sensibility to intellection, from mere experiencing to an initial understanding. We have moved from the single-rayed intentionality of perception to the many-rayed intentionality of judgment. We have entered into categorial thinking.

In the first and second stages, the whole and the parts were experienced or lived through, but they were not made thematic. Strictly speaking, they were not yet articulated. Even in the second stage, when the part was brought to the fore, it was highlighted, but it was not yet acknowledged explicitly as a part. The part was brought to the fore, but its being a part was not brought to the fore. In this second stage the part is being prepped, so to speak, to become acknowledged as an attribute, but it has not been so identified as yet. In the third stage the whole and the parts are explicitly articulated.

We should note, however, that the third stage could not be reached without the preparation afforded in the second, without the first blush of structure, the concentration on a feature, that goes beyond simple continuous perception. The first stage is not differentiated enough to yield a categorial structure directly. The special focus that occurs in the second stage is needed. We have to begin to experience a part within the whole (the abrasion) before we can articulate it as such ("The car is damaged!").

A lot of philosophical material is contained in what we have just described. We have described the shift in intentionality that occurs when we go from simple perception to categorial intending, to thinking. The intentional achievement we have described is the thoughtful basis for human language and speech. Language does not float by itself on top of our sensibility; the reason we can use language is that we are capable of the kind of intending that constitutes categorial objects. The syntax that defines language is grounded on the articulation of wholes and parts that takes place in categorial intending. Syntax in language simply expresses the relations of part and whole that are brought out in categorial consciousness. The reason we can communicate, the reason we can tell someone, "that car over there is damaged," is that we have the power to go from perception to categorial thinking. It is not the case that we can think because we have language; rather, we have language because we can think, because we have the ability to achieve categorial intentions. The power of rational consciousness underlies the capacity for language. It is true that the language we inherit pressures our categorial activities in this direction or that, into these or those categorial forms, but the very ability to have language is based on the kind of intentionalities that we enjoy in the categorial domain.

It will take us some time to unpack the implications of this transition from experience to judgment. First of all, we should note that the move into the categorial domain is obviously discontinuous with the experiencing that preceded it. The move into the categorial is not just more perception; it is not just a further unrolling of the manifolds that are given in perception. In the third stage noted earlier, when we go back to the whole and register it precisely as the whole containing the part in question, we interrupt the continuity of perception. We start again on a new level; we go back over what we had been experiencing and initiate a new level of identity. This new beginning installs a new kind of consciousness and a new kind of object, the state of affairs, as the objective correlate of that consciousness.

Second, the state of affairs that is registered, the car's being damaged, is a "one," a unity in a way that is different from the identity that was given in perception. It is a heightened unity. It is more discrete and identifiable. The continuous perception just went on and on as more and more profiles were given, in a process that could have continued indefinitely. Now, however, we have a single state of affairs ("the car is damaged") that can be picked up and carried around, so to speak; it can be detached from the immediacy of perception and from our present situation. It can be conveyed to someone else in a communication (in contrast, we cannot really hand our perceptions or our memories over to someone else). It can be logically related to other states of affairs that we register. The theme of identity, which was so important even in perception, where an identity is given through manifolds, acquires a new sense and a new level of intensity. We now have identity in categorial consciousness, the kind of identity that is presented, preserved, and transported through speech.

Third, the identity of the categorial object is presented all at once. In perception we have a process in which profiles follow one another sequentially, but in categorial registration the whole and the part are given simultaneously. It is not the case that we first have the whole all by itself ("the car") and then, as a separate achievement, the part or the predicate ("damaged"), and then a relation drawn between the two ("is"). Rather, even as we register the car as the whole, we must already have the part in mind. The whole-with-part comes all at once, synchronously. When we have an articulated whole given to us, we do not have the whole first and then the articulation. The whole as such is presented only as articulated. This simultaneity of the categorial object is a further aspect of its discreteness, which must be contrasted with the continuous character of perceptual experience.

In phenomenological terminology, the establishment of categorial objects is called their *constitution*. The term "constitution" should not be taken to mean anything like a creation or an imposition of subjective forms on reality. In phenomenology, to "constitute" a categorial object means to bring it to light, to articulate it, to bring it forth, to actualize its truth. We cannot manifest a thing any way we please; we cannot make an object mean anything we wish. We can bring a thing to light only if the thing offers itself in a certain light. The thing has to show up with certain aspects that we can spotlight if we are to be able to declare that it has certain features. If we did not experience something like the abrasions in the car, we would not be able to constitute the car as damaged. Of course, we might be misled by false appearances, in which the car merely seems to be scraped, and we might erroneously declare that it is damaged when it is not; but then we remedy this situation simply by further and closer experience of the car, or by listening to what other people have to say about it, or by figuring out what must really be the case; we will then come to see that we were wrong. We have to submit to the way things disclose themselves. To submit in this way is not to place limitations on our freedom, but to achieve the perfection of our intelligence, which is geared by its nature to disclosing the way things are. To submit in this way is to bring about the triumph of objectivity, which is what our minds are supposed to do. To "constitute" a state of affairs is to exercise our understanding and to let a thing manifest itself to us.

Some further remarks on terminology: the development of categorial objects from experience is called *genetic* constitution, because of the stages through which the higher objectivities come to be from the lower. The categorial objects and intentions are obviously *founded* on the simple objects and intentions. They are *nonindependent* parts. Human intellectual activity is based on the sensible. Finally, *predicative* intentionality, in which we predicate a feature of an object and declare that "S is p," is the preeminent form of categorial activity; the term *prepredicative*, in contrast, is used to designate the kind of experience and intentionality that precedes the categorial. One of the major topics in phenomenology is that of *prepredicative* experience, the sort of experiencing that precedes but also leads up to categorial achievements.

NEW LEVELS OF IDENTITY, NEW MANIFOLDS

We have remained with predication in our analysis of categorial intentionality, but there are many other kinds of articulation that can take place once we move into this higher-level form of consciousness. Besides saying "the car is damaged," we can articulate other internal features of the car: "the car is large," "it is old," "it is a Ford." We can articulate its external relations: "it is in the parking lot," "it is next to the Honda," "it is smaller than my truck." We can include it in a collection: "there are five cars," "three of the cars seem to be damaged." We can introduce independent and subordinate clauses, conjunctions, prepositions, relative pronouns and relative clauses, adverbs, adjectives, and many other grammatical features, all of which express various ways of allowing things to be articulated. The range of the categorial is very wide, as extensive as the grammar of human language.

This whole domain of categorial articulation, in all its variety and nuances, rests, together with picturing and symbolizing, upon the "lower" intentionalities of perception, imagination, remembering, and anticipation. The categorial linguistic intentionality humanizes our perception, imagination, remembering, and anticipation; it raises them to a more rational level than they achieve in the animal kingdom. Categorial intending introduces new manifolds that supplement and penetrate the manifolds found in prepredicative experience.

Categorial intentionality is itself a new kind of identification, a new kind of identity-synthesis, that also supplements and penetrates those achieved in prepredicative experience. When we categorially intend the cube, we have not just the identity of a cube that is perceived through a manifold of sides, aspects, and profiles, and through the manifolds of memory, imagination, and anticipation; we also have the identity achieved through the statements we can make about it, the statements we can hear others make about it from their points of view, and the fulfillments we can achieve when we listen to what others say and then try to confirm their opinions by going and looking and directly articulating for ourselves. A whole new range of manifestation and truth is opened up in the categorial domain. Even our imaginings, memories, and anticipations take on a categorial complexity: we can anticipate not only "water" but "the cool water from the mountain spring." In human consciousness, perception, imagination, remembering, and anticipation all show the effects of being ordered toward their completion in rational thinking. The way we exercise these forms of intending is shaped by their involvement in categorial intentionality.

What happens in categorial intentions is that the things we perceive become elevated into the space of reasons, the domain of logic, argument, and rational thinking. Categorial experience is the transit point leading from perception to intelligence, where language and syntax come into play. Through categorial articulation, the things we perceive become registered and admitted into the field of reasoning and conversation. Simple perception is more of a physiological and psychological process, while categorial registration is the first move into logic.

When we speak about the object as an identity within a manifold of presentation, we insist that the identity itself never shows up as one of the sides, aspects, and profiles through which it is given. Its identity belongs to another dimension. It is this identity, however, that we refer to when we name the object and bring it into categorial articulation. Thus, the cube that is perceptually given in and through a manifold of sides, aspects, and profiles is the identity that we refer to when we utter the words "the cube" and begin to predicate features of it. The identity of the cube is the bridge between perception and thought.

CATEGORIAL OBJECTS

Through our categorial intentions, we establish categorial objects. We constitute states of affairs, such as the fact that the car is damaged. These categorial objects truly are objects; they are not just arrangements of concepts or ideas. They are not "intramental" objects; they are intellected crystallizations that take place in the things we encounter. In categorial activity we articulate the way things are presented to us; we bring to light relationships that exist in things in the world. We have this world-directed focus, moreover, whether we intend things that are present to us or things that are absent. We must emphasize the fact that categorial objects are ways in which things appear; they are not subjective, psychological "things in the mind."

To bring out the objectivity of categorial objects, let us examine a few other examples. We have already talked about the state of affairs expressed by the statement, "this car is damaged." As another example, suppose I am engaged in a discussion with two other people. The discussion progresses, but then something fishy begins to surface; something smells strange in what they are saying and the way they are saying it. This intermediate stage is like the stage, in our previous example, when the abrasions on the car begin to attract our attention. Then, suddenly, I register the situation: "They are trying to put something over on me!" The state of affairs clicks into place, a categorial intuition is achieved, the wholes and parts are articulated, syntax is installed into what I experience.

Again, suppose I am walking along a trail, looking at the rocks along the side. Suddenly I realize that the thing over there is not a rock but a fossil. The rather passive level of perception, the continuous identification of one and the same object through many profiles, gives way to a registration of the state of affairs, "that is not just a rock; it's a fossil in the ground!"

The examples we have examined—the damaged car, the deceptive behavior, the fossil and not the rock—are articulations of things that are before us. They are not mental entities, they are not just meanings in the mind; they are modifications in the way things are being presented to us. These modifications, these changes in the mode of presentation, are "in the world," but obviously they are not in the world in the manner in which a tree or a table is in the world. Rather, they are higher-level objects. They are "out there" as more complex modes of presentation, more intricate ways of being manifested. The states of affairs expressed by the words that we use ("the car is damaged," "they are deceiving me") are truly parts of the world. They are how certain segments of the world—this car, this behavior—can be articulated.

The states of affairs in these examples are there directly before us. We intuit them. Most of the time that we speak, however, the states of affairs that we express are absent from us. We talk about what is not present: yesterday's football game, how our congressman is voting, what happened at the Battle of Sharpsburg. The human possession of language gives us enormous reach; we can talk about things long ago and very far away, even about galaxies that are incredibly distant from us and periods of time billions of years ago. Most of our talk does not reach quite that far; most of it is much more local ("What did she do after you slammed the door?" "Was the dentist careful?"), but it still reaches largely into what is absent.

An extremely important point is the fact that when we speak about the absent, we still are articulating a part of the world. We are not turning to our ideas or concepts as substitute presences for the things that are absent. We are so constituted that we can intend things in their absence as well as in their presence. The intentionality of consciousness is such that it reaches outward all the time, even when it targets things that are not before it. If I give a speech about the Battle of Antietam, I and my audience intend that battle even though it happened more than 130 years ago; if you and I, here in Washington, D.C., talk about the Empire State Building, it is the building we are talking about, not some meanings or images that might come to mind during our conversation.

Our discourse about the absent is, however, punctuated by episodes in which we speak about what is present. Sometimes we might just have something to say about the objects that are nearby, objects that we can perceive. At other times, our speech about absent things might demand that we go and find out whether what we say is true or not. We might be questioned about what we say, and at least in some cases we can resolve the question by going to see what is the case, that is, by going somewhere and categorially registering the situation in its presence ("see; I told you that an owl was nesting in this barn"). When we cannot do this, we may resort to the witness of others, to documents, to relics, and to other forms of indirect confirmation, but many of these in turn will have been based on direct categorial registrations that were carried out by someone else.

Thus, although our speech is mostly directed toward things that are absent, it can turn to things that are present to confirm or disconfirm what we say about the absent. An identity-synthesis takes place between the state of affairs that we intended in its absence and the same state of affairs we now intend in its confirming presence. We identify the situation given now as the same as the one we intended when we only spoke about it.

THE ELIMINATION OF MEANINGS AS MENTAL OR CONCEPTUAL THINGS

In discussing the transition from categorial actions dealing with the absent to those dealing with the present, we have introduced the issue of truth. We noted that in our worldly experience we try to see whether the statements made in the absence of the objects are true or not. But something seems to be missing in our analysis so far.

Where does "the meaning" of our words exist? Where are the judgments we perform? Traditionally, the meaning of our words, the judgments or the propositions that we make, the ideas that we possess, have all been taken as some sort of mental or conceptual things, something closer to us, some sort of things that are never absent. Because such things were thought always to be directly present to our minds, they seemed able to serve as a bridge between us and what we intend, especially when we intend something that was absent. These things could explain how we could be directed toward that which was not near us. This understanding of meanings and propositions can be found in some medieval thinkers, in Descartes, the British Empiricists, and Kant, in contemporary cognitive science, and in many philosophers of language.

Furthermore, the issue of truth seems to require some sort of meaning or concept or judgment between us and the thing: when we claim we have told the truth, we imply—do we not?—that what we said, the meanings we had, correspond to what is out there. If there are no meanings and propositions apart from the things we know, how can we ever say that our judgments conform to things as they are? What is there that could conform to the facts? How can we explain what truth is if we do not posit meanings and judgments as some sort of mental things? Common sense seems to demand that we posit meanings as some sort of entities in the mind.

And yet, although we seem forced to posit meanings and judgments as mental or conceptual things, such things turn out to be philosophically embarrassing and perplexing. We never directly experience them. They are postulated as something we cannot do without, but no one has ever seen one of them. They are theoretical constructs rather than familiar entities. They are postulated, not given, and they are postulated because we think we cannot explain knowledge and truth without them. How do they exist? What sort of entities are they? Are they in the mind or in some sort of third realm between the mind and the world? How do they do their work of referring us to objects? How many of them do we have? Do they come into actual existence and then go out of it, moving from virtual to actual and back to virtual again, as we call them up? They seem to be duplicates of the things and states of affairs outside us; why do we need to posit them? But how can we avoid doing so? Propositions and meanings as mental or representational entities seem to be a *pis aller*, a cul de sac, an aporia. We are boxed into them by philosophical confusions.

I believe that one of the most sophisticated and most valuable contributions of phenomenology to philosophy lies in its treatment of judgments and meanings. Phenomenology is able to show that we need not posit judgments and senses as mental entities or as intermediaries between the mind and things. We need not introduce them as the philosophically perplexing, strange beings that have the magical power of relating our consciousness to the world outside. Phenomenology provides a new interpretation of the status of judgments, propositions, and concepts, one that is simple, elegant, and true to life. It does so in the following manner.

Suppose you tell me that the flatware you are showing me is sterling silver. At first I simply go along with what you say and see it as silver. Following your lead, I register the state of affairs, "this flatware is silver." Then I begin to have doubts. The whole thing does not add up; how could you have so much silverware? Besides, it does not look or feel like sterling; it is too light; it is too tinny.

What happens at this point is that I have changed my attitude toward the state of affairs that I had just constituted. Originally, I simply intended the flatware's being silver; I intended it naively and straightforwardly. Now I begin to hesitate. I enter into a new, reflective attitude. I still intend the flatware as silver, but now I add the qualifier, "as proposed by you." I no longer simply believe; I suspend belief, but I still intend the same thing-and-feature. I have changed the state of affairs, "this flatware is silver," into the mere judgment or meaning, "this flatware is silver." It is no longer a simple state of affairs for me; it is now, for me, a state of affairs *as being presented by you;* this qualifier makes it into just your judgment, not the simple fact.

The change from being a state of affairs to being a judgment occurs in response to a new attitude I have adopted. Let us call my new attitude the "propositional attitude," and let us call the reflection that establishes it the "propositional (or judgmental) reflection." It can also be called *apophantic* reflection, because it establishes and turns toward the judgment, which is called *apophansis* in Greek. The judgment, the proposition, the meaning, the sense arise in response to this new attitude. The judgment, proposition, or concept is not there ahead of time as a kind of mediating entity before it is reflected upon. It is not there beforehand doing its epistemological work of relating us to the real world. It is not there already, waiting for us to turn to it or to infer its presence. Rather, it is a dimension of presentation, a change in the mode of presentation, that arises when we enter into the propositional attitude by means of a propositional reflection. It arises when we change our focus. The proposition is not a subsistent entity; it is part of the world being articulated, but being taken as just someone's presentation: in this case, it is being taken as your presentation. It is your judgment.

The benefit of this new explanation of how propositions and meanings come to be is that it avoids the need to posit propositions and meanings as mysterious mental or conceptual entities. It preserves the world-directedness of all intentionality; even when we refer to a judgment, we are referring to the world, but to the world precisely as it has been proposed by someone.

This phenomenological analysis of judgment also allows us to clarify the correspondence theory of truth. Usually, the biggest problem discussed in the correspondence theory of truth is how to explain the "match" between the proposition and the state of affairs. But in fact, a deeper problem is the question of what propositions are in the first place; how do they come to be? What mode of existence do they have? Before we say how they can correspond to things, we have to say what they are like.

Instead of postulating judgments, propositions, and senses as mediating entities, phenomenology sees them as correlated to a propositional attitude and propositional reflection. They arise in response to our taking a state of affairs as being merely proposed by someone. In this analysis, not only is a state of affairs "in the world"; even a proposition is "in the world," but in the world only as being projected by someone. It is how the world is being projected as being, through what someone is saying.

We have reached the following point in our phenomenological analysis: we have moved from naively intending the state of affairs to reflectively taking the same state of affairs "as stated or proposed by you." The flatware "is" silver, but only as stated or presented by you; I am no longer intending it purely and simply as such. What happens next? At this point we have a state of affairs as intended by you. We do not yet have the truth of the question resolved.

What happens next is that I go back to the flatware and inspect it more closely, look at its bill of sale, look for inscriptions on it, perhaps ask other people's opinion, and so on. Then, after sufficient inspection of my own, I might conclude, "yes, it is silver after all." If this is the outcome of my inquiry, then I find that your judgment does correspond to the way things are. I no longer take the state of affairs as just being proposed by you. I go back to a straightforward intending of the "being silver" of the flatware, but my return is not like the original naive intention. I now have the state of affairs as confirmed, as having gone through the acid test of propositional reflection and confirmation. The state of affairs is the same one I originally intended, and the same I took as just proposed by you; but now it takes on a new layer of sense, a new noematic dimension: it is now a confirmed fact and not just a naively intended state of affairs.

This explanation of the correspondence between judgment and fact can be called a "disquotational" theory of truth, because it involves the step of first merely "quoting" the state of affairs (during the critical analysis, when I take the state of affairs as merely proposed by you) and then removing the quotation marks, annulling the propositional reflection, leaving the propositional attitude, and going back to the straightforward acceptance. However, it is a disquotational theory that deals with more than the merely linguistic phenomenon of introducing and removing the quotation marks; the theory provides more than a linguistic explanation, because it describes the shifts in intentionality that underlie the quotation and disquotation. We begin with the state of affairs simply, then move to the state of affairs as proposed, then move to the state of affairs as confirmed.

Of course, my investigation might well result in the conclusion that the flatware is not silver after all; then the "state of affairs as proposed" continues permanently. I do not disquote, I do not annul the propositional reflection; the flatware never was silver, it was only proposed as such by you. Therefore, that particular "state of affairs" was and is only your proposition, only your judgment, only your meaning, never the way the things are. The state of affairs becomes permanently disqualified from being truly the case; it will always remain just your opinion, and a false one at that. It is interesting to note, incidentally, that an opinion or a judgment is usually attached to someone whose proposition it is, while a fact is not the possession of anyone in particular; it is there for everyone.

This phenomenological theory of truth, instead of moving between mental or semantic entities and real entities, operates entirely in the domain of presentation. It distinguishes varieties in the kinds of presentation (the simple, the categorial, the propositional, the confirmatory) and speaks about the identities that are achieved within the new manifolds that these varieties introduce. The perceptual object, given through profiles, is now further identified through categorial articulation and heightened still further as an object through the moves of critical reflection and confirming identification.

The dimension of linguistic categorial verification also introduces great richness and variety because it involves an intersubjective dimension. We have not only the other side of the cube that someone else can see while I see this side; we also have, say, the statements made by people centuries ago, confirmed or disconfirmed by people now, or statements made by people very different from us, living in different times and places, and yet understood and to some degree verified or falsified by our own thoughtful experience. We also have the statements made by us that will be confirmed or disconfirmed by others in other places and times. Speech allows intersubjective exchanges that range far more widely than do the exchanges based on simple common perceptions.

The steps in intentionality that we have considered—of naive, categorial intending, of critical, propositional reflection, and of the return to confirmation or disconfirmation—are all carried out in the natural attitude. The phenomenological theory of truth and meaning analyzes these steps and their elements from the vantage point of the transcendental, phenomenological attitude. From this perch, it reflects on the true and false intentionalities that are carried out in our prephilosophical engagements and clarifies what goes on in them.

FURTHER REMARKS ON CATEGORIAL ACTS AND OBJECTS

Obviously, we are more active when we enter into categorial intentions than when we simply perceive, imagine, remember, and anticipate things. There is something like a new "product" in categorial intentionality, the categorial object, whether that object be taken as a state of affairs or a judgment (which is a state of affairs taken as proposed). The new product, the categorial object, can be detached from its immediate context and related somewhere else through the use of language. By speaking to you, I can "give" you the same categorial object that I see and articulate now. You can articulate that selfsame object even in its absence. This sort of distancing is much more radical than that which occurs in the displacements of remembering or imagining, in which I can also present things to myself in their absence. Remembering and imagining give us an original sense of the absent, but they do not allow the sort of communication of the absent, and the kind of control we can have over it, that occur in speech.

Categorial intentionality elevates us into a properly human form of truth, the truth that involves speech and reasoning. But if it allows this form of truth, it also allows a properly human abuse of truth; it makes possible errors and falsehoods on a scale that dwarfs the misperceptions, failed memories, and misimaginings of the lower intentions. If I can "give" you a state of affairs that you have not experienced, I can also "give" you a false version of it in my speech, or I can "give" you a state of affairs that never happened at all. Also, I can even contradict, that is, speak against, my own self. I can have one conviction and then have another that annuls the first. I may hold as true the state of affairs that this person is good to be with, and also hold as true the state of affairs that this person is hateful to be with. I can believe that "S is p" and also hold, at least by implication, that "S is not p." Often, such contradictions are caused by emotional involvements, in which we desire two things that cannot be possessed together and we do not wish to face up to the fact that we cannot have both; they can also be caused by confusion, inattention, and inability to master the intellectual material of the thing at hand. We will examine this intellectual root of contradiction when we come to the topic of vagueness.

Entry into the categorial domain also permits the introduction of logic. Logic does not belong to the lower level of perception and its variants, but it does come into play on the categorial level. Once we have constituted categorial objects, we can formalize those objects and pay attention to the consistency or inconsistency of the forms that result. Instead of dealing with the categorial object, "the car is damaged," we can deal with the pure form, "S is p," in which the content of the object is rendered indifferent and the syntax is kept in place. Instead of "car" we deal with "any object whatever," and instead of "damaged" we deal with "any attribute whatever." Then we can examine the relations among various forms and see, for example, that the form "S is not p" is not consistent with the form "Sp is q." If we were to assert the latter and then go on to assert the former ("this red house is expensive; this house is not red"), we would be contradicting ourselves. Logical consistency is a necessary condition for the truth of statements; if statements contradict themselves by virtue of their logical form, then *a priori* they cannot be verified by our experience of the things themselves.

A distinction is introduced in phenomenology between two kinds of formal systems, those belonging to objects and states of affairs and the "ontological" side of things, and those belonging to judgments or propositions and the region of sense or meaning. The science of the formal structures of objects and states of affairs is called *formal ontology*, while the science of the formal structures of senses and propositions is called *formal apophantics*.

Let me make one more comment about the doctrine that takes concepts, judgments, meanings, or senses as mental or conceptual entities, the doctrine that I have attempted to refute. To think that such entities are needed to explain knowledge betrays a failure to recognize the intentionality of consciousness. It is to take consciousness as simple, sheer awareness, conscious only of itself, and to assume that intentionality must be added to it by the insertion of some kind of representation: a concept, a word, a proposition, a mental image, a symbol, a sense, or a "noema." In this view, it is not consciousness that is essentially intentional, but the representation. It is the insert that makes consciousness intentional and specifies what the consciousness intends and how it intends it: the insert establishes an intention, a reference, and a sense. The representation relates us to the objects "outside" and gives them a certain meaning. But how could such an additive bestow intentionality on our awareness? How could we know that what is given to us is a word or image or concept, and that it represents something "beyond" itself? How would the very dimension of an "outside" arise for us if it were not there in the beginning? If consciousness does not start out being intentional, it could never figure out how to become so.

THE PHENOMENON OF VAGUENESS

We have been discussing categorial intentions and their correlative objects, as well as truth, meaning, judgments, states of affairs, verification, and logic. Phenomenology also treats another topic that plays a strategic role in this network of phenomena, one that is only infrequently and marginally treated by most philosophers. It is the phenomenon of *vagueness*. Vagueness is important not only in regard to the more scientific issues of logic, meaning, and verification, but also in regard to the ordinary use of language and the establishment of a responsible speaker.

When we say or read something, it is usually assumed that we think through what we say or read. This is often not the case. Words are frequently used without thought. We might be superficially reading something, or we might hear someone talk but fail to pay attention to what he says, we might even say things ourselves without being properly aware of the meaning of what we say, or we might be reciting something by rote. Sometimes the material we are talking about is beyond us; we really do not understand what we are saying. Much of what people say about politics, for example, is like this. Much of what they say is vague: slogans are repeated, favorite ideas are trotted out, statements made by others are stated verbally but without comprehension. Most public opinion polls measure vague thinking. The human power of speech, the noble power that gives us our dignity as human beings, also makes it possible for us to seem to be thinking when we really are not. This is a specifically human way of failing to be what we should be, and it is very important in human affairs.

What occurs in thoughtless speech is that the categorial activity that should accompany the speech is not adequately achieved. There is some categorial activity, but it is not up to the issues being discussed and asserted. There is a succession of ideas but not a thought. If I speak vaguely, someone who listens to me and who is more thoughtful than I am will usually find, as time goes on, that what I am saying makes no sense. It is garbled. He will ask me to clarify what I mean, to make sense out of the hodgepodge I am presenting. If he tries to argue with me he will be continuously frustrated; arguing with someone who speaks vaguely is like trying to use hand grenades to disperse a fog. A listener who is no more thoughtful than I am, however, will not perceive that I am speaking vaguely. In his own vagueness, he will, if he likes the position I seem to take, feel that I am successfully articulating our common belief: "Un fou trouve toujours un plus fou qui l'admire." If the listener does not sympathize with what I seem to be saying, he will be upset with me and express what seems to be another viewpoint. But in all this, neither his mind nor mine is truly active; we are expressing something like emotional attitudes rather than distinct opinions. There is no real argument, only a collision of half-formed thoughts.

Vagueness should be distinguished from two other failures in regard to truth and categorial objects, ignorance and error. In ignorance we simply do not try to articulate the categorial objects in question: we just are silent about the issue. We do not pretend to think about it, and we do not seem to be thinking. When we are in error, we formulate an opinion about something, and we do so explicitly, but it turns out to be incorrect. Our opinion would not stand up if we went to the things we are talking about and tried to experience and register them as we state them to be. Our propositions would be disconfirmed. In such error, we do achieve distinct thinking and we do articulate a categorial object, but the thinking and the object are false. We must have overcome vagueness and reached distinctness if we are to be incorrect.

Vagueness comes between ignorance and error. It is inchoate thinking. It is an attempt to think that does not quite get there, but it uses the words that generally indicate thinking, and hence it dissimulates, however unintentionally. The words are paraded and give the impression of thought, but there is insufficient thought behind them.

In some cases it is possible for the speaker who begins with vagueness to think through the things he is saying and to articulate the states of affairs and judgments that he wishes to declare. In this case, the speaker has moved from vagueness to *distinctness*. He successfully achieves the categorial objects he was striving to constitute. He now thinks distinctly. He now presents the state of affairs or the judgment he was earlier trying to present.

When the speaker goes from vagueness to distinctness, he may find that the judgment he finally achieves is indeed the same one he had been vaguely stating; the judgment is the same in the two modes of presentation, the vague and the distinct. But he may also find that the distinct judgment is not the same as the vague one; rather, he may find that the vague judgment harbored contradictions within itself, and now that distinctness has been achieved, the contradictions come to the fore; they had been hidden, precisely because of the vagueness. Thus the possibility of logical contradiction or consistency demands that we have brought the judgment to distinctness, that we have distinctly articulated it. Until a judgment is brought to distinctness, we cannot really say whether it is true or false, or even consistent or inconsistent with itself and other judgments, because we do not yet really know what the judgment is. It does not yet exist as a distinct meaning, one that could be true or false, consistent or inconsistent. We have to know what someone is saying before we can determine whether what he says is true or false.

Vagueness can harbor inconsistency, but it can also harbor *incoherence*. Inconsistency means that one part of what we say contradicts another part in regard to formal logical structure: we say both "S is p" and "S is not p." Incoherence, on the other hand, means that the content, as opposed to the form, of our judgments is not properly assembled. It means that we are using content words that make no sense when they are put together: we might, for example, say that, literally, the nation is a big family, or that a political constitution guarantees a job for everyone, or that the brain knows who is coming through the door (it is the person, not the brain, that knows things). Contradiction deals with the form of judgments, incoherence deals with their content, and both can occur in the fog of vagueness. Words mean things, but it is possible to put the words together in such a way that the whole does not mean one thing. Some parts of the whole "speak against" other parts, or some parts are not blended properly with other parts (features that belong to families are blended with nations, feature of the whole person are blended with one of the person's organic parts).

Everyone is vague at some time, and there is nothing regrettable about that. We have to start with vagueness when we enter into a new domain of thinking. Ideas that come to mind are almost always vague at first and ask to be brought to distinctness, when the inconsistencies and incoherences in the idea will be filtered out. The student beginning mathematics is usually quite vague about the categorial objects he is articulating. If he is a good student, he will move on to distinctness. Some people can get to distinctness more easily and more quickly than others. Some people can never get out of vagueness in certain domains, while other people can hardly ever get out of vagueness in any domain. They just do not think clearly and distinctly, and yet they use language, which might make it seem to others that they are thinking properly. A chatterbox is a living example of vagueness. Public opinion is awash with vagueness, demanding contradictory things from public figures. What "they" say, what "on dit," what "man sagt," is notoriously vague, but it is still the starting point for authentic thinking. Our thoughts, the categorial objects we constitute, do not come finished and polished from the start.

Finally, our treatment of vagueness has dealt with its appearance in speech and thought, but vagueness also occurs in action. Someone who chronically speaks without thinking is likely to act in the same manner, lurching from one half-baked move to another and making a royal mess of things. In this case it is deliberation and choice that are pervaded by the inconsistency and incoherence that vagueness brings. The spectacle of such conduct, whether in personal, institutional, or political affairs, arouses either pity or grief in the observer, depending on how he is affected by the action in question.

CATEGORIAL OBJECTS AND HUMAN INTELLIGENCE

Instead of closing with the theme of vagueness, which is a deficiency in human thinking, let us end on a more positive note and consider some of the excellences of the domain of categorial objects.

Human language differs from animal sounds because it contains syntax. Human language contains sound, but its sound is structured by phonemic patterns and by grammatical particles, inflections, and placements. It is the grammatical ordering of language that makes the linguistic sign system amenable to human control, that makes it a system of such exquisite complexity and refinement, and that lets it become the vehicle for the exercise of truth. Syntax elevates animal sounds into human discourse. In phenomenology the syntactic elements of language have been called the *syncategorematic* parts of language, because they "come along with" the expressions that merely name objects and features, the *categorematic* parts of speech.

The syntactic parts of language obviously serve to link words. They are the grammar of a language. This linguistic work, however, is not all that they do. They also function in intentionality: the syntax of language is related to the way things can present themselves to us, to the way we can intend and articulate them. Syntactic parts of language serve to express the combinatorics of presentation, the way things can be presented to us in various part-whole relationships. Phenomenology does not just consider the linguistic role of grammar, as structural linguistics does; it also relates syntax to the activity of being truthful, to evidencing.

The nonsyntactic elements of language (terms such as "tree" and "green") simply name things and features, but the syntactic elements express the manner in which the things and features are displayed. The syntactic parts of expressions have objective correlates. In the statement "the tree is green," the terms "tree" and "green" obviously name things and features that can be given to perception, but the copula "is" also has objective reference, because the statement does not just present the tree and the green color: it presents the tree's being green, or the state of affairs that the tree is green. The "being featured" of the tree corresponds to the copula "is." The copula "is" does not just link the words "tree" and "green," but also allows the tree's being green to be intended by us, even in its absence. To take another example, if we were to conjoin two terms, such as "pepper and salt," the grammatical particle "and" would correspond to the "being together" of the two items: the two are not just individually presented but are presented as being together, as taken as one.

Thus, the way things can be articulated for us, the way they can be intended in either presence or absence, the way they "fall apart" and "fall into wholes" for us, is made possible by the syntax of language, and the grammatical genius of each language provides a style of presentation that is distinctive to that language. Phenomenology relates syntax to the modes of presentation.

When we register a categorial object, we move from the continuity of perception to the more abrupt, discontinuous presence of intellected objects, with wholes and parts being explicitly recognized. We present higher-level, categorial objects, and such objects come in discrete packets. There are many of them, expressed in the many statements we make, and they are all interrelated. The objects given to intellection form a network. We document each categorial object when we express it; we put ourselves on record, we state precisely this or that. We say one thing, then another, then yet another, but as we move on to other statements the ones we made earlier remain in force, and what we say subsequently has to be consistent with what we said before. The connections among all these categorial objects are logical and not just associative. We can ask whether this categorial object or sense is consistent with that one; we can call upon the speaker to avoid contradiction (that is, to avoid saying something "against" what he said before). We can also call upon the speaker to explain what he has articulated, to give reasons and clarifications for it. The categorial domain is the space of reasons, and phenomenology explores the intricate intentionalities that constitute it.

When we succeed in lifting the objects we experience into the precision of categorial objects, we do not fragment them into pieces disconnected from one another. Rather, we make available a more profound continuity among things. Instead of a perceptual flow we are given interrelated states of affairs and, behind them, the sense of a world or a cosmos. The categorial domain brings a new, articulated sense of the whole; it is not the case that only the precategorial is holistic. Precision and distinctness in thinking do not atomize things but yield a much keener appreciation of the whole picture, allowing us to apprehend the forest precisely because we apprehend trees.

Syntactic parts of speech express categorial forms, and in doing so they help express the way the world presents itself to us, but they also serve another function. They also serve to *indicate* or to signal that the speaker is carrying out the acts of thinking that constitute the categorial objects. They signal that the speaker is speaking and voicing an opinion, and not just groaning or burping. When we listen to someone speak, we hear more than sounds; we also hear the grammatical ordering of sounds. By virtue of this encoding we have the world and the things in it expressed to us, and we also have given to us the presence of a speaker who takes responsibility for their being expressed in this way. Language and syntax are used to reveal a world and the things in it, but they also, in a different way, reveal the speaker who is using the language and syntax at the moment. They reveal a transcendental ego, a responsible agent of intentionality and evidence.

We have discussed categorial intentionality, the form of intending that supervenes on the more basic forms of perception and its variants. Categorial intending is the domain of reason or logos. It establishes categorial objects, objects that are pervaded by syntax, with parts and wholes explicitly registered. Categorial objects are found on the ontological side of things (states of affairs, things, attributes) and also on the apophantic side (judgments, propositions, senses, subjects, predicates). Verification moves between these two sides, between the ontological and the apophantic. States of affairs and judgments have to be brought to distinctness before they can be confirmed or disconfirmed, and even before they can be understood (indeed, to bring them to distinctness is precisely to understand them). They are brought to distinctness out of the matrix of vagueness, which is a sort of basement and source for categoriality.

Our attention has been directed to categorial objects, but, as we have noted, the domain of the categorial also involves the emergence of a responsible speaker. It requires a self elevated beyond the self constituted in perception, memory, and imagination. Categorial objects involve categorial activity, which requires in turn an agent of truth who carries it out: the transcendental ego.

14   Carving Up Reality

BARRY SMITH

1. THE PROBLEM OF THE MANY

Think of Mont Blanc, with its rabbits and foothills and its slurries of moistened rock. We can carve up the reality around Mont Blanc in different ways. If we are hunters, we might include rabbits as parts of the mountain; if we are geologists we might include only rock, perhaps together with a certain amount of air in the crevices and tunnels that have been formed beneath the mountain surface. If we are soil chemists we might include also a surrounding thin layer of organic matter; if we are skiers, we will want some snow; and if we are French or Italian government surveyors, then our respective maps of the mountain might include slightly different determinations as to where, precisely, its borders lie. If we are armed with a microscope we will discover that the closer we approach the surface of the mountain, the more questionable does the belongingness or non-belongingness of microscopic particles to the mountain itself begin to appear. What could make it true, given some atom or molecule very near the surface of the mountain, that it is, or is not, a *part* of the mountain? Reflection on such puzzles suggests the hypothesis—expounded in the literature on vagueness under the heading "supervaluationism"—that there is no single answer to the question what it is to which "Mont Blanc" refers. Rather, there are at any given time many answers, many parcels of reality that deserve the name "Mont Blanc."

Something similar applies also to you yourself, and indeed to every other organism. When you refer to John, you do not think of all the parts of John or of his immediate surroundings. You do not think of the cells in John's arm, or the fly next to his ear, or the neutrinos that pass through his body. These things do not fall under the beam of your referential searchlight. Rather, they are traced over. You apprehend John as a single, unitary object. His dermatologist, though, has a different perspective, for he is all too well aware that, like Mont Blanc, John has questionable parts and that there are at the molecular level many overlapping aggregates of matter, all of which have a claim to being John. Notice that this is not an epistemological matter. Even an omniscient being would be in the same predicament as you or I concerning where the boundaries of John, or Mont Blanc, precisely lie.

That John is losing or gaining molecules from one moment to the next is of no consequence, however, for our everyday purposes: it falls below our normal threshold of concern. Our cognitive habits have thus developed in such a way that they relate to reality in a *coarse-grained fashion,* and this allows us to ignore questions about the lower-level constituents of the objects foregrounded by our referential searchlight. This in turn is what allows such objects to be specified, not precisely, but rather in such a way that a range of alternative but nearly identical objects are simultaneously comprehended within the scope of what we see or refer to. We do not recognize this "many" because we are focused precisely on those parts and moments of the matters in hand that lie above the pertinent granularity threshold. On the level of granularity we embrace in our everyday cognitive activities it is as if only one object serves as the focus of our attentions.

The acts in which we make reference to objects in reality thus bring about a partitioning of reality into two domains: the foreground domain, within which the relevant object is located, and the background domain, which comprehends all entities left in the dark by the operating perceptual or referential searchlight. But how is this partitioning to be understood? Certainly it cannot be understood in terms of any simple pigeonholing of reality into jointly exhaustive and mutually exclusive parts, either of the sort that is involved in a system of categories like that of Aristotle or of the sort that underlies the periodic table of the chemical elements.[1] Nor can the foreground-background partition be understood along geographical lines (by analogy with the sort of partition that might be depicted on a map). Thus it is not as if one connected, compact (hole-free) portion of reality is set in relief in relation to its surroundings, as on old maps of the known world surrounded by *terrae incognitae,* or on contemporary maps in which Beverly Hills is represented as something set into relief within the wider surrounding territory of Los Angeles. For if an object is included in the foreground domain, this does not imply that all the parts of the object are also included therein. This is because each partition comes with its own granularity, and this means that it does not recognize parts under a certain size. It is for this reason that each partition is compatible with a range

---

1. See the essays by Sanford, Lang, and Sim on Aristotle's system of categories, Chapters 1, 2, and 5 of this volume.

of possible views, and indeed with no view at all, as to the ultimate constituents of the objects included in its foreground domain.

2. THE GRANULARITY PROBLEM POSED

If, however, partitions are effected not in any simple geographical way but rather in such a way as to be marked by a certain granularity, then this presents a serious problem to our standard views of how reference and perception work—a new variant on older problems connected with intentionality, opacity, and substitution. The problem turns on the fact that the relation of a part to its whole is transitive. Consider the question of what Mary sees when she sees John raising his hand. The following must all simultaneously be true:

A. The molecules inside John are parts of John.
B. John is part of what Mary sees.
C. The molecules inside John are not a part of what Mary sees.

These sentences cannot be simultaneously true in the presence of the (independently attractive-seeming) principle of the transitivity of parthood:

D. If x is part of y, and y is part of z, then x is part of z.

Counterpart triads can be constructed in regard to a host of other types of entities: truth makers, facts, states of affairs, situations, surfaces, aspects, pluralities, shadows, visual fields, persons, Husserl's "noemata,"[2] Kant's "phenomenal world," Fine's "qua objects," and so on. Thus we might have:

A'. The molecules inside John are parts of John.
B'. John is part of what makes it true that John is raising his hand.
C'. The molecules inside John are not a part of what makes it true that John is raising his hand.

Clearly, if we are to do justice ontologically to the facts of granularity, then some way must be found to explain how the sentences in each of these triads can be simultaneously true, and this means that some way must be found to block the transitivity of parthood (thus, for example, to block the move from "x is visible" and "y is part of x" to: "y is visible"). We can formulate an analogous triad also in relation to entire domains, for example, in relation to the domain of what might be called "common-sense reality":

2. On Husser's noemata, see Føllesdal's and Sokolowski's essays, Chapters 8 and 13 of this volume.

A. The molecules inside John are parts of John.
B. John is part of common-sense reality.
C. The molecules inside John are not a part of common-sense reality.

One way to resolve the problem is to refuse to take expressions like "fact," "sense datum," "what Mary sees," or "common-sense reality" seriously as referring to special sorts of entities. One is then simply not allowed to ask, for example, whether molecules of paint are or are not a part of the sense data which John sees when he focuses on a painted wall. To suppose that a part-whole relation might obtain (or not obtain) here is to be guilty of what some like to call a "category mistake."

Those interested in ontology will persist in raising such questions nonetheless, which means that in regard to at least some of the types of entities mentioned, they will take such entities seriously from an ontological point of view. Sentences involving category mistakes (for example, "cardinal numbers are green") they will classify simply as unproblematic falsehoods. One standard ontological approach, then, uses the phrase "under a description" or some comparable locution. The idea is that it can be the case that some given molecule is part of John under one description (for example, *physical body*), but that it is not a part of John under some other description (for example, *object visible with the naked eye*). Again, however, ontological persistence reveals a problem with such approaches. For if John under these different descriptions is indeed one and the same entity, then he thereby also has, under each description, all the same parts. If, on the other hand, John under this description is a different entity from John under that description, then we are still in need of an account of how this difference is to be understood, and this brings us back to the puzzling triad with which we began.

Another popular starting point for the resolution of our puzzle rests on using set theory as a means of blocking the principle D of the transitivity of parthood. The set-membership relationship is after all not transitive. But to use set theory as a means of blocking transitivity brings too great a cost. For if set theory is taken realistically, then this forces us to identify *Urelemente*—elements of sets that are not themselves sets—from out of which the larger worldly structures which concern us would be constructed by set-theoretical means. But what would such elements be in the case of a complex event such as *John raising his hand*? And even if appropriate elements—ultimate subatomic particles, for example—did present themselves for purposes of set-theoretic reconstruction, problems would still arise because we would then find that our ontology is cluttered with multiple copies of reconstructed objects existing at different times and at different levels of granularity (for example, John as set of atoms, John as set of molecules, John as set of cells; this set of atoms at a time when it constitutes John, this same set of atoms at a time when its elements are scattered to the four winds; and so on). This problem of supernumerary copies does not arise for standard mereologies, i.e., theories of part and whole, since the mereological sums of the atoms, molecules, cells, and so forth constituting John at some given time are all one and the same object. It is precisely this, however, that makes the mereological approach susceptible to the puzzle captured in our triad. Mereology as an instrument of ontology is, furthermore, in no better a position than set theory when it comes to the problem of doing justice to the fact that John preserves his identity from one moment to the next even in spite of the fact that he gains and loses parts.

3. THE GRANULARITY PROBLEM SOLVED

Consider what happens when you observe a chessboard. You are working with a partition of the world into that, in the region of the chessboard, which you are focusing on, and that which is traced over. Your focus brings with it, again, a certain granularity: you are interested not in the atoms or molecules within the board and its pieces, but only in the board and the pieces themselves. Moreover, you are interested in the latter not as constituting a mere list, or set, but rather as they exist within a certain arrangement. The board is divided into squares. In some of these cells pieces of specific kinds are located.

To understand what is going on here, we need to focus in more detail on the notion of a partition and on the associated notion of cell. The first thing we need to recognize is that partitions have their granularity built in, as it were, from the very start. An administrative map of France depicting its ninety-one *départements* or its 311 *arrondissements* provides a close approximation to a partition in the sense we have in mind. Such a map is the result of applying a certain coarse- or fine-grained grid of cells—the minimal units of the partition—to a certain portion of reality.

A partition is the ontological analogue of the sort of labeled grid we might find in a large post office or automobile component warehouse. For a partition to do its work, it needs to have cells large enough to contain the objects that are of interest in the portion of reality that concerns us; but at the same time these cells must somehow serve to factor out the details that are of no concern. A partition is accordingly a device for focusing upon what is salient and also for ignoring or masking what is not salient. We can think of it as being laid like a net over whatever is the relevant object-domain, and, like a net or grid (or a latticed window of the type depicted in Renaissance manuals of painting), it is to a large degree transparent. Thus, significantly, it does not in any way change the objects to which it is applied. The sorts of carvings up of reality that are effected through our partitions are comparable not to those effected by surgeons, but rather to those we find in atlases of surgical anatomy, or indeed in the various tables of categories prepared by Aristotelian philosophers and by Linnean biologists.

A partition is like a map. It is an artifact of our perceiving, judging, classifying, or theorizing activity, and it exists only as a product of the cell boundaries by which it is determined. The reality partitioned, in contrast, is what and where it is, and it has all its parts and moments, independent of any acts of human fiat and independent of our efforts to understand it theoretically. Granularity as it has been treated above is thus properly at home precisely in the realm of our partitions: granularity pertains not to the objects themselves on the side of reality but rather to the ways we partition those objects in different sorts of contexts.

The arrangement of cells in a partition may be purely spatial, as in a map, where the relative positions of neighboring cells are determined by the corresponding positions of those portions of geographic reality to which the cells relate. Or it may be determined by a linear ordering, as for example where partitions are determined via quantitative scales reflecting age cohorts or temperature bands. The arrangement may also be determined in more complex (for example, hierarchical) ways, as in the case of a partition determined by *biological kinds* (for example, a multilevel partition of the animals in your local zoo into *lions, tigers, spiders, small marsupials, vertebrates,* and so on). The partitions that come closest to sets (or to mere lists) are those associated with our uses of proper names, partitions that we are able to project onto reality in such a way that their cells keep track of the corresponding objects in the world as objects that are identical from one moment to the next, and this in spite of the fact that these objects change and that parts are gained and lost.

Complex multidimensional partitions arise through the combination of these different types of demarcations and cell arrangements. A map of the zoo, for example, might indicate not only the places where animals are located but also the sorts and sizes and proper names of the animals located in those places.

4. TOWARD A THEORY OF PARTITIONS

The cells in a partition may have sub-cells.[3] Thus, for example, the cell *rabbit* is a sub-cell of the cell *mammal* in a partition of the animal kingdom. The cell *Florida* is a sub-cell of the cell *United States* in the standard geopolitical partition of the surface of the globe. The sub-cell relation, then, is an analogue of the subset relation in standard set theory. An example of a chain of cells ordered by the sub-cell relation is your address (Oval Office, The White House, 1600 Pennsylvania Avenue NW, Washington, D.C., 20500, USA).

Those cells in a given partition that have no sub-cells within that partition are called minimal cells. The closest counterparts to sets within our present framework are those ideal sorts of partitions that can be identified as the mereological fusions of such minimal cells.[4] The corresponding minimal cells will, again in the ideal case, constitute a perfect tiling—a jointly exhaustive and pair-wise disjoint decomposition—of the pertinent domain of objects, and each cell in such a partition is itself the mereological sum of one or more of those minimal cells.

Not all partitions have these nice properties, however. This is because our partitions are artifacts of our theorizing and classifying activity and thus are often incomplete. Thus we can imagine a partition of the animal kingdom containing a cell labeled *mammal* and other cells labeled *rabbit*, *dog*, etc., which is yet not such as to provide a complete accounting of all the species of mammal that exist. There are gaps in the partition, analogous to the no-man's-lands between the zones of civilization represented on ancient maps.

Each partition will characteristically contain cells that are empty *per accidens*—because they have no objects located in them (as a chessboard will contain squares empty of pieces, and as a hotel may, on any given night, contain rooms empty of guests). *Dodo* is an empty cell in

---

3. The formal details underlying the ideas in this section are set out in Thomas Bittner and Barry Smith, "A Taxonomy of Granular Partitions," in *Spatial Information Theory, Proceedings of COSIT 2001, Morro Bay, Calif., September 2001*, ed. Daniel Montello (New York: Springer, 2001). They were inspired on the one hand by the theory of location developed by R. Casati and A. C. Varzi, *Parts and Places: The Structures of Spatial Representation* (Cambridge: MIT Press, 1999), and on the other hand by the machinery of granular partitions in R. Omnès, *The Interpretation of Quantum Mechanics* (Princeton: Princeton University Press, 1994). Omnès's theory is summarized in Barry Smith and Berit Brogaard, "Quantum Mereotopology," in *Annals of Mathematics and Artificial Intelligence* 35 (2002): 153–75, which also contains indications as to how the theory of partitions can be extended to deal with time and change.

4. Minimal cells play the role played by singletons in the theory of classes as the mereological sums of singletons, advanced in David Lewis, *Parts of Classes* (Oxford: Blackwell, 1991).

one standard partition of the animal kingdom. There are thus many empty cells within the domain of partitions taken as a whole.

For some partitions, which we can call *distributive*, if object x is a part of object y, and if y is located in a cell z, then x is also located in that cell.[5] Distributive partitions satisfy a principle to the effect that, if two objects are located in two different cells, then the sum of these objects is located in the sum of these cells.

Spatial partitions are always distributive in the sense specified. If John is in Salzburg and Mary is in Salzburg, then their sum is in Salzburg and so, too, are all their bodily parts. A set, on the other hand, is a simple example of a nondistributive partition, and a partition generated by kinds or concepts is also nondistributive. A partition recognizing cats does not ipso facto recognize parts of cats. Moreover, if Bruno is a cat and Tibbles is a cat, then the mereological sum of Bruno and Tibbles is not itself a cat.

We can define the notion of recognition that is at work here as follows. We shall say that x is recognized by A if and only if A is a partition and x is located in some cell in A.

Suppose John is recognized by a nominal partition A consisting of a single cell labeled "John." This is consistent with its being the case that each member of a whole family of distinct though almost identical aggregates of molecules is recognized by A. This is because A does not care about the small (molecule-sized) differences between these different aggregates: it traces over John's molecular structure. The cell *John* captures *all* the aggregates that are almost identical to John, but it does so in such a way that it cannot apprehend those different aggregates as different. Only a more refined partition would have the resources necessary to apprehend the differences in question.

We now have the machinery we need in order to explain how the three sentences of our triad can be simultaneously true. All three clauses are retained, but now they take the following forms:

A. The molecules inside John are parts of John.

B. John is recognized by a partition associated with Mary's act of seeing.

C. The molecules inside John are not recognized by any partition associated with Mary's act of seeing.

---

5. Here "part" is to be understood according to the usual axioms of classical extensional mereology, as set forth, for example, in P. Simons, *Parts: An Essay in Ontology* (Oxford: Clarendon Press, 1987).

The fact that the partitions available to Mary lack appropriately fine-grained cells yields a solution to our puzzle which does not require the abandonment of the transitivity of parthood.

5. PARTITIONS, SETS, AND FUSIONS

The notion of a partition turns out to be in some respects a generalization of the notion of set, and we have in effect exploited an analogue of the transitivity-blocking feature of set theory in resolving our puzzle. A set is the ontological analogue of a mere list. The elements of a set exist within the set without order or location—they can be permuted at will and the set will remain identical. A partition, by contrast, typically comes with a specific order and location of its constituent cells. Its cells fit together in a determinate arrangement, like pieces in a jigsaw or molecules in a strand of DNA.

Partitions differ from sets also in this: that there are many different sorts of partitions, reflecting the many different sorts of relations between objects and cells. Set theory, as Lewis shows, rests on just one central relation: the relation between an element and its singleton. Unfortunately, as Lewis himself concedes, this relation is enveloped in mystery:

> [S]ince all classes are fusions of singletons, and nothing over and above the singletons they're made of, our utter ignorance about the nature of the singletons amounts to utter ignorance about the nature of classes generally.... What do we know about singletons when we know only that they are atoms, and wholly distinct from the familiar individuals? What do we know about other classes, when we know only that they are composed of these atoms about which we know next to nothing?[6]

The machinery of partitions, by contrast, rests not just on one mysterious relation between element and singleton but on a multiplicity of different (and quite unmysterious) ways we have of carving up reality. The relation between an object and its proper name is one such. Others include the relation between an object and its spatial location (for example, in relation to a grid on a map), or between an object and a concept under which it falls, or between an object and a kind to which it belongs.

Objects as they exist in nature stand to each other in various relations. They have hooks of various sorts that link them together; these include common boundaries and also relations of dependence and of

---

6. Lewis, *Parts of Classes*, 31.

functional or causal association. The operator of mereological fusion, when it is properly handled, preserves these interobject relations, and it thus preserves the order and location of objects that fall within its charge: if two objects are linked together in nature, then they are linked together also within their mereological fusion.

A set is a mereological fusion of singletons, and mereological fusion preserves order and location. How can it be, then, that the elements within a set can be permuted at will and the set remain identical? The answer is that the set is built up mereologically not out of elements but out of singletons, and the latter are—according to standard philosophical conceptions of the nature of sets (which are in turn inspired by the axioms of set theory itself)—mere homeless *somethings*, outside time and space. The singleton operator has the effect of stripping away the various sorts of linkages that obtain between the objects to which it is applied and also of setting them apart from their surroundings and from time and change.

Partitions are distinct from sets however (and from mereological fusions) also in this: that they are not constituted out of (not made or built out of) the objects located in their cells. Rather, they belong to the level of our theorizing and classifying activity. Like maps, they can in an easily understandable fashion remain the same even though the objects toward which they are directed are subject to constant change. Moreover, it is no less easily understandable how distinct partitions can arise in relation to one and the same initial stock of objects. Some partitions are like sets in the sense that they will apprehend the objects that are located in their respective cells independent of order or arrangement or linkage or time. Other partitions, however, inherit from mereology the ability to comprehend their objects in ways that map the different kinds of relations that obtain among them. The cells in such partitions project their objects not in isolation but in tandem with other objects located in related cells within the same partition. Such partitions will apply to pairs of entities only in reflection of the specific relations in which they stand to each other. John and Mary, before they wed, are not, but after marriage they will be, located in the two-celled partition *married pair*. Yet other two-celled partitions—for example, the partition capturing the relation between the two terms of an ordered pair—apply to pairs of objects only in reflection of our ways of conceiving them. A three-celled partition is needed to capture the way in which, in an action of kissing or congratulating, two objects become bound together by a third object—a relational event—in which the one occurs as agent, the other as patient.

Partitions, as we have seen, have built-in granularity. The theory of partitions is thus unlike both mereology and set theory in that it has a direct and natural way of dealing with the fact that three-dimensional objects such as cats and human beings are many, but almost one.[7] It thus also, again unlike both mereology and set theory, promises to offer a way to do justice to the ways in which three-dimensional objects such as cats or human beings can preserve their identity from one moment to the next even in spite of gaining and losing parts. A human organism is at any given time a certain family of distinct aggregates of atoms, molecules, and cells, but we are not in general aware of this fact because, as we saw, the differences between the latter are traced over in our standard ways of dealing with them.

Partition theory does not in and of itself give an account of what trans-temporal identity—for example the trans-temporal identity of human organisms—is. Rather, it tells us what is involved when cognitive subjects track identity through the sorts of changes by which human (and of course other) organisms are affected. If, however, the trans-temporal identity of organisms is in part a function of the types of (small) changes by which they are affected from moment to moment, then the framework of partitions may provide a new path toward resolving the problem of what makes it true that organism a at time t_1 is identical to organism b at time t_2, namely via an accounting of the sorts of (small) changes that affect (and do not affect) the identity of the entity in question.

The theory of partitions can do justice also, in a way that is precluded for set theory, to the phenomena of time and change. This is because, whereas sets are abstract entities existing outside time and space, partitions are human constructions that can be applied to the very same domain of objects at different points in time. In this way we can construct entire histories of partitions tracking the temporal evolution of (for example) physical systems of different sorts at different levels of granularity.[8] In this way also we can use the machinery of partitions to represent not only the way objects are related together at a time but also how they evolve from one time to the next.

---

7. Cf. David Lewis, "Many, but Almost One," in *Ontology, Causality, and Mind: Essays in Honour of D. M. Armstrong*, ed. J. Bacon, K. Campbell, and L. Reinhardt (Cambridge: Cambridge University Press, 1993), 23–38.

8. See Smith and Brogaard, "Quantum Mereotopology."

6. A CODA ON REALISM AND THE OBJECTIVITY OF TRUTH

That scattered portion of the world that is made up of rabbits, that which is made up of rabbit stages, and that which is made up of undetached rabbit parts, are all three just the same scattered portion of the world. The only difference, as Quine sees the matter, "is in how you slice it."[9] What Quine does not recognize, however, is that there are two sorts of slicings: the bona fide and the fiat.[10] Bona fide slicings reflect boundaries existing in nature, for example, the boundaries of tennis balls or planets. Fiat slicings reflect boundaries that we ourselves have introduced into reality through our more or less arbitrary demarcations, for example, the boundaries of census tracts or tax brackets. Both kinds of slicing are represented in our partitions. For even though the cells of the latter are entirely fiat in nature—they are artifacts of our cognitive activities—some of them are coordinated with bona fide demarcations on the side of objects in reality.

Different philosophers have different views as to which slicings are bona fide and which are fiat.[11] Quine himself holds a view that implies that the metaphysical distinctions between continuants, stages, and undetached parts belong in the realm of fiat slicings. Since reference is behaviorally inscrutable as concerns such distinctions—this is the moral of Quine's "gavagai" fable in *Word and Object*—Quine concludes that there is no fact of the matter that they might reflect—no fact of the matter on the side of the objects themselves as these exist before we address them in our language.

Notice that this is not an epistemological thesis. Quine must hold that even an omniscient being would be in the same predicament as you or I as concerns referential inscrutability. That is, he must hold that continuants, parts, and stages do not differ from each other in virtue of any corresponding (bona fide) differences on the side of the entities in reality. Rather, they differ from each other in the way in which, when asked to count the number of objects in the fruit bowl, you can say either one orange or two orange halves or four orange quarters, and so on—and you will give the right answer in every case. The distinctions in question are merely the products of our distinct slicings (our purely fiat partitions) of one and the same reality.

---

9. Willard V. O. Quine, "Ontological Relativity," in *Ontological Relativity and Other Essays* (New York: Columbia University Press, 1969), 32.

10. See Barry Smith, "Fiat Objects," *Topoi* 20 (2001): 131–48.

11. See, for example, DeMarco's and Gracia's reflections on this in Chapters 15 and 16 of this volume.

But note that Quine is being too hasty when he asserts that there is *no* fact of the matter as concerns the reality to which we are related when using singular referring terms. For it follows from his own doctrine that it is a fact of the matter that this reality is intrinsically undifferentiated as far as the mentioned metaphysical distinctions are concerned. This is just the other side of the coin of the fact that the corresponding boundaries are entirely fiat in nature.

Quine indeed comes close to a view according to which all boundaries on the side of objects in reality are of the fiat sort. Objects of reference, for him, can comprise any content of some portion of space-time, however heterogeneous, disconnected, and gerrymandered this may be. This is not so for Lewis, on the other hand, whose perspective on these matters I find more congenial:

> Among all the countless things and classes that there are, most are miscellaneous, gerrymandered, ill-demarcated. Only an elite minority are carved at the joints, so that their boundaries are established by objective sameness and difference in nature. Only these elite things and classes are eligible to serve as referents.[12]

Elite things and classes are, in these terms, the things and classes captured by those partitions that track bona fide boundaries and relations in reality. It is the job of fundamental science and of fundamental metaphysics to move us in the direction of partitions of this sort. Even when scientists and philosophers have completed this job, however, there will still be room for partitions of the lesser sort, partitions that track boundaries—for example, the boundary of Quebec, of Tibbles's tale, or of the no-smoking section of your favorite restaurant—which exist only as a result of our acts of fiat.[13]

---

12. David Lewis, "Putnam's Paradox," *Australasian Journal of Philosophy* 62 (1984): 227.
13. Thanks go to Berit Brogaard for invaluable assistance in the working out of the ideas in this essay. Thanks also to the National Science Foundation, which supported work on the theory of partitions under Research Grant BCS-9975557: "Geographic Categories: An Ontological Investigation," and to the American Philosophical Society, for the award of a Sabbatical Fellowship.

15   The Generation and Destruction of Categories

C. WESLEY DEMARCO

Philosophers often behave like aboriginal peoples who count, "one, two, three, four, five, many." Quite a few count, "one, two, many." Dialectical sophisticates take pride in reckoning "one, two, *three*, many." Contemporary thinkers arrive at indefinite multiplicities with alarming speed. Some philosophers of knowledge observe a couple of large revolutions and project indefinitely forward the enumeration of epistemic overturns. Some philosophers of language observe a handful of discursive functions and conclude that since there are not one or two, there must be countless kinds of language—think of Wittgenstein, who celebrates not only a multiplicity but a changing multiplicity, as "new types of language . . . come into existence, and others become obsolete and get forgotten" (*Investigations* #23). Similarly with categories: it is undeniable that there is more than one category set in evidence, though it is a big jump from that observation to the conclusion that there are indefinitely many. Even if we infer their multitude from the evidence of a few, need we surmise that categories are simply handy organizers, merely manufactured amenities? Such is the trendy—and hasty—conclusion.

Human thought and language are category-hungry, so much so that category sets are multiple and variable, coming into and passing out of service as philosophical systems and conceptual regimes come and go. Nature in itself is category-friendly, so much so that a range of category sets can translate nature's intelligible content for us. The point of this essay is metaphysical: I wish to consider what being must be like in order that both these statements be true.[1] In Part I, I set forth the idea that categories are best understood when we see them not merely as

---

1. For discussions of the connection between mental categories and ontological categories, see Chapters 4, 7, 13, and 14 of this volume.

ways of establishing order within a domain but as ways of mediating intelligibility between domains;[2] I also argue that categories do this only when they are "qualified" by pertinent distinctions and clarifications. In Part II, I spell out further aspects of qualification and its importance for some classic debates about realism and idealism. In Part III, I propose an explanation for our sometime success in translating content from nonhuman domains. The conjecture is that the most elementary operations evident in human category formation are formally identical with some of the most primitive acts of nature. The fact that nature is built up in its own reality by means of such acts is what qualifies it for categorization. Finally, in Part IV, I draw things together to explain how category sets can at once be variable and convey truth.

This is an account of categories that turns to generative activities underlying category formation. The key point is that when we look in human experience for something that answers to nature in and of itself, it is not, in the first instance, our categorial frameworks or classification schemes. What answers most directly is a group of formative acts that people use flexibly to generate various categories and concepts. In short, I shall argue for a moderate realism about categories that depends on a direct realism about the elementary operations that generate those categories. The main virtue I claim for the account is that it resolves in a natural way and at one stroke the two most difficult problems about categories: their multiplicity and their applicability. Language and reality do not share a fixed categorial template that represents a single underlying order. Being and thought meet in the formative activities that give rise, on the one hand, to nature's various structures and functions and, on the other hand, to the variable structures and functions of human thought and language.

---

2. The language of "translation" is probably more precise than the language of "mediation" for at least two reasons. First, mediation has come to imply continuity, while translation sometimes marks and sometimes brooks discontinuities. Second, mediation is often taken to imply change. If knowing and even questioning are modes of mediation, and if mediation always involves change, then knowing and even questioning would change their objects in their every effort to approach them. That spells philosophical trouble. This claim is sometimes made for translation, but the idea of translation, taken generally, is neutral with respect to the alteration of content. Some translations (adaptations, for instance) do and others do not alter content. In this essay I use both terms, saying typically that truth translates being for thought and that categories mediate content between domains in ways that facilitate the articulation of truths.

I

Too often, when thinking about categories, we fasten on a single domain and consider how a given set of structures frames and organizes it. (This is true even when the domain is as large as "language," "thought," or "experience.")[3] The rationale for categorization then shrivels to orderliness, and we find ourselves tempted either to insist that a single categorial ordering is the true one, or to maintain that a multiplicity of categories entails their conventionality. Either option sticks us with riddles. Thought about categories will stray if focused on a single domain and its organization. Considering categories in relation to two or more domains helps to show that, more than a filing system for a given field, categories function to mediate intelligibility. They facilitate the translation of content between domains and fit language for the conveyance of truths.[4]

A category set is an arrangement. By "arrangement" I mean a settlement between two or more domains (areas of experience, language, thought, or what have you) that are disparate enough to need mediation. The media may even be of the same kind—two languages, for instance—so long as they are alien enough to require translation, so long as there are risks of confusion and jumble, so long as there is the danger of "category mistakes" that might be avoided with reference to some canonical partitioning. The statement "the triangle is silver" appearing in a mathematical domain involves a category mistake that ineptly predicates a sensible quality of a geometric abstraction, while in reference to musical instruments the statement makes sense. "The cat is on the mat" describes a felled pugilist no less than a reclining feline, though the meaning shifts conspicuously between the two domains of discourse. Categories help resolve issues about meaning and truth by composing modes of predication, arranging sortals, and aligning schemes of identification and individuation, all in the name of calibrating features of interest so that content can be clarified and conveyed across domains. In every auspicious categorial arrangement different

3. I refer to domains, fields, and media. Roughly, fields are areas of study such as different arts and sciences; domains are topical regions, such as different domains of discourse within a language or domains of experience within the human province; media are materially disparate zones of receipt such as perception and writing. The usage is loose and nontechnical; no sharp division between these terms is required for my purpose, as nothing essential hangs on it.

4. I want this claim to hold broadly; therefore, I include in the scope of the assertion such large domains as language and experience. Even if there were a single category set that held for all forms of experience at all times or even all languages, it would still be better to understand those categories in their work of mediating two or more domains.

media come to an agreement—that is, an understanding—and this involves compromises. The specific terms of the settlement will depend on the characteristics of the domains needing mediation. Concessions or adjustments might pertain to one or both sides.

Natural language translation provides some useful examples. Say that we wish to translate a segment of a source language into several different target languages, and say for the sake of argument that we wish to make the translations as literal as possible. If those target languages have very different lexicons and grammars, the translations may look quite different from each other. That is because different target languages may require different modifications to express the same source. They might even require devices from disparate grammatical categories. For example, if we wish to translate segments of a language with verb tenses into a language with no verb tenses, we will not use "tenses" to mark temporal content in the target domain. One such language might use an adpositional marker; another might use a nominal device as simple as adding "yesterday," "today," or "tomorrow." The use of such devices may or may not involve some loss of content. (That is fine, since translation is not an all-or-nothing proposition.)[5] We might need to paraphrase, or add explanatory notes that are not strictly speaking part of the translation. Any number of adjustments or explications might be needed to ready a target language to express the source. Again, distinct target languages may need to invoke different devices or employ different categories to translate a single source, however literally.

Understanding may on occasion be thwarted by the mere arrangement of contents, particularly if, in addition to different membership lists within two similar schemes, we are faced with dissimilar schemes with disparate structures of classification (such as tree structures as op-

---

5. This simple point has serious consequences for views that understand truth in reference to translation. There are, as a matter of fact, different standards of translational faithfulness, from free translations that play off of a particular text while departing from it, through adaptations that conserve the thrust of a text but alter content, to stylistic variations that preserve core content while admitting incidental amendments, to the most verbatim term-by-term representation that strives to transfer every detail. Once we admit that there are different translational standards, we should consider invoking a similar spread of standards for truth. There are, after all, notions of truth, from deconstructive truth as differential reading (which is supposed to exhibit the "movement" of truth) and hermeneutical transfiguration, through pragmatic truth as "adaptation" and empiricist truth in its indeterminacies, to the most mulish of correspondence views. I advise that we take note of all of these options and observe that each is apt in a limited range of domains (aesthetic, political, religious, moral, sciences soft and hard). Rather than insist that one of these is the sole legitimate theory of truth, it is better to qualify each view, discerning its assets and liabilities, its home fields and limitations. Truth translates being for thought. If we understand truth in connection with translation, then our accounts of truth should track these same qualifications.

posed to grids, radial structures, networks, or what have you).[6] Consider, for instance, the translation of commonsense biological classifications into a technical taxonomy that uses tree structures and requires necessary and sufficient conditions of membership. Commonsense categories are usually quite loose; most, moreover, use radial structures where a class is defined by reference to a paradigmatic focal case. Translating between the commonsense classification and the technical one, even in the same natural language, is not always straightforward. Adjustments will have to be made; the two classifications will have to be calibrated if they are to come to an understanding. It is not as simple as noting that what we ordinarily call "starfish" are not fish or that sweet potatoes are not potatoes.[7] What we commonsensically call "species" are more like technical genera and families, and the standards and procedures of classification differ significantly between the two sorts of case. We may need to modify the categories of the target medium, augment them, or perhaps simply clarify and point up their limits. In any case it is categories we shall have to work with in order to carry content over from the source to the target.

Like difficulties dog translations between natural languages. The ordinary Chinese idiom for "giraffe" (chang jing lu) translates into English literally as "long neck deer." We could regard this as a simple error in classification (since giraffe are not deer), or we could translate "lu" not as "deer" (which is the standard practice) but rather as "antlered animal." Any number of adjustments might serve, but fine-tuning is often needed to translate a source into a target language. In no case can we avoid working with categories, and in no case can categories do the job without the qualifications that bend them to the source.

This point is germane to philosophical categories. It is now fashionable to believe that Aristotle derived his categories by culling some features of Greek grammar and setting them up, rather naively, as generic features of being. In this view substances are just what answer to nouns; "quantity and quality" are adjectives that answer to pronouns, while relations are just adjectival comparisons; "where and when" are adverbs of place and time, action and passion are verbs in the active and passive

---

6. One way of categorizing classifications is in terms of their general format. Some use tree structures (genus/species is one familiar example that involves nesting or containing as well as branching). Others use radial structures (including definition by focal meaning and classification by central case). We also find groups and sets, webs and networks, strata or layered sheets (especially pertinent to historical studies), lattices and rings of concepts. These conceptual configurations are generated by the operations of interest, which create structure along with significant form.

7. They are not just different genera but belong to different families. Sweet potatoes are relatives of the morning glory, while potatoes are members of the nightshade family.

voice, and so on. People like Benveniste, who argue—wrongly, I think —that Aristotle simply codified features of his native Greek, miss the point that even if other languages do suggest or require other categories, it still might be that Aristotle's categories mediate ways of saying in *that* language to ways of being generally.[8] Just as Aristotle needed to coin a few neologisms to tender his list of virtues, he needed to upgrade the grammatical structures of his native Greek to forge his list of general forms of predication-contents. Aristotle's categories are best understood as facilitating the translation into language of certain features of substantial wholes and their properties. Other languages may require different adjustments and refinements for the same purpose. A copula-free language like early Chinese may need quite different devices to translate this same content.[9]

Any language in its historical specificity has limited expressive resources. Categories are not best understood as merely the jelling of these limitations. This is one-sided; it views categories in relation to only one domain. When categories are understood to assist the work of intelligible crossover, they need to be profiled against at least two media. Once categories are understood to be means of mediation, the fact of their diversity is no longer evidence of their caprice. Only a naive re-

---

8. See Emile Benveniste, *Problems in General Linguistics*, trans. Mary Elizabeth Meek (Coral Gables: University of Miami Press, 1971). For more on Aristotle's categories, see Chapters 1 and 2 of this volume. We may find that many or maybe all of these categories remain pertinent for *our* language. That, by itself, is not evidence of their ontological import; it may be the merest byproduct of the history of languages that Aristotle's categories are still serviceable. And even if all languages did share these same categories, this could be an accident of human cognitive evolution. None of this would trouble the proposed account.

9. May Sim's thesis (Chapter 5 of this volume) that Aristotle's categories are implicit in Confucian thought is not best understood as the thesis that Confucian Chinese actually employed those categories, nor is it the thesis that Han language and thought harbor them as depth structures, nor is it the thesis that they contain the categories immaturely so that Aristotelian thought would aid and improve them. Her work does show that key aspects of Confucian thought can be mediated successfully to one prominent Western idiom. It shows that an Aristotelian can in fact translate intelligible content from Confucian thought to Aristotelian thought by means of Aristotelian categories that organize and highlight important features of this source for *that* target idiom. Success does not in the least imply that Aristotelian categories make for a uniquely adequate translation or an exclusively true rendering. We could express a different arrangement of the same Confucian content with Peircean categories, or with the "categories" of the *I Ching*. Rather than insist that the use of Aristotelian categories must be a distorting imposition (as David L. Hall and Roger T. Ames might say; see their *Thinking from the Han: Self, Truth and Transcendence in Chinese and Western Culture* [Albany: State University of New York Press, 1998]), rather than insinuate those categories into Confucian idioms as clarifications or improvements (as Sim implies), it is better to appreciate that different categories may be used to mediate the same Confucian sources to different target media and can, with qualification, do so successfully.

alism requires that the features of both source and target media must remain fixed so that they might reflect one true permanent and complete ordering. I cannot stress this point enough. Given a single source medium, different target media with disparate initial features may well require quite different devices to translate this same source. Categories are chief among the devices of thought and language that may vary, and may even need to vary, precisely so that they can mediate the same content.

Like commonsense categories, if in more specialized ways, philosophical categories are means of mediation that apply with qualification. They are patently diverse, and it is not at all clear that they service the same tasks. Quite the contrary: Aristotelian categories mediate ways of saying to the ways of being of natural wholes. Kantian categories, more broadly, mediate the sensible and the intelligible within transcendental subjectivity. Peircean categories, more broadly still, articulate phenomena with a logic of relations and so mediate phenomenology ("phaneroscopy") and semiotic. Hegelian categories mediate objects and subjects at various stages of development toward a comprehensive and necessary system of modes of mediation within the one absolute subject-object. Once one appreciates that philosophical category sets are not all summoned to perform the same chores of mediation and translation, it is more obvious why such categories might vary.

With philosophical categories above all, devices that look on the surface dissimilar may be used to mediate similar content. The converse, however, is also true: categories that look quite similar may have quite different functions in their home contexts and may be used to render quite different content. It all depends on the task of mediation and ultimately on the qualifications we make to help that mediation go through. This is a prime source of confusion. Philosophical categories, like others, mediate intelligibility and facilitate the translation of points of significance from one domain to some other. Grant that many—though plainly not all—of these philosophical devices succeed well enough in their tasks. But particularly when there are disparate philosophical systems at issue, the different category sets may not calibrate to each other well or at all. In such cases it is especially clear that categories apply, when they apply, with qualifications.

By "qualifications" I mean, in the first place, the sense-delimiting operations that serve to specify utterances and sort out meaning-variations. Qualifications in the intended sense are not hedges or dodges. Evasions and prevarications are common abuses of qualification. In the main, they are the moves we use to discern divergences in interpretation, to survey usage and thereby sort out the elements of dissension. They are the contrasts and comparisons we make in the name of clarification. We make qualifications to point up the discourse- and argument-shaping purposes of interlocutors, to discern the meaning-modifying circumstances of controversies, to articulate differences in significance that often go unmarked. We employ qualifications to identify aspects and situate events and experiences with respect to each other and their backgrounds. Vehicles of questioning and interpretation and translation, qualifications are more basic than categories. They prime media for mediation and so facilitate the categorizations that assist the truthful translation of being for language and thought.

Consider how we prime a common language to serve as an instrument of predication by making type distinctions among predicates that help resist contradiction and confusion. These arrangements may be made with logical standards in view, as when we translate into a logical idiom. To make the motley of daily discourse serviceable for logical purposes, we need to make distinctions of respects-in-which that often remain unmarked in ordinary language. We identify times and persons, standardize the individuation of objects and properties and events, and so on. Natural languages rarely translate directly and without adjustment into logical idioms. Moreover, different languages require different kinds and degrees of tinkering to become amenable to PC formatting (that is, symbolizing in predicate calculus of first or higher order.) Sometimes this is merely a matter of clarification and fine-tuning. Other times the needed amendments run deeper, amounting to a more radical re-smelting of symbols. We may need to reclassify. We may even need to re-individuate, so that different items count as the focal "individuals" (as when we quantify over predicates in a formal idiom, or when we shift the focus of discussion from commonsense objects to particles or from particles to fields). When we prime a language to serve as an instrument of predication, we individuate entities and attributes in some canonical mode, sort out what belongs to logical and grammatical form, and so on, to help us avoid muddle and misunderstanding. We frame contexts and aspects to discern and to reconcile diverse modes of classification (such as phenetic and biogeographic and genetic taxonomies in biology) or individuation (as in the logical examples above). Once apt qualifications are made and limits are discerned, categorization and classification schemes that seem wholly disparate on the surface can become jointly legitimate, each a good vehicle for conveying truths.

Categories express neither the hidden essence of being nor a single deep structure of language nor necessary posits of subjectivity. Categories nevertheless can mediate content truthfully. This point demands that we renounce the habit of considering categories in relation to one domain merely. It also requires that we cease presuming that categories are structures that can be understood in isolation, are true or false in themselves, or are a locus of ontology without further ado. No, categorization leans on qualification. Neither reflections of a single objective order of being nor merely serviceable amenities, categories are translation devices that work with qualifications that let us identify aspects, relate situations, and array the elements of significance. Qualifications make categories go. In truth, categories are germane or not, articulate or not, successful or not, depending upon the qualifications we make. To convey truths across domains we must identify contexts, make distinctions of respect-in-which, specify times and persons, clarify functions and roles, and so on. Categories come to be of service or pass out of service accordingly. Once we take stock of the wide range of variations in the ways things and features, subjects and objects, circumstances and events can be articulated in different fields, theories, languages, etc., we can turn attention to the qualifications that inform those articulations and let categories make sense.[10] Categorization presumes qualification.

I have argued that categories mediate intelligible content between domains, and therefore that we need to profile categories against two or more domains to appreciate how they work. I have argued that it is not structures of sorting or predication that do the work of mediation, but *qualified* categories, categories made functional and fine-tuned by acts that finesse their limits and adjust them to the matter at hand. I next wish to argue that some key philosophical problems traditionally handled with reference to categories are better handled with reference to the qualifications that fit categories for truthful employ.[11]

---

10. A phenomenologist might understand this as a sort of eidetic reduction on the range of plausible philosophical category sets. What emerges from the variations is not a single set of categories but a set of operations by which all category sets are constituted. (I say "sort of" because in this exercise the categories almost seem to dissolve, or rather their noematic form becomes as *hyle* for a higher-order group of noetic acts.) Those are the forms of qualification, which under a transcendental reduction appear as noetic acts *and* in the natural attitude appear as primitive forms of natural process.

11. If we say in a Wittgensteinian vein that categories are "techniques" of our practice with language, then qualifications are the activities that make of these techniques a philosophical art. They allow us to employ our conceptual and categorial devices skillfully and calibrate these in the pertinent ways. If categories are techniques, then philosophical qualifications transmute such devices into skillful means and turn utility to truth. This may come to pass on the condition that the acts by which we work with technique (and ultimately may transcend technique) are nature's own acts of being. If we recognize this, we can accept much of what Wittgenstein was inclined to avow while retaining something of the metaphysical philosophy he was tempted to eschew. (For another discussion of Wittgenstein, see Chapter 9 of this volume.)

11

Categorization is more than a matter of controlling unruly diversity by instituting canonical collections. By aligning discourse and experience, calibrating thought and being, categories mediate intelligibility. Catalogues of concepts and the filing systems of experience do not do this job on their own. Only qualified categories mediate content. These qualifications are not always a matter of adjustment or fine-tuning merely, since sometimes the turns and twists we need will run quite deep, involving alternate individuation or entification schemes as well as different patterns of predication and classification. We may, moreover, need to consider disparate modes of presentation or standards of meaningfulness, as for instance between profoundly alien cultures or disparate philosophical systems. Such large-scale schemes are, I want to argue, traceable to the same formative acts. That is, the cognitive functions underlying human category formation employ the same operations we use when making qualifications. Qualifications resolve issues about meaning and truth by making determinations about relative interiors and exteriors, situations and contexts, features and emphases, functions and roles. Established categories are simply settled patterns of such determinations. Categories are frozen acts of thought, congealed feats of articulation. Adducing qualifications performatively to fit some set of categories for use amounts to revisiting the operations that generate categorial structures we normally take for granted. When qualification is keen, dead metaphors come to life and the sediment in the riverbed of usage is loosened and stirred up; cognitive structures are made supple and adaptable to their sources, and the fund of concepts gains liquidity.

In the sense of interest to this essay, categories are definitive determinations that settle a domain so that intelligible features might be conveyed from some other domain. Categories help us sort things and relations, parse properties, array events and interactions, and so on. Somewhat more narrowly, by "categories" we mean generic kinds of predicates or predicate-contents, or the most inclusive kinds of these kinds, and typically the target domain is linguistic or cognitive.[12] In the

---

12. Jorge Gracia takes categories, as neutrally as he can, to be predicate-contents; that is, as what is expressed by predicates of whatever sort. See Chapter 16 of this volume; see also his *Metaphysics and Its Task: The Search for the Categorial Foundation of Knowledge* (Albany: State University of New York Press, 1999). The category for X is simply X-as-X, distinct from the "meaning" of X (which makes it relative to language), or the "idea" X (which yokes it to mind), or the "universal" X (which makes it an instantiable abstraction; instantiability is sufficient but not necessary for categoricity). That is of course unimpeachable as a stipulative definition aimed to further a philosophical project, though

most nontechnical sense, however, categories are generic classifications of whatever sort. To categorize is to classify. The best empirical work shows that classification patterns and practices of categorization do vary culturally,[13] though that is not to say different languages must make for inimical modes of thought or experience or incomparable "worlds."

Color categories provide a well-worked example. Vocabularies vary widely both in numbers of basic terms and where the lines between colors are drawn. Patterns of inclusion and exclusion, the segmenting of virtual spectra, and the parsing of color aspects such as hue, intensity, sheen, and so on, have proved quite disparate. On the other hand, Berlin and Kay have demonstrated that there are some focal colors discernible throughout the species. (Though we must admit that such commonalities do not argue the objective realism of the categories.) Given the diversity of color vocabularies, then, the fact of some species-wide saliences does not preclude the wildest diversity. Similarly, research shows that most individuals can perceive "just noticeable differ-

---

philosophical and ordinary usage would tend to find "categories" not in the predicate contents but in their more generic types. *Types* of Gracian categories, which are more like what most people would call "categories," are a matter for further thought on his view. He notes rightly that orders of dependence and inclusion determine these larger types. At this point one must ask: might there be more than one order of dependence and inclusion? Gracia's argument against binding categories to language or mind or material existence exclusively implies there must be.

Gracia asserts that the unity of metaphysics is the unity of a collection of things considered as related in certain ways. We need to note, however, that in philosophical contexts particularly, the things and the relations are posed in many, and often inimical, ways. For instance, to the transcendental idealist, categories of causation and time and matter will be dependent on and less general in scope than those of subjectivity itself. On the other hand, for the physicalist, categories of subjectivity—if any—will be dependent on and less general than physical categories, even if they are irreducible. No matter; so soon as we notice that there is no single fixed order of dependence and inclusion, we can track "qualifications" in the moves by which we make sense of the differing orders and priorities and dependencies. Once we track the qualifications, we can focus metaphysical interest there.

I think Gracia must accept the variability of dependence-orderings and generality-orderings on pain of reinstating the kind of metaphysics he wishes to avoid. Suppose for the sake of argument that metaphysics deals with categories (as distinct from words, concepts, properties, universals, etc.). Now, if categories did have a single definitive ordering, then contrary to his original supposition that order would turn out to mark the province of metaphysics, whatever the source of that order (linguistic, conceptual, physical, etc.). To deny that any of these fields is the one true province of metaphysics, Gracia must deny that there is a single ordering. Then the question becomes how we can account for the variable typings and orderings of predicate-contents. What accounts for the different orders of dependence and inclusion, what sets priorities of whatever sort, is "qualification." Therefore, whether the issue is predicate-contents or their types, things categorize and categorize variously because qualification qualifies and so qualifies them for categorization.

13. See John A. Lucy, *Language Diversity and Thought: A Reformulation of the Linguistic Relativity Hypothesis* (New York: Cambridge University Press, 1992).

ences" between hues even when their home languages lack the terms that would mark out those hues as distinctive. This finding is compatible with the truth that recall, cognitive processing, and discourse are all shaped by habits of lexis, of classification, of categorization.[14] These habits facilitate cognitive processing and articulation and in some cases even perception. That is not to say they make rigid limits for thought and experience, but only that they influence them. Still, this influence is often profound. Cognitive habits may prevail to the extent that a customary categorization scheme comes to seem "natural" and the alternatives uncanny.

Supposing categories mediate intelligibility, there is a problem, one that hounds philosophical categories particularly. Schematically and simplistically, let two items A and B be externally related, so that A is to B as language to nature, or consciousness to reality (understood so that there is no necessary bond between them). Next, let two other items be internally related, and call them A' and B,' so that A' stands to B' as proposition to fact, noesis to noema, *signifié* to *signifiant*, or any other mutually determined or co-defined couple. Now, when we turn to a philosophical theory to explain how categories facilitate the crossover of intelligible content between A and B, we often find a subtle substitution of (A', B') for (A, B). This substitution occurs because it is easier to see how a single set of categories might apply to the pair (A', B') than to the externally related pair. In the hands of a deft philosopher, this substitution is almost undetectable. However, it is a trick of misdirection.

When it comes to knowledge, where A is an inquiring subject and B some real article, idealists (whether psychological, sociological, or transcendental) typically give up on the external relation altogether. They may bracket out one or (more recently) both items. Thinkers who sincerely doubt whether Aristotle's categories—or Peirce's, or Hegel's—truly apply to independent nature have little trouble conceding that they apply within one domain, internal to a zone of appearances (Peirce's phanera) or language (Aristotle's Greek). If we reconceive objects or referents so that they are internally related to subjectivity or language, the categories would then apply to "objects" or "referents," but only because of the reconception and concomitant internalization. Even a hickory-tough skeptic can accept the applicability of categories to internally related items while rejecting the pertinence of the internal to the external relation. This restriction of the applicability of cate-

---

14. See John A. Lucy and Richard A. Schweder, "Whorf and His Critics: Linguistic and Nonlinguistic Influences on Color Memory," *American Anthropologist* 81 (1979): 581–615.

gories to the internally related items limits their relevance, if it does not trivialize them outright. Any claim about categories' applying to the externally related items then seems suspect, and the question of how categories might mediate the externals might seem meaningless. "Categories" look like a setup. The deck seems stacked.

Think of "facts" as understood in Analytic traditions; that is, as discrete configurations of particulars that obtain all or none and so answer to determinate propositions. ("Facts" so conceived might be situations or states of affairs or eternal possibilities in logical space or what have you, according to the favored theory.) If "facts" are mere posits stipulated into being to serve as correspondence correlates for propositions, then categories of "fact" would likewise seem to be fabrications that tell us nothing about the world in its independence from human involvement. Or (switching now to a Continental idiom), if signifiers and signifieds are mutually definitive, so that signifieds are put-ups posted to shadow human signifiers, the categories internal to a scheme of signs would reveal nothing about "transcendental signifieds." Categories would then be only cover-ups of the failure of mediation rather than touchstones of its success—a sham.

How categories mediate the externally related items, via the internally related items, without circularity or regress, is the hard question. To make a start on this issue, focus on the pair (A, A'). This is neither an internal nor an external relation; we will misconstrue (A, A') if we force it into either mold. A' is still A, is A qualified so that it is primed for the pertinent mediations—as we might consider an event under different aspects, or retool the common language for some logical use, or refine perception for art appreciation. A' is a guise of A, or is A-with-respect-to . . . , or A-to-the-extent-that . . . , or A-insofar-as . . . , or what have you. This is not the supposed internal relation between A' and B', so beloved of idealists. Nor is it the supposed external relation between A and B, much reserved by realists. Rather, (A, A') and (B, B') mark variations in standing or role or function of some articles A and B. Internal relations do mediate the external relations, but we cannot merely assert this without account. Vicious circles appear if we pass from (A', B') to (A, B) without attending to the qualifications that turn A into A' and B into B'. The qualifications are pivotal.

By priming A and B, qualification facilitates the transition (A', B') that mediates (A, B). Since A and A' are not separate articles needing relation, there is no regress. No extra entities or fantastic objects are posited here. Since qualifications are not "categories," strictly speaking, but acts that articulate respects and roles, relative interiors and exteriors, distinctions of function and significance and so on, there is no circularity. We need not appeal to categories to explain how categories mediate content. Categories can articulate qualified content in ways the target can track. These ways might vary widely between linguistic or other media; again, I have argued that different target media may require quite different categories to translate truly. Categories mark out the settlement a medium needs to convey the qualifications of things. Categories in this account are derivative. They are, in fact, byproducts of our acts of qualification. Settled categories codify some of the work of qualification; they mark the general terms of agreement where disparate media have come to an arrangement and mediation can go through. Structures of categorization, configurations of sortals and classes of predicates and so on, do not mediate content all by themselves; they are placeholders for the work of thought that is "qualification."

Suppose, at least for the sake of argument, that the priming of A and B lets mediation go through without regress or circularity. We quickly bump into a second problem: how to understand the relation—if it is a relation—between, on the one hand, the qualifications that turn A into A', and on the other hand those that turn B into B'. Having stipulated that A and B appear on different sides of some philosophically significant divide, if categories fail to mediate this rift all by themselves, how can so-called forms of qualification fare any better?

The admission that different media may require different categories makes more sense of the observation that as the media change, so may the categories. Both theses were tabled above in the name of a qualified realism that recognizes that different target media may need different categories precisely to ready them to mediate the same source. The moral of this story was that media are mediated according to the state of the target medium. Starting with examples of natural language translation, I claimed that assorted styles of experience, different sciences and arts and so on, may need to employ quite different categories to perform the tasks of mediation relevant in their domains. In every case, we prime a medium for mediation by making qualifications that ply its structures and limits. Say that qualification is prior to categorization in the ways described. How are the qualifications we make in the course of adjusting categories related to the qualifications that inform the content we use those categories to convey? If the qualifications that prime the A-side were related to the qualifications that prime the B-side as A is related to B, this external relation might account for the variability of categories but not for their applicability. On the other hand, if the qualifications that prime the A-side were related to the qualifications that prime the B-side as A' is related to B', this internal relation might account for the applicability of categories but would leave their variability murky.

Consider that the qualifications on the B-side stand to those on the A-side rather as A stands to its many A-primes. This bond between the qualifications on the A-side and the qualifications on the B-side is neither an internal nor an external relation. (It is not best thought of as a relation at all, though in a special sense or for limited purposes one can style most any sort of identity a "relation.") This is the case: acts of segmenting, branching, nesting, networking, etc., as they function in natural phenomena (that is, the A-side) stand to psychological acts of segmenting, branching, nesting, networking, etc., as they function in category formation (that is, the B-side) *not* as A is related to B *or* as A' is related to B', but rather as A stands to A' or B stands to B'.

The problem is that these forms of qualification are so inclusive and ungarnished that they tell us virtually nothing about the distinctive determinations of the domains needing mediation. To that end we need further articulation. That is where categories come in. Categories settle some clear-cut shapes the unbound brands of qualification might take. Experience and language are category-hungry just because the forms of qualification that define their most basic operations need additional specifications if they are to express the specific qualifications of particular media. Acts of qualification can prime different media for mediation because the categorization schemes of disparate domains specify in distinctive ways the same primitive *forms* of qualification. Again, category sets stand to the forms of qualification not as A stands to B or as A' stands to B', but rather as many A-primes stand to A. This is neither an external nor an internal relation in the senses of these terms used above. Once the forms of qualification are as natural to the A-side as to the B-side, they can prime the transitions that convey content. Once the forms of qualification can prime the transitions, they will be transcategorial and so will not be captured adequately in either categorization scheme.[15]

Human animals inherit the forms of qualification as cognitive operations used flexibly to forge units and linkages and fields of all sorts. Their variability makes for alternative identification and entification schemes,[16] variant parsings of features, discretionary groupings, and

15. I address a few paragraphs below to the point that the forms of qualification are not identical with any category set or any set of all category sets or any system or organic totality of categories. I argue elsewhere that they appear most sharply in a survey of categorial alternatives. The purest and most ungarnished forms of act appear in the shifts and switches we must make to cross between the most disparate philosophical idioms.

16. An entification scheme is an order of beings that marks out individuals and kinds, parts and wholes, things and features, and so on. There are a number of alternative en-

further arrangements otherwise. Categories are codifications that dispose these arrangements; the codification may be a product of individual design (as with philosophical systems) or a side effect of social practice. Cut off and considered by themselves, categories seem to be interposed between thought and things—part of a screen of signs or iron curtain of representations. But qualified categories are not interposed as some *tertium quid* between thought and things.[17] There is no truth-thwarting interposition because the qualifying operations that fit categories for use are formally identical with acts of nature that compose the categorized content in the first place. That cuts out the middleman in our commerce with the world. With the dissolution of an intervening *tertium quid*, the supposed screen of signs or wall of representations vanishes, and truth is intelligible again.[18]

III

All vigorous realisms invoke something able to play a dual role in knowledge and the known. Categories are often taken to play this double role. Gracia's "categories" (predicate contents as neutral between language, mind, and nature) provide one candidate.[19] Weissman's infinities of eternal possibilities provide another.[20] Both are neutral thirds

---

tification schemes in evidence in the history of thought. Those schemes that are products of philosophical design are relatively systematic, while those that are byproducts of social practice are relatively loose and multifarious and usually hard to frame in any tidy way.

17. Think again of the translation examples. When I render a source language in a target language, I do not need some third language in which to compare them. It is rather the categories of the target language—*as qualified*—that mediate the source. For some reason this point is often overlooked; discussions too often either insist on a *tertium quid* or insist that if there is no viable *tertium quid* then there could in principle be no translation troubles or *bona fide* incommensurability.

18. Donald Davidson's way to cutting out the middleman in an economy of truth takes truth structure to distal content wholesale; see his *Inquiries into Truth and Interpretation* (New York: Oxford University Press, 1984). His argument is that because of "indeterminacy" we can use our own categories to understand any other, and that because of "charity" we must use our own categories to understand any other. Hence deep categorial disparities or differences in conceptual scheme will seem either impossible or unintelligible. Davidson's gambit has trouble with philosophical language, at least, where categorial and schematic differences are in abundant evidence. The account that roots categories in qualifications is an account that unblocks truth while making sense of deep categorial and conceptual disparities.

19. See note 12 above.

20. David Weissman, *Eternal Possibilities: A Neutral Ground for Meaning and Existence* (Carbondale: Southern Illinois University Press, 1977). In general, Weissman distinguishes between space-time, its powers of self-determination and self-dirempt ion, and eternal possibilities; the view is neatly summarized in his "First Considerations" in *Creativity and Common Sense*, ed. Thomas Krettek (Albany: State University of New York Press, 1989), 92–110. Very roughly, space-time is his One, its powers do the generating, and eternal possibilities do the mediating (in the sense of interest to this essay). The proposed alternative

able to be instantiated equally in linguistic and material media (or mental and extra-mental media) and thereby to mediate them. Fregean *Gedanken* and Husserlian *noemata* understood in Føllesdal's Fregean way are also contenders.[21] Aristotelians like Sim instead invoke *eide* that function as the substance of things and also as forms known universally that translate the being of beings for thought.[22] Hegelian categories unfold in time as the formative principles of "peoples" according to a succession of negations that replicates the eternal dialectical sequence in the Absolute's own self-thinking. Here is another option: it is in its most primitive operations that thinking coincides with being. Categories and concepts are derivative and variable. Feats of situation and re-situation, acts of inclusion and exclusion, operations of sampling and segmenting and so on make (and unmake) what function as categories. They compose the items and relations and fields that define the patterns and ranges of human symbolic life. The admission that these are all multiple and variable, constructed and so deconstructable, may seem a sop to postmodernists; if so, it is limited by the conjecture that the operations ultimately responsible for all the varieties are in reality forms of

---

is, I think, more parsimonious. Platonizing a handful of primitive acts loosens the compulsion to summon up organized infinities of abstracta to anticipate every contingency.

That leads to another advantage I wish to claim for the proposed account. Weissman has argued forcefully and provocatively against what he calls "intuitionism," a virus he believes has infected most philosophers: even Aristotle became obsessed with noûs; Peirce could not quite break free; Weiss wandered; one wonders who is left free of the bug. See David Weissman, *Intuition and Ideality* (Albany: State University of New York Press, 1987); Weissman seems to have changed his mind about Peirce. The hard U-turn to subjectivity has indeed produced many gaffes and absurdities, but transcendental and psychological and sociological constructionisms need not be so stoutly opposed. For if we follow these views to their limit, out beyond all the wily tactics and polemical maneuverings, there is useful information about the operations of mind. Any naturalizing account ought after all to hold that mind is a sort of wildlife; its operations therefore ought to be understood to be natural acts. If there is evidence that these are highly supple, productive of all sorts of categorial and conceptual differences, so be it. The intuitionist disease only becomes morbid from an insistence that these acts are exclusive properties of human mind, and therefore that their products too (what we know "by inspection") have no standing outside of the human sphere. The hypothesis that operations of mind track natural forms of act tames intuitionism and constructivism. As a consequence, the mind-obsessed can be thought allies rather than fools; they are simply tracing the forms of qualification to another locus of operation. Relative to that locus there is much in what they say. Physics and chemistry, politics and economics and so on are indeed human constructs with a history we can trace. Once conceptual schemes, categorial frameworks, etc., are outsourced to natural forms of qualification, we can accommodate this fact while appreciating their openness to truth as realistic as you like.

21. See note 10 above.

22. Notice that the form informing the being and the form in the soul, while formally identical, are not identical in every way. Even in reference to the Stagirite, talk of translation is apt, since the *way* a form is known (universally) is not the way it is, in the being as its cause.

activity that are not exclusive possessions of human language or mind.

See the list below. The headings at the top of the chart—enaction, transaction, proaction, etc.—are my candidates for the most basic forms of activity pertinent to human and nonhuman nature.[23] These "forms of qualification" give rise to the "acts of nature," itemized in the body of the chart.[24] These function as cognitive operations or as generic forms of natural process, depending.[25] "Enaction" consists of acts of bounding and binding and so on that establish series of relative interiors and exteriors in thought and things. "Transactions" are acts of transfer that yield patterns of exchange in an economy of motions.[26] Faction (or "facture," as I sometimes call it for want of a better term)

---

23. For the purposes of this essay, I use "forms of activity" and "forms of qualification" interchangeably. Strictly, though, to speak of "forms of activity" or "acts of nature" is already to take sides, at least in so far as we contrast activity with passivity, action with reception, act with potency, and so on. The emphasis on activity is useful for the purpose of this essay, but it does have its limits, since activity has only a conditional ontological priority. The most neutral way to describe these "forms" is to use the idiom of qualification and speak of "forms of qualification." As I explain elsewhere, the language of qualification—also used by A. N. Whitehead, Paul Weiss, and Stephen David Ross (*Transition to an Ordinal Metaphysics* [Albany: State University of New York Press, 1980]) for their own quite different ends—seems peculiarly well suited to symbolize something prior to essence (the definitive "qualifications" of something) and accident ("qualifications" as modifications), prior to process and substance, prior to subject and object, mind and nature, language and world, and so on, for other infamous disparities.

It might help to notice the distinction between qualification, qualifications, acts of qualification, and forms of qualification. Qualifications are the characteristics of things (by bequest or conversion more or less central or peripheral, intrinsic or extrinsic, salient or incidental). Acts of qualification are the operations productive of the qualifications of things, events, properties, relations, situations, and so on. "Forms" are the common principles in these acts ("form of qualification" is hence short for "form of the act of qualification"); forms are not structures; structures are derivative. The root term "qualification" may be used abstractly or concretely; abstractly it refers to all of the above together, generically, while concretely it refers to the act of being that generates and destroys them.

24. At first blush some of these items may seem close if not indistinguishable, as arranging and arraying are close to aligning and orienting. But, in the intended sense, to arrange is to situate items with regard to mutual position, while to align is to situate items relative to lines of force or a vector field or a common attractor. Opening and closing are not the same as entering and exiting, exposing and shielding, or beginning and ending. Segmenting is not sequencing. To divide is not yet to distribute; to end is not necessarily to satisfy. Opening is not the same as exposing, enclosing not the same as securing, importation not tantamount to integration. Even when particular cases of looping and waving are explained by mechanisms of pushing and pulling, as forms they are distinct.

25. Compare: group theoretic operators can be given an abstract or a physical interpretation, neither of which is in principle more basic than the other. The metaphysical forms at issue are more general and inclusive still. See also note 6 above.

26. Transactions may prove more basic in limited respects than the agents doing the exchanging; it depends on the conditions at issue. It is fruitless to argue whether things (or events) or patterns of exchanges must necessarily always and in principle be more fundamental. It is a consequence of the hypothesis being considered that such priority claims hold only with qualification.

FIGURE 15. A ROSTER OF ELEMENTARY ACTS OF NATURE

Humanly inherited as cognitive operations productive of assorted categories and concepts.

ENACTION	TRANSACTION	FACTION	COACTION	PROACTION
(acts of binding and bounding that define relative interiors and exteriors in thought and things)	(acts of exchange producing patterns of transference in an economy of motions)	(internal rationing that makes for multiple relations & roles, properties & aspects; source of bias in the universe)	(field-constituting acts of situation &interplay responsible for context effects in nature, history, language)	(function-fixing acts generative of state-defining attractors, success-marking standards, and purposes of all sorts)
↓	↓	↓	↓	↓
gather/scatter, converge/diverge; center/decenter	give/take, (send/receive, acquire/donate, borrow/lend, etc.)	ration, allot, apportion, partition; divide, fraction, section, sector; facet; parse	networking, webbing	minimize/maximize, optimize
fission/fusion; merge/emerge, resolve/dissolve; concresce, coalesce	deliver, carry, channel, convey	segmenting, chunking	nesting/embedding	coordinate, subordinate, prioritize
integrate/segregate; in/externalize, include/exclude; in/out-grouping	import/export, insource/outsource	sample, select; filter, strain, sift	placing/displacing, setting/besetting, array, arrange	balance/unbalance; equalize/disequalize
grasp/release; absorb/discharge, capture/emit, assimilate/alienate, (possess/dispossess or own/other)	substitute; swap, switch, trade	phase, stage, periodize	implicate, entangle	harmonize, reconcile
insert/delete, attach/detach, join/separate; blend/isolate	push/pull; collide/swerve; wave/pulse;	feature, mark; stress, weight; emphasize, press, accentuate, appoint	fielding, environing	adopt, adapt, adjust
string & sequence, layer, stratify, sheet; settle & sediment; forking & branching	cycle, loop; feedforward/back	focus/fade, clarify/obscure; simplify/elaborate; sharpen/dull	scening, framing	fit, suit, attune
fill/empty, (endow/divest, infuse/evacuate, ingest/void, etc.)	toggle, oscillate; reciprocate, circulate	refine/defile (cleanse/dirty, purify/taint, etc.); clash/concur; tense/relax	sinking (energy sinks, etc.), draining	orient, align; regulate/deviate
condense/dilute, intensify/attenuate	rotate/translate; reverse, return; turn, spin; shift	supplement/detract; complement/contrast	basing (as a natural place, home base, or Vavilovian center)	mean (establish a central tendency)
open/close; radiate/draw	warp, twist, flex/ply/crease	exhibit, display, expose	grounding (establish dependence on a field of relations,; loops of reliance become a reserve)	promote (selection-by-consequences)
extend/retract; contract/expand (spread, stretch swell/shrink)	flow/stow; pass/block, loose/impede	partaking in, sharing out	funding, resourcing; backing/stocking	develop/devolve; grow/decay; advance/retreat
skin, coat, seal; contain, engulf, encapsulate, encase	thrust/recoil, penetrate/withdraw	retain, save, store, conserve, reserve; secrete, suppress, withhold	settle, normalize, standardize	attract/repel; tend/aver, incline/shun
	insist/admit, resist/yield; access/deny, allow/restrict; restrain/assist	occlude, cache, shield, screen (hence masking and camouflage, etc.)	acclimate (mutual adjustment of participants reinforces an environment)	lead/follow; direct/demur; dominate/submit
	support/weaken (catalyze/damp, etc.)		collect/ distribute (reproducing a field of trade)	finalize (establish an attractor; set an end)
	come/go; enter/exit; venture/return		conform/contend, comply/contest	apply, implement; use, accessorize (execute an end by making the means)
			compete/cooperate	satisfy, fulfill; finish, complete, succeed; peak, culminate (meet a measure, achieve an end)
				outdo, overcome; transcend, surpass (exceed the end)

consists of acts of rationing that yield features and aspects, parts and phases and moments. Facture is the source of bias in the universe. Whenever it is in play, relations are fractional, perspectives partial, and accomplishments incomplete. That is, facture is the principle of partitivity in experience and reality. Proaction consists of the function-fixing acts that constitute state-defining attractors, success-setting standards, norms and purposes of all kinds. Coaction is instead a matter of field-constituting acts of situation, responsible for context effects in nature, history, and language. This pervasive form of activity makes positions to involve circumstances, changes to involve interchange.[27]

The roster is merely a list; various more systematic arrangements are possible, but no one arrangement will serve all charges.[28] For instance, most of the "elementary acts" appear on the chart in contrasting pairs; sometimes triads would do better, while at other times there is reason to prefer longer strings of examples that display series of transitions. I have found no reason to suppose that triads or dyads or strings or anything else constitute a superior design as a matter of principle. All the various acts are derivatives, dependent upon the forms of qualification, and each more specific form exhibits the influence of several more basic forms. This influence appears on the chart. Reading each column down, there are clusters of act-forms due to the mutual qualification of the more basic forms. For instance, "insourcing" and "outsourcing" are enaction in transition to transaction; opening and radiating are enaction in transition to facture; spreading and scattering are enaction in transition to coaction, and so forth. The roster does not exhibit one uniform pattern of influence or transition, however, so the clusters

---

27. Again, it is dubious to argue that because fields are in some ways and in some domains more fundamental than particles, or social contexts more basic than (because constitutive of) specific powers of political agency, fields or contexts must in all ways or in general be more elemental. Priority obtains only with qualification. The acts of thought by which we sort out matters of priority and dependency and inclusiveness and so on are just the "qualifications" themselves. For that reason these acts come into prominence whenever the issue at stake is a question of priority, "significance," or the like.

28. The given arrangement trades on contrasts, though not exclusively. Arrangements of triplets highlight floating midpoints that mediate contrasts, or elaborate the form of processes (as with exchange-reciprocation-circulation or adjusting-balancing-harmonizing or beginning-turning-ending). Longer chains highlight strings of transitions (e.g., "separate-withdraw-avoid-approach-contact-overlap-mix-interpenetrate-merge"). Most of the mentions of the act-forms in this essay, notice, use these longer chains or act-strings. Evolutionary arrangements emphasize the sequential emergence of more specific shapes from the primitive form (as when we arrange "binding and loosing" as particle capture and emission, chemical absorbing and exuding, animal ingestion and excretion, psychological attachment and release, social bonding and shunning, etc.). I make use of some of the evolutionary arrangements below. All these orderings are incidental to the task at hand.

found on the chart are merely examples of the ramifications of qualification. Again, various arrangements are possible and, relative to specific projects, desirable.

I elsewhere elaborate the thesis that the operations by which we form and transform symbols of all sorts are pliable employments of elementary forms of activity with a fully natural standing.[29] And I argue that the act of qualification is primitive; discernible forms of qualification are specializations that are in principle innumerable. That we inevitably make use of limited numbers of qualifying operations is one restriction on human experience and symbolic processing. That a single group of operators can give rise to disparate forms of articulation, modes of presentation, and alternative category sets is a second limit. A deep appreciation of both kinds of limit helps us to sort out philosophical issues about realism and idealism, fallibilism and fictionalism, constructionism, and deconstructionism.

A set of categories will remain useful so long as the media remain sufficiently uniform, and so long as we make—at least tacitly—the germane qualifications. Now, what about the forms of qualification? Is an array of such forms merely another set of categories? It surely may seem so, especially when faced with a list.[30] It is good to be clear about what is

29. See C. Wesley DeMarco, *Wittgenstein and Philosophical Signification* (Ph.D. diss., Vanderbilt University, 1991). In a series of conference papers I have elaborated key points of this account, showing how the forms of qualification account for basic modes of signification, with attention to issues about how they give rise to various sorts of value and significance. Chapter 4 revisions Peircean semiotic in ways that draw on Wittgenstein and Heidegger as well as Plato and Aristotle. First, I add a fresh emphasis on aspect and context. Second, I make formulaic the basic elements of signification, so that signification consists of signing something of something in some respect to some others in some context for some purpose. Third, I construe these elements as being due to a number of primitive signitive operations (sign = A of I in C to T for P, or in a formula: S{A, I, T, C, P}). Last, I take the operations symbolized in this formula (importing, aspecting, transacting, situating, purposing) to exemplify natural forms of act. A focus on categories leads us to discernible patterns of inclusion and exclusion, forking and branching, nesting and embedding, and so on, and thence to the speculation that the operations that produce these patterns are natural forms of act. A focus on semiotics takes us rather from a "general form of signification" valid across categorial domains to the broadband forms (enaction, proaction, coaction, etc.) more directly.

30. The roster of elementary acts of nature bears some resemblance to other lists. Goodman's "ways of worldmaking" (composition and decomposition, addition and deletion, expansion and contraction, warping and deformation, division and ordering, weighting and reweighting) capture some of the acts, though his interpretation makes for conceptual relativism and a strongly internal sense of "rightness." See Nelson Goodman, *Ways of Worldmaking* (Indianapolis: Hackett, 1978). A number of people in cognitive linguistics—George Lakoff and Mark Johnson above all—get part of the list, but their interpretations continue to psychologize the forms, making of them mental operations merely; see, for starters, their *Metaphors We Live By* (Chicago: University of Chicago Press, 1980). René Thom's categories are naturalistic but are not linked to cognitive tropes in ways that account for conceptual variations. Thom's classification of smooth non-Morse

at stake in calling a group of qualifications "categories." If any highly general, internally ordered formatives can be categories, then these are categories. But it is better to be more exact. If categories mediate special domains, translating content between media, then the forms of qualification are not yet categories. They are, by themselves, too primitive and nonspecific to settle particular agreements between disparate fields. That requires categorization. Qualifications are not categories. They are acts we draw upon when we make determinations and articulate partitions and segmentations, complements and supplements, particular patterns of inclusion and exclusion, and so on. Settled into replicable patterns, these more specific determinations can mediate content and translate truths. The settled shapes are what function as categories. We use qualifications performatively to fit and finesse them.

On the side of content, too, the broadband forms of act (enaction and transaction and coaction and so on) play different roles in different domains. In physics, the formatives yield particles and their properties, forces and interactions and fields of the kinds studied in that domain. In biological studies the broadband forms mark the determinations of organisms, functions, and environments, emergent qualities and natural histories. In narrative and drama, we find instead characters, their purposive actions, scenes, images, and plots. In psychology the same formants are determined as persons and actions, contexts and relationships, intentions and perspectives. It is impossible to deduce the domain-specific forms from the primitives. Every field has some sort of "situating" and "transaction." None lacks internalizings and ex-

---

functions (fold and cusp, swallowtail and butterfly, elliptic, hyperbolic and parabolic umbilics) does get part of the list, though; see his *Structural Stability and Morphogenesis: An Outline of a General Theory of Models* (Reading, Mass.: W.A. Benjamin, 1975). His fold function temporalizes in beginnings and endings and generates (spatially) borders, the butterfly temporalizes in filling and emptying and generates (spatially) pockets, and so on. But Thom takes his categories naively as well as naturalistically. Moreover, he insists on their algebraic nature. A mathematical correlate is nice, but is simply not available for most *philosophical* categories and concepts. Gregory Bateson and Tyler Volk speak of metapatterns (spheres, cycles, sheets, tubes, arrows, breaks, centers, borders, layers and "calendars") that appear in all sorts of domains; see Volk's *Metapatterns* (New York: Columbia University Press, 1995). Though their list is useful in bridging Gestalt forms and D'Arcy-Thompson-type natural structures, their "patterns" are abstract and inert and hence help neither with morphogenesis (as do Thom's) nor with cognitive processes (as do Lakoff's and Johnson's), nor with conceptual variations (as do Goodman's). A number of other lists capture some of the elementary forms of act, going all the way back to the ancient Chinese *Book of Changes,* whose unchanging forms of transformation seem to me now to be the great-grandfather of this type of category. But none suggests an interpretation that helps with philosophical questions about the variability and applicability of concepts and categories, the mediation of content and translation of truth, etc. I have tried to offer both a decent go at a list and a useful philosophical interpretation of them.

ternalizings—but we must distinguish capturing and emitting of photons, chemical absorption and discharge, animal ingestion and excretion, social assimilation and ostracizing, and so on. Such determinations define the *particular* qualifications of each domain.[31]

Forms of activity such as situating, transacting, appropriating, equalizing, rending, opening, releasing can play quite different roles in different domains. On the cognitive side, they give rise to disparate categories. Thanks to enaction we have things and features, parts and wholes, insides and outsides of different sorts in different settings. Purportive operations induce beginning-middle-end, means-end, and means-extremes differences—these likewise vary in meaning, depending on the domain. Importive acts internalize and externalize in various ways to yield boundaries and enclosures, gatherings and scatterings, fusions and fissions, and so on, of different shapes in different media. In each case there is a generic "form" in evidence, but it is not allied with one field—say, physics (or psychology, or history)—in ways that would lend that field metaphysical priority. Nor can the primitive form mediate, by itself, determinate content between domains. That task requires categories, along with the acts of qualification that calibrate them.

An indefinite mélange of phenomena will exhibit tendencies to equilibrium, but the character of the balance (and of the tendency, actual or ideal) will vary with the specific nature of the exchange. With social phenomena, for instance, the shape of the attractors varies in real time; moreover, the tendency to equilibrium is *expectational*—it depends on a state of knowledge and on psychological circumstances of anticipation. This feature is lacking in chemical systems. Selection-by-consequences is a general category of purportive explanation; there is a big difference, however, between natural selection in large-scale evolutionary biology and the operant conditioning of individual human

---

31. There are problems with using this stock spread of fields (physical, chemical, geological, biological, anthropological), but it suggests the point. Supposing there to be an order of generation in time and an order of dependence in respect of material basing that lends priority in *these* respects to physics and its categories, there is no need to suppose the same arrow of dependence (with physics as fundamental if not foundational) in respect of *significance*. Supposing there to be an order of genetic constitution within subjectivity and an order of dependence in respect of understanding that displays the sciences as achievements of and for subjectivity, there is no inference to the same arrow of dependence (with consciousness or intentionality as fundamental if not foundational) in respect of other sorts of priority or importance. Philosophical qualifications sort out these issues about significance and priority. Significance, not "presence," is the *being* of nature, and the forms of qualification array its dimensions. Even if we believe that being is presentable in itself, it has presence only in relation to consciousness. On the other hand, being is signifiable, but it also has significance in and of itself.

behavior. Operant conditioning is no less a form of selection-by-consequences, though we must invoke quite different qualifications to make it applicable as a category of explanation. Similarly, appeals to social evolution that hang on mechanisms of selection require a host of qualifications to delimit the formative and to specify the respects in which the mechanism and the idea might apply in this domain.

It is a fact of life that such specific determinations emerge at some point in time and in time may pass away. Part of the advance of thinking is to model these large-scale changes. Physical fields, biological environments, historical contexts, and psychological "scenes" all ring changes on the themes of nesting and networking, placing and displacing, complying and contending, but we need to track those changes. To track these differences is to trace speciation-events within the dimension of coaction. This is a matter of what Weissman would call "categorial form."[32] Here these speciation events—the large-scale changes within some broadband act of nature—are traced to the work of generative operations. But if the forms of act are so mercurial, why not rest content with categories and nature's categorial form? First, it is simply an observation that there are general forms that cut across structured domains: equilibrium principles in various sciences (physics, chemistry, biology, psychology, sociology, etc.) appear in survey to be variations on a single theme. The same is true for the various types of selection-by-consequences. It is true above all for the most general forms of nesting, gathering, centering, rationing, and so on. Second, these forms of qualification are not more at home in any one domain in particular, do not favor one field of study above the others, are not aligned with any special standpoint in a way that would accord it philosophical indulgences. This claim is an alternative to the now more standard idea that "selection by consequences" has a home base in, say, biology, and is applied to other domains only by extension—or that teleological categories are merely projections of human intent ascribed to nonhuman nature only by a sort of metaphor. The truly elementary forms are not the special property of any one domain. Philosophers are particularly guilty of vio-

---

32. Weissman is right that "categorial form" (see Chapter 11 of this volume) traces layers of specifications of variables and relations, but his way to categorial form either makes everything dependent on physics by a series of one-way dependences, or it leaves dark the relations between levels and domains. Once we appreciate that "categorial form" *also* marks out specifications of primitive acts of qualification, there is more room for philosophizing of a more traditional cast. We can go directly to ethics and aesthetics, for instance, since they also turn on forms of qualification. Because human arts and action exhibit the forms of qualification in their own ways, insight into these forms lends insight into the content of ethics and the arts and to their own ontological import. See also note 20 above.

lating this tenet and as a result wander into various sorts of category mistake.[33]

No, the forms of qualification are not categories. They are modes of activity more primitive than categories. Still, since these broadband formatives can be expressed and arrayed, we might want to call a group of qualifications a set of "categories." If we were to say that qualifications are categories, we would be saying that they *mediate* being—but "being" does not mark out a separate field like other fields. Nothing existing is strange from being, and so, when the issue is being, there is no domain crossing that requires a categorial ferry. I have urged here that the acts that make for intelligibility and being appear first off and for the most part in the operations by which we construct and reconstruct and deconstruct categories, rather than in any particular set of categories or categorial settlement. It is better, instead, to focus the term "categories" on those definitive determinations that facilitate the translation of truth and the crossover of content between media. Still, if we simply *must* say that a roster of elementary operations is a set of categories (in some airy philosophical sense), then what they mediate is the being of nature. In this broader or looser sense of the term, qualifications would be the primary categories of being, considered in its own acts of being.[34]

---

33. We err if we take categories specific to some domain and ascribe them too broadly, as when we do metaphysics in mentalistic or even organic categories. We stray when we try to take specifically organic sorts of wholeness and purpose and ascribe them to the cosmos at large. We err too if we focus on the more generic notions (such as segmenting and sequencing, nesting and embedding, expansion and contraction, etc.) but then understand these to have a home base in a particular domain, as when we take segmenting and sequencing to be first and foremost information-theoretic concepts, or expansion and contraction to be most at home in thermodynamics. Applications of the notions outside the putative home domains then appear to be metaphorical extensions at best. We likewise blunder by limiting the relevance of the forms of qualification to select domains. Philosophers do this when they suppose that "aspects" are found only or primarily in the human estate or "ends" only or primarily among living things. We wander into confusion when we take a form specific to one domain and (on the basis of an intuition that there is a common form of activity afoot) apply it to some other domain without apt adjustments, as when take the kinds of layering and stratification specific to geologic phenomena and apply them without qualification to human social structuring. These are all category mistakes.

34. The suggestion that the forms of qualification can be understood to be primary categories of being as act (though it is better still to avoid calling them "categories," for the reasons noted above) is intended as an alternative to going straight from primordial power or *esse in se* to divine ideas or species forms or what have you. Instead, ideas and structures, species and types are generated (and destroyed) when forms of activity are deployed in definite conditions. There is, however, a connection between the forms of act

IV.

The great mass of philosophers post-Kant have found ample evidence that categories and concepts are human constructions, that models and theories are heavy with theory and laden with language, and so that the "objects" about which we speak or theorize are no less forgings of the human thoughtsmith. It then seems as if the best sort of realism we should hope for is a pragmatic realism that turns categories into useful amenities answering to nothing with a standing independent of our own craft. So much argument and evidence have been amassed for this opinion, and so many learned people have been persuaded by it, that I do not wish to dispute the point directly. Rather than resist it, I have instead aimed to nudge it along just a little bit.

Throughout this essay I have admitted that categories may vary between philosophical systems and sometimes even between cultures, and I have argued that we can account for them by appeal to generative operations that make category sets to be upshots of individual design (as in the philosophical case) or side effects of social practice. But the fashionable inference that this encloses us in a charmed circle of language, or a magic cloak of experience, is a *non sequitur*. For there remains the alternative explanation that the most basic operations evident in category formation are the functioning, in human thought, of natural forms of activity that play constructive roles in nonhuman domains. This explains the variability and the applicability of categories at one go. If categories were simply abstracted from things, it would be hard to see why they vary as they do, and harder still to see how more than one category set might articulate truths about the world. If categories were constructs fabricated out of whole cloth, it would be hard to account for their ability to mediate content and translate truth. But if the operations by which we draft and delimit categories are formally identical with elementary acts of nature, we have an answer to the twin questions why our understanding is so category-hungry and why nature in itself is category-user-friendly.

Particular category sets are dynamic configurations with psychologi-

---

and traditional transcendentals that is worth remarking. I have mentioned that qualifications yield orders of priority, standards of meaningfulness, and norms of signification. In relation to traditional transcendentals, enaction is allied with unity, facture with beauty, coaction with justice, transaction with otherness, and proaction with goodness. The main trouble with traditional transcendentals is that they are hypostatized qualities and so are inert. Moreover, even on a *pros hen* approach it is hard to see how quite different kinds of goodness or beauty or unity might rise and fall historically or serve as conjointly legitimate. A turn away from species and properties, from special categorial and conceptual constructs, and toward qualifying forms of activity can help in both respects.

cal and social histories. It is misleading to ask whether, as social-psychological compositions, they are true or false in and of themselves. Categories in this sense are props for truth. Different category sets emerge as we turn out alternative patterns of inclusion and exclusion, variant segmentings and sequencings, different orders of subordination and coordination, and so on. Any of these can serve as the struts and buttresses we need to speak meaningfully, articulately, and truly. But speaking truly requires more than categories; it needs the qualifications that calibrate categories. Though they are psychologically engendered and socially stabilized and normalized, any number of category sets can—with qualification—succeed in mediating intelligible content and conveying truths between media. This does not imply, however, that categories are mere tools or sheer conventions. Functional categories are neither mere serviceable utensils of our practical coping nor direct representations of reality. They are means of mediation, due ultimately to formative operations that elaborate some primitive acts of nature.

To categorize is to structure thoughts about things in a particular way, though of course a given category set can be used in a range of ways under a range of interpretations.[35] Sorting out these senses and construals is part of the work of qualification. In any case, the fact that one way of structuring things yields truths about those things does not imply that it is the only truthful way to structure them. The success of one category set does not imply the failure of others. Categories apply only because category sets can be sensitive to features of the things to be categorized, but those features are specified neither uniquely nor exhaustively by a single category set. This is why it is good—particularly when the interest is ontological—to switch focus from the categories and concepts internal to various philosophical frameworks to the qualifications that make them go. A turn to qualifications can explain the diversity and applicability of such frameworks as it explains the diversity and applicability of their elements.

The specific structures used to articulate particular truths are part of our means of mediation. But the structures (and hence the categories) are derivative on the acts that make for the qualifications themselves. This is true on the side of the categorized items, where the structures are derivative on acts of being, and on the side of categories, where the structures are derivative on generative acts of thought. (Strictly speak-

---

35. I trust it is clear by now that "things" is a shorthand for natural wholes, their features and parts and stages, events and processes, functions and structures, relationships and situations, and so on for anything else that qualifies for categorization in some respect. For another look at "things," see Chapter 3 of this volume.

ing, once we focus on qualification and the forms of qualification themselves, talk of "sides" is moot, but here the issue concerns the mediation of divisions already established.) Because primitive acts of nature are responsible for the qualifications of things, and because structures are derivative on the qualifying acts, when we try to capture the qualifications of things we find that more than one category set can articulate truths about those things.

A color in a picture might be called black in one color system, deep violet in a second system more sensitive to the pigments used to create the effect, and a non-color in a third (i.e., if it is called black in that system and if black is counted as not a color but as the absence of color). A particular organism might be deemed an animal in one taxonomy and not an animal (a "protist," perhaps) in some other.[36] Once qualified, any number of categories can mediate content and translate truths. No category set can prescribe to others what its structures must be (trees, radial structures, grids, lattices, etc.) or how its divisions should run. None can exclude the possibility of others that relate things differently. None can exclude there being others that individuate, relate, and classify in ways so alien it will find them unintelligible. In fact, once we learn that the ability of categories to mediate content and translate truths hangs on the qualifications that fit and finesse them, we should rather infer from the actuality of one to the possibility of others.

Nature categorizes variously because the forms of activity qualify variously.[37] That is a conjecture that squares with the best science of the

36. We say that a living thing must be a plant or an animal, and then encounter the euglena; or say that something must be living or nonliving and then confront viruses; or say that something must be a liquid or a solid or a gas, and then face plasmas and colloids. In response to new phenomena, we can choose to allow for borderline cases, amend existing membership criteria, or add new categories altogether. We should, however, resist the suggestion that the world can never challenge or ultimately quash a particular set of categories that can over time and with repeated assaults be undone. This is not a matter of pragmatics only. The apparent indefinite plasticity of a good system of categories evinces its roots in the pertinent cognitive operations; the limited utility of any system betrays the fact that its special structures and concepts may not track a domain of interest well or at all.

37. "Nature categorizes variously" is a deliberately ambivalent phrase that rings changes on Aristotle's infamous "being is said in many ways." Unambiguously it means that nature is categorized by us in different ways *and* that nature accepts many of these categorizations as true to itself. Compare this with a traditional point about quantity. Beings are quantifiable because they are "signed" deeply in their inmost potencies ("deeply" because signate matter—*materia signata quantitate*—is supposed to be closest to prime matter). And once beings are quantifiable, any number of systems of measure can serve. And though some measures (light years, miles, meters, Angstrom units, etc.) will prove more efficient for a given task, most any can be used once suitable adjustments are made. As a matter of fact, the application of *any* system of measure is possible only with some suit-

day while it resolves at a stroke a number of hoary philosophical problems. Rooting categories in qualifications addresses both the applicability and the multiplicity of categories at one go. Nature is category-friendly because being's own formative acts are inherited by us as primitive operations of thought—part of our evolutionary endowment. Human thought and language are category-hungry because we use these operations with a high degree of freedom to yield multiple and sometimes even inimical products. The resulting category sets sometimes look wholly disparate, disjoint, or "incommensurable," especially if we abstract them from their work of mediation and compare them directly with each other. Truth translates being for language and mind, but more than one translation is always possible, and sometimes alternatives are indispensable.[38]

I argued in Part I that categories mediate content between domains. Of special importance was the point that different target media may need quite different devices to translate the same content from a given source medium. In Part II I turned to the qualifications we invoke to fit categories for use, and linked these to generative operations. In Part III I argued that the most primitive of these acts are not special human possessions. Far from it: language and nature do not coincide in any particular category set but in the formative activities that in nature give rise to different kinds of beings and in language and thought give rise to different kinds of categories. Nature's being is based in forms of activity more fundamental than taxa or types. It is a philosophical error to locate the being of nature in categories and concepts or even in the structures of real articles that correspond to them. Since the structures are derivative, the qualifications of things can be categorized in any

---

able calibration. In the account on offer, qualified categories can apply truly because being itself "qualifies"; that is, it enacts itself in and through the several forms of qualification. Being in its own act "signs" so that all beings are "signed." Once beings are "signed," different systems of signification—including different category sets—can be used to articulate pertinent truths, provided we make the qualifications that calibrate the categories. A particular category set might prove more efficient for a given task, but any number can be made to serve, given the appropriate adjustments.

38. The thesis of incommensurability (loosely, that there is not even one adequate translation of one system in a second) is not really inimical to the thesis of the indeterminacy of translation (loosely, that there are many adequate translations for any one system), though it is often taken to be. That is because translation admits of a range of standards of adequacy. Therefore, though on the highest standards of adequacy a given system may fail to translate a second, there is always some lower standard on which a translation is possible and some range of contents successfully conveyed. And any standard that allows for one translation will *ipso facto* allow for more than one. Problems of incommensurability are especially acute in philosophy and comparative studies where the point is the translation and comparison of alien category sets themselves.

number of ways according to any number of patterns. Thought and being are identical in this way: nature's own acts of construction and qualifying acts of mind are formally identical. These are, in reality, elementary forms of activity that discharge the act of being. We draw upon them whenever we make the qualifications that fit categories to mediate meanings and translate truths. A variety of categories can mediate intelligible content in selected respects, but the qualifications that make categories go actually exemplify some of the most primitive acts of nature.[39]

39. Thanks to Jim Swindler for reading an earlier version of this essay, and to the late Paul Weiss for reading several much earlier versions. Thanks to Jorge Gracia for encouraging words. Many thanks to Jonathan Sanford and especially Michael Gorman for detailed comments on the draft. I am grateful to the audience at the 2001 meeting of the Metaphysical Society of America for grinning and bearing a stumbling and half-improvised presentation and still coughing up a number of helpful questions.

16 Are Categories Invented or Discovered? A Response to Foucault

JORGE J. E. GRACIA

Sometimes the philosopher is allowed a certain latitude to explore and perhaps even to preach, rather than to present a completely worked out position. So I am going to do a bit of both. My chapter and verse is a passage from the preface to Foucault's *The Order of Things*, in which he argues that categories are a matter of invention.[1] This text has had an enormous impact on the issue I wish to address here, and in many ways has helped to define it and to establish as definitive, in the minds of many of our contemporaries, the view that categories are invented.

I. FOUCAULT'S POSITION

Foucault writes:

This book first arose out of a passage in Borges, out of the laughter that shattered, as I read the passage, all the familiar landmarks of my thought—*our* thought, the thought that bears the stamp of our age and our geography—breaking up all the ordered surfaces and all the planes with which we are accustomed to tame the wild profusion of existing things, and continuing long afterwards to disturb and threaten with collapse our age-old distinction between the Same and the Other. This passage quotes a "certain Chinese encyclopedia" in which it is written that "animals are divided into: (a) belonging to the Emperor, (b) embalmed, (c) tame, (d) sucking pigs, (e) sirens, (f) fabulous, (g) stray dogs, (h) included in the present classification, (i) frenzied, (j) innumerable, (k) drawn with a very fine camelhair brush, (l) *et cetera*, (m) having just broken the water pitcher, (n) that from a long way off look like flies." In the wonderment of this taxonomy, the thing we apprehend in one great leap, the thing that, by means of the fable, is demonstrated as the exotic charm of anoth-

---

1. Michel Foucault, *The Order of Things: An Archeology of the Human Sciences* (New York: Vintage Books, 1973), hereafter cited parenthetically in the text by page number.

er system of thought, is the limitation of our own, the stark impossibility of thinking *that*. (xv)

After this extraordinary statement, Foucault proceeds to ask himself about the "kind of impossibility" Borges's preposterous classification forces us to face. And he answers that it consists in that "[e]ach of these strange categories can be assigned a precise meaning and a demonstrable content" (xv). This is exactly what we expect of our most cherished and accepted categories; indeed, it is the mark of a category and the whole world that we have built on them. Yet this Borgesian classification, according to Foucault, destroys the common ground on the basis of which our own categories are based. It is not the propinquity of the categories that is destroyed, but the very site on which the propinquity is based, precisely because "the distance separating" the categories is too narrow (xvi). What has been removed is the table "that enables thought to operate upon the entities of our world, to put them in order, to divide into classes, to group them according to names that designate their similarities and their differences—the table upon which, since the beginning of time, language has intersected space" (xvii). When we say that "a cat and a dog resemble each other less than two greyhounds do, even if both are tamed or embalmed, even if both are frenzied, even if both have broken the water pitcher, what is the ground on which we are able to establish the validity of this classification with complete certainty? On what 'table,' according to what grid of identities, similitudes, analogies, have we become accustomed to sort out so many different and similar things?" (xix).

Consider the case of "aphasiacs" [*sic*], who, "when shown various differently colored skeins of wool on a table top, are consistently unable to arrange them" according to their color patterns (xviii). They earnestly attempt to classify them in various ways, but as soon as they begin one classification, they start another. For them, the field of identity that sustains the various classifications they consider is too unstable. So they can never settle on one. And how is this different from what we do? It is different, according to Foucault, in that we have a table that makes our task possible, although the table in question is just one among many others. The table is the grid we use to make our classifications, to operate on the world; it is what produces the categories we employ (xix).

What does this tell us about our particular categories, according to Foucault? They are myths resulting from the system of classification we employ (xviii). This system is a historical *a priori* (xxii). It is historical, Foucault seems to be saying, because it is the product of our history, and it is *a priori* because it precedes the ways in which we classify the world (more on this later). From all of this Foucault concludes that the various classifications we use are inventions governed by historically contingent events. Indeed, this is true even of what is perhaps our most cherished category, "man."

> Strangely enough, man—the study of whom is supposed to the naïve to be the oldest investigation since Socrates—is probably no more than a kind of rift in the order of things, or, in any case, a configuration whose outlines are determined by the new position he has so recently taken up in the field of knowledge. Whence all the chimeras of the new humanisms, all the facile solutions of an "anthropology" understood as a universal reflection on man, half-empirical, half-philosophical. It is comforting, however, and a source of profound relief to think that man is only a recent invention, a figure but yet two centuries old, a new wrinkle in our knowledge, and that he will disappear again as soon as that knowledge has discovered a new form. (xxiii)[2]

These words have resounded deeply in modern thought and have been put to many uses, including the call for the elimination of particular categories. Indeed, they have been employed as means for the liberation from what some consider the tyranny of invented categories that have been used in the past and continue to be used for the oppression of selected members of society. The attack has been systematic. If humanity itself is nothing more than a passing historical invention—"a new wrinkle," as Foucault puts it—then we can certainly do away with such other categories as male and female, race, ethnicity, and individuality, let alone duty, honor, goodness, beauty, rationality, and truth. Plato, of course, was wrong in thinking that there are some immutable categories, independent of history and human thought; Aristotle was wrong in holding that there are natures that things have and that establish the necessary and sufficient conditions of their being what they are;[3] Aquinas was wrong in believing that these natures are grounded in God's thought;[4] Kant was wrong in claiming that these categories are common to all human thinking even though we can never know if they characterize reality as it is itself,[5] considered independently of human thought; and Ryle was wrong in proposing that they are semantic spaces in the logic of propositions. All these philosophers, so the argu-

---

2. The point is repeated in the conclusion of the book (386).
3. See Sanford's, Lang's, Sim's, and Garver's essays for perspectives on Aristotle's view of categories, Chapters 1, 2, 5, and 9 of this volume.
4. See Stump's essay for Aquinas's view of categories, and McMahon's for how other medieval philosophers challenged Aquinas's view of categories, Chapters 3 and 4 of this volume.
5. See Quinn's and Garver's essays for reflections on Kant's categories, Chapters 6 and 9 of this volume.

ment goes, make similar mistakes: they do not realize that categories are inventions, resulting from systems of classification that are *a priori* but historically contingent.

The motivation for both Foucault's proposal and the success it has had derives from the way categories function. Surely one of the obvious ways in which they do is that they limit our thinking. Categories function as ruts in which we fall and from which it is often impossible to escape. Once in a rut, we just continue along it to wherever it leads us. In some cases the end result is obviously nefarious. Consider for a moment the racial category "black" as used in the United States to think of persons in terms of the so-called one-drop rule: if X has a drop of black blood, X is black. The consequences of the use of this category have been disastrous. It has prevented Americans from thinking the obvious, that if one has just one drop of black blood and the rest of the blood is white, then one is mostly white; it has demonized blackness; it has prevented some persons from escaping a circle of discrimination, poverty, and oppression; it has coupled the notion of blackness with that of impurity, and so on. Do I need to provide another example? The point should be clear: the use of categories can have pernicious consequences, particularly when categories are applied to persons. This has been amply demonstrated by sociologists in the context of race and ethnicity.[6]

But it is a mistake to think, as some followers of Foucault appear to do, that the use of categories is always nefarious or counterproductive, or that we can actually dispense with them. We need categories, for without them we cannot think or speak. There is not one sentence or one thought that can be formed without it depending on categories. Moreover, categories can also function beneficently by making us see and understand things we did not see or understand before. After all, isn't what we do in school largely to learn about new categories and the

---

6. See, for example, the following studies about Hispanics: H. H. Fairchild and J. A. Cozens, "Chicano, Hispanic, or Mexican American: What's in a Name?" *Hispanic Journal of Behavioral Sciences* 3 (1981): 191–98; Martha Giménez, "'Latino?/Hispanic?'—Who Needs a Name? The Case against a Standardized Terminology," *International Journal of Health Services* 19 (1989): 557–71; David E. Hayes-Bautista and Jorge Chapa, "Latino Terminology: Conceptual Bases for Standardized Terminology," *American Journal of Public Health* 77 (1987): 61–68; G. Marín, "Stereotyping Hispanics: The Differential Effect of Research Method, Label, and Degree of Contact," *International Journal of International Relations* 8 (1984): 17–27; Suzanne Oboler, *Ethnic Labels, Latino Lives: Identity and the Politics of (Re)Presentation in the United States* (Minneapolis: University of Minnesota Press, 1995); Fernando Treviño, "Standardized Terminology for Hispanic Populations," *American Journal of Public Health* 77 (1987): 69–72; and Jorge J. E. Gracia, "¿Qué son las categorías?" trans. Emma Ingala Gómez, in series *Opuscula philosophica* (Madrid: Ediciones Encuentro, 2002).

correspondingly new ways of seeing and understanding the world? The use of categories can also be beneficial in matters of social concerns. For example, the use of racial and ethnic categories can serve to empower disempowered groups and reverse discrimination, oppression, and economic disadvantage. Historically, the category black has served to unite persons who, constituted as a group, have been able to change longstanding patterns of discrimination that otherwise would not have been changed.

The issue, then, is not whether we can do without categories, but (1) what they are, (2) the validity of particular categories, and (3) the ways in which they should be used. Naturally, the answers to these questions are all related to the issue we are addressing here: are categories invented or discovered? Before I attempt to resolve this issue, however, let me briefly characterize Foucault's own answer.

II. FOUCAULT'S POSITION IN BRIEF

First, Foucault has a very inclusive understanding of the extension of the term "category." He is not talking, as Aristotle and so many other philosophers have done, of a small group of very general, or even most general, items. Aristotle thought that there were roughly ten of these: substance, quality, quantity, relation, and so on.[7] The Stoics reduced their number to four.[8] And there has been constant bickering in the history of philosophy about the number and identity of categories. But most of these authors thought of categories as most general and of their number as very small. Foucault, by contrast, casts a very wide net. He speaks of such things as "dog" and "man" as categories, as well as of all the items contained in Borges's list. There is nothing wrong with this. But it is important for us to keep it in mind, for what we conclude about categories if we understand them broadly, as Foucault does, will be significantly different from what we will conclude if we adopt a narrower view as encompassing only the most general categories.[9]

Second, for Foucault, categories are found in knowing subjects. They are ways in which we slice, arrange, carve, or cut up—depending on the metaphor one wishes to use—the world. One could say, then, that they are concepts in terms of which one thinks about the world

---

7. Aristotle, *Categories*, 1b25.
8. H. F. A. von Arnim, *Stoicorum Veterum Fragmenta*, vol. 2 (Stuttgart: B. G. Teubner Verlagsgesellschaft, 1964), 369.
9. I am on record as advocating a similarly broad extension for the term "category" in Jorge J. E. Gracia, *Metaphysics and Its Task: The Search for the Categorial Foundation of Knowledge* (Albany: State University of New York Press, 1999), 132–33.

and their function is primarily epistemic (xxii). This is, of course, not the only way of understanding categories, although it is one of the most common ways of understanding them today.[10] Let me mention three other ways of understanding them that are pertinent to our topic if we aim at a judgment that extends beyond Foucault's position.[11]

One of these is as the way in which things are, or, as some proponents of this view say, as properties of things.[12] This is a realistic understanding of categories if by realism one means that a category is something in the world independent of the way humans may think. In this sense, the category "cat," for example, is taken to be the way in which certain things are, that is, the way the things we call cats are, or put in a different way, it is a property common to all cats and responsible for them being so.

Another common view is that categories are words, although again there is considerable disagreement about what this means exactly.[13] Regardless of disagreements about details, however, this view holds minimally that a category is a linguistic entity rather than a way in which people think, or a way in which the world is. So let us assume, then, for present purposes, that this means that the category "cat" is nothing more than the word "cat." This view is often put in terms of predicates, so that a category is said to be a predicate when a predicate is understood to be no more than a linguistic entity of a certain sort. For this reason, one might call this position a nominalist view of categories.[14]

---

10. For a conceptualist view of categories arising from a different philosophical tradition from that of Foucault, see Stephan Körner, "Thinking, Thought, and Categories," *Monist* 66, 3 (1983): 353–66, and Stephan Körner, *Categorial Frameworks* (Oxford: Blackwell, 1970).

11. I have explored these and other ways in Gracia, *Metaphysics and Its Task*, 181–99, and "The Ontological Status of Categories: Are They Extra-Mental Entities, Concepts, or Words?" *International Philosophical Quarterly* 39 (1999): 249–64.

12. Cf. Aristotle, *Metaphysics*, 1017a23; David Pole, "'Languages' and Aspects of Things," *Philosophical Quarterly* 12 (1962): 306–15; and Kenneth Livingston, "Concepts, Categories, and Epistemology," *Philosophia* 19 (1989): 265–300, who argues for a modified version of realism.

13. For different views, see Peter Abelard, *Dialectica*, ed. Lambert M. de Rijk (Assen: Van Gorcum, 1956), 69, 112; John Searle, *Speech Acts: An Essay in the Philosophy of Language* (Cambridge: Cambridge University Press, 1969), 105, 120. See also Gilbert Ryle, "Categories," in *Collected Papers*, vol. 2 (New York: Barnes and Noble, 1971), 174, 180; and Rudolph Carnap, "The Elimination of Metaphysics through Logical Analysis of Language," trans. Arthur Pap, in *Logical Positivism*, ed. A. J. Ayer (Glencoe, Ill.: Free Press, 1959), 68.

14. The three views of categories I have outlined here (i.e., as properties, words, and concepts) are in fact three of the four traditional interpretations of Aristotle's view as presented in his *Categories*. The fourth is an inclusive view that tries to integrate the other three. See Christos Evangeliou, *Aristotle's Categories and Porphyry* (Leiden: Brill, 1988), 29–33.

Finally, there is the way I have proposed in *Metaphysics and Its Task*.[15] In this way, a category is whatever is expressed by a term or expression, simple or complex, that can be predicated of some other term or expression. According to this formula, a category *qua* category is not necessarily a linguistic entity, although linguistic entities are used to express categories, and it is possible for some categories to be linguistic entities. Nor is a category necessarily a property of things in the world, although some of them may be so. And a category is not necessarily a concept or way in which we think about the world, although a category can be that, and it is through concepts that we think about categories. Consider three examples of categories: indefinite article, capacity to laugh, and opinion. The first is a linguistic entity, for indefinite articles, such as "a" and "an," are words; the second is a property of certain animals, namely, human animals; and the third is a way in which someone thinks about something or other. In each case there are corresponding linguistic entities, namely, the terms "indefinite article," "capacity to laugh," and "opinion." And in each case there are also concepts through which we think about the indefinite article, the capacity to laugh, and an opinion. But the categories are not these words, or concepts, but what is expressed by the words and thought about through the concepts. And these are sometimes words, sometimes concepts, and sometimes properties of things, as the examples given indicate.

It is quite obvious that Foucault does not consider categories to be either properties or what predicates express. His view explicitly challenges "realistic" views of categories and my view never occurred to him. But it is not perhaps as clear that he does not propose a linguistic view of categories. After all, he takes pains to indicate the importance of language, telling us, for example, that the categories of Borges's Chinese encyclopedia can be "juxtaposed" only "in the non-place of language" (xvii). And in an attempt to distance his view from that of phenomenologists, he describes it as "a theory of discursive practice" (xiv). Still, we should not be led astray by these comments, for Foucault explicitly states that the task of language is merely to spread categories before us (xvii), and this entails that categories are not the linguistic entities through which they are spread. Indeed, categories "make it possible for us to name, speak, and think" (xix), which suggests that they precede language (i.e., names and speech) but is consistent with the interpretation that they are conceptual in some sense, although Foucault never quite makes clear in what sense. I shall return to this later.

---

15. Gracia, *Metaphysics and Its Task*, 199–202.

Third, for Foucault, categories are the result of *a priori* historical systems of classification. They do not appear to be the systems themselves but rather the results of systems. The categories listed in Borges's Chinese encyclopedia cut up the world in the way they do because they presuppose a system of classification that is used in producing them. And it is because the system is presupposed that it is called *a priori;* the system precedes the process of classifying. But the system is historical because, unlike the Kantian *a priori*, which is universal and common to all human knowers, it is the result of historically contingent events, and therefore historical and contingent itself. Categories, then, are the result of the application of the system. In a sense, the system is like a set of criteria (he calls them "rules," xi) that, when applied in experience, make us think of the world in certain ways.

Foucault does not explain how exactly this system of classification can both be the product of history and *a priori*. Indeed, if one thinks in terms of experience, this may appear impossible. For, how can the system be *a priori* and thus precede experience and at the same time be the result of history, which presumably includes experience? One way to solve this puzzle is to distinguish between what might be called "causing experiences" and "affected experiences." The first are the experiences that play a causal role in the development of the system of classification; the second are the experiences that are affected or structured by that system once it is in place. Understood thus, there is no contradiction in Foucault's view insofar as one could say that the experiences causing the system are not the experiences affected by the system.[16]

To return to a point mentioned above in passing, it should be clear that categories, for Foucault, are not personal, and certainly not arbitrary. Foucault was quite annoyed when his view was interpreted as a kind of phenomenology, in which the observing subject and his individual consciousness are given absolute priority (xvi). The systems that produce the categories through which we view the world are not particular but general, and they are revealed in discourse rather than in consciousness. Moreover, in virtue of the fact that they are the result of systems, they are not arbitrary creations of individual persons but rather the results—although Foucault does not tell us whether necessary or contingent—of those systems.

Finally, we come to Foucault's most important claim for our purpos-

---

16. This does not solve other problems with Foucault's proposal, of course. For example, the problem of how change is possible is one that requires further tinkering. Foucault is aware of it and attempts an answer in the foreword to the English edition of *The Order of Things*, xii.

es, namely, that categories are invented. They are ways we invent to think about the world. But what exactly does Foucault have in mind with this? First, a question of extension: does he mean to say that only categories, and not the systems of which they are the products, are invented, or are the systems whose application gives rise to categories also invented? In characteristic style, Foucault does not explicitly ask or answer this question, but much of what he says suggests that not just categories but also the systems that are used to produce them are invented. For our purposes, the claim that is particularly important is that *all* categories, not just some, are invented. But here we face another question, this time concerned with invention: what does "invented" mean? Again, in characteristic fashion Foucault does not openly tell us. And his many disciples follow his lead, although they often complicate matters by also, and frequently, using the term "constructed" instead of "invented." A favorite claim these days, for example, is that race is a "social construction," although many also speak of it as a "social invention."[17] For the sake of simplicity and parsimony, however, I shall discuss only invention, not construction.[18]

From what we saw earlier, however, there seem to be at least two conditions Foucault has in mind when he writes about the invention of categories. First, categories are the products of human activity. So let us express this condition by saying that, according to him, categories are human products. Second, humans are not just responsible for producing categories, they also seem to be responsible in some sense for making categories what they are. Like myths, categories are made up, although as we saw earlier, they are made up not by individual persons but by societies. This suggests an element of creativity or design. So let us express this condition by saying that categories are designed by humans or are the products of human design. Anything that meets these two conditions is presumably invented, and this is why categories are said to be so.

From this conception of invention, we can surmise its distinction from discovery. An invention is distinct from a discovery in that something discovered is neither the product of the discoverer nor designed by him or her.[19] The discoverer of King Tut's tomb did not produce or

17. I discuss this particular issue in detail in Jorge J. E. Gracia, *Surviving Race, Ethnicity, and Nationality: A Challenge for the Twenty-First Century*, forthcoming.

18. For the use of "construction" in racial studies, see Michael Omi and Howard Winant, "Racial Formation in the United States," in *The Idea of Race*, ed. Robert Bernasconi and Tommy L. Lott (Indianapolis: Hackett, 2000), 197 and passim.

19. These two conditions suggest that categories are artifactual. The notion of artifact, however, is one of the most difficult to pin down in philosophy. I have discussed several

design it. Obviously we have here a rather broad sense of discovery, for one can discover such different things as the genetic structure of humans, an ancient artifact, or the concept of zero.

III. ARE CATEGORIES INVENTED OR DISCOVERED?

With these clarifications in mind, we can now turn to the central question: are categories invented or discovered? I shall assume in the present discussion that the notions "invented by X" and "discovered by X" are mutually exclusive and jointly exhaustive in the domain in which they are applied. This means that if a category is invented by X, it is not discovered by X, and vice versa. A fortunate consequence of this is that an answer to the question of whether categories are invented is enough to tell us if they are discovered or not. So we might as well just ask whether categories are invented.[20] Now, from what we saw earlier, this question can be more pointedly asked, in accordance with Foucault's view: are categories both produced and designed by humans?

Even in this form, however, the question is not sufficiently clear for our purposes, for categories can be understood in many different ways, and this complicates matters. In order to simplify and facilitate things, however, I shall consider only the four ways suggested earlier, and in addition I shall frame the question in terms of a concrete example, say, the category "cat." Thus we have the following four questions:

1. Is the word "cat" both produced and designed by humans?
2. Is the concept cat both produced and designed by humans?
3. Is the property catness both produced and designed by humans?
4. Is what the predicate "cat" expresses both produced and designed by humans?

Distinguishing among these questions makes it easier to answer them. The answer to 1, for example, is quite clear insofar as words are always produced by humans and include an element of design in them. Words are conventional signs constituted by various kinds of entities, such as

---

attempts at formulating its necessary and sufficient conditions, all of which turn out to be inadequate in some ways, in Jorge J. E. Gracia, *A Theory of Textuality: The Logic and Epistemology* (Albany: State University of New York Press, 1995), 44–52. For other discussions of artifacts, see George Dickie, *Aesthetics: An Introduction* (Indianapolis: Bobbs-Merrill, 1971); William R. Carter, "Salmon on Artifact Origins and Lost Possibilities," *Philosophical Review* 92 (1983): 223–32; Hilary Kornblith, "Referring to Artifacts," *Philosophical Review* 89 (1980): 109–14; Steven Schwartz, "Putnam on Artifacts," *Philosophical Review* 87 (1978): 566–74; and Randall Dipert, *Artifacts, Art Works, and Agency* (Philadelphia: Temple University Press, 1993).

20. On this see DeMarco's essay, Chapter 15 of this volume.

sounds, gestures, lines drawn on a page, actions, pebbles, and so on. The entities that constitute words can be anything whatever, including mental images of some kind. The word written as "cat" is constituted by black lines; when I utter "cat," the word is made up of certain sounds; when I imagine the written word, it is constituted by the images of the lines that make up the written word, and so on. These groups of lines, sounds, or images become words when they are used together with other words to say something.[21] The sound I utter when I say "cat" becomes a word when I use it to say "the cat is on the mat." The conventional character of words comes from their intentional use by humans as signs in order to say something. The connection between the sound I utter when I say "cat" and its meaning is the result of human design and activity. In some cases, words are designed and produced by individual persons, as happens with the terms of some logical languages (e.g., $\supset$), but in others they are products of cooperative efforts among members of a group within a society or among members of the society at large (e.g., "cat"). From all this we can conclude that the word "cat" was invented rather than discovered by those who first introduced it into English, although it is always possible that someone else may discover it later (the case of a Mayan glyph). Something similar could be said about all other categorial words and indeed about *all* words.[22]

The situation with question 2 is particularly difficult because the notion of a concept is quite contested.[23] There are, in fact, many different views of concepts, but let me mention only two for the sake of brevity. In one sense, a concept is taken to be an act of thinking itself through which we understand something; in another sense, it is conceived as a certain idea or view one entertains when one thinks about something. If one adopts the first view of concepts, then it should be clear that we have a human act, but not one designed by humans. Concepts in this

---

21. Pole, "'Languages' and Aspects of Things," 315.
22. Obviously there are words that are not categorial, such as "Jorge," "this," and "or." This raises the question of which words are categorial and which are not. My view is that only words that can function as predicates can be categorial. This follows from my description of a category as "what a predicate expresses." Proper names and indexicals appear in third place only in identity sentences, not in predicative ones. And the case of connectives and quantifiers should be obvious.
23. For different views, see Michael Dummett, *The Logical Basis of Metaphysics* (Cambridge: Harvard University Press, 1993), 1, 15; Peter F. Strawson, *Analysis and Metaphysics* (Oxford: Oxford University Press, 1992), 7, 18, 22, and 34; Gilbert Ryle, "Systematically Misleading Expressions," in *Logic and Language*, ed. Antony Flew (Oxford: Blackwell, 1968), 11–12, 29; Willard V. O. Quine, "On What There Is," in *From a Logical Point of View* (Cambridge: Harvard University Press, 1953), 2; and William of Ockham, "On the Notion of Knowledge or Science," in *Philosophical Writings: A Selection*, trans. and ed. Philotheus Boehner (London: Nelson, 1967), 11.

sense are not invented by us, although they are produced by us. We produce concepts in a way similar to how we produce acts of digestion or sensation. This means that a concept in this sense is discovered rather than invented. If by the category "cat" we mean the very mental acts whereby we think of cat or cats, then we have something that is not invented to the extent that those acts are not designed by humans.

On the other hand, by "concept" one may mean a certain idea or view one entertains about something, and indeed this is what Foucault seems to have in mind. If this position is adopted, then whether we have something invented or not depends on the idea or view in question. If the idea or view has not been produced or designed by humans, then it is not invented. But if the idea or view has been produced and designed by humans, then it is invented.[24] The ideas of phoenix (a bird that rises from its ashes) and coat hanger (a thing that serves to hang coats in a certain way—nails are not coat hangers and yet also serve to hang coats), for example, are both invented, although the first one is an idea of something that does not exist except in the imagination, and the second is an idea of something that exists outside the mind. Both ideas are invented, because there could be no such ideas were it not that someone came up with them.

But are all ideas like the ideas of phoenix or coat hanger? Consider the idea of cat. Is it like the idea of phoenix, like the idea of coat hanger, or like neither? The first two possibilities are interesting. If the first, then we have a situation in which it is a fictional invention—a mere mental model to which nothing outside the mind corresponds (or perhaps even could correspond). If the second, then it is a nonfictional invention—a mental model that has been used (or perhaps even could be used) to create something outside the mind. Before we can answer the question we have asked, then, we need to answer question 4 above, for this answer will reveal the status of that to which the categorial term refers and which we understand through the corresponding categorial concept.

So, turning to question 4: is what the predicate "cat" expresses—that is, cat—something produced and designed by humans? But perhaps it would be better to separate the two conditions. So, first, let us ask: is cat the product of human action? The temptation is to answer yes *or* no, where "or" is taken exclusively. Instead, I submit that the sensible answer is yes *and* no. It is affirmative because many of the historical events that gave rise to what we call cats are the result of human actions; but it

24. For purposes of this paper I am not considering cases of nonhumans, whether divine, angelic, Martian, or nonhuman animals.

is negative because many of them are not. Likewise, there are many human choices that contribute to the creation of cats—such as the invasion of a territory and capturing cats, the selective breeding of cats, and so on—but there are others that do not—such as a natural cataclysm that kills an entire population of certain kinds of cats. Thus cat appears to be the result of both human action and factors that have nothing to do with such actions.

The second condition of inventions is human design. So we need to ask whether cat is a human design. Again the temptation is to answer yes *or* no, but the sensible answer is yes *and* no. The negative answer is justified because it is hard to find evidence that either a person, a group of persons, or an entire society ever set out to design, or actually did design, what we call cats. But, on the other hand, affirmatively, it is clear that there have been attempts at designing some individual cats (e.g., Hunter and Peanut) and some kinds of cats (e.g., Siamese or Pekinese). Genetic engineering certainly vouches for this.

So now we have an answer to question 4 about what the predicate "cat" expresses (it expresses something that appears to be partly invented and partly not invented), and this can be applied, *mutatis mutandis*, to other predicates. Moreover, we can go back to the property catness and the answer to question 3: is catness invented or not? To the extent that this property is the result of human action and has been designed by humans, we must conclude that catness is invented. Moreover, to the extent that catness is invented, the concepts (as ideas) that we have of cats are also invented. So here we have the answer to the part of question 2 we had left unanswered earlier. This does not mean, however, that the concept cat is an invented fiction (like phoenix) or that it is a nonfictional invention (like coat hanger). And if we follow a similar procedure with categories other than cat, we should be able to come up with appropriate answers.

Let me summarize the conclusions we have reached in general terms:

1. If categories are conceived as words, then they are invented but not discovered (except in cases in which the discoverer is other than the inventor).

2. If categories are conceived as mental acts, then they are discovered but not invented.

3. If categories are conceived as ideas or views, then whether they are invented or discovered depends on the kind of idea or view in question.

4. If categories are conceived as properties, whether they are invented or discovered depends on the kind of property in question.

5. If categories are conceived as what is expressed by a predicate, then whether they are invented or discovered depends on what is expressed by the predicate.

From this it follows that the claim that all categories are invented, or discovered, is confusing. One must engage in some analysis before the question to which this claim aims to be a response can be answered. And if we do, we see that only when categories are conceived as words can one sensibly argue that they are always invented, but not discovered (with the proviso made earlier); only when categories are conceived as mental acts can we argue sensibly that they are always discovered, but not invented; and the adequacy of other claims about categories when they are conceived as ideas, properties, or what is expressed by predicates, depends on the particular kinds in question. Naturally, other theories of categories will yield other alternatives.

IV. RESPONSE TO A FOUCAULTIAN RETORT

Still, Foucault, along with some of his followers and sympathizers, may not be persuaded by my arguments. I have introduced some distinctions that may be useful, but at bottom the matter remains unresolved insofar as one can still argue, with Foucault, that categories, considered as the ways we think about things (what I called ideas or views earlier), are the products of historically contingent systems of classification. Let me address this position directly through the following arguments:

First, the very notion that *some* categories are invented requires that at least some others not be invented, or at least that it be possible that some not be invented. The notion of a design, which is intrinsic to invention, requires the notion of elements that are part of the design but are not themselves designed. The notion of designing something involves ordering, but an ordering involves putting things in relations with each other, and a new order involves the notion of putting things in new relations with respect to each other. This means that there is something new and something old in a design. The new is the order; the old is the things that are being placed in order. To design a coat hanger is to twist a wire (or carve wood, or whatever) in a certain way, so that it can serve to hang clothes. But I must begin with the wire. Of course, one could say that the wire itself is a design. And indeed it is. But if I go back far enough, eventually I will find some stuff that is not designed.

Second, consider the category "invented." Is this category itself invented or is it not? If it is itself invented, then according to Foucault it is the result of a particular *a priori* and contingent historical system of classification. But this means that this category may not be operative in other systems. So why should I use it? In short, why should I pay any attention to Foucault? Particularly when I find that what he says goes against some of my most fundamental basic intuitions, which are presumably based on the particular *a priori* system of classification that regulates the ways in which I think about the world? Of course, if the category "invented" is not invented, then we have a conclusion that contradicts the view that all categories are invented, and we have the result I favor.

Third, one of the things that Foucault seems to be arguing is that the invented character of categories necessarily undermines their universal validity. But this argument surely rests on a fallacy. That something is produced and designed by humans does not mean that it is valid only within particular historical circumstances. A coat hanger serves to hang clothes in any place where there are clothes to be hung.

Of course, Foucault might object that the three arguments I have given against his view are based on certain assumptions taken from the particular *a priori* system of classification under which I operate. My criticisms, then, are internal to my system and therefore beg the question. Indeed, so the argument would go, they depend on such things as the principle of identity that is a result of historically contingent circumstances.

Let me answer this objection with a fourth argument, based precisely on the principle of identity: A is identical to A. Am I justified in accepting this principle? Why should I not say that the category "identity" is merely invented and the product of historical contingencies? Why can't we dispense with it? And on what bases can I argue, through this example, against categories resulting from some other system, including Foucault's?

The answer is very old, although it has proved ineffective in convincing hardcore skeptics: to deny identity is impossible without using it. The critic who tries to deny it must accept it. And if he accepts it, then that is all that we need to show that he is wrong. The critic, then, faces an inescapable dilemma: he can either remain silent or speak, but if he speaks, he must accept the very rules he rejects.[25]

---

25. The standard skeptical retort that a critic can use identity methodologically to undermine the positions of those who accept it, but need not accept it himself, works only to a limited extent. It works in that identity may indeed be used to undermine the views of those who accept it, but it does not work insofar as the critic cannot, without using it, put forth a positive view of her own.

V. CONCLUSION

In conclusion, let me list the things I have attempted to do. First, I have tried to clarify, and I have criticized, Foucault's position. This is important because of Foucault's prominent historical place in the debate concerning the issue of the invention and discovery of categories. Second, I have tried to clarify the notions that play a role in the controversy: invention, discovery, and category. This is significant because most discussions that use these concepts do not explain them, thus generating confusion and solving nothing. Third, I have drawn certain conclusions about the issue under discussion, from which, in turn, follows perhaps the most important thesis I have tried to defend, namely: claims that all categories are either invented or discovered are suspect pending careful analysis and investigation; for some categories appear to be invented, some discovered, and some mixed. Indeed, the third kind is most significant, for those categories that affect our social and political lives generally seem to be of this sort. Those authors who feel entitled to reject or modify the categories we ordinarily use because they regard all categories as inventions, and those authors who argue for their uncritical acceptance because they regard them as discovered, need to take a second look. If they do, they will realize that the matter is not as simple as they think. A fruitful approach to categories must start, then, with an analysis of the sort I have provided here. So, even if I have failed in the particular details I have provided, I hope I have succeeded in charting a course that all those who wish to determine whether categories are invented or discovered should follow.[26]

26. Let me express my gratitude to Peter Hare, Robert Mayhew, and Jonathan J. Sanford for some suggestions prompted by an early draft of this paper, and to Richard Gale, Dagfinn Føllesdal, Eleonore Stump, Brian Martine, Mariam Thalos, and Marcus Marenda for various comments and criticisms they offered when I presented the paper at the 2001 meetings of the Metaphysical Society of America.

Bibliography

Abelard, Peter. *Dialectica*. Ed. Lambert M. de Rijk. Assen: Van Gorcum, 1956.
Ackrill, J. L. *Aristotle's "Categories" and "De Interpretatione."* Oxford: Clarendon Press, 1963.
Adams, Marilyn McCord. "Things versus 'Hows,' or Ockham on Predication and Ontology." In *How Things Are*, ed. James Bogen and James E. McGuire, 175–88. Dordrecht: Reidel, 1985.
———. *William Ockham*. 2 vols. Publications in Medieval Studies, Medieval Institute, University of Notre Dame, 26. Notre Dame: University of Notre Dame Press, 1987.
Aertsen, J. A. *Medieval Philosophy and the Transcendentals: The Case of Thomas Aquinas*. New York: Brill, 1996.
Albertus Magnus. *De Praedicamentis*. In *Omnia Opera*, vol. 1, ed. August Borgnet. Paris: Ludovico Vives, 1890.
———. *Liber de Sex Principiis*. In *Omnia Opera*, vol. 1, ed. August Borgnet. Paris: Ludovico Vives, 1890.
Ames, Roger T. "The Focus Field Self." In *Self as Person in Asian Theory and Practice*, ed. Roger T. Ames, Wimal Dissanayake, and Thomas P. Kasulis. Albany: State University of New York Press, 1994.
Aristotle. *The Basic Works of Aristotle*. Ed. Richard McKeon. New York: Random House, 1941.
———. *The Complete Works of Aristotle: The Revised Oxford Translation*. 2 vols. Ed. Jonathan Barnes. Princeton: Princeton University Press, 1984.
Arnauld, Antoine, and Pierre Nicole. *The Art of Thinking*. Trans. James Dickoff and Patricia James. Indianapolis: Bobbs-Merrill, 1964.
Baker, Lynne Rudder. "Why Constitution Is Not Identity." *Journal of Philosophy* 94 (1997): 599–621.
———. "Unity without Identity: A New Look at Material Constitution." *Midwest Studies in Philosophy* 23 (1999): 144–65.
Bambrough, Renford. "Universals and Family Resemblances." *Proceedings of the Aristotelian Society* 61 (1960–61): 207–22.
Beal, M. W. "Essentialism and Closed Concepts." *Ratio* 16 (1974): 190–205.
Benveniste, Emile. *Problems in General Linguistics*. Trans. Mary Elizabeth Meek. Coral Gables: University of Miami Press, 1971.
Bittner, Thomas, and Barry Smith. "A Taxonomy of Granular Partitions." In *Spatial Information Theory: Foundations of Geographic Information Science, Proceedings of COSIT 2001, Morro Bay, Calif., September 19–23, 2001*, ed. Daniel Montello. New York: Springer, 2001.
Boethius, Anicius Manlius Severinus. "*De Trinitate*." In *The Theological Tractates*, trans. H. F. Stewart and E. K. Rand, 2–31. London: William Heinemann, 1918.

Borges, Jorge Luis. "The Analytical Language of John Wilkins." Trans. Ruth L. C. Simms. In Jorge Luis Borges, *Other Inquisitions, 1937–1952*. Austin: University of Texas Press, 1993.

Brentano, Franz. *Psychologie vom empirischen Standpunkt*. Leipzig: Duncker und Humblot, 1874. Reprinted in *Philosophische Bibliothek*. Hamburg: Felix Meiner, 1955.

———. *Psychology from an Empirical Point of View*. Trans. D. B. Terrell. In *Realism and the Background of Phenomenology*, ed. Roderick M. Chisholm. Glencoe, Ill.: Free Press, 1966.

Brestzke, James T., S.J. "The Tao of Confucian Virtue Ethics." *International Philosophical Quarterly* 35 (1995): 25–41.

Buridan, John. *Quaestiones in Praedicamenta*. Ed. Johannes Schneider. Munich: Verlag der Bayerischen Akademie der Wissenschaften, 1983.

———. *Summulae in Praedicamenta*. Artistarium 10:3. Ed. E. P. Bos. Nijmegen: Ingenium, 1994.

Bursill-Hall, G. L. *Speculative Grammars of the Middle Ages; The Doctrine of the Partes orationis of the Modistae*. Approaches to Semiotics 11. The Hague: Mouton, 1971.

Campbell, Keith. "Family Resemblance Predicates." *American Philosophical Quarterly* 2 (1965): 238–44.

Carnap, Rudolph. "The Elimination of Metaphysics through Logical Analysis of Language." Trans. Arthur Pap. In *Logical Positivism*, ed. A. J. Ayer, 60–81. Glencoe, Ill.: Free Press, 1959.

Carter, William R. "Salmon on Artifact Origins and Lost Possibilities." *Philosophical Review* 92 (1983): 223–32.

Casati, R., and A. C. Varzi. *Parts and Places: The Structures of Spatial Representation*. Cambridge: MIT Press, 1999.

Colapietro, Vincent. *Peirce's Approach to the Self*. Albany: State University of New York Press, 1989.

Confucius. *Confucian Analects, the Great Learning and the Doctrine of the Mean*. Trans. J. Legge. Oxford: Clarendon Press, 1893. Reprint, New York: Dover Publications, 1971.

———. *The Analects of Confucius*. Trans. R. Ames and H. Rosemont Jr. New York: Ballantine Books, 1998.

Danto, Arthur. "Naturalism." In *The Encyclopedia of Philosophy*. 8 vols. Ed. Paul Edwards, 4:448–50. New York: Macmillan, 1967.

Davidson, Donald. *Inquiries into Truth and Interpretation*. New York: Oxford University Press, 1984.

DeMarco, C. Wesley. "Wittgenstein and Philosophical Signification." Ph.D. diss., Vanderbilt University, 1991.

De Rijk, Lambert M. "On Buridan's View of Accidental Being." In *John Buridan: A Master of Arts*. Artistarium Supplementa 8. Nijmegen: Ingenium, 1993.

Dickie, George. *Aesthetics: An Introduction*. Indianapolis: Bobbs-Merrill, 1971.

Dipert, Randall. *Artifacts, Art Works, and Agency*. Philadelphia: Temple University Press, 1993.

Dummett, Michael. *The Logical Basis of Metaphysics*. Cambridge: Harvard University Press, 1993.

Dupré, John. "Natural Kinds and Biological Taxa." *Philosophical Review* 90 (1981): 66–90.

Ebbesen, Sten. "The Paris Arts Faculty: Siger of Brabant, Boethius of Dacia,

Radulphus Brito." In *Medieval Philosophy*, vol. 3 of *Routledge History of Philosophy*, ed. John Marenbon, 269–90. London: Routledge, 1998.
Evangeliou, Christos. *Aristotle's Categories and Porphyry*. Leiden: Brill, 1988.
Fackenheim, Emil C. "Kant's Concept of History." *Kant-Studien* 48 (1956): 381–98.
Fairchild, H. H., and J. A. Cozens. "Chicano, Hispanic, or Mexican American: What's in a Name?" *Hispanic Journal of Behavioral Sciences* 3 (1981): 191–98.
Fales, Evan. "Natural Kinds and Freaks of Nature." *Philosophy of Science* 49 (1982): 67–90.
Fingarette, Herbert. "Comment and Response." In *Rules, Rituals, and Responsibility: Essays Dedicated to H. Fingarette*, ed. Mary I. Bockover. La Salle, Ill.: Open Court, 1991.
———. "The Problem of Self in the *Analects*." *Philosophy East & West* 29 (1979): 129–40.
Føllesdal, Dagfinn. "Husserl and Heidegger on the Role of Actions in the Constitution of the World." In *Essays in Honour of Jaako Hintikka*, ed. E. Saarinen, R. Hilpinen, I. Niinilnoto, and M. Provence Hintikka. Dordrecht: Reidel, 1979.
Foucault, Michel. *The Order of Things: An Archeology of the Human Sciences*. New York: Vintage Books, 1973.
Frawley, William. *Linguistic Semantics*. Hillsdale, N. J.: Lawrence Erlbaum, 1992.
Frede, Michael. "Categories in Aristotle." In *Essays in Ancient Philosophy*, 29–48. Minneapolis: University of Minnesota Press, 1987.
Frege, G. *The Foundation of Arithmetic*. Trans. J. L. Austin. Oxford: Blackwell, 1950.
———. *The Frege Reader*. Trans. Michael Beaney (Oxford: Blackwell, 1997).
Garver, Newton, and S. C. Lee. *Derrida and Wittgenstein*. Philadelphia: Temple University Press, 1994.
Genova, C. A. "Kant's Epigenesis of Reason." *Kant-Studien* 65 (1974): 259–73.
Gilbert, Margaret. *Living Together: Rationality, Sociality, and Obligation*. Lanham, Md.: Rowman & Littlefield, 1996.
———. *On Social Facts*. Princeton: Princeton University Press, 1992.
Gillespie, C. M. "The Aristotelian Categories." *Classical Quarterly* 19 (1925): 75–84.
Giménez, Martha. "'Latino?/Hispanic?'—Who Needs a Name? The Case against a Standardized Terminology." *International Journal of Health Services* 19 (1989): 557–71.
Gorman, Michael. "Subjectivism about Normativity and the Normativity of Intentional States." *International Philosophical Quarterly* 43 (2003): 5–14.
———. "Intentionality, Normativity, and a Problem for Searle." *Dialogue: Canadian Philosophical Review* 41 (2002): 703–13.
Goodman, Nelson. *Ways of Worldmaking*. Indianapolis: Hackett, 1978.
Gracia, Jorge J. E. *Philosophy and Its History: Issues in Philosophical Historiography*. Albany: State University of New York Press, 1992.
———. *A Theory of Textuality: The Logic and Epistemology*. Albany: State University of New York Press, 1995.
———. *Metaphysics and Its Task: The Search for the Categorial Foundation of Knowledge*. Albany: State University of New York Press, 1999.
———. "The Ontological Status of Categories: Are They Extra-Mental Entities, Concepts, or Words?" *International Philosophical Quarterly* 39 (1999): 249–64.

———. *The Challenges of Race, Ethnicity, and Nationality: A Foundational Analysis for the Twenty-First Century.* Forthcoming.
Graham, A. C. "Relating Categories to Question Forms in Pre-Han Chinese Thought." In *Studies in Chinese Philosophy and Philosophical Literature,* ed. A. C. Graham, 360–411. Albany: State University of New York Press, 1986.
Hall, David L., and Roger T. Ames. *Thinking from the Han: Self, Truth and Transcendence in Chinese and Western Culture.* Albany: State University of New York Press, 1998.
Hanna, Robert. "What Categories Are Not." *The Monist* 66 (1983): 422–38.
Hassing, Richard F., ed. *Final Causality in Nature and Human Affairs.* Studies in Philosophy and the History of Philosophy, vol. 30. Washington, D.C.: Catholic University of America Press, 1997.
Hausman, Carl R. "Eros and Agape in Creative Evolution: A Peircean Insight." *Process Studies* 4 (1975): 11–25.
Hayes-Bautista, David E., and Jorge Chapa. "Latino Terminology: Conceptual Bases for Standardized Terminology." *American Journal of Public Health* 77 (1987): 61–68.
Henninger, Mark G. *Relations, Medieval Theories, 1250–1325.* Oxford: Clarendon Press, 1989.
Henrich, Dieter. "The Proof-Structure of Kant's Transcendental Deduction." In *Kant on Pure Reason,* ed. R. C. S. Walker, 66–81. Oxford: Oxford University Press, 1982.
———. "Kant's Notion of a Deduction and the Methodological Background of the First Critique." In *Kant's Transcendental Deductions: The Three Critiques and Opus Postumum,* ed. Eckart Förster, 29–46. Stanford: Stanford University Press, 1989.
———. "Identity and Objectivity." In *The Unity of Reason,* ed. and with an introduction by Richard Velkley, 123–208. Cambridge: Harvard University Press, 1994.
———. "The Concept of Moral Insight and Kant's Doctrine of the Fact of Reason." In *The Unity of Reason,* ed. and with an introduction by Richard Velkley, 55–87. Cambridge: Harvard University Press, 1994.
Henry of Ghent. *Summa (Quaestiones ordinariae).* In *Opera Omnia,* vol. 27, ed. R. Macken. Leuven: Leuven University Press, 1991.
———. *Quodlibeta.* Louvain: Bibliotheque S.J., 1961.
———. *Quodlibet VII.* In *Opera Omnia,* vol. II, ed. G. A. Wilson. Leuven: Leuven University Press, 1991.
Hoffman, Joshua, and Gary Rosenkrantz. *Substance among Other Categories.* Cambridge: Cambridge University Press, 1994.
Horgan, Terence, and John Tienson. "Soft Laws." *Midwest Studies in Philosophy* 15 (1990): 256–79.
Hull, David L. *The Metaphysics of Evolution.* Albany: State University of New York Press, 1989.
Husserl, Edmund. *Ideen zu einer reiner Phänomenologie und phänomenologischen Philosophie.* Vols. 1–3. Ed. Walter Beimel. The Hague: Martinus Nijhoff, 1950–52.
———. *Ideas: General Introduction to Pure Phenomenology.* Trans. W. R. Boyce Gibson. London: Allen & Unwin, 1931.
———. *Ideas Pertaining to a Pure Phenomenology and to a Phenomenological Philosophy.* Trans. Fred Kersten. The Hague: Kluwer, 1983.

———. *Erfahrung und Urteil*. Hamburg: F. Meiner, 1972.
———. *Experience and Judgment*. Trans. James S. Churchill and Karl Ameriks. Evanston: Northwestern University Press, 1973.
———. *Die Krisis der europäischen Wissenschaften und die transzendentale Phänomenologie*. Husserliana VI. Ed. Walter Beimel. The Hague: Martinus Nijhoff, 1976.
———. *The Crisis of European Science and Transcendental Phenomenology*. Trans. David Carr. Evanston: Northwestern University Press, 1984.
John Duns Scotus. *God and Creatures, the Quodlibetal Questions*. Trans. Felix Alluntis, O.F.M., and Allan B. Wolter, O.F.M. Princeton: Princeton University Press, 1975.
———. *Ordinatio*, book II, dist. 1-3. In *Omnia Opera*, vol. 7, ed. Carolo Baliæ, Cherubino Barbariæ, Stanislao Buseliæ, Barnaba Hechich, Luca Modriæ, Sebastiano Nanni, Rogerio Rosini, Saturnino Ruiz de Loizaga, Caesare Saco. Vatican City: Typis Polyglottis Vaticanis, 1973.
———. *Quaestiones Super Libros Metaphysicorum Aristotelis*, books 1-5. In *Opera Philosophica*, vol. 3, ed. R. Andrews, G. Etzkorn, G. Gál, R. Green, F. Kelley, G. Marcil, T. Noone, and R. Wood. St. Bonaventure: Franciscan Institute, 1997.
———. *Quaestiones Super Praedicamenta Aristotelis*. In *Opera Philosophica*, vol. 1, ed. R. Andrews, G. Etzkorn, G. Gál, R. Green, T. Noone, and R. Wood, 147-652. St. Bonaventure: Franciscan Institute, 1999.
Johnston, Mark. "Constitution Is Not Identity." *Mind* 101 (1992): 89-105.
Kant, Immanuel. *Gesammelte Schriften*. 8 vols. Berlin: Prussian Academy of the Sciences, 1902-10.
———. *Critique of Pure Reason*. Ed. and trans. Werner Pluhar. Indianapolis: Hackett, 1996.
———. *Critique of Practical Reason*. 3d ed. Trans. Lewis White Beck. New York: Macmillan, 1993.
Katz, Jerrold J. *The Philosophy of Language*. New York: Harper and Row, 1966.
Kern, Iso. *Husserl und Kant. Eine Untersuchung über Husserls Verhältnis zu Kant und zum Neukantianismus*. Phenomenologica 16. The Hague: Martinus Nijhoff, 1964.
Kincaid, Harold. "Defending Laws in the Social Sciences." *Philosophy of the Social Sciences* 20 (1990): 56-83.
Klima, Gyula. "Buridan's Logic and the Ontology of Modes." In *Medieval Analyses in Language and Cognition, Acts of the Symposium, "The Copenhagen School of Medieval Philosophy", January 10-13, 1996*, ed. Sten Ebbesen and Russell L. Friedman, 473-95. Copenhagen: C. A. Reitzels, 1999.
Kornblith, Hilary. "Referring to Artifacts." *Philosophical Review* 89 (1980): 109-14.
Körner, Stephan. *Categorial Frameworks*. Oxford: Blackwell, 1970.
———. "Thinking, Thought, and Categories." *The Monist* 66 (1983): 353-66.
Lakoff, George, and Mark Johnson. *Metaphors We Live By*. Chicago: University of Chicago Press, 1980.
Lewis, David. *On the Plurality of Worlds*. Oxford: Blackwell, 1986.
———. *Parts of Classes*. Oxford: Blackwell, 1991.
———. "Many, but Almost One." In *Ontology, Causality, and Mind: Essays in Honour of D. M. Armstrong*, ed. J. Bacon, K. Campbell, and L. Reinhardt, 23-38. Cambridge: Cambridge University Press, 1993.

———. "Putnam's Paradox." *Australasian Journal of Philosophy* 62 (1984): 221–36. Reprinted in *Papers in Metaphysics and Epistemology*, 56–77. Cambridge: Cambridge University Press, 1999.
Lipton, Peter. "All Else Being Equal." *Philosophy* 74 (1999): 155–68.
Livingston, Kenneth. "Concepts, Categories, and Epistemology." *Philosophia* 19 (1989): 265–300.
Loux, Michael. *Primary OUSIA*. Ithaca: Cornell University Press, 1991.
Lowe, E. J. "Sortal Terms and Natural Laws." *American Philosophical Quarterly* 17 (1980): 253–60.
———."Laws, Dispositions, and Sortal Logic." *American Philosophical Quarterly* 19 (1982): 41–51.
———. *Kinds of Being*. Oxford: Blackwell, 1989.
Lucy, John A. *Language Diversity and Thought: A Reformulation of the Linguistic Relativity Hypothesis*. New York: Cambridge University Press, 1992.
Lucy, John A., and Richard A. Schweder. "Whorf and His Critics: Linguistic and Nonlinguistic Influences on Color Memory." *American Anthropologist* 81 (1979): 581–615.
MacIntyre, Alasdair. "Incommensurability, Truth, and the Conversation between Confucians and Aristotelians about the Virtues." In *Culture and Modernity: East-West Philosophic Perspectives*, ed. Eliot Deutsch, 104–22. Honolulu: University of Hawaii Press, 1991.
Maierù, Alfonso. "Significatio et connotatio chez Buridan." In *The Logic of John Buridan*, ed. Jan Pinborg, 101–14. Copenhagen: Museum Tusculanum, 1976.
Mann, Wolfgang-Rainer. *The Discovery of Things: Aristototle's Categories and Their Context*. Princeton: Princeton University Press, 2000.
Marín, G. "Stereotyping Hispanics: The Differential Effect of Research Method, Label, and Degree of Contact." *International Journal of International Relations* 8 (1984): 17–27.
Maynard-Smith, John. *Evolution and the Theory of Games*. New York: Cambridge University Press, 1982.
McMahon, William E. "Albert the Great on the Semantics of the Categories of Substance, Quantity, and Quality." *Historiographia Linguistica* 7 (1980): 145–57.
———. "Radulphus Brito on the Sufficiency of the Categories." *Cahiers de l'Institut du Moyen-Age Grec et Latin* 39 (1981): 81–96.
———. "The Categories in Some Post-Medieval Spanish Philosophers." In *Medieval and Renaissance Logic in Spain, Acts of the 12th European Symposium on Medieval Logic and Semantics*, ed. Ignacio Angelelli and Paloma Perez-Ilzarbe, 355–70. Hildesheim: Georg Olms, 2000.
Mehl, Peter J. "In the Twilight of Modernity: MacIntyre and Mitchell on Moral Traditions and Their Assessment." *Journal of Religious Ethics* 19 (1991): 21–54.
Millikan, Ruth Garrett. *White Queen Psychology and Other Essays for Alice*. Cambridge: MIT Press, 1993.
Minio-Paluello, Lorenzo, ed. *Anonymi fragmentum vulgo vocatum* Liber Sex Principiorum. In *Aristoteles Latinus. I.6–7: Categoriarum supplementa: Porphyrii Isagoge et Liber Sex Principium*, 35–59. Bruges: Desclée de Brouwer, 1966.
Mohr, Richard. "Family Resemblance, Platonism, Universals." *Canadian Journal of Philosophy* 7 (1977): 593–600.

Moody, Ernest A. *The Logic of William of Ockham.* New York: Russell & Russell, 1965.
Mumford, Stephen. "Normative and Natural Laws." *Philosophy* 75 (2000): 265–82.
Oboler, Suzanne. *Ethnic Labels, Latino Lives: Identity and the Politics of (Re)Presentation in the United States.* Minneapolis: University of Minnesota Press, 1995.
Olson, Eric. *The Human Animal.* Oxford: Oxford University Press, 1997.
Omi, Michael, and Howard Winant. "Racial Formation in the United States." In *The Idea of Race*, ed. Robert Bernasconi and Tommy L. Lott. Indianapolis: Hackett, 2000.
Omnès, R. *The Interpretation of Quantum Mechanics.* Princeton: Princeton University Press, 1994.
Owen, G. E. L. "Logic and Metaphysics in Some Earlier Works of Aristotle." In *Logic, Science, and Dialectic: Collected Papers in Greek Philosophy*, ed. Martha Nussbaum, 180–99. Ithaca: Cornell University Press, 1986.
Owens, Joseph. "Aristotle on Categories." *Review of Metaphysics* 14 (1960): 73–90.
———. *The Doctrine of Being in the Aristotelian* Metaphysics. 3d ed. Toronto: Pontifical Institute of Mediaeval Studies, 1978.
Parsons, Kathryn Pyne. "Three Concepts of Clusters." *Philosophy and Phenomenological Research* 33 (1973): 514–23.
Paulus, Jean. *Henri de Gand, Essai sur des Tendances de sa Métaphysique.* In *Etudes de Philosophie Médiévale*, vol. 25. Paris: J. Vrin, 1938.
Pears, David. "Universals." *Philosophical Quarterly* 1 (1951): 218–27.
Peirce, Charles Sanders. "The Doctrine of Necessity Examined." *The Monist* 2 (1892): 321–37.
———. *Collected Papers.* Ed. Charles Hartshorne and Paul Weiss. Vols. 7–8, ed. A. W. Burks. Cambridge: Belknap Press of Harvard University Press, 1958–66.
Pepper, Stephen. *World Hypotheses: A Study in Evidence.* Berkeley and Los Angeles: University of California Press, 1970.
Peterson, Roger Tory. A Field Guide to the Birds of Eastern and Central North America. 4th ed. Boston: Houghton Mifflin, 1980.
Plato. *Parmenides.* In *Platonis Opera*, vol. 2, ed. J. Burnet. Oxford: Clarendon Press, 1900–1907. Reprint, Oxford: Oxford University Press, 1995.
———. *Timaeus.* In *Platonis Opera*, vol. 4, ed. J. Burnet. Oxford: Clarendon Press, 1900–1907. Reprint, Oxford: Oxford University Press, 1995.
Pole, David. "'Languages' and Aspects of Things." *Philosophical Quarterly* 12 (1962): 306–15.
Popper, Karl. *The Logic of Scientific Discovery.* London: Hutchinson, 1959.
Porphyry. *Porphyry the Phoenician, Isagoge.* Trans., introduction, and notes by E. W. Warren. Toronto: Pontifical Institute of Mediaeval Studies, 1975.
———. *Isagoge.* In *Five Texts on the Mediaeval Problem of Universals.* Trans. and ed. Paul Vincent Spade. Indianapolis: Hackett, 1994.
Putnam, Hilary. "The Analytic and the Synthetic." In *Mind, Language, and Reality: Philosophical Papers*, vol. 2, 33–69. Cambridge: Cambridge University Press, 1975.
Quine, Willard V. O. *From a Logical Point of View.* Cambridge: Harvard University Press, 1953.
———. *Word and Object.* Cambridge: MIT Press, 1960.

———. "Ontological Relativity." In *Ontological Relativity and Other Essays*, 26–68. New York: Columbia University Press, 1969.

Rorty, Richard. "Pragmatism." In *Routledge Encyclopedia of Philosophy*, ed. Edward Craig. http://www.rep.routledge.com.

Rosenthal, Sandra B. *Charles Peirce's Pragmatic Pluralism*. Albany: State University of New York Press, 1994.

Ross, David. *Transition to an Ordinal Metaphysics*. Albany: State University of New York Press, 1980.

Ruse, Michael. "Biological Species: Natural Kinds, Individuals, or What?" *British Journal of the Philosophy of Science* 38 (1987): 225–42.

Russell, Bertrand. *Problems of Philosophy*. New York: H. Holt & Co., 1912.

Ryle, Gilbert. "Systematically Misleading Expressions." In *Logic and Language*, ed. Antony Flew, 13–40. Oxford: Blackwell, 1968.

———. *Collected Papers*. Vol. 2, *Collected Essays, 1929–1968*. London: Hutchinson, 1971.

Sanford, Jonathan J. "An Aristotelian Critique of Gracia's View of Metaphysics." In *Revisiting Metaphysics: Essays on Jorge J. E. Gracia's* Metaphysics and Its Task, ed. Robert Delfino. Amsterdam: Rudopi, 2004.

Schwartz, Steven. "Putnam on Artifacts." *Philosophical Review* 87 (1978): 566–74.

Searle, John. *Speech Acts: An Essay in the Philosophy of Language*. Cambridge: Cambridge University Press, 1969.

———. *The Construction of Social Reality*. New York: Free Press, 1995.

Sim, May. "Dialectical Communities: From the One to the Many and Back." In *From Puzzles to Principles?: Essays on Aristotle's Dialectic*, ed. May Sim, 183–214. Lanham, Md.: Lexington Books, 1999.

———. "Ritual and Realism in Early Chinese Science." *Journal of Chinese Philosophy* 29 (Dec. 2002): 495–517.

———. "Harmony and the Mean in the *Nicomachean Ethics* and the *Zhongyong*." *Dao: A Journal of Comparative Philosophy* 3 (2004): 253–80.

———. "The Moral Self in Confucius and Aristotle." *International Philosophical Quarterly* 43 (Dec. 2003): 439-62.

Simons, P. *Parts: An Essay in Ontology*. Oxford: Clarendon Press, 1987.

Smith, Barry. "Relevance, Relatedness, and Restricted Set Theory." In *Advances in Scientific Philosophy: Essays in Honour of Paul Weingartner*, ed. G. Schurz and G. J. W. Dorn, 45–56. Amsterdam: Rodopi, 1991.

———. "Fiat Objects." *Topoi* 20 (2001): 131–48.

Smith, Barry, and Berit Brogaard. "Quantum Mereotopology." *Annals of Mathematics and Artificial Intelligence* 35 (2002): 153–75.

Sokolowski, Robert. *Pictures, Quotations, and Distinctions: Fourteen Essays in Phenomenology*. Notre Dame: Notre Dame University Press, 1992.

Stenius, Erik. *Wittgenstein's "Tractatus."* Ithaca: Cornell University Press, 1960.

Strawson, Peter F. *Scepticism and Naturalism: Some Varieties*. New York: Columbia University Press, 1985.

———. *Analysis and Metaphysics*. Oxford: Oxford University Press, 1992.

Stroll, Avrum. *Twentieth-Century Analytic Philosophy*. New York: Columbia University Press, 2000.

Stroud, Barry. "The Charm of Naturalism." *Proceedings and Addresses of the American Philosophical Association* 70 (1996): 43–55.

Thom, René. *Structural Stability and Morphogenesis: An Outline of a General Theory of Models*. Reading, Mass.: W. A. Benjamin, 1975.

Thomas Aquinas. *Quaestio disputata de unione verbi incarnati.*
———. *Expositio super librum Boethii De trinitate.*
———. *Quaestiones disputatae de anima.*
———. *Quaestiones disputatae de malo.*
———. *Quaestiones disputatae de potentia.*
———. *Quaestiones quodlibetales.*
———. *Sententia super Metaphysicam.*
———. *Summa Contra Gentiles.*
———. *Summa theologiae.*
———. *Super I ad Corinthios.*
Thompson, Manley. "Categories." In *The Encyclopedia of Philosophy.* 8 vols. Ed. Paul Edwards, 2:46–71. New York: Macmillan, 1967.
Trendelenburg, Adolf. *Geschichte der Kategorienlehre.* Berlin: G. Bethge, 1846. Reprint, Hildesheim: Georg Olms, 1979.
Treviño, Fernando. "Standardized Terminology for Hispanic Populations." *American Journal of Public Health* 77 (1987): 69–72.
Velkley, Richard. *Freedom and the End of Reason.* Chicago: University of Chicago Press, 1989.
Volk, Tyler. *Metapatterns.* New York: Columbia University Press, 1995.
Von Arnim, H. F. A. *Stoicorum Veterum Fragmenta.* Vol. 2. Stuttgart: B. G. Teubner Verlagsgesellschaft, 1964.
Watson, Walter. *The Architectonics of Meaning: Foundations of the New Pluralism.* Chicago: University of Chicago Press, 1993.
Wedin, Michael V. *Aristotle's Theory of Substance: The* Categories *and* Metaphysics Zeta. Oxford: Oxford University Press, 2000.
Wehrle, Walter E. *The Myth of Aristotle's Development and the Betrayal of Metaphysics.* Oxford: Rowman & Littlefield, 2000.
Weissman, David. *Eternal Possibilities: A Neutral Ground for Meaning and Existence.* Carbondale: Southern Illinois University Press, 1977.
———. *Intuition and Ideality.* Albany: State University of New York Press, 1987.
———. "First Considerations." In *Creativity and Common Sense,* ed. Thomas Krettek, 92–110. Albany: State University of New York Press, 1989.
———. *Truth's Debt to Value.* New Haven: Yale University Press, 1993.
Willard, Dallas. "Who Needs Brentano? The Wasteland of Philosophy without Its Past." In *The Brentano Problem,* ed. Roberto Poli, 15–44. Aldershot: Ashgate, 1998.
William of Ockham. *Expositio aurea et admodum utilis super artem veterem.* Bononia: Benedictus Hector, 1946. Reprint, Ridgewood, N.J.: Gregg Press, 1964.
———. "On the Notion of Knowledge or Science." In *Philosophical Writings: A Selection,* ed. and trans. Philotheus Boehner. London: Nelson, 1967.
———. *Ockham's Theory of Terms: Part I of the Summa Logica.* Trans. Michael J. Loux. Notre Dame: University of Notre Dame Press, 1974.
———. *Summa Logicae.* In *Opera Philosopha et Theologica,* ed. Philotheus Boehner, Gedeon Gál, and Stephen Brown. St. Bonaventure: Franciscan Institute, 1974.
Wippel, John F. "Thomas Aquinas's Derivation of the Aristotelian Categories (Predicaments)." *Journal of the History of Philosophy* 25, no. 1 (1987): 13–34.
———. *The Metaphysical Thought of Thomas Aquinas.* Washington, D.C.: Catholic University of America Press, 2000.
Wittgenstein, Ludwig. *Tractatus Logico-Philosophicus.* Trans. David F. Pears and Brian McGuinness. London: Routledge and Kegan Paul, 1961.

———. *Notebooks, 1914–1916*. 2d ed. Ed. G. E. M. Anscombe and G. H. von Wright and trans. G. E. M. Anscombe. Oxford: Basil Blackwell, 1979.
———. *Philosophische Untersuchungen*. Ed. Joachim Schulte. Frankfurt am Main: Suhrkamp Verlag, 2003.
Wolterstorff, Nicholas. *Works and Worlds of Art*. Oxford: Clarendon Press, 1980.
Wubnig, Judith. "The Epigenesis of Pure Reason." *Kant-Studien* 60 (1969): 147–52.
Yao, Xinzhong. "Self Construction and Identity: The Confucian Self in Relation to Some Western Perceptions." *Asian Philosophy* 6 (1996): 179–96.
Yu, Jiyuan. "*Tode Ti* and *Toionde* in *Metaphysics Z*." *Philosophical Inquiry* 16 (1994): 1–25.
———. "Two Conceptions of Hylomorphism in *Metaphysics ZHΘ*." In *Oxford Studies in Ancient Philosophy*. Vol. 15, ed. C. C. W. Taylor, 119–45. Oxford: Clarendon Press, 1997.
———. "What Is the Focal Meaning of Being in Aristotle?" *Apeiron* 34 (2001): 205–31.
Zimmerman, Dean. "Temporary Intrinsics and Presentism." In *Metaphysics: The Big Questions*, ed. Peter van Inwagen and Dean Zimmerman, 206–19. Malden, Mass.: Blackwell, 1998.

List of Contributors

C. Wesley DeMarco (Ph.D., Vanderbilt University) teaches philosophy at Clark University. His research interests include metaphysics and ethics, and he has published a number of articles, including "Knee Deep in Technique: The Ethics of Monopoly Capital" (*Journal of Business Ethics*, 2001), "On the Impossibility of Placebo Effects in Psychotherapy" (*Philosophical Psychology*, 1998), and "The Greening of Aristotle," in *Greek Roots of Ecological Thinking*, ed. T. M. Robinson and L. Westra (1997).

Dagfinn Føllesdal (Ph.D., Harvard University) is the C. I. Lewis Professor of Philosophy at Stanford University and Professor Emeritus of Philosophy at the Philosophical Institute of the University of Oslo. He has published extensively on the philosophy of logic and language, phenomenology, existentialism, and hermeneutics. Most recently he has edited and written introductions for *The Philosophy of W. V. Quine*, 5 volumes (2001); republished his 1961 dissertation, *Referential Opacity and Modal Logic* (2003); and assembled many of his most critical papers in *Selected Papers* (forthcoming).

Newton Garver (Ph.D., Cornell University) is SUNY Distinguished Service Professor and Professor Emeritus of Philosophy at the State University of New York at Buffalo. A leading interpreter of Wittgenstein, he has also published many articles on various topics in the philosophy of language and ethics. He is the co-editor, with P. H. Hare, of *Naturalism and Rationality* (1986), and, with J. B. Brady, of *Justice, Law, and Violence* (1991). He is the co-author, with Seung-Chong Lee, of *Derrida and Wittgenstein* (1994). He is also the author of *This Complicated Form of Life: Essays on Wittgenstein* (1994).

Michael Gorman (Ph.D., State University of New York at Buffalo; Ph.D., Boston College) is Assistant Professor of Philosophy at The Catholic University of America. He has authored more than a dozen publications on metaphysics, philosophy of mind, Christology, and other topics, among them papers in *Ratio International Philosophical Quarterly*, *Dia-*

logue: *Canadian Philosophical Review, Traditio, Philosophical Quarterly,* and *Hume Studies.* He is currently working on a book on essence.

Jorge J. E. Gracia (Ph.D., University of Toronto) is the Samuel P. Capen Chair and a SUNY Distinguished Professor of Philosophy at the State University of New York at Buffalo. He is the author of more than two hundred articles and has written or edited more than twenty-five books. His recent books include *Metaphysics and Its Task: The Search for the Categorial Foundation of Knowledge* (1999), *How Can We Know What God Means? The Interpretation of Revelation* (2001), and *Old Wine in New Skins,* Aquinas Lecture 2003 (2003). He is the co-editor, with Timothy Noone, of *The Blackwell Companion to Philosophy in the Middle Ages* (2003). His specializations include medieval philosophy, metaphysics, hermeneutics, and Latin American philosophy.

Carl R. Hausman (Ph.D., Northwestern University) is Professor Emeritus of Philosophy, the Pennsylvania State University. His interests focus on the philosophy of Charles Peirce, especially his views of evolution, realism, and semeiotic. His interests are equally focused on philosophical understandings of creativity and metaphor in the arts. His books include *Metaphor and Art* (1989), *Charles S. Peirce's Evolutionary Philosophy* (1993), and *A Discourse on Novelty and Creation* (1984). He also was a co-editor of *The Creativity Question* (1976), *Classical American Philosophy* (1999), and other works, as well as articles on Peirce, creativity, metaphor, and aesthetics in various professional journals.

Helen Lang (Ph.D., University of Toronto) is Professor of Philosophy at Villanova University and is currently the chair of the Department of Philosophy. She is an authority on topics in ancient and medieval philosophy and has held visiting positions at the Institute for Advanced Study in Princeton and the Dibner Institute for the History of Science and Technology at MIT. In addition to numerous articles, she is the author of *Aristotle's Physics and Its Medieval Varieties* (1992) as well as *The Order of Nature in Aristotle's Physics: Place and the Elements* (1998). Her most recent book, with A. D. Macro, is an edited Greek text, translation, and introduction to Proclus's *On the Eternity of the World* (2002).

William E. McMahon (Ph.D., University of Notre Dame) is Professor Emeritus of Philosophy, University of Akron. He works in the philosophy of language, medieval philosophy, and philosophy of science. His publications include *Hans Reichenbach's Philosophy of Grammar* (1976), "Albert the Great on the Semantics of the Categories of Substance, Quantity, and Quality" (*Historiographia Linguistica* 7, 1980), and "The

Categories in Some Post-Medieval Spanish Philosophers" (*Medieval and Renaissance Logic in Spain, Acts of the 12th European Symposium on Medieval Logic and Semantics*, 2000).

Timothy Sean Quinn (Ph.D., The Catholic University of America) is Associate Professor of Philosophy at Xavier University of Cincinnati. He is the former director of the Honors Bachelor of Arts Program and remains involved with the honors program. His specializations include Aristotle, Kant, aesthetics, and metaphysics. He has published on Aristotle, Kant, and Boethius, including "Kant's Apotheosis of Genius," *International Philosophical Quarterly* 31 (1991). He is currently writing on the relationship between philosophy and myth.

Jonathan J. Sanford (Ph.D., State University of New York at Buffalo) is Assistant Professor of Philosophy at Franciscan University of Steubenville. His publications include "An Aristotelian Critique of Gracia's View of Metaphysics," in *Revisiting Metaphysics: Essays on Jorge J. E. Gracia's* Metaphysics and Its Task, ed. Robert Delfino (2004); "Anselm: *Ratio quarens beatitudinem*," co-written with Jorge J. E. Gracia, in *Rationality and Happiness: From the Ancients to the Early Latin Medievals*, ed. Jiyuan Yu and Jorge J. E. Gracia (2003); and "Affective Insight: Scheler on Feelings and Values," in *Proceedings of the American Catholic Philosophical Association* 76 (2002).

May Sim (Ph.D., Vanderbilt University) is Associate Professor at College of the Holy Cross. Her specializations include ancient philosophy and comparative philosophy. She is the author of numerous articles on Aristotle and Confucius and the contributing editor of *The Crossroads of Norm and Nature: Essays on Aristotle's Ethics and Metaphysics* (1995) and *From Puzzles to Principles?: Essays on Aristotle's Dialectic* (1999). She is currently finishing a manuscript entitled *From Master to Master: Aristotle and Confucius on Ethical Life*.

Barry Smith (Ph.D., University of Manchester) is the Julian Park Professor of Philosophy and member of the Center for Cognitive Science at the State University of New York at Buffalo, as well as a research scientist at the National Center for Geographic Information and Analysis. He has been the editor of *The Monist* since 1991. His more than 150 articles have ranged over such areas as formal and applied ontology, mereology, and Austrian and German philosophy. He is the author of *Austrian Philosophy: The Legacy of Franz Brentano* (1994). He has edited more than thirteen books, including *The Cambridge Companion to Husserl*, with David W. Smith (1995), and *Formal Ontology and Informa-*

tion Systems, with Christopher Welty (2001). He is currently the director of the Institute for Formal Ontology and Medical Information Science at the University of Leipzig.

Robert Sokolowski (Ph.D., Université de Louvain) is the Elizabeth Breckenridge Caldwell Professor of Philosophy at The Catholic University of America. His main areas of research are phenomenology, metaphysics, philosophy of language, philosophy of human nature, and theology. He has published more than seventy articles and nine books, including *Husserlian Meditations* (1974), *Presence and Absence* (1978), *Moral Action* (1985), *Pictures, Quotations, and Distinctions: Fourteen Essays in Phenomenology* (1992), and *Introduction to Phenomenology* (2000).

Eleonore Stump (Ph.D., Cornell University) is the Robert J. Henle Professor of Philosophy at Saint Louis University. She has written, edited, or co-edited more than a dozen books and written or co-written more than ninety articles in medieval philosophy, philosophy of religion, philosophy of mind, and other areas. Her publications include *Dialectic and Its Place in the Development of Medieval Logic* (1989) and *Aquinas* (2003). She gave the Gifford Lectures in 2003 under the title "Wandering in Darkness: Narrative and the Problem of Suffering."

Mariam Thalos (Ph.D., University of Illinois, Chicago) is Professor of Philosophy at the University of Utah. She taught at the State University of New York, Buffalo, before joining the faculty at Utah in 2001. Her research focuses on foundational questions in the sciences, especially the physical, social, and decisional sciences, as well as on relations between the sciences and between the sciences and common sense. She is the author of numerous articles on causation, explanation, and the relations of micro and macro in the sciences, and on political philosophy, epistemology, logical paradox, and feminism. She is a former fellow of the National Endowment for the Humanities, the Institute of Advanced Studies of the Australian National University, and the Tanner Humanities Center. She is currently writing two books, *The Natural History of Knowledge* and *The Natural History of the Will*.

David Weissman (Ph.D., University of London) is Professor of Philosophy at the City College of New York. His main areas of research interest include metaphysics, epistemology, and ethics. His numerous publications include *Lost Souls* (2003), *A Social Ontology* (2000), *Truth's Debt to Value* (1993), *Hypothesis and the Spiral of Reflection* (1989), and *Eternal Possibilities: A Neutral Ground for Meaning and Existence* (1977).

Author Index

Abelard, Peter, 273n
Ackrill, J. L., 22n, 139-40
Adams, Marilyn, 50n, 55
Albertus Magnus, 45-46, 48-49
Allunti, Felix, 51n
Amerik, Karl, 126n, 127n
Ames, Roger T., 58n, 59n, 60n, 65n, 243n
Andrews, Robert, 51n, 52
Angelelli, Ignacio, 45n
Anscombe, G. E. M., 144n
Aquinas, Thomas, xii, 33-46, 169n, 170n, 270
Aristotle, vii-viii, x-xii, xiv, 3-20, 21-32, 45n, 46, 47n, 48n, 53-77, 86n, 97, 118, 136-47, 164n, 169n, 170-72, 226, 242-44, 249, 258n, 265n, 270, 272, 273n
Arnauld, Antoine, 53n
Arnim, H. F. A. von, 272n
Austin, J. L., 138n
Ayer, A. J., 273n

Bacon, J., 235n
Baker, Lynne Rudder, 38n
Baliae, Carolo, 52n
Bambrough, Renford, ix, 153n
Barnes, Jonathan, viiin, 22n
Bateson, Gregory, 259n
Baudin, Abbé, 122
Beal, M. W., 154
Beany, Michael, 138n
Beck, Lewis White, 81n
Benveniste, Emile, 59n, 243
Bernasconi, Robert, 276n
Biemel, Walter, 119n, 130n
Bittner, Thomas, 231n
Bockover, Mary I., 66n
Boehner, Philotheus, 54n, 278n
Boethius, 36, 44, 48n, 51n
Bogen, James, 50n
Bolzano, Bernard, 134
Borges, Jorge Luis, 118, 268-69, 272, 274-75

Brentano, Franz, 119-21
Brestzke, James T., 58n
Brito, Radulphus, 49
Brogaard, Berit, 231n, 235n
Brown, Stephen, 54n
Buridan, John, xii, 46, 53-57, 64n
Burks, A. W., 98n
Bursill-Hall, G. L., 50n

Campbell, Keith, 153n, 235n
Carnap, Rudolf, 190-92, 273n
Carr, David, 130n
Carter, William R., 277n
Casati, R., 231n
Chapa, Jorge, 271n
Chisholm, Roderick M., 120n
Chomksy, Noam, 137
Churchill, James S., 126n, 127n
Confucius, xii, 58-77, 118, 243n
Cozens, J. A., 271n
Craig, Edward, 196n
Cummings, E. E., 141

Danto, Arthur, 147n
Davidson, Donald, 202, 253n
Delfino, Robert, 19n
Democritus, 172
Descartes, René, 56, 212
Deutsch, Eliot, 58n
Dewey, John, 196
Dickie, George, 277n
Dickoff, James, 53n
Dipert, Randall, 277n
Dissanayake, Wimal, 65n
Dummet, Michael, 278n
Dupré, John, 165n

Ebbesen, Sten, 47n, 50, 56n
Einstein, Albert, 179
Evangeliou, Christos, 273n

Fackenheim, Emil, 94n
Fairchild, H. H., 271n
Fales, Evan, 157n

299

AUTHOR INDEX

Fingarette, Herbert, 64n, 65n, 66n
Flew, Anthony, 278n
Føllesdal, Dagfinn, 129n, 254
Förster, Eckart, 82n
Foucault, Michel, 118, 268–83
Frawley, William, 56n
Frede, Michael, 3n, 6n, 9n, 10n, 64n
Frege, Gottlob, 137–38
Freud, Sigmund, 128
Friedman, Russell L., 56n

Gál, Gedeon, 54n
Genova, C. A., 86n
Gettier, Edmund, 186
Gibson, W. R. Boyce, 122n
Gilbert, Margaret, 196n
Gillespie, C. M., 3n
Giménez, Martha, 271n
Gómez, Emma Ingala, 271n
Gracia, Jorge J. E., 19n, 271n, 274n, 276n, 253
Graham, A. C., 59n
Guilfoy, 53n

Hall, David L., 58n, 59n, 243n
Hanna, Robert, 5n
Hansen, Chad, 59n
Hartshorne, Charles, 98
Hausman, Carl R., 117n
Hayes-Bautisa, David E., 271n
Hegel, Georg Wilhelm Friedrich, 113, 115, 249
Heidegger, Martin, 258n
Henninger, Mark G., 48n
Henrich, Dieter, 82n, 84n, 93, 94n
Henry of Ghent, xii, 46–51
Hobbes, Thomas, 89, 180
Hoffman, Joshua, viiin
Hull, David L., 156n, 164n
Hume, David, xiv, 96, 192, 196; 143–44, 146–47, 182
Husserl, Edmund, xiii, xv, 100, 118–35, 227n

Inwagen, Peter van, 44n
Ivanhoe, P. J., 77n

James, Patricia, 53n
James, William, 193n, 196
Jastrow, Joseph, 122
Johnson, Mark, 258n–59n
Johnston, Mark, 38n

Kant, Immanuel, xii–xiii, 53n, 81–97, 121, 136–37, 142–47, 174–75, 178–79, 182, 190, 212, 227, 263, 270n

Kasulis, Thomas P., 65n
Katz, Jerrold, 53n, 137
Kern, Iso, 122n, 130
Kersten, Fred, 119n, 126n, 129n, 130n
Kincaid, Harold, 156n
Klima, Gyula, 56
Kornblith, Hilary, 277n
Körner, Stephen, 273n
Krettek, Thomas, 253n

Lakoff, George, 258n, 259n
Lee, S. C., 137n
Legge, J., 66n
Leibniz, Gottfried, 44n, 120
Lewis, David, 44n, 231n, 233, 235n, 237
Lipton, Peter, 156n
Livingston, Kenneth, 273n
Locke, John, 180
Lott, Tommy L., 276n
Loux, Michael, 13n, 54n
Lowe, E. J., 161–62
Lucy, John A., 248n, 249n
Luther, Martin, 176

MacIntyre, Alasdair, xii, 58, 67–70, 76
Macken, R., 46n
Maierù, Alfonso, 54n
Mann, Wofgang-Rainer, 10n
Marenbon, John, 47n
Marín, G., 271n
Marx, Karl, 171
Mauritius de Portu Hibernico, 52
Maynard-Smith, John, 197n
McGuinness, Brian, 145n
McGuire, James E., 50n
McKeon, Richard, 47n, 169n, 178
Meek, Mary Elizabeth, 243n
Mehl, Peter J., 58n
Meinong, Alexius, 121
Mill, John Stuart, 181
Millikan, Ruth Garrett, 161, 170
Minio-Paluello, Lorenzo, 45n, 48n
Mohr, Richard, 160n
Montello, Daniel, 231n
Moody, Ernest, 55n, 56n
Müller, Friedrich Max, 53n
Mumford, Stephen, 161–62

Newton, Isaac, 179
Nicole, Pierre, 53n
Nussbaum, Martha, 3n

Oboler, Suzanne, 271n
Olivi, Peter John, 52
Olson, Eric, 39n, 42n
Omi, Michael, 276n

AUTHOR INDEX

Owen, G. E. L., 3n, 5n, 15n
Owens, Joseph, 4n, 21n

Pap, Arthur, 273n
Parmenides, 23
Parsons, Kathryn Pyne, 153n
Paulus, Jean, 48n, 51n
Pears, David F., 145n, 153n
Peirce, Charles Sanders, xiii, 97–117, 196, 249, 254n, 258n
Pepper, Stephen, 178
Perez-Ilzarbe, Paloma, 45n
Peterson, Roger Tory, 154n
Pinborg, Jan, 54n
Plato, xi, 22–31, 35, 42n, 128, 171, 258n, 270
Pluhar, Werner, 81n
Poincaré, Henri, 192
Pole, David, 273n, 278n
Poli, Roberto, xn
Popper, Karl, 192–93, 194n, 196–98
Porphyry, 6, 31
Putnam, Hilary, 159

Quine, William V. O., 56, 202–3, 236–37, 278n

Rand, E. K., 51n
Reinhardt, L., 235n
Rijk, Lambert M. de, 55n, 273n
Rorty, Richard, 196n
Rosemant, H., Jr., 60n
Rosenkrantz, Gary, viiin
Rosenthal, Sandra, 104, 115
Ross, Stephen David, 255n
Ross, W. D., 22n
Rousseau, Jean Jacques, 181
Ruse, Michael, 156n–57n
Russell, Bertrand, 121, 137, 186
Ryle, Gilbert, 143, 270, 273n, 278n

Schneider, Johannes, 53n, 64n
Schulte, Joachim, 152n
Schweder, Richard A., 249n
Scotus, John Duns, xii, 46, 51–52
Searle, John, 163n, 273n
Sim, May, 60n, 64n, 65n, 66n, 118, 243n, 254
Simms, Ruth L. C., 118n
Simons, P., 232n

Smith, Barry, 231n, 235n, 236n
Smith, J. A., 169n
Sokolowski, Robert, 187–92, 199–203
Spade, Paul Vincent, 6n
Spinoza, Benedict de, 171
Stenius, Erik, 147
Stewart, H. F., 147n
Strawson, Peter F., 147n, 278n
Stroll, Avrum, xn
Stroud, Barry, 163n

Terrell, D. B., 120n
Thom, René, 258n
Thompson, Manley, 21, 26
Tienson, John, 156n
Todes, Sam, 128n
Trendelenburg, Adolf, 53n
Treviño, Fernando, 271n

Varzi, A. C., 231n
Velkley, Richard, 84n, 93n, 94n
Volk, Tyler 259n

Walker, R. C. S., 84n
Warren, E. W., 31n
Watson, Walter, 178n
Wedin, Michael, V., 4n
Wehrle, Walter E., 3n
Weiss, Paul, 98n, 255n
Weissman, David, 253, 261
Wellbery, David, 128n
Whitehead, A. N., 255n
Whorf, Benjamin Lee, 174
Willard, Dallas, xn
William of Ockham, xii, 46, 53–55, 278n
Wilson, G. A., 49n
Winant, Howard, 276n
Wippel, John F., 46n
Wittgenstein, Ludwig, xiv, 122, 138, 144–45, 152–54, 238
Wolter, Allan B., 51n
Wolterstorff, Nicholas, 161
Wright, H. von, 144n
Wubnig, Judith, 86n

Yao, Xinzhong, 65n
Yu, Jiyuan, 5n, 15n, 16n

Zimmerman, Dean, 44n

Subject Index

a priori: and Foucault, 269–71, 275, 282; and Kant, 82–85, 88–89, 142, 174, 275
absence. *See* presence
absolute: chance, 111, 117; categorical terms, 55; divinity, 254; and extrinsic principles, 45; and Foucault, 275; and Hegel, 244; and relative properties, 47–52, 55; requirement of thought, 143, 145, 147; and substance, 10
abstraction: in formation of Peirce's categories, 100–101. *See also* induction
accident: absolute, 49; and Aquinas, 35–39, 43–44; and Aristotelian categories, 5–6, 8, 12, 47, 76; and Confucius, 67; and dependent reality, 48; individual accidents, 56; intrinsic and extrinsic, 48–50; and Kant, 93; ontology 50–51, 56; and Peirce, 104, 111. *See also* properties
action: and agape, 116; as an Aristotelian accident, 9, 21, 56–57, 59, 64, 72–74, 76, 242; and beliefs, 128; and bodily movement, 124, 126; categorial, 212; and Confucius, 62–67, 71–74, 76; elemental, 257; and invention of categories, 11, 279–80; and Kant, 87–95; man of, 107–9; and narrative, 259; and nature, 171; normative, 114; and norms, 158; as object, 123; and partitions, 234; and phenomenalism, 105; purposive, 116; practical, 189; and signs, 278; and struggle, 102, 115, 117; and vagueness, 221–22; and value, 126
agape: in Peirce's evolution, xiii, 111–17; and *eros*, 113–17
agapasm, 112
agapasticism, 111
anancasticism, 111
anamnesis, 128
anancasm, 109
appearances: and Aristotle's categories, 249; in Husserl, 123, 205, 208, 221; in Kant, 84–86, 89
apophansis, 214
apophantics, 218
apperception: transcendental, 84–85, 93
arguments: nature of, 7n, 8n, 10n, 23, 72, 210. *See also* logic; syllogism
Aristotelian: conceptual system, 51; logic, 137, 143; naturalism, xiv, 146–47; notion of final causes, 85, 200; ten category scheme, x–xiii, 21, 33, 38, 55–56, 59, 67, 73, 77, 151, 244; necessary truth, 159–60; primary substance, 176; tension between practical and disciplinary life, 187, 194–95; theme in Wittgenstein, xiv, 136, 147; understanding of change, 43; view of soul, 168
atomism, 176, 178, 181
attitude: emotional, 220; natural, 246n; pre-philosophical, 164; propositional, 214–15; reflective, 214

Bayesianism, 191–96
being: act and potency and Ockham, 54n; analogical character of, 48n; and Aquinas, 33; Aristotle's science of being, xi, 3–4, 9, 12–19, 81; and becoming in Plato, 23; as consciousness, 119; degrees of, 52; four senses of, 5n, 15n; generic features of, 171; and mentalism, 172; modal interpretation of being, 50; modes of, 105, 114; participation in, 27; and qualifications, 262, 267; and signification, 265n; and soul, 254n; transcendent, 119
belief, 128, 167, 179, 198n, 214; justified true, 203
biology, 164, 165, 170
bracketing, 100

categorical/categorial: activity, 219; articulation, 209–10, 216; being, 5–6, 18;

303

SUBJECT INDEX

classification, 140; concept, 279; consciousness, 206–7; division, xvi, 12; domain, 223; etymology, 204; features of reality, 171, 173, 178; form, 172, 171, 173, 175, 178–82; formation, 239, 263; formulations, xvi; functions, 84; imperative, 81, 87, 93; intending, 206, 216; intentionality, 217, 224; intentions, xv, 219; intuition, 210, 206; level, viii; morality, 81; objects, xv, 206, 210, 217, 218, 220, 223; metaphysics, viii; registrations, 212; settlement, 262; terms, 55, 279; thinking, 207

categories: abstracted, 263; and accidents, 67, 76; and Ackrill, 139; and Aristotle, xi–xii, xiv, 9–10, 13, 33, 45–46, 49, 118, 141; biological, 155n, 156, 157n, 164, 170; of causality, 89; characterological/non-characterological approaches, 156–57; closed, 143; common to all human thinking, 270; commonsense, 242–44; conceptual, 273n, 274; as constructs, 263; derivative, 251; discourse, 139; eidetic, 134; elimination of particular categories, 270; epistemic function of, 273; and ethics, 22n (*see also* normativity); etymology of, vii, 139; evaluative, 166–67; of family resemblance, 153; of freedom, 88, 91; and function, 161; functional, 264; generation and destruction of, 236–37; and Hegel, 244, 254; as historically contingent systems of classification, 281; and Husserl, 118–35; as ideas/views, 280; of intelligibility, 117; intrinsic, 46; as inventions, 271, 276; and Kant, 143, 244; language and logic, 139, 278 (*see also* language); and linguistics, 143, 273; logical, 93, 134–35, 143; loose theories of, 157; and mediation, 250, 266; as mental acts, 238n, 280; and metaphysics, 4n, 22n (*see also* metaphysics); of modality, 92; modistic account, 56; natural fact, 143; natural norm-constituted, 170; as necessary features of reality, 144, 159; noetic, 134; nominalist view of, 273; as norm-constituted, 151, 159–69; normative variations of, 154–58; optional/non-optional features of, 153–60; ontological, 134; open-ended, 142; and parts of speech, 50; and Peirce, 244; pernicious consequences of, 271; and persons, 271–72; phenomenological approach to, 99, 106; practical, xiii, 82, 86, 89–96; as predicate, 247n, 273, 281 (*see also* predication); as products of human design, 276–77; as properties, 273, 280; and qualification, 251–53, 259; realism of, 248; of relation, 61, 89; rigid, 152–54, 157–59; scheme, viiin, ix–x, xvi, 45; semantic, 54, 137; set, 238–40, 263; and social-psychological compositions, 264; substance, 67, 76, 161; teleological, 262; theoretical, xiii, 81–82, 86–96; transcendental requirement of, 143; unity of, 151, 160; validity of, 282; variations, 152–53; and Whorfian outlook, 56; as words, 273, 280

causality: and agape, 112; and categories, 11; causal reciprocity, 176; efficient, 116; final, 16–17, 68, 102, 116; first, 4; formal, 3, 13–14; and freedom, 89–92; modes of, 92; and sciences, 172

cells, 229, 231–34

chance, 110; absolute, 111, 112

change, 24; evolutionary 104; nature of, 43

chaos, 111

character formation, 76

choice, 222

class, xvi, 16, 26, 151, 242. See also species

coaction, 256–57, 261

commensurablity, xii, 59, 63

communitarianism, xv, 175–81

concept, 70, 76, 136, 263, 277–79; as ideas, 280; in categories, 272; contextualist conception of, 69; derivative 254; development in history, 70; original pure concepts, 83; sorts of, 137; status of, 213; universal conceptions of, 98; variable, 254

conceptual: system, 46, 175, 178; and theoretical systems, 92; things, 213

confirmation, 216; and identification, 216; indirect, 212

consciousness, 91–93, 120, 123–27, 131–32, 209; background of, 127; individual, 275; intentionality of, 211, 218; rational, 207; of something, 121

contemplation, act of, 189

contextualism, 178

continuity, 113–17

conventionalism, 54, 192, 196; and groupings, 165, 189

cosmology, 97, 106

cosmos, xi, 23–25, 112, 116, 223

custom, 75–76

SUBJECT INDEX

dao, 6on, 64n
Darwinism, 108, 111, 196; social, 171
decision: of collective, 197; of individuals, 197; making, 194; procedure, 193; theory, 191
deduction, xiii, 6–12, 16; empirical/physiological, 84; and Kant, 83n, 87n
definition, 8, 12, 141, 188, 199, 201
democracy, 75
demonstration, 5–7, 12, 17
determination, 88; and arrangement, 233; definitive, 247, 262; and dimensions, 36; real, 49; specific, 261; teleological, 112; and time, 29
determinism, 108, 112
dialogue, x, 59, 77; and categorical hypotheses, 174; and inquiry, 173
differentia, 14, 138, 141
directedness, xiii, 120–23
disciplines: boundaries of, 201
discourse, 275; possibilities, 141
discovery: *vs.* invention, 283
disposition, 127; and ascription, 162; and notions, 128
distinction, xv, 189, 199, 202, 221; absolute/relative, 48; between knowledge and fact, 185–87; judgment's reliance upon, 188; making, 201–2; and reality, 52; and semantics, 54; theoretical, 189
domain: of presentation, 216; of reason, 224
duty, 180
dyad, 97; and relation, 102, 107

ego, transcendental, 93, 224
eidetic reduction, 130–33
eidos, 130–34
empiricism, 96, 132, 174, 191–92, 196; and deduction, 84; and information, 172; and test, 179; and world, 84
enaction, 255–57, 260, 263n
epistemic: knowledge, 8, 17–18; point, 168; position, 195
epistemology, x–xi, xv–xvi, 5, 11, 14, 20, 81, 100, 186, 196–205; and doctrine, 190; foundationalist, 196; work, 214
eros, and agape, 113–17
esse, 46, 48
essence, 9, 46, 122, 130–31, 133, 245
ethics, xii–xiv, 59, 63–64, 73, 76, 99. *See also* normativity
evolution, xiii, 98, 106–8, 112, 164n, 165, 257n; agapastic, 111, 116; anancastic, 111; cosmic, 109–10, 117; law of, 114; and love, 111; principle of, 117; process, 105; social, 261; tychastic, 111
experience, 85–89, 96, 117, 122, 127, 131–32, 174, 204, 252; affected 275; causing, 275; mature, 200; moral, 93; of illumination/disclosure, 200; possible, 83n; prepredicative, 208–9; structuring of, 123

fact, xv, 213, 250; and properties of things, 126; and pure reason, 95
faction/facture, 255–57
fiat boundaries, 236–37
firstness, 97, 100–103, 106–15
form, 18, 33–35, 41–42, 125, 134, 199–200; categorial, 171–82; of disclosure, 200; elementary, 262; essential, 179; generic, 255; intrinsic accidental, 50; of intuition, 142; and soul, 254n; and species, 62
freedom, 91–92, 96, 110, 116, 180–81

Golden Rule, 61
government: aristocratic, 69; oligarchic, 69, 75; timocratic, 69
grammar: and Buridan, 57; and Wittgenstein, 144. *See also* syntax; language
granularity, 226–30; built-in, 234; levels of, 229

habit, 61–62, 103
habitus, 64, 72–73
haecceitas, 51
happiness, 89; and flourishing, 166
holism, xv, 175–81
horizon, 127
human: action, 11, 279, 280; activity, x–xii, xiv; associations, 67; behavior, 181; beings, xii, xv, 34, 35, 37, 42, 43, 44, 67, 205; category formation, 239; constructions, 263; design, 279; intelligence, 105; inventions, 11; language, xvi, 238; life, xv, 181; nature, 35; products, 276; symbolic life, 254; thought, xvi
hyle, xiv, 125, 131
hylomorphism, 16, 40, 50, 125; and constitution, 48; dynamic and static, 16–18; and substance, 3; theory of, 67
hypoicons, 107. *See also* signs
hypostasis, and *suppusit*, 39

idealism, 139, 171, 239, 249–50, 258; distinction with realism, 122; transcendental, 142

SUBJECT INDEX

identity, xii, 38–41, 44, 185, 207, 210, 212, 235, 269, 282
imagination, xii, 209, 217
immaterial intelligence, 34
imperative: categorical, 81, 87, 93; of prudence, 88; technical, 88
indexes. *See* signs
individualism, xv, 70, 175–76, 179–80
individuals, 34, 37, 39, 43, 64n. *See also* particulars
individuation, xii, 34–36, 42–44
induction, 7n, 14, 11n, 127, 173, 192, 196
inference, 124, 127, 144, 192, 203, 260n, 263; abductive *vs.* inductive, 173
intellection. *See* understanding
intelligibility: of world, 12, 19, 70, 92, 97, 113–17, 170n, 262; mediating, 239–40, 244, 247
intension, and extension, 47
intentionality, xiii, xv, 47–49, 54, 105, 119–23, 128, 204–24, 227, 260n
intersubjectivity, 129–30
intuition, 83–86, 89–93, 137, 142, 164, 282; categorical, 206, 210; manifold of, 96; prescientific, 157

judgment, vii, xv, 83, 93, 136, 142, 187, 212–15, 219–21; and distinction making, 201; faculty of, 143; and intentionality, 206; and logical function, 92; moral, 94–96; phenomenological analysis of, 214; practical, 90; reliance on distinctions, 188; synthetic, 83n; theoretical, 94. *See also* thinking
junzi, 61, 64n

kinds, 26–27, 47–48, 52–53, 151, 156, 165, 187, 191, 229–34, 247, 252n, 259, 281
knowledge, x, 5–7, 17–19, 61–62, 81–82, 83n, 93, 185–86, 203, 213; definite, 17; of fact, xv; paradigm of, 196; scientific, 5, 14, 17; supersensible, 86; universal, 18. *See also* science; thinking; understanding

language, vii, x, xvi, 23, 138, 205–6, 217, 222–24, 239, 245, 252, 266; games, xiv, 145–47, 263; of participation, 28; logical analysis of, 134; natural, 241, 245; primary and primitive elements of, 137; relation to logic, 138; requirement of, 145; syncatagorematic parts of, 222; syntatic and nonsyntatic parts

of, 222. *See also* grammar; semantics; syntax
law, 74–76, 103–6, 110, 114–16, 172; *a priori* practical, 88; *ceteris paribus* laws, 156; of freedom, 90; of growth, 114; moral, 88–89, 94–95; natural, 90, 95, 162, 172; ontological status of, 172; physical, 171; reality of, 107; of the will, 87
li, 58, 63, 67–69, 73–76
logic, 31, 98, 138, 142, 200, 210, 217–19; and categories, 3–4, 9, 19–20, 97; and consistency, 218–20; and contradiction, 220; and decision, 192, 196; and grounding of science of being, 15–16; and idioms, 245; of induction, 92, 196; and language, 138; modern, 137–38; nature of, 137–38; operations, 204; Port Royal, 53; primary and primitive elements of, 137; of relations, 98–99; subject-predicate, 136; of terms, 137; truth-functional, 137. *See also* arguments; validity

manifold: of desires, 91; identity of, 205; of intuition, 96; synthesis of, 85; synthetic unity of, 89, 123
matter, 3, 13, 18, 30, 33–37, 41–44; prime, 35–36, 40
meaning, xv, 5n, 103, 131–32, 137–38, 144, 178n, 202, 214, 216, 218–19, 240, 247, 253n, 260, 269, 278; of nature, 95. *See also* perception; semantics
mechanism, 178
mediation: and entities, 215; means of, 244
mental: acts, vii, 120; entities, 14, 211, 216; phenomena, 120; skills, 128; things, xv, 213
mentalism, 172
mereology, 229, 235; approach of, 229; and fusion, 231, 234. *See also* part. *See also* whole
metaphysics, vii–xiv, 22n, 39–42, 49–50, 82–83, 99, 104–5, 133, 138–39, 144, 146, 171–73, 178–79, 186, 200; and Aquinas, xii, 33–44; and Aristotle, xi, xiv, 3–20, 31; and epistemology, 204–24, 225–37, 238–67, 268–83; and ethics, xiv, 151–70, 171–82; fundamental, 237. *See also* ontology
mind, 20, 172, 177; Cartesian, 176; and materiality, 171
modes, 51–52; of activity, 262; of being, 50; of categories, 50; of classification, 245; and Kant, 142; of mediation,

244; of predication, 77; of presentation, 220; of signification, 53
monad, 97–99
moral: acts, 74; doctrine, 81; imperatives, 180; implications, 179; and morality, x, 182 (*see also* normativity); systems, 64
motion, 24–29, 50, 165, 177

natural: attitude, 130–31, 216; category, viii, ix; history of sciences, 197; kinds, 165; phenomena, 172; philosophy, 24; selection, 164; things, xi, 24; worldview, 163
naturalism, xiv, 138, 146, 147n, 163n
nature, viii–x, xvi, 14, 22–27, 34–37, 46, 91–95, 105–6, 122, 159, 177, 234, 238, 266, 270; acts of, 255; of classes, 233; independent, 249; laws of, 94, 112, 162; primitive acts of, 239, 265; rational, 44. *See also* physics
necessitarianism, 109–10, 117
necessity, 86, 111, 146, 177; and Hume, xiv; logical, 146; as matters of fact, 146
noema, xiii 123–25 128–32, 218, 227, 254
noematic, xiii, 134; dimension, 215; modification, 125
noesis, 131–32
nominalism, 53, 56, 106
norm, xiv, 163; and approach, 170; and kinds, 161; and subservience, 169
normativity, xi, xiv–xv, 162, 168–70; and actions, 73; and causes, 164; and differences, 156; and features, 160, 163–66, 168–69; and traits, 165–66; and unity problem, 155–57, 162, 169; and variations, 160. *See also* ethics; moral; practical

Object: Dynamical, 103, 105; Immediate, 105
objectivity, 120–23, 127, 131, 202, 208, 233, 263; and correlation, 219; and domain, 230; intramental objects, 210; perceptual objects, 216; simple, 205; three-dimensional, 235; and validity, 84
observation: fundamental, 193; primary, 193; statements, 193
ontology, viii–x, xiii, 6, 9–11, 15–16, 33, 82, 97, 133, 224; accident, 50; analogue, 233; and approach, 228; and distinctions, 119; formal, 133–34, 218; of layers, 50–51; and material,

133; and priority, 17–18; and thing, 55. *See also* metaphysics
organicism, 178

part, xii, 38, 136–37, 164, 176, 205–6, 210, 223, 232n; and individuality, 176; integral, 33, 40–41; metaphysical, 41–42; *nonindependent*, 208; and part-whole relationships, 222, 228; primary, 14; transitivity of parthood, 233. *See also* mereology
particulars, 17, 39–42; self-sufficient, 176. *See also* individuals
partitioning, xvi, 227–37, 240; and arrangement of cells, 230, 240; and arrangement of contents, 241; and *bona fide* slicings, 236; boundaries, 237; and *fiat* slicings, 236; foreground-background, 226; nominal, 232; spatial, 232
perception, xv–xvi, 89, 97, 121, 125, 137, 204–9, 227; and categorical thinking, 207; and intentionality, 206; passive level of, 211; simple, 206. *See also* meaning
person, 39–44, 66, 71, 74, 121–24
phaneron, 99–101
phaneroscopy, 99, 244
phenomenal: realm, 86; world, 81–82, 227; *vs.* noumenal, 89
phenomenological: approach to categories, xiii; attitude, 216; examination, 99, 105; method, 98; realism, 122; reduction, xiv, 119, 132
phenomenology, xiii, 98, 104–5, 121–22, 130–32, 205, 213, 222–23
physics, 171; of Aristotle, xi, 22, 24. *See also* nature
place, xi, 5, 9–11, 22–25, 30, 59, 63, 69–74
potential: and actual, 4–6, 14–18, 35
practical: end, 189; life, 69; origin, 189; reasoning, 197; singular subject position, 196; tension with theoretical, 189. *See also* normativity
pragmatism, 97, 116, 145, 193, 196–98
predication, xi, 5, 8–14, 17–21, 24, 62, 106–7, 139–40, 153n, 187, 209, 277–80; categories of, 22, 26; common predicables, 53–54; contents, 243; empirical, 142; generic kinds, 247; instrument of, 245; modes of, 240; prepredicative, 208; primary, 81–82; and saying, 141; species of, 136; substantial, 141

presence: and absence, 210–12, 217, 233; qualitative, 117
principle, 4, 14, 17, 92; first, 11–12, 52; moral, 92; practical, 89–92; primary, 7; rational, 88; six, 49; of transitivity of parthood, 227
proaction, 256–57
property, 8, 277, 280; and value, 126. *See also* quality
proposition, 5–8, 137, 212–15; and reflection, 214–16

qi, 75
quaestio facti, 82–84, 91
quaestio juris, 82, 91
qualification, xvi, 239, 244–46, 250–51, 259, 264–66; acts of, 252; and acts of nature, 253; forms of, 252, 255–57, 261–62; operations, 253, 258; transcategorical, 252; as specializations, 258
quality, 54, 59, 62–64, 70–74, 142, 242
quantity, 59–60, 70–74, 242; continuous, 60; discrete, 60; as predicates of equality and inequality, 60; and Kant, 142
quantum theory, 175

realism, ix–x, 56, 122, 171, 174, 239, 250, 253, 258, 263, 273n; direct, 239; evolutionary, xiii, xvi, 97; moderate, xvi, 239; naïve, 139, 144, 244; ontological, 105; pragmatic, 263; scientific version of transcendental, 122; skeptical, 144
reality, viii, xi, xiii, xvi, 11–12, 46, 49, 97, 105, 110–11, 138–39, 144, 171, 180–81, 208, 225–26, 229–30, 237–39; as array of systems, 177; commonsense, 227–28; corporate, 180; dependent, 48–50; derivative, 48; extra-mental, xvi; partitioning of, 226; of relations, 54
reason, xiii, xvi, 82, 85, 88, 92–93; epigenesis of, 82; immoderacy of, 96; practical, 87–92, 191; pure, 94–96; theoretical, 96, 191–92, 197; unity of, 93n, 96
relation, vii, xii, 16, 49, 59, 62–64, 72–76, 125, 176, 185, 206, 233; of categories and ethical thought, xii; of element and singleton, 233; external, 252; human, 61; internal, 250–52; interobject, 234; and Kant, 142; of part to whole, 227; of past, present, and future, 27; of Peirce's categories and

evolutionary realism, xii, 97–117; of place and where, 25; and real things, 51; in reality, 237; of syntax to modes of presentation, 223; of time and now, 29
remembering, as mode of perception, 124, 209, 217
ren, 58, 61–63, 65n
res, 46–47
resemblance, family, 153

science, 4, 7, 11–12, 16–17, 144, 196; of being, 15, 18–20, 172, 197; empirical, 173; logic of, 192–93; natural, 179, 187; universal, 18. *See also* knowledge
secondness, 97, 100–110, 113
self, 64–66, 94–96, 102, 180, 217; identity, 84; substantial, 67
semantics, 49; and entities, 216; and inclusion in categories, 10, 138–40; and syntactic language, 57; lexical, 56; and markers, 137–38; of ordinary language, 56; and spaces, 270. *See also* language; meaning
semiotic, and Peirce, 103, 107–8, 244, 258n
sense, 90–92; activity, 120; and data, 228; experiences, 125; and layers of phenomenology, 215; organs, 125; power, 122. *See also* meaning
set, 232–34; and member relationship, 228; as philosophical category, 244; theory, 228, 234–35
shu, 62, 65
signs, Peirce's classes of, 107–8
sometime, as Aristotelian category, 21–32. *See also* when
somewhere, as Aristotelian category, 21–32. *See also* where
soul, 15n, 32n, 59, 71–72, 102, 155n, 168–69, 254n
space, 125, 142, 253n; and continuity, 36; and location, 36; and time, 177
species, xvi, 34–35, 41–42, 86, 164–66; biological, 163–65; boundaries, 166; and properties, 35. *See also* universal
speech, 11, 139, 206–7, 216–19; acts, vii, xiv, 139; categorematic parts of, 222; true, 264. *See also* language
state of affairs, 215, 219
substance, xi–xii, 3, 4n, 6n, 9–11, 13–18, 21, 22n, 30, 33–35, 37, 39–40, 44, 46, 48, 49n, 50, 52, 54–57, 59, 61–64, 67, 71–72, 74, 76, 140–41, 161, 254, 255n, 272
substratum, 9n; and now, 28–29

suppposit, 39–42
syllogism, 7; demonstrative, 5; dialectical, 7–8. *See also* argument
syntax, 204–6, 210, 218, 222–24. *See also* grammar; language

Table of Judgments, in Kant, 142
teleology: Aristotle's, 16, 65n, 67; Peirce's, 108–13, 116
theology, 4, 17, 67; Aquinas and individuation, 44; rational, 172
thing, 33, 42, 176; Aquinas's theory of, 33, 34; and Henry of Ghent, 51n
thinking, vii, xiv, xvii, 12, 120, 204–6, 210; and Kant, 142. *See also* judgment; knowledge; thought
thirdness, 97, 100–105, 108, 113–17
thought, 11–12, 63n, 97, 178, 266–67. *See also* thinking
tian, 72
time, xi, 5, 9–11, 22–29, 59, 63, 70, 74, 125, 142
transcendental, xiii, 132; attitude, 216; deduction, 82–83, 87; ego, 131–32; reductions, xiv, 119, 131–33; subjectivity, 244
translation, 21, 76, 241n; of being, 245; commonsense and technical classification, 242; theory of, 120
truth, xv, 5, 58, 59n, 196n, 204, 213–19, 222, 240, 266. *See also* meaning
tychasm, 111

understanding, 204, 206, 223; pure concepts of, 143. *See also* knowledge
unity, viii, 13–17, 123, 207; category of, 84; of a category, xiv, 153; forms of, 83; individual, 72; problem, xiv, 3–4, 151–61, 165–66, 169; scientific, 14; of self-consciousness, 85; synthetic, 84–85
universals, 17, 22–23, 37, 160n; generalizations, 192. *See also* species
unmoved mover, 26, 30
Urelemente, 228

vagueness, xvi, 219–22
validity, 50–51. *See also* logic
virtue, 58–62
void, 24–27

when, as Aristotelian category, xi, 9, 21–32, 242. *See also* sometime
where, as Aristotelian category, xi, 9, 21–32, 242. *See also* somewhere
whole, xi, 16, 40, 136–37, 164, 176, 205–6, 210, 223; articulated, 208; and part, 208; natural, 244; substantial, 243. *See also* mereology
will, 88–92, 105; *a priori* determination of, 89; free, 90, 93; general, 181
world, ix–xiv, xvii, 10–16, 19–20, 26, 32–33, 81–82, 121, 124–31, 142, 146, 174, 223, 272; external, 171; features of, 129; and intentionality, 214; intersubjective, 129; and Kant, 179; material, 173; natural, 95, 172; phenomenal, 90; real, 122, 214; and role of practical, 129; of sense, 90–91

xian, 74
xiaoren, 61

yi, 62, 65
yu, 16

zhing, 65
zhou, 74–75